Countryside Conflicts

In nature there are neither rewards nor punishments; there are consequences.

Robert Ingersoll
(1833–1899)

Countryside Conflicts

The Politics of Farming, Forestry and Conservation

Philip Lowe
Graham Cox
Malcolm MacEwen
Tim O'Riordan
Michael Winter

Gower/Maurice Temple Smith

Published by

Gower Publishing Company Limited,
Gower House,
Croft Road,
Aldershot,
Hants GU11 3HR
England

Gower Publishing Company,
Old Post Road
Brookfield
Vermont 05036
U.S.A.

British Library Cataloguing in Publication Data
Countryside conflicts: the politics of farming,
    forestry and conservation.
    1. Nature conservation—Great Britain
    2. Agricultural ecology—Great Britain
    I. Lowe, Philip
    639.9′0941   QH77.G7

ISBN 0 566 05088 9
ISBN 0 566 05089 7 (pbk)

Printed in Great Britain by Blackmore Press,
Shaftesbury, Dorset

Contents

Introduction   **1**

Section 1   The Conflict in Context   *9*

1. Changing conflicts in the countryside   11
2. The political economy of post-war agriculture and forestry   31
3. The impact of agriculture and forestry on the countryside   55

Section 2   The Political Background   *83*

4. The farming, landowning and timber-growing lobbies   85
5. The conservation movement   113
6. The Wildlife and Countryside Act   133
7. The implementation of the Act   157

Section 3   Case Studies in Conflict and Compromise   *187*

8. Moorland preservation in Exmoor   191
9. Afforestation and SSSI designation of the Berwyn Mountains   209
10. Wetland reclamation in West Sedgemoor   231
11. Ploughing into the Halvergate Marshes   265

Section 4   Proposals for Reform   *301*

12.   Changing direction in agriculture and forestry   303
13.   A new deal for the uplands   325
14.   Sticks and carrots   345

Index   371

Introduction

The decision by the European Economic Community to cut back milk production almost overnight in the spring of 1984 came as a fearful shock to many British farmers. Their organisations, the National Farmers' Union and the Country Landowners' Association, had failed to prepare them for the inevitable. But it came as no great surprise to the authors of this book or to many other observers to whom it had been apparent for some time that the Common Agricultural Policy (CAP) was on a one-way road to bankruptcy. It is not, therefore, entirely an accident that this book appears at a moment in history described in May 1984 by the President of the NFU, Sir Richard Butler, as 'a watershed' for farming, and the end of an 'era' in which 'agricultural expansion was automatically accepted as a desirable goal'. For the five authors had all been studying the conflict between agriculture and conservation for some years, had a detailed knowledge of both the farming and the conservation lobbies, and would have been politically blind had they not seen that the CAP was heading for trouble. The question even two or three years ago was no longer *whether* agricultural policies should be radically changed, but *when* and *how* the changes would be effected. We all felt that the time would be ripe in 1985, in a new climate, for a book that would set the conflict in its historical, political, social and ecological context; examine the strengths and weaknesses of the contending parties; illuminate the issues by detailed studies of some of the crucial cases; discuss the genesis and operation of the Wildlife and Countryside Act 1981; and bring forward alternative policies for farming and the conservation of our precious landscapes and natural resources.

The EEC decision to cut back milk production presaged a series of decisions over the next few years which will greatly reduce the level of financial support for the farming industry. As we show in Chapter 7, the immediate response of both the NFU and the CLA was to review their policies, and within a few months to publish reports outlining the new directions that they thought agricultural policy should take. One has only to read earlier policy statements emanating from these organisations over the past 20 years (many of them quoted in these pages) to appreciate the extent to which the NFU, and even more the CLA, have seen the need to adopt a far more sympathetic and accommodating attitude towards conservation. At the same time, both the Countryside Commission for England and Wales and the Nature Conservancy Council — the two agencies primarily responsible for the conservation of nature and natural beauty — markedly sharpened their hitherto rather timid representations to government, once it became apparent to them that the EEC decision had suddenly opened a door that had seemed closed against any major changes in conservation funding or policy.

The voluntary conservation bodies, which until then had been far more outspoken and percipient, have welcomed both the initial shifts in the positions of the NFU and the CLA and the indications of greater boldness on the part of the conservation agencies. But the emphasis is on the word 'initial'. Nobody is as yet committed irrevocably to anything. Everybody is feeling their way towards new stances and policies appropriate to new situations that cannot yet be predicted precisely. The voluntary conservation and recreation lobby, whilst delighted at the turn of events, is acutely aware of its weakness and lack of influence in government, when contrasted with the inside influence exercised by the NFU and CLA, analysed in Chapters 4 and 5.

While welcoming the belated shift in attitude by the NFU and CLA, and the prospect that this unfolds for collaboration rather than confrontation, conservationists will continue to be wary until the realities behind the fairer words become apparent. There is clearly an element of opportunism. For example, in its document, *The Way Forward: New Directions for Agricultural Policy*, the NFU make no secret of their view that farming profitability is their primary concern and that they are looking to conservation principally as an alternative source of income to compensate farmers' lost income as cuts in production subsidies bite more and more deeply. If the NFU had spent less time in the past attacking the conservationists, and put more effort into preparing their members for an inevitable shift towards farming methods that need less financial support and make fewer demands on the natural environment, they would not have been taken so much by surprise when the blow finally fell.

But the Ministry of Agriculture, Fisheries and Food (MAFF) is even more culpable. Right up to the day that the EEC cut back milk production, MAFF continued to lure dairy farmers into a financial trap. It encouraged small producers, with limited financial reserves, to buy more land and to invest in new buildings, equipment and livestock to expand production on borrowed money. Farmers who accepted the bait of capital grants found themselves trapped in six-year expansion plans, with mortgages round their necks that could only be serviced out of the projected expanded production that the EEC had suddenly prohibited. Although some of the more extreme cases have been helped, the result can only be widespread hardship, bankruptcies and forced decisions by the smaller and more indebted farmers to abandon farming. The sense of betrayal felt throughout the farming community, and the way in which confidence has been undermined, can hardly be exaggerated. The farming community is having to pay heavily for its leaders' pugnacious refusal, over many years, to listen to those who warned them of the way things were going.

Although a cutback in financial incentives for agricultural intensification has for some time been a central plank in the proposals of conservationists for resolving the conflict

between farming and conservation, it does not follow that
a reversal of the policy of subsidising increased productivity will necessarily have beneficial results, or by itself resolve the conflict. On the contrary, for reasons that will be
readily apparent to those who read this book and are
familiar with governmental attitudes and the roles of the
respective lobbies, there is a real risk that sharp and progressive reductions in farming support could push many
farmers into environmentally and socially damaging practices. The essence of the suggestions coming from the
conservation side is that the large sums of money needed
for positive programmes to conserve or enhance the natural environment, and to rehabilitate the rural economy,
should be obtained by diverting money currently going to
the agricultural and forestry programmes. To accept one
half of this package — the cuts — but not the other — the
expanded support for conservation and the rural economy
– could prove the worst of both worlds.

The situation at the beginning of 1985 was a highly fluid
one, with few signs that it would settle down. The government in particular seems beset by contradictory forces,
and part of the job that books like this one must do is to
help those who influence governments — whether by
their authority or by their numbers and political status —
to understand the problems better and to make their
weight felt. Both the Labour Party and the Liberal/Social
Democratic Alliance have made significant changes in
their policies towards farming and conservation, although
it remains to be seen what these commitments would be
worth if either party was in office. The Conservative Party,
too, is showing signs of change, ranging from the unprecedented number of fringe meetings on conservation
issues at its 1984 conference to the publication of a number
of books and pamphlets by Conservatives. As William
Waldegrave, Minister for the Environment, observed, the
sound of ambitious politicians climbing on the Green
bandwagon can be heard distinctly. The critical question,
given the probability of the Conservative administration
staying in power until 1988, is how Mrs Thatcher and her
colleagues are likely to react. The signs are contradictory,
which suggests that much may turn on the way in which
the growing conservation movement develops and exerts

its influence in Whitehall, in Westminster and in the constituencies.

There are clear indications that, despite growing lip-service to conservation, the government does not yet feel it politically expedient to take a strong stand on environmental issues. In December 1984 alone, it refused to subscribe to the international convention regulating, *inter alia*, the exploitation of the seabed; it rejected a European proposal to reduce acid rain emissions; and it permitted water authorities to disregard the limits imposed by the EEC on levels of nitrate polluting water supplies. And while the government is committed to closing the loophole in the Wildlife and Countryside Act 1981 that gives farmers a three months' period in which to destroy new Sites of Special Scientific Interest, the Queen's Speech in 1984 did not mention the conservation of the environment. Ministers looked instead to a Private Member's Bill to close the loophole, and declined to take the other urgently needed steps to put conservation on a stronger legal and financial footing.

The free-market and monetarist ideology now dominant in the Conservative Party has had the unexpected result of generating a powerful movement to cut down or even eliminate subsidies for agricultural production, except in the designated Less Favoured Areas. Unfortunately, the same ideology seems to inhibit the government from diverting the money thereby saved into positive programmes for conservation of natural resources or rural rehabilitation. There is a very serious risk that the Treasury, with its ruthless attitude to public expenditure, will swallow the savings whole.

In this situation, where the solid ground has gone, there seems to us to be a need for a book such as this that covers the area, addressing the problems from our distinctive point of view. No book in this field is entirely new, and we make no apology for the fact that we pull together a good deal of work that each of us has done in different fields to make a coherent whole. We obviously owe a substantial debt to others, far too numerous to mention, who have gone before and laid the foundations on which we are building. But we believe that anybody who is concerned about the future of farming and forestry, about our landscape, wildlife and natural resources, will find it both useful and stimulating to read the chapters that follow. The information that is provided and analysed, and the conclusions that are reached, cover a range that has not been attempted in any other publication. A coherent package of reforms is also presented, designed to integrate farming and forestry with conservation and sustainable land management. Some of the conclusions are more tentative than others, because we do not pretend to be absolutely certain of the right course of action to recommend in every instance. But all of them are, in our view, a constructive contribution to one of the most important debates ever to be held on the future of the British countryside.

Some readers may be surprised that five authors have managed to arrive at an agreed text on such controversial issues. That we were able to do so was only partly due to the broad agreement on many aspects that we shared when we decided to write the book. On other issues similar agreement was secured following the mutual criticism and discussion which was an essential element in our genuinely collaborative project. We all subscribe, therefore, to the factual information, analyses and broad conclusions presented, though each of us has reservations about some minor points of detail. In addition to achieving consistency of content and revising the text as new developments occurred, the task of integrating the work of five authors and ensuring a uniformity of style was inevitably a demanding one and, in so far as each of these tasks has been accomplished, particular credit and special thanks are due to Philip Lowe who undertook responsibility for coordinating our efforts.

This book could not have been produced without a great deal of help from many people and institutions. We are deeply grateful to them all, but wish to single out the following for special mention: the Nuffield Trust, for a grant which enabled us to develop the Berwyn Mountains study and to undertake other work; Geoffrey Sinclair, on whose research data for *The Upland Landscapes Study* (Environment Information Services, 1983) Chapter 12 is largely based, and which he developed with Malcolm MacEwen in *New Life for the Hills* (Council for National Parks, 1983); Professor Tim O'Riordan, who pioneered some of the ideas in this book in 'Putting Trust in the Countryside', his contribution to *The Conservation and Development Programme for the UK* (Kogan Page, 1983); Philip Lowe and Jane Goyder, for permission to draw on their work in *Environmental Groups in Politics* (George Allen & Unwin, 1983) in drafting Chapter 5; Ann and Malcolm MacEwen, for permission to adapt material from *National Parks: Conservation or Cosmetics?* (George Allen & Unwin, 1982) in several chapters; University College London's Bartlett School of Architecture and Planning, for the facilities and support provided to Philip Lowe and in administering the Nuffield grant; Tracey Clunies-Ross who compiled the index; and Sue Fairhurst of the Educational Services Unit, at the University of Bath, who prepared the maps of the case-study areas. Photographs are credited where they appear.

In addition, the following people have assisted us in our background researches or have commented on parts of the book in draft, and we would like to record our thanks for their help: Susan Bell, Roger Bradley, Denis Britton, David Conder, Stan Davies, Andrew Flynn, Sue Forsyth, Dorothy Gibbins, Anthony Gibson, Barney Holbeche, Stuart Housden, Reggie Lofthouse, Roger Lovegrove, Richard MacDonald, Jo Meredith, Rick Minter, Richard Munton, Peter Nicholson, Philip Oswald, Fiona Reynolds, Alan Rugman, Alistair Scott, Geoffrey Sinclair, Bill Slee, Alan Smith-Jones, John Taylor, Sir Ralph Verney, Alan Vittery, Peter Walters-Davies, Haydn Williams and Rob Williams.

Section 1
The Conflict in Context

1. Changing Conflicts in the Countryside

In recent years the countryside has become a source of considerable political contention. Rural issues and conflicts have become a central feature of local and national politics, and are hotly contested in public inquiries, council chambers, Parliament and the press. It has not always been so. For several decades the countryside presented an image of harmony and political consensus, though this often masked deep social divisions and inequalities. The consensus was carried over into national politics, where agricultural policy and the protection of the countryside enjoyed considerable bipartisan support. Conflicts seemed to arise not from within rural areas but from external pressures and demands emanating from towns and cities.

Gradually, over the past 20 years, the rural consensus has broken down. Urban/rural conflict still remains a potent feature of rural political issues, but what has also become apparent is conflict within the countryside — between the political parties, between government bureaucracies, between locals and newcomers, and between farmers and conservationists. One consequence has been a major shift in the focus of political debate about the British countryside, from an emphasis on the antagonism between town and country to an emphasis on the conflicts between different rural interests. This chapter discusses what lies behind these developments.

THE RURAL PRESERVATION MOVEMENT

Rural preservation emerged as a powerful force in British politics with the formation of the Council for the Preservation of Rural England (CPRE) in 1926. Though the CPRE quickly established county branches, it was predominantly a metropolitan-centred movement comprising a small but influential group of intellectuals, members of the artistic and literary establishments, and the landed aristocracy. They were able to tap a strong strain in English culture, deeply antipathetic to industrialism and all its creations, particularly the modern city. Early industrialism, by depopulating the countryside, had made it a potentially powerful cultural symbol. Indeed, the less practically important rural England became, the more it could stand simply for an alternative set of values.

Rural preservation was essentially an aesthetic movement expressing social pessimism and other-worldliness. In the words of one of its leading figures, the social historian G.M. Trevelyan, 'It is a question of spiritual values. Without vision the people perish and without sight of the beauty of nature the spiritual power of the British people will be atrophied.' The true national spirit was presented as residing, not in British commerce and industry, but in the past and in the country. It was important, therefore, that the latter should be preserved from the rampant spread of urban industrialism and its utilitarian values. As Patrick Abercrombie, the pioneer planner, argued, 'the greatest historical monument that we possess, the most essential thing which *is* England, is the Countryside, the Market Town, the Village, the Hedgerow Trees, the Lanes, the Copses, the Streams and the Farmsteads.' These words appeared in the *Clarion* pamphlet, 'The Preservation of Rural England', which he published in 1926, and which led to the establishment of the CPRE.

The CPRE set about lobbying vigorously for controls over urban sprawl and ribbon development, and for the creation of green-belts and national parks. Its leaders saw themselves fighting against an avalanche of bricks, concrete and asphalt. The motor car, new trunk roads and commuter railway lines were allowing residential development to break loose from the city boundaries. Suburbs mushroomed as cheap mortgages and depressed land prices enabled many white-collar workers to buy a villa or a bungalow, with a garden and a garage for their new Ford 8 or Austin 7.

The need to protect agriculture and create conditions in which it could flourish was part of the conventional wisdom of rural preservation. The preservationists tended to have a highly romantic and idealised view of farming, summed up by G.M. Trevelyan in his *English Social History* in the following terms: 'Agriculture is not merely one industry among many, but is a way of life, unique and irreplaceable in its human and spiritual values.' Agriculture had been in a chronic state of depression since the 1880s, and farming practices seemed to pose no threat to other rural interests and pursuits. On the contrary, it was felt that the debilitated condition of farming exacerbated many other threats to the countryside, such as urban encroachment, the decline of rural communities and the flight from the land. Not only was the countryside under attack from the towns, but rural life was disintegrating from within. A secure and revitalised farming was seen as the essential conserver of both the social life and the natural beauty of the countryside.

Support for protecting the countryside came from two other groups — open-air enthusiasts and naturalists. Hiking, previously a bohemian pursuit, became a popular pastime in the 1920s and 1930s, attracting young people equally from working-class and middle-class backgrounds. The bicycle, the motor car and the charabanc made the countryside more accessible, while reductions in the working week and declining religious observance gave people more free time and the opportunity for at least temporary escape from drab, smoky and overcrowded towns. The popularity of hiking derived from the vogue for health and physical fitness and from the new sense of social permissiveness which had emerged in the wake of the Great War. By the early 1930s it was also attracting many of those who were being subjected to the enforced idleness of mass unemployment.

A number of organisations were formed to represent and cater for this burgeoning interest. The Ramblers' Association, established in 1935, brought together some

600 local rambling clubs with 50,000 members, strongly concentrated in London and the South-East and the industrial areas of the Midlands, Yorkshire, Lancashire and Central Scotland. 'Hiking has replaced beer as the shortest cut out of Manchester,' quipped Cyril Joad, an influential figure with the Ramblers' Association, in his book *The Untutored Townsman's Invasion of the Country*. For the accommodation of this new army of townsfolk seeking the country, the Youth Hostels Association was set up in 1931, with Trevelyan as its President. By the summer of 1939, it had 300 hostels and 83,000 members. These and older organisations, such as the Camping Club, the Holiday Fellowship, the Co-operative Holidays Association and the Cyclists' Touring Club, gave their backing to the protection of the countryside, especially the campaign for national parks.

For the Ramblers' Association, however, the main political cause was access to open country. The lack of rights of way, particularly over the grouse moors of the Southern Pennines, was a major source of resentment, and occasioned various mass trespasses and protest demonstrations. The most famous — on Kinder Scout in April 1932 — was organised by the British Workers' Sports Federation, an offshoot of the Young Communist League. Several hundred trespassers clashed with gamekeepers and the police. Prison sentences totalling 17 months were meted out to five of the leaders. Though the official rambling clubs had boycotted it, they and their members were aroused by the severity of the punishment, and this fuelled a broad political campaign to amend the law of trespass.

The other source of support for rural preservation was from naturalists interested in wildlife protection. The largest and most active group was the Royal Society for the Protection of Birds. In the 1930s, its membership stood at about 4000. It had been formed in 1889, initially as a crusade against the fashion for exotic feathers in women's hats which threatened the survival of many of the colourful birds of the Tropics. However, it had broadened its interests to encompass all aspects of wild bird protection, and had played a key role in promoting protective legislation. The main threats to bird populations were seen to come from the excesses of hunting, gamekeeping, egg-collecting and human cruelty. By the 1920s, though, other hazards to birdlife had begun to exercise the RSPB, including oil pollution and the use of arsenic sprays by fruit-growers.

A threat to wildlife of a different kind was recognised by the Society for the Promotion of Nature Reserves, which had been set up in 1912. It was concerned at the loss of wild and natural areas and their attendant species, through such causes as building, land drainage and woodland clearance. The Society's outlook was influenced by the understanding emerging from the new science of ecology of the causal relationship between habitats and animal and plant communities, which indicated the need to protect habitats to preserve species. It was a relatively inactive group and certainly made no popular impact, but its small membership included leading naturalists and influential public figures.

The cause of rural preservation was greatly boosted by the outbreak of the second world war. The demand for a 'better Britain', to replace the Britain of the dole queue, means tests and social strife, exerted pressure on the wartime coalition government to demonstrate that it contemplated some decisive changes when the war was over. Planning and the promise of greater prosperity and security, it was realised, could play a major role in stimulating the war effort, so the need to preserve the British countryside was embraced, at least in principle, as part of a general commitment to a comprehensive land-use policy. It was a cause which commended itself to the government for its obvious symbolic value in helping sustain morale during a period of intense national sacrifice.

Official preparations for post-war reconstruction provided unprecedented opportunities to influence the formulation of government policy. The major focus for opinions on the future of the countryside was the official Committee on Land Utilisation in Rural Areas appointed in October 1941 by the Minister of Works and Buildings, Lord Reith, to consider 'the conditions which should govern building ... in country areas consistent with the maintenance of agriculture ... having regard to ... the well-being of rural communities and the preservation of rural amenities.' The Committee's Chairman was Lord Justice Scott, who had been Vice-President of the CPRE.

Formulated at the height of the war, the Scott Report's thinking contributed crucially to the post-war ideology of urban containment and green-belts, the establishment of national parks and nature reserves, and state support for farming. Its essential thesis was that the rural community was an agricultural community, dependent on the continuance and revival of the traditional mixed character of British farming. The assumption was that a prosperous farming industry would preserve both the rural landscape and rural communities. 'Farmers and foresters are unconsciously the nation's landscape gardeners', declared the report, adding emphatically, 'there is no antagonism between use and beauty.'

The major threat to rural areas, apart from government neglect, was seen to arise from building and industrial pressures which, it was argued, threatened to mar the countryside, take land out of farming and entice labour away from agriculture. The chief author of the Report was the Committee's Vice-Chairman, the geographer L. Dudley Stamp. His 'Land Utilisation Survey' had recently revealed that, in the years 1927–39, there had been an average annual loss of 25,000 ha. of open land — much of it good farm land — to urban and industrial development. The Report was optimistic that, if these pressures could be resisted, farm incomes boosted and modern services provided in villages, then rural life would be resuscitated and the countryside preserved.

Herein lay the fatal contradiction of the Scott Report, for it wished to have the best of all worlds — traditional mixed farming, rural living standards raised to urban levels and the 'traditional' landscape. But, in a dissenting report, the economist, Professor S.R. Dennison, flatly challenged the basic assumptions of the rest of the Committee. He denied that the rural community was still agricultural, and anticipated the course of post-war farming by arguing that agricultural prosperity depended on efficiency, which could be achieved only by specialist farming and by reducing the number of agricultural workers. He looked to industry to provide the jobs that agriculture would lose, and suggested that farmers could be paid to conserve landscape as 'landscape gardeners and not as agriculturalists'. Dennison clearly regarded as nonsense the dictum of the Majority Report that 'the cheapest, indeed the only way, of preserving the countryside in anything like its traditional aspect would be to farm it'. He regarded traditional farming as incompatible with prosperity and was happy to see it disappear.

THE POST-WAR PLANNING SYSTEM

The assumptions made by the Scott Committee had far-reaching consequences, particularly in shaping the philosophy and objectives of post-war policy for agriculture and land-use planning. Thus the Town and Country Planning Act 1947 accorded farming and forestry a pre-emptive claim over all other uses of rural land. There were two underlying motives: to regenerate agriculture and to protect the countryside from urban development. Britain, more than any other country, had relied on imported food. The war, however, clearly demonstrated the strategic importance of increased home supplies of food and timber, as well as the role government could play in stimulating production, and this became the basis of post-war agricultural policy as set out in the Agriculture Act 1947. This Act and the Town and Country Planning Act of the same year, were complementary, in that the former achieved a secure environment for investment in farming and the latter ensured security of land-use for agriculture.

The Planning Act introduced the principle that new development and changes in land-use were to be subject to control, to ensure their conformity to plans to be prepared by the local planning authorities. In rural areas these were the county councils. The definition of 'development' in the Act specifically excluded 'the use of any land for the purposes of agriculture or forestry (including afforestation), and the use for any of those purposes of any building occupied together with the land so used'. The Act also made possible the undertaking of agricultural operations without planning permission, through the provisions of the general development order. Agriculture's exemption occasioned no dispute at the time — reflecting the romantic view of farming encapsulated in the Scott Report and the overriding political commitment given to the expansion of home food production at a time when rationing was still in force.

The new planning system sought to protect agriculture not only as an end in itself, but also as a means of achieving the wider aims of rural preservation. The latter objective was elaborated in the National Parks and Access to the Countryside Act 1949. This provided the machinery for the designation and administration of national parks, to be chosen for their landscape and recreational value; areas of outstanding natural beauty (AONBs), chosen on landscape grounds alone; and national nature reserves and sites of special scientific interest (SSSIs) to safeguard places with a special flora, fauna or geology.

Though the rural preservation movement had been highly effective in shaping the broad philosophy and objectives of the new system of land-use planning, it was disappointed with the specific measures introduced to protect and open up areas of great natural beauty. The official Dower and Hobhouse Reports, which followed up some of the recommendations of the Scott Report, had called for the establishment of a central National Parks Commission with executive powers to designate national parks and to acquire and manage land within them. This suggestion was pre-empted, however, by the responsibilities given to the county councils by the Town and Country Planning Act: they had become the planning authorities for rural areas, including the intended national park areas. The county councils declined to surrender any of this recently won power to a new central body. Moreover, the Labour government was keen that legislation for national parks should go through as an agreed measure enjoying bipartisan support, and ministers were not prepared to include any powers that were not acceptable to the agricultural and landowning interests. The consequence was that the National Parks Commission established by the 1949 Act lacked executive, administrative, land-owning or land-managing functions, and was little more than a sop to the amenity and preservation interests. Apart from designating national parks and AONBs (subject to ministerial confirmation), its role was to be entirely advisory and supervisory. The administration of these designated areas was to be in the hands of the local planning authorities.

In contrast, those interested in nature conservation achieved their highest hopes. The Society for the Promotion of Nature Reserves had quickly responded to the wartime challenge to plan for post-war reconstruction. Somewhat ironically, it benefited from the fact that nature reserves had never emerged as a popular cause during peace-time. The very popularity of the national parks' cause over the years, and its emphasis on access and recreation, had allowed ample time for opposition to develop among farmers, landowners and local authorities and within some government departments. The Society for the Promotion of Nature Reserves avoided controversy by divorcing the case for nature reserves from that for national parks and by concentrating on the scientific aspects of nature conservation.

During this period — the 1940s — ecologists gradually assumed the leadership of the nature conservation movement. They were anxious to institutionalise their discipline, and nature conservation seemed a potential vehicle for achieving government recognition. The British Ecological Society established its own Committee in 1943, under the chairmanship of Arthur Tansley, to investigate the need for nature reserves and nature conservation. The Committee, in its report, reasoned that the formulation and implementation of conservation policies must be based on sound ecological advice.

These and other suggestions were considered by two official committees: one for England and Wales, under the chairmanship of Julian Huxley with Tansley as his deputy, which reported in 1947; and the other for Scotland, under James Ritchie, which reported in 1949. The committees drew up lists of proposed nature reserves and stressed the importance of selecting and managing reserves on scientific principles, recommending for the purpose the setting up of an official 'Biological Service'. The government acted on their recommendations by establishing, in 1949, the Nature Conservancy as a chartered research council. This new government agency combined the functions of conducting and sponsoring ecological research, giving advice and information on nature conservation, and acquiring and managing nature reserves.

Nature conservation thus became a scientific matter to be administered by scientists. Not only did this separate the protection of natural beauty from the protection of nature, but it also divorced nature conservation from the realms of land-use planning. The only exception related to sites of special scientific interest (SSSIs). These were to be areas of conservation value which were not being managed as nature reserves. The Nature Conservancy was given the duty of notifying local planning authorities of SSSIs so that they could be marked on development plans and their value taken into account in the exercise of development control. However, during the following 20 years, the main thrust of nature conservation activity was concentrated elsewhere — on the purchase of land for nature reserves and the development of techniques of reserve management.

Apart from nature reserves, the main instruments for protecting natural beauty or wildlife habitats depended upon the exercise of planning powers by local authorities. Developments in agriculture and forestry were therefore outside their remit. This did not seem anomalous to the advocates of nature conservation and landscape protection. John Dower, in his Report to the government, *National Parks in England and Wales (1945)*, maintained that 'Agriculture, landscape preservation and recreational provisions must march together. There should be no substantial difficulty in working out the necessary practical arrangements, for in all major matters there is a community and harmony of purpose.' The war-effort had necessitated extensive reclamation of marginal land, the ploughing-up of old pasture, and the exploitation of non-commercial woodlands. Most observers sanguinely assumed this would cease once peace returned. As Arthur Tansley wrote in *Our Heritage of Wild Nature: A Plea for Organized Nature Conservation*, published in 1945, 'it is scarcely probable that the extension of agriculture will go much further, for the limits of profitable agricultural land must have been reached in most places.'

The creation of the Nature Conservancy and the

enactment of the National Parks Act 1949 should not blind us to the fact that it was the two earlier pieces of legislation — the Agriculture Act 1947 and the Town and Country Planning Act 1947 — that established the basic context of post-war rural planning. The crude statistics suggest that both have gone some way towards achieving at least their primary objectives. Prior to the war, British agriculture supplied approximately a third of the food requirements for a population of 47 million. Today this has risen to about two-thirds of the food requirements for a population of 56 million, and, in terms of temperate foodstuffs, Britain is rapidly approaching self-sufficiency. The achievements of the planning system in curbing urban sprawl can be seen in the statistics for the loss of farmland to urban development. In the 1930s, the average annual rate was over 25,000 ha. Since the war, this has been cut back to an average annual rate of less than 16,000 ha. In achieving these primary objectives, however, profound changes have occurred to both agriculture and the rural preservation movement — changes which have set these two interests increasingly at odds with one another.

SOCIAL AND POLITICAL CHANGE IN THE COUNTRYSIDE

The post-war period has brought considerable social change to rural areas, and, in the process, perceptions of the countryside have altered. Rural depopulation continued as in earlier decades, with the number of full-time agricultural workers declining by 400,000 (70 per cent) between 1950 and 1980; and it is still falling at over 10,000 per annum. The new prosperity which state support brought to agriculture did not ensure a place in the sun for farm labourers: their wages have lagged consistently behind the average for industrial workers. Moreover, the whole thrust of technological development in agriculture has been to replace labour with machinery. This has favoured the larger farmers with capital to draw on, and most of them have expanded their holdings, squeezing out the small farmer.

The loss of population as small farmers and farm

workers, or their sons and daughters, sought a better living in urban areas has been more than matched by the movement of the middle class into the countryside. Growing affluence and car-ownership have enabled more and more people to realise their dream of a home in the country. Tight planning controls around the major cities and the construction of motorways have pushed housing pressures further and further out into free-standing towns and villages. The line dividing rural pressure areas (i.e. those experiencing net population growth) from declining rural areas has spread steadily outwards from the conurbations as commuter hinterlands have expanded and as people have looked to more and more remote areas for retirement cottages and second homes. By the 1960s, the whole of lowland England was part of the rural pressure area. By the mid-1970s, it embraced most of rural Britain, including such classic areas of out-migration as mid-Wales and the Scottish Highlands, though many isolated settlements are still suffering decline. Thus, since the second world war, the historic role of the countryside as a net exporter of people, established in the early stages of industrialism, has been reversed.

Migration into the countryside has been very much a movement of middle-class owner-occupiers with their own transport. A fair proportion have enjoyed subsidised mobility — such as the company car and the payment of removal expenses on appointment or promotion, which are among the standard perks enjoyed by those above the lower rungs of the managerial ladder. Tax relief on mortgage payments for those buying their own homes was also available to those acquiring second homes until 1974. In addition, home improvement grants to private owners have aided the modernisation, extension and gentrification of much, previously sub-standard, rural property.

The operation of the planning system has reinforced the selective effect of people's private means on migration into the countryside. The spread of the rural pressure areas has quickly taken up the slack in the housing market created by rural depopulation. This has involved the transfer of much of the existing housing stock from the private, rented sector catering for the rural working class to the owner-occupied sector catering for the ex-urban middle class. Once the housing surplus had been taken up, the rural pressure areas began to experience growing demand for new private housing, but those who have settled in the countryside have sought to use the preservation procedures of the planning system to safeguard their own residential amenity. Thus, most of the expansion which has been permitted for villages and small towns has consisted of small, low-density estates, mainly of bungalows, semis and detached houses. Many of the prettier villages have been designated as conservation areas; in these, housing development has usually been limited to sensitive in-filling of vacant sites. Such policies simultaneously enhance the attractiveness of the area and restrain new development. The consequent shortage, high quality and hence high cost of housing tend to restrict residential access mainly to higher income groups. Moreover, most rural councils have shown a marked reluctance to build low-cost housing for rent, thus further restricting the housing opportunities for those with low incomes.

The great exodus from the cities of retired people, commuters and second-homers, though still continuing, peaked in the 1960s. This massive population movement has disrupted established social hierarchies and provoked new divisions and tensions in rural communities. Though agriculture remains the dominant land-use, rural society is no longer mainly an agrarian society. The countryside, in the words of the rural sociologist Howard Newby, has been transformed 'into a predominantly middle-class territory'.

The ex-urban newcomers show none of the political quiescence of the rural working class. Invariably, they have challenged the political and social leadership of farmers and landowners. Gradually they have taken over many of the established institutions — such as the parish council, the Women's Institute and the local Conservative Association. They have also established new institutions which reflect their interests and particular visions of the rural community. Indeed, many of the rural issues which have arisen in recent years derive from the expectations which the middle classes have taken with them into the countryside — such as the expectations of urban standards of service provision and an unchanging countryside.

One of the most pervasive political expressions of the middle class in the countryside is local amenity and conservation groups. Once settled in their chosen town or village, they are understandably reluctant to see changes that might adversely affect the environmental standards which first attracted them there. Most towns and villages now have an amenity or preservation group, formed in the period between 1955 and 1975, and concerned with safeguarding the character and physical appearance of the locality from any unpleasant developments. They are particularly thick on the ground in the South-East, the most prosperous region in Britain, and the area which has experienced the greatest pressures for development; and in retirement areas, such as the West, the Isle of Wight, Cumbria, North Yorkshire and East Anglia. In comparison, there are few in remote rural areas, which have not yet experienced the full impact of retirement or commuter pressures. All in all, there are about 1200 local amenity societies in Britain with a combined membership of about 300,000.

The other prominent local groups concerned with environmental protection are the county trusts for nature conservation. Most of these were set up in the late 1950s and early 1960s. There are now 46 trusts covering the country and their total membership stands at 150,000. As well as helping to identify and protect local habitats of importance to wildlife, the trusts acquire sites of their own which they run as nature reserves.

Many who join these local groups have swollen the support for groups such as the RSPB, the National Trust and the CPRE. The consequence for the power and standing of the national groups will be discussed in Chapter 5. One of them, the Society for the Promotion of Nature Reserves, has been transformed into a body to coordinate and represent nationally the interests of the county trusts and is now known as the Royal Society for Nature Conservation.

By virtue of their own predominantly middle-class membership, many local environmental groups are able to draw on an impressive array of professional expertise, organisational skills and political contacts, and this often gives them considerable influence, especially within local government. Across most of the countryside they are a significant political force, treated with wary respect by officials and developers. They are particularly effective at working within the planning system, making use of the opportunities provided for public participation and the various protective designations in order to stave off unwanted urban development.

THE THREAT FROM WITHIN

To the latter-day rural preservationists, however, there is a worm in the bud threatening their vision of an unchanging countryside, and that is modern agriculture. As we have seen, few people anticipated the rapid transformation in agricultural practices which was to occur in the post-war period. Even so, agricultural intensification, fostered by government and realised through the adoption of new technologies, the spread of mechanisation and the consolidation of holdings, has transformed the rural environment. As the scale of the post-war revolution in agriculture has become apparent, there has been a shift in emphasis in preservationist circles from a focus on urban and industrial pressures as the main threat to landscape and wildlife to a preoccupation with the destructive effects of changing farming and forestry practices and technologies. This shift has involved profound changes in the popular image of agriculture. The sheer pace of development has destroyed any illusions that it is intrinsically an unchanging or slowly evolving activity. Nowadays, many conservationists regard agriculture as austere and capitalistic, no longer the embodiment of rural simplicity and rustic virtue. In the title of a recent, highly publicised book by Marion Shoard, a former staff member of the CPRE, farmers are accused of *The Theft of the Countryside*. Indeed, even farmers themselves tend to refer to agriculture as an industry, to the farm as a business, and to their fields as a factory floor.

Yet disillusionment on the part of those concerned about the protection of the countryside has come about in a slow and piecemeal fashion, so strong was the romantic view of farming. To the inter-war preservationists, the countryside was an abstract symbol. What actually happened in the real countryside mattered less than that it should be defended from the incursions of urban industrialism. As the middle classes have moved into rural areas, so the realities of the countryside have gradually impinged on their Arcadian vision.

Initially, in the period of austerity of the early post-war years, increased home food production was an unquestioned priority to save on the country's import bill. Changes in agricultural practice were becoming apparent, but their impact on the fabric of the countryside was at first limited. Indeed, under the impression that mechanisation would adapt to existing field boundaries and farm buildings, the prominent rural economist Gerald Wibberley could write, in 1950:

> Casual travellers will see few drastic changes in the appearance of our fields in the near future. The patchwork quilt of colours and the different types and breeds of livestock will continue.

He anticipated major technological developments in agriculture but presumed that 'so many people will pass them by unheeded and talk of Britain's "unchanging" countryside'.

Since the late 1950s, through a series of controversies, the image of the farmer as the conserver of the countryside has gradually disintegrated, to be replaced by the image of the agri-businessman. It was the introduction of factory production methods, particularly broiler houses from the mid-1950s onwards, that first aroused alarm, drawing attention to the anomaly whereby industrial-type buildings — often badly sited and of poor design — could be erected without any form of consultation if intended for agricultural use. Pressure from amenity societies, planners and the County Councils' Association secured an amendment to the general development order in 1960 which brought agricultural buildings of more than 5000 sq.ft in area within the remit of development control. A further modification in 1967, in this case in response to the threat of tower silos, brought agricultural buildings over 40 ft in height under development control.

The deaths of thousands of birds in 1960 and 1961 after the spring sowing of seeds dressed with Aldrin and Dieldrin prompted concern over the threat that agriculture posed to wildlife. The resultant public outcry prompted the chemical manufacturers to establish a voluntary system restricting the availability of the more toxic pesticides. In an effort to avert criticism, the manufacturers suggested that other factors might be contributing to the decline in bird numbers and even funded research into the effects of hedgerow removal. The loss of hedgerows reached its peak in the 1960s at 10,000 miles/per annum and is still perhaps the most unpopular consequence of mechanisation in agriculture. Investigations by naturalists, however, suggested that this was of marginal importance to wildlife populations in the lowlands compared to the diminishing area of deciduous woodland, so attention was again switched to another facet of modern agricultural practice.

Agricultural intensification has pressed more and more upon marginal land, as new technology and grants from the Ministry of Agriculture have encouraged the improvement of land which previously was relatively unproductive. In the early 1960s, public attention was first directed to the ploughing-up of moorland in Exmoor. The Exmoor Society, a branch of the CPRE, commissioned a study of the extent of change and this suggested that the very fabric of the national park was under threat (see Chapter 8). Ever since, the Exmoor issue has been at the forefront of debate on the future of the countryside, though concern has also been aroused since the mid-1970s at the conversion of moorland in other national park and upland areas. In the late 1960s, the reclamation of old pasture and the ploughing-up of lowland heaths and downland were also brought into focus; and in the 1970s the drainage of wetland habitats received some of the most concentrated publicity (see Chapters 10 and 11).

Thus over a period of about 20 years the various environmental implications of agricultural intensification have been recognised, one by one, first by conservationists and then by others, including an increasing number of farmers. Because each issue was viewed separately, the response of the conservation organisations was to seek specific remedies through isolated campaigns. It is only within the last decade that a global concept of agricultural change seems to have been fully grasped. The Countryside Commission's *New Agricultural Landscapes* study (1974) was influential in demonstrating that changes in agriculture could comprehensively alter 'the landscape' rather than just individual features of it, though the Commission was optimistic that, with proper guidance, modern agriculture could produce a new, though equally attractive, countryside, largely through planting or conserving the bits the high-tech farmers had no use for. Since then opinions have hardened, as evidence of a general destruction of habitats has accumulated — evidence first marshalled in the Nature Conservancy Council's report, *Nature Conservation and Agriculture* (1977), which concluded that 'all changes due to modernisation are harmful to wildlife except for a few species that are able to adapt to the new simplified habitats'.

The sweeping impact of agricultural development on the rural environment has drawn attention to the failure of existing protective measures to moderate or deflect the tide of change. National parks and AONBs cover 19 per cent of England and Wales; and SSSIs 5 per cent. Farming and forestry occupy 90 per cent of the land so designated, but local planning authorities lack any control or influence over these uses. This means that the measures intended to safeguard the countryside are impotent in relation to the forces now recognised as dominant in the creation or destruction of landscape and habitats. Moreover, MAFF and the Forestry Commission continue to give grants in designated areas to encourage agricultural intensification and afforestation.

With the growing appreciation of the totality of agricultural change, the whole system of agricultural support has come under attack as the root cause of intensification, rather than the activities of individual farmers. The system of protective designations has also been questioned, not only because of its ineffectiveness, but also for neglecting the ordinary countryside and its depredations by dividing the country into areas where conservation mattered and areas where it could be ignored with impunity. Pressure has thus built up for general powers to regulate the environmental impact of agricultural and forestry development. In seeking these and other changes, the conservation lobby now confronts a powerful set of interests which it once regarded as its closest allies.

Though farmers and landowners may have suffered some diminution in their local influence since the 1940s and the influx of the middle classes into the countryside; their influence in national and European politics has grown immensely. The large farmer who might once have played an active part on the county council often has less time for local affairs nowadays because of the calls of Whitehall and Brussels. The influence of the farming lobby on agricultural matters is paramount, and the policies which have promoted agricultural prosperity have also strengthened the farming lobby and nurtured its unique link with government.

FURTHER READING

Howard Newby is the leading authority on social change in the countryside. His book *Green and Pleasant Land?* (Pelican, 1980) is a synthesis of his work and serves as a good introduction to his more specialised studies.

The place of the countryside and rural imagery in national culture is analysed in Martin Wiener, *English Culture and the Decline of the Industrial Spirit 1850–1980* (Cambridge University Press, 1981) and Raymond Williams, *The Country and the City* (Chatto & Windus, 1973).

The history of nature conservation in Britain is retailed in John Sheail, *Nature in Trust* (Blackie, 1976), whereas Gordon Cherry presents, from official sources, the history of countryside legislation in *Environmental Planning 1939–1969. Vol. II, National Parks and Recreation in the Countryside* (HMSO, 1975).

Howard Hill, a veteran rambler, provides a spirited account of the struggle for access to open countryside in *Freedom to Roam* (Moorland Publishing, 1980).

The changing patterns of land-use in Britain were carefully monitored over many years by the late Robin Best, and a summary of his findings is *Land-Use and Living Space* (Methuen, 1981).

Finally, a useful compilation of countryside legislation, developments in rural politics and reviews of recent books and reports is included in *The Countryside Planning Yearbook*, ed. Andrew Gilg (Geo-Books, annual publications).

2. The Political Economy of Post-War Agriculture and Forestry

No industry operates in a completely free and unfettered market, and agriculture and forestry are no exceptions. The farmer is constrained on the one hand by his own personal circumstances and on the other by the policies and economic management of government. The structure of the farming industry, with its myriad of small and large producers, can give the impression of free competition — an impression reinforced by the keen entrepreneurial spirit displayed in livestock markets, pick-your-own enterprises and farm shops up and down the country. Often farmers imply that this activity and competitive drive for efficiency are the sole basis for the industry's success. But the truth is that farmers have received more state aid from the British government, and latterly also from the European Community, than any other industry outside the state sector.

Although the political management of farming may not be as obvious as it is with the nationalised industries, the agricultural economy is very much a political economy, in that it is subject to the political and administrative decision-making of Whitehall and Brussels. Decisions of government are as important to the hill farmer selling his lambs in a remote market as they are to a coal miner or NHS hospital worker. The massive expansion of British agriculture since 1945 has been the result of deliberate government policy. In its scale, speed and impact, this state-supported expansion matches or surpasses the agricultural revolution of the eighteenth century which saw the demise of open-field agriculture.

THE SECOND AGRICULTURAL REVOLUTION

By 1945 there was already a new outlook amongst British farmers. For the first time since the onset of the great agricultural depression in the 1870s, all sectors of agriculture were prospering. Wartime support for the industry and the promise of continued support in peacetime fostered in farming circles a confidence and optimism unknown for three generations. But farming practices had altered little. Desperate measures had been taken to increase food supplies during the war to overcome the U-boat blockade. The tractor had begun to displace the horse, but the technological revolution, with its economic, social and environmental concomitants, had hardly begun. Agriculture in 1945 was closer technically to the farming of the 1880s than the 1980s.

It was still reliant on human labour and, to a major extent, on horse power. The 1949 edition of the agriculturalist's Bible, *Fream's Elements of Agriculture*, could confidently assert the indispensability of farm horses for many tasks, and they still greatly outnumbered tractors. A majority of farmers hand-milked their cows and fed them with unbaled hay. Chemical fertilisers were not widely used and chemical sprays were largely unknown outside fruit farming. The number of combine harvesters may have increased tenfold between 1941 and 1947, but with only 5000 in the country by 1947 they were still a rare sight away from the cornlands of the East. Perhaps even more telling is that yields of many crops had scarcely increased over 40 or 50 years.

The traditional maxims of good husbandry — crop rotation and tidy farming — still prevailed. The straggly hedges of pre-war days had been cut back, but few had yet been grubbed out. Some ecologically interesting downland had been lost to the plough, but most wartime ploughing had resulted in cropping land which had reverted to pasture in the 1870s and 1880s or had been cropped briefly during the first world war. Agriculture was largely characterised by small farms and fields. The soil's natural fertility was supplemented by manure, marl and lime. Physical constraints, such as steep slopes, heavy clay, infertile sand or wetness, kept land out of cultivation, and large areas were used only for rough grazing. Within the overall pattern of arable cultivation concentrated in the East and pastoral dominating in the West, established agricultural practices and mixed farming maintained a rich diversity of landscapes and natural habitats.

All this has changed during the past 40 years. The organisation and practices of farming have been transformed with dramatic results. Yields of wheat and barley, for example, have virtually trebled. In spite of the massive emphasis on the production of grain during the war, the area under the plough in 1945 was considerably less than today. The combined acreage of wheat and barley has more than doubled, and in the last 15 years output too has been boosted, particularly by new strains. Between 1975 and 1981 alone, the total volume of wheat harvested doubled to 8,600,000 tonnes. With similar developments in other European countries, it is small wonder that there is now a huge stockpile of surplus grain in the EEC.

Meat and dairy production have also expanded. Though the area of grassland has shrunk considerably through the expansion of arable cropping in the lowlands and afforestation in the uplands, the number of livestock has not decreased. On the contrary, improved grassland yields have enabled the number of cattle to increase, from 8,616,000 in 1945 to 13,137,000 in 1981. Even the beasts themselves are more efficient: on average a cow now produces 8500 pints of milk a year; in 1945 it would have been 4000 pints.

The basis for these changes has been the mechanisation of agriculture, the use of artificial fertilisers and pesticides, selective plant and animal breeding, and more efficient and capital-intensive farming. Not all these developments are unique to the agricultural industry but they have taken a particular form in agriculture because of its social and economic diversity and its dependence on land. As a primary industry, agriculture has been encouraged to pay special attention to the efficiency of its use of labour. Post-war policy was designed not just to increase food production, but also to release labour (in order to provide for the manpower needs of other sectors of the economy) and to improve the profits and incomes of those remaining in agriculture.

The intensification of production has inflicted tremendous pressure on the rural environment, but the decline in the work force, as fixed capital has displaced labour, has meant additional strains. Labour-intensive methods of production and farm management may be capable of producing yields per hectare as good as or better than today's, and they are often particularly well suited for conservation management, but they have been largely superseded by labour-saving practices which are usually environmentally harmful. The Countryside Review Committee, on which MAFF was represented, commented in 1978 that 'the really significant new dimension' of recent developments in agriculture 'is that virtually all of them have been un-favourable to wildlife and landscape'. Capital grants to save labour, though justifiable in the 1950s and 1960s when labour was in short supply, are of dubious value today when mass unemployment prevails. Similarly, production payments to farmers made sense in the 1940s and 1950s when Britain was short of food and critically dependent on food exports, but current price-support policies which create butter and grain mountains and milk and wine lakes are an anachronism. Before looking in more detail at the legislative background to some of these policies, it is as well to contemplate the scale of change in farm structure and workforce attendant on the second agricultural revolution.

FARM LABOUR AND FARM STRUCTURE

The proportion of the UK workforce employed in agriculture has long been one of the smallest in the world. By 1977 it had dropped to 2.2 per cent compared with 2.4 per cent in the USA, 9.5 per cent in France and 11.4 per cent in Western Europe as a whole. Even as far back as 1851, only a quarter of the UK's working population was employed in farming, and the proportion has declined remorselessly since. Two phases of particularly marked shrinkage can be identified. The first was the late-Victorian period, when the prosperity of farming slumped in the face of growing competition from imported food, particularly from North and South America. The second phase has been the post-war period of state-supported agricultural expansion. It is ironic that the working population engaged in agriculture should have fallen so rapidly during such contrasting periods for farming fortunes, though in both cases farmers were subject to sustained price pressures which stimulated their efforts to cut labour costs.

The more 'rational' utilisation of labour has been a preoccupation of policy-makers throughout the post-war period. As Britain has moved from food shortage to surplus and the overall emphasis of policy has shifted from increased food production to improved efficiency, a recurring objective has been to facilitate the flow of labour from the land. As we shall see, this is in sharp contrast to the policy rationale of state-supported forestry, which is to augment rural employment in order, in part, to mop up some of the surplus labour generated in remoter rural areas by contemporary agricultural policies. Between 1960 and 1979 the number of agricultural workers fell by a half, and of farmers by a third. Nearly three-quarters of UK farms now employ no full-time hired workers at all, and are run by family labour, often just the farmer and his wife and sometimes a son, with occasional help from casual labour or farm contractors. But this relative resurgence of family farming should not be romanticised — the modern family farmer is not the peasant or yeoman of yesterday; rather, he is a highly specialised, technologically sophisticated producer. Nevertheless, it is important to bear in mind that many producers are family producers. Critics of farming often seem to imply that *all* farmers in modern Britain are large and exploit both land and workers. It is as well to remember, in the search for new directions in agricultural policy, that many family farmers have to struggle hard for economic survival. With a quarter of farms comprising less than 10 ha., there are still a large number of relatively small farmholdings, although their agricultural importance has declined rapidly in recent years.

In the 1950s, farm sizes were almost static. With generous price support, the small farmer flourished and was
able to modernise his holding with the help of capital
grants. In the 1960s and 1970s, however, farming became
subject to a cost–price squeeze, and a number of policy
measures were specifically designed to speed up the rate
of farm amalgamations. As a result, the number of small
farms declined rapidly. By the late 1960s farms of 8–40 ha.
were disappearing at a rate of nearly 3 per cent per
annum. Since the early 1950s the proportion of land in
England and Wales farmed in units of over 120 ha. has
risen from a quarter to a half. One consequence is that a
small minority of farms produces a disproportionate
quantity of our food; the largest 1 per cent of holdings —
just 2100 in total — account for 15 per cent of agricultural
output.

Associated with these developments has been a steady
growth in the proportion of farms in owner-occupation. In
the early 1920s, about one-fifth of the land was owned by
farmers, rather than by landed estates; now it is close to
two-thirds. The taxation system does not favour private
landowners and, over the past 60 years, many of them (or
their heirs) have either sold out to their tenants or have
taken over the running of the farms as tenancies have
fallen vacant. Big estates remain in the hands of such
bodies as the Crown, the Church Commissioners and Ox-
bridge colleges. Since the 1960s, rising land values have
attracted a new class of institutional landowners — the
pension funds and insurance companies. These are happy
to hold tenanted land but, given the opportunity, will
usually take land in hand and instal a farm manager.

Changes in land tenure have increased the pressures to
intensify production. A farmer who has recently acquired
land faces heavy mortgage repayments, and so must consider any possibilities for increased output and income.
Similarly, the pension fund manager must justify his
investment. This usually means boosting both the profitability and the value of the land through grant-aided
capital improvements. In addition, the constraints formerly imposed by traditional landlords on their tenants in
the interests of game, amenity and good estate management have also largely disappeared.

Not only have farms been getting bigger, but they have also become more specialised at the expense of mixed farming. Between 1968 and 1974 alone, the average number of enterprises per farm declined by some 10 per cent. Pig and poultry production have become intensely concentrated in factory-farming enterprises. Most of Britain's 60 million broilers are housed in units of over 100,000; and most of the 8 million pig population in units of over 1000. Milk production has remained a key enterprise on many small and medium-sized farms — the average herd size is now around 50–60 cows, still a family-sized enterprise. Nevertheless, that represents a 70 per cent increase over the past decade, during which the number of holdings with dairy cows has halved. Linked to farm specialisation has been greater regional specialisation. The eastern counties, in particular, are more intensively devoted to tillage cropping than ever before, and arable farming has steadily engulfed the areas of mixed and dairy farming in central and southern England.

All these changes can be linked to particular policy developments and the manner in which farmers have responded to the changing political and economic climates in which they operate. In the 1950s and 1960s, increased production demanded greatly increased capital inputs, particularly of machinery and fertiliser. Though this may have created short-term demands for additional labour on individual farms, the long-term effect was to enable the more capital-intensive farms to shed labour. Numerous farm tasks were mechanised, and traditional buildings were replaced by modern units designed to use less labour, leading to rapid increases in gross fixed-capital formation. These grant- and price-induced developments, encouraged by the National Agricultural Advisory Service and the manufacturers of farm machinery and chemicals, have enhanced the pressures to specialise and expand. For the small farmer, these are often the only means by which new capital equipment or specialist buildings (usually acquired with borrowed money) can be justified; and for the large farmer, tax incentives are a powerful inducement to plough profits back into farm expansion and the purchase of new equipment. British agriculture is one of the most capital-intensive in the world, and, if the value of land is included, the amount of capital employed per worker is amongst the highest for any industry in Britain.

It would be a mistake to see all these developments as the inevitable consequence of rational economic adjustments, for there is considerable evidence that government measures designed to facilitate capital expansion have gone beyond the goal of more 'efficient' resource use. Indeed a number of commentators have argued that the capital which has flowed into agriculture would have yielded a better social return if invested elswhere in the economy. Such 'over-capitalisation' has speeded up the reduction of the agricultural labour force, hastened rural depopulation, and done harm to the environment. It has been promoted by successive grant schemes, encouraging the purchase of machinery and construction of buildings, and by advantageous capital depreciation and taxation allowances for these investments. Price support also affects the pattern of resource distribution in agriculture: farm incomes and land prices are boosted, thus facilitating further capital-intensification, especially on larger farms, and depressing the demand for labour. Capital accumulation in farming has created a countryside in its own image. With the expansion and amalgamation of holdings, the rationalisation of farm lay-outs and buildings and the enlargement of fields to accommodate the new machinery, many familiar and natural features have been obliterated, transforming both the rural scene and the natural resources of the countryside.

These processes are all part of the story of unparalleled growth in agricultural productivity of the past 40 years — growth which has been checked only by extreme weather conditions, notably the harsh winters of 1947/8 and 1962/3 and the dry summers of 1975 and 1976. There have been a number of shifts in the details of government policy over the years, but the overall commitment to agricultural expansion and rationalisation has rarely been questioned. Underlying all the changes has been a powerful ideology which gives farmers a special place in the life of the nation. They have frequently been presented as fine examples of free enterprise — notwithstanding the degree of financial support they receive — as well as the producers of the nation's food and the custodians of the countryside. In government circles, the costs of agricultural support have rarely been questioned. On the contrary, a succession of Official Reports and White Papers have affirmed the importance of an expansionist agriculture, although the reasons given have changed. As food shortages gave way first to abundance and then to over-production, so the ideological arguments for support shifted, and import savings or the balance of payments took the place of the earlier strategic arguments.

Underlying the case for special treatment for agriculture has been the notion of farming 'efficiency' as something to be encouraged, supported and emulated elsewhere in the economy. The doctrine has been pedalled successfully by the National Farmers' Union and the Ministry of Agriculture and, until recently, has been accepted uncritically by conservationists. In fact, the word 'efficiency' has been used in a highly selective way to refer solely to the output per man employed in agriculture. It is not a measure of the efficiency with which land, capital or energy are employed in the industry; nor does it take account of the long-term effects of current practices on soil fertility or water quality, or of the sustainability of technologies that are heavily dependent on oil or oil-based derivatives. If these other efficiency criteria are taken into account, agriculture's performance is far less rosy. Indeed, the argument that British agriculture presents a model of efficiency for other nations to follow has been convincingly challenged. Nevertheless, the notion that British farmers are somehow uniquely efficient remains a prominent component of the political ideology surrounding agriculture. This reflects the continuing strength and purpose of the National Farmers' Union. The high profile of agriculture in government thinking and in government expenditure is an abiding testament to the influence of this most successful of pressure groups (see Chapter 4).

THE ORIGINS OF POST-WAR POLICY

The legislative basis for post-war agricultural policy was provided by the Agriculture Act 1947, but the origins of the approach adopted in the Act were much earlier. The

period of the first world war and the inter-war years provide examples of policy initiatives designed to encourage
agricultural production in the face of shortages, overseas
competition or problems of internal organisation, price
fluctuations and depressed markets. In agriculture, as in
other sectors, the 1920s and 1930s saw a gradual reassess-
ment of the *laissez-faire* economics which had prevailed for
the previous 70 years. In 1917 the Selborne Committee had
made recommendations for the limited introduction of
guaranteed prices. The Agriculture Act 1920 embodied
some of its suggestions, but the cost to the Exchequer led
to its repeal a year later. The potential cost of support
having bedevilled attempts to formulate new policy initiatives, attention turned in the 1930s to the less costly techniques of market regulation. The Agricultural Marketing
Acts of 1931 and 1933 paved the way for one particularly
important feature of British agricultural policy, the product marketing boards. The Milk Marketing Boards, by
providing a guaranteed outlet for all milk production, a
secure income and advice based on research, gave a
powerful impetus to a massive expansion of dairy production, bolstered by new forms of intensive grassland
production.

The 1930s also saw the introduction of subsidies for a
small number of products, as well as limited import
protection. Government financial support remained
modest, and 80 per cent of it went on wheat and sugar
beet. The situation was dramatically changed by the onset
of war. Agriculture was placed on a war footing. This
entailed strict market regulation of all crops, guaranteed
prices and central purchasing. In each county, War Agricultural Executive Committees were established, mainly
comprising leading local farmers, to supervise the drive
for greater production and to encourage, cajole and if
necessary compel farmers to cooperate. Farming boomed
and, as the war ended, farmers held their breath for fear of
a return to the conditions of the 1920s and 1930s.

It fell to the new Labour government, elected on a tide
of post-war optimism, to provide a comprehensive legislative framework for British farming that would achieve the
hitherto conflicting aims of supplying cheap food to the
consumer and guaranteeing secure markets and prices for

farm products to the farmer. The 1947 Act was designed to assist farmers to adjust to changing markets and demands, and to provide the nation and farmers alike with the benefits of a productive and expansionist agriculture. As government wanted cheap and secure food supplies and farmers a secure income, the idea of partnership (first conceived by the Selborne Committee) came to fruition. The Act was also supposed to benefit farmworkers, but they were never included in the partnership.

An expansionist agriculture was to be based on a system of guaranteed prices for all major agricultural products. The Act detailed the means by which prices were to be arrived at, and the National Farmers' Union was given a statutory right of consultation in the *Annual Review and Determination of Guarantees*. The other side of the partnership found its true expression in the requirement of the Act — a legacy of Selborne and the operation of the 'War Ags' — for farmers to comply with 'rules of good husbandry', and landowners with 'rules of good estate management'. Failure to comply rendered them liable to supervision orders by the county executive committees, and ultimately to notices to quit. Between 1947 and the repeal of these provisions in 1958, 5000 farmers were placed under supervision orders and 400 were dispossessed. George Marten, who was reported in 1952 for failing to make full productive use of downland (which conservationists would be protecting today), has described the climate which was created:

> politicians spoke disparagingly of farmers who failed to clear land for higher production. The Inland Revenue were urged to investigate farmers who failed to make reasonable profits. Agricultural education was geared to the same ends.

POLICY DEVELOPMENTS SINCE 1947

Initially, expansion of output was pursued regardless of public cost, in order to provide food in conditions of continuing shortage when war-time controls over the purchase and sale of food were still needed. The cost to the

Exchequer was considered of minor importance in such circumstances. It was, in any case, relatively modest as home demand rose with the revival of the economy under conditions of full employment. Support prices paid were distributed fairly widely and evenly in such a way that all farmers received identical payments per unit of commodity produced, irrespective of their costs or market acumen. Government control in the market encouraged a confident increase in production, but it could neither give special reward to the more efficient or the needy, nor stimulate a restructuring of the industry to improve its long-term viability.

Gradually, however, it was accepted that certain sectors of production, for political, social or economic reasons, were deserving of special treatment. In 1951, the Livestock Rearing Act extended to lower ground the grants for capital investment that had already been made available to upland farmers under the Hill Farming Act 1946. In 1952, fertiliser subsidies, ploughing grants and beef-calf subsidies were introduced. Not only did these measures acknowledge the need for selective encouragement of certain sectors of food production, they also indicated a growing awareness that agricultural support must also stimulate increased efficiency.

An important tool in the drive for efficiency was the encouragement of better marketing, especially through the Milk and Egg Marketing Boards. But grants and marketing were not enough to stimulate the changes that government required. For that, alterations in the price support mechanism were essential. By the mid-1950s fixed prices, payable to all producers, had been abandoned in favour of *minimum support prices*. Henceforth guaranteed prices would only come into operation if the market price for a commodity fell below the minimum support price, in which case producers would be recompensed for the shortfall through what were termed *deficiency payments*. What this meant was that equality of prices received by farmers was at an end. The minimum support price provided a base-line below which no one could fall, but above that line there was scope for the adventurous or favoured farmer to cash in on high free-market prices. The policy was designed to encourage efficiency and hence limit Exchequer expenditure in a context in which world food supply had greatly eased. This was in line with contemporary Conservative economic thought which, as the problems of post-war scarcity receded and wartime controls continued by the Labour government were abolished, emphasised de-control and economic freedom.

The changes were enshrined in the Agriculture Act 1957, which the then Minister of Agriculture, Heathcote Amory, described as 'a logical development of the Agricultural Act, 1947 . . . agricultural development must concentrate on ever-improved efficiency and reducing unit costs of production . . . farmers must have two things: capital and confidence'. The key to the Act lay in the idea that the annual price awards would never reimburse the farmer for all the increases in his costs of production. The Act defined in some detail the proportion of these costs that he was expected to absorb each year through increased efficiency. The farmer was required, in effect, to run up the down escalator; only if he could run faster than the escalator would he remain solvent or increase his profits. Caught in this cost–price squeeze, farmers had little option but to take up the grants on offer, and to invest capital in new buildings, plant and machinery, to adopt new technologies, to make more use of hitherto unproductive land, to remove any features that stood in the way of maximising production, to dispense with much of their labour force, and to concentrate production in larger units – in short, to carry through the second agricultural revolution. Those who did so prospered. Those who could not went under.

In 1959, a Small Farmers Scheme was introduced, supposedly to help the smaller producers improve efficiency and attain economic viability: in short to become bigger producers. As with subsequent schemes of a similar nature, it was abused by and benefited the larger producers. By the time it was fully in operation, however, the ground had shifted again.

As growing surpluses on world commodity markets pushed prices lower and lower, the cost of compensating farmers for the difference between market prices and the minimum support prices escalated. Steps were taken to curb the level of deficiency payments beyond a certain level of domestic production, but policy-makers also became convinced that deficiency payments and an 'open door' for imports that depressed market prices could no longer coexist. In 1963, therefore, the government breached one of the basic principles of British trading policy since the repeal of the Corn Laws — that there should be an open door for imports of cheap foodstuffs. This involved the introduction of *minimum import prices*, which had the bizarre effect of paying foreign suppliers prices above the world market level, so as to maintain British farm prices without resorting to import quotas which might provoke retaliation against British exports.

These initial and halting steps towards protectionism were fully consummated when Britain entered the EEC in 1972, and British agriculture became subject to the Common Agricultural Policy. In principle there is a common system of pricing throughout the EEC, although in practice most countries have used various devices which seriously undermine this principle. The pricing policy presents a bewildering variety of terms — target price, guide price, intervention price, withdrawal price, minimum price, deficiency payment, threshold price, sluice-gate price, variable levy, restitution, and so on! But most of these represent variations on a common theme. Thus, there are basically two types of pricing mechanism — the external and the internal. Internally, the Community sets *target prices* annually as the desired or normal prices for most commodities. Other prices, including guaranteed prices, are derived from them. A minimum guaranteed price is provided by the *intervention price*: when the market price slips to a certain level, the Community buys into intervention sufficient quantities of the product to ensure that prices do not fall below the intervention level; ideally, stocks should be released onto the market when the prices have risen again. Externally, threshold prices are set annually as prices which must be reached by imports, and they are maintained by variable levies or duties which are charged on imported goods.

These pricing policies are similar in their effect to the earlier policies adopted by the British government, although particular problems are associated with their operation in a European context. So too there has been an essential continuity in the various capital grants available to farmers. One important development has been the formal linking of such grants to farm development schemes, of which the capital input is only one ingredient. Britain's accession to the Common Market gave agriculture considerable prominence in national politics. With the burden for the payment of guaranteed prices shifting from the Exchequer to the consumer, the costs of agricultural support became much more visible in the form of dearer food. The CAP accounts for some two-thirds of the EEC budget and, with its explicit protectionism, high prices and embarrassing surpluses, is an object of considerable contention and popular resentment. However, its reform faces major political obstacles, not least on account of the range of organisations involved, including all the EEC member governments, the European Commission, the European Parliament and various major national and transnational lobbies, such as consumer interests and food manufacturers, as well as farmers and conservationists.

Agriculture benefits from state support in other ways, including favourable taxation arrangements for both capital and income, subsidised credit, the de-rating of farmland and buildings, and exemption from most planning control. Education and research receive massive support through the network of county agricultural colleges and a number of university departments. An Agricultural Training Board assists on-farm training. The ministry maintains its own research farms and disseminates free technical advice to farmers through the Agricultural Development Advisory Service (ADAS). The industry is also uniquely privileged in being the only individual industry to be served by its own government-funded research council, the Agricultural and Food Research Council. The total cost of state support for agriculture, including these indirect subsidies, has been variously estimated at between £3 billion and £5 billion per annum. Although the level of direct state support has begun to fall since 1983, there is no sign as yet of any radical rethinking of the aims and pattern of this expenditure — only ad hoc and crude budgetary cuts imposed either to satisfy the Treasury or to comply, as in the case of milk levies and quotas, with unprincipled compromises thrashed out in Brussels.

FORESTRY POLICY

Although the sums of public money spent on forestry are a fraction of those which go into agriculture, the state has much more direct involvement through the operation of the Forestry Commission, which is both a nationalised industry and the national forestry authority. It was established in 1919 in a climate of concern over Britain's strategic vulnerability to the disruption of timber supplies, akin to the concern that prompted agricultural support. In the case of forestry, however, more radical action was called for than support for private producers. Landowners were reluctant to invest in a crop which might not show a return for 100 years. They had also manifestly failed to maintain Britain's woodlands, which had dwindled for centuries, thus making this country one of the least wooded in the world.

In the last 60 years the area of forest plantations and woodland in the United Kingdom has doubled to 2 million ha., half of which is owned by the Forestry Commission. But the change has been far more dramatic than even these figures imply, for many of the woods which existed in 1919 have been replanted with different species. Large acreages of ancient and semi-natural woodlands, containing traditional deciduous species and of great ecological merit, have been replaced by coniferous plantations. The implications for conservation are discussed in the next chapter. At this stage it is important to grasp the underlying political reasons for these developments.

Although responsible to the Minister of Agriculture and the Secretaries of State for Wales and Scotland, the Forestry Commission has a high degree of autonomy in discharging its twin functions as the state forestry enterprise and as the responsible authority for all aspects of forestry in Britain. The Commission is empowered to purchase land on the open market, afforest it and sell the timber produced. Its primary responsibility is the production of timber. Since 1967, it has also had a special responsibility to cater for public recreation and to enhance the beauty of the countryside. This shift in policy objectives was partly the result of pressure from environmentalists, but it was also a consequence of the increasing irrelevance of the earlier strategic arguments for a rapid programme of afforestation. Rates of afforestation, though substantial, have never been as high as periodic reviews have proposed. The 1943 target of 2 million ha. of productive forests (including private woodlands) by the early 1990s is unlikely to be reached until the end of the first decade of the next century. Rather than strategic considerations, it is the import-cost consequences of British forests supplying only 8 per cent of domestic needs that are now emphasised by the lobby. But if the revenue supporting forestry were diverted to other industries, critics claim, greater import savings might be achieved. Nevertheless, even in the face of such criticism the lobby has done well.

In 1972 a major review of forestry policy was conducted. The Treasury produced a devastating cost-benefit critique of the forestry programme which indicated that new planting was not economically or socially justified in terms of its expected timber yield or job opportunities and served no strategic need, whether defence or commercial. The Treasury's case rested, in part, on a contentious technique of discounting: at a test discount rate of 10 per cent nobody would ever plant any trees. Also, it assumed that afforestation would take place on marginal land in the uplands, whereas there is a strong case for more planting in the lowlands (see Chapter 12). The Commission and the timber-growing lobby were able to withstand the Treasury's assault only by recourse to social and environmental arguments, chiefly concerning the role of afforestation in stemming rural depopulation through the provision of employment, and in providing opportunities for public access and recreation in the countryside. The Commission emerged relatively unscathed from the 1972 review: a government policy statement called for only a 10 per cent reduction on its planting targets.

In its 1977 Report, *The Wood Production Outlook in Britain*, the Forestry Commission again concluded that large expansion of forestry (of the order of 36,000 ha./per annum — an increase of more than 50 per cent on existing targets) would be a 'prudent investment'. But even more extravagantly expansionist in outlook were the recommendations of the Centre for Agricultural Strategy at Reading University, whose *Strategy for the UK Forest Industry* (published in

1980) envisaged an increase in the forest estate at a rate of 60,000 ha./per annum. Such recommendations, based on 'guesstimate' forecasting of future world timber demands, have tended to command more respect than they perhaps warrant, and continue to underpin the Commission's case for doubling the area of productive forestry.

Since the late 1970s the Commission's budget has been squeezed by successive rounds of public expenditure cuts. As a nationalised industry, it has been subject to calls for 'privatisation' and to more rigorous scrutiny of its finances and operations. The Forestry Act 1981 effectively transferred to the minister the right to sell land in the Commission's ownership. Land is being sold to realise the full market price, without any safeguards either for recreational opportunities the public has enjoyed or for continuing the Commission's policies for nature conservation. The minister is also empowered to transfer the Commission's profits to the Treasury. Such a major attack on the Forestry Commission represents something other than a logical development of the 1972 critique, for the Commission has been singled out for *special* restrictions on expansion, whereas the private sector, which was also subject to heavy criticism in the 1972 cost–benefit analysis, has been encouraged to increase rates of planting. Indeed, should large-scale sales of Commission plantations take place, the private sector's role is likely to be an expanding one. As in the case of agriculture, however, this 'private' sector is heavily supported by the state at a high cost to the public purse. That the government should support such a continued cost whilst severely curtailing the Commission's activities reveals an inconsistency based on ideological bias rather than pure monetarist economics. Nevertheless, the Forestry Commission continues to have an important role in this private expansion by virtue of its other role, as forest authority.

The Commission has the general duty of promoting forestry in Britain. To this end, it conducts research and supports the education and training of forestry personnel. It also has control over licences for the felling of trees (beyond a certain acreage and/or quantity of timber), which gives it an important role in regulating the use or agricultural reclamation of existing deciduous woodlands in private hands, although it has been reluctant to use its powers to achieve conservation instead of 'commercial' woodland management. By far its most significant power in its relations with private landowners is the awarding of grants for afforestation. Since 1947, most grants have been payable under the Dedication Scheme operated by the Commission, whereby the owner of land agrees to adhere to particular management practices and to keep the land as woodland in perpetuity in return for grants for a number of key forestry operations, including planting, maintenance and thinning. The Forestry Grant Scheme, which replaced the Dedication Scheme in 1981, excludes the Commission from any involvement in management decisions once the initial plan has been agreed, and fundamentally weakens the Commission's influence over the management of grant-aided plantations. Although grant-aided schemes often have landscape and nature conservation objectives, and can be used to improve degraded woodlands, they *must* be designed to produce marketable timber and cannot just protect ancient woodlands whose economic potential is small and whose character is at odds with commercial forestry. Despite the importance of grants, the decisive factor encouraging private afforestation is the concessions on income, capital transfer and capital gains taxation.

An individual in a high tax bracket can use investment in forestry as a tax shelter to bring down the marginal rate of tax; and treatment of investment in forestry as a business under Schedule D enables businesses to offset expenses against corporation tax. In principle, choosing to offset establishment costs against tax incurs liability for a substantial tax bill when the trees are felled. But in practice a private woodland is almost always sold or inherited before it matures and the new owner can elect to be taxed under Schedule B, which allows a purely notional income tax based on the rental value of the land to be paid while the trees are maturing in return for complete exemption when the windfall profit day eventually arrives. It is not surprising that, since 1982, private growers have attracted 'hundreds of millions of pounds of investment', according to the chief executive of Timber Growers UK, the private forestry lobby (see Chapter 4).

Forestry development is necessarily a long-term enterprise though, so the timber-growing lobby has had to be successful in securing the tax advantages and maintaining the level of grant aid necessary for making the activity profitable. But such achieved incentives have been open to manipulation by high-rate taxpayers. In 1979 Sir William Pile, the former Chairman of the Inland Revenue, estimated that tax avoidance in forestry was costing the Revenue £10 million annually, a view of forestry syndicates which was corroborated in 1981 by the Parliamentary Committee of Public Accounts. None of these tax incentives, it should be noted, encourages the landowner to provide public access or conservation management.

CONCLUSION

It should be apparent by now that agriculture and forestry operate in an economic climate heavily determined by political considerations and decisions. In the period since the war, both sectors have been insensitive to the wider functions of the countryside. Agricultural policy has promoted a relentless increase in production and in the intensity of land use, which has degraded much of the rural landscape. Afforestation in certain circumstances can be beneficial for conservation, but much of the story since the war has been of the coniferisation of valuable ancient woodlands, plantations which are unsympathetic to the landscape and the loss of upland areas valued for their wildlife or recreational use. The various environmental impacts of contemporary agriculture and forestry are reviewed in the next chapter. What is now beyond dispute is that the post-war era of agricultural expansion came to an end in 1984.

The warning signals, had, of course, been apparent for some years, although neither the NFU nor MAFF had been willing to recognise them. It is instructive to go back over the record of the decade 1974–84, and observe their obstinate resistance to the growing evidence of the need for drastic changes in agricultural policy, and the growing strength of the conservation lobby. The warnings given by the Nature Conservancy Council in 1977, by the interdepartmental

Countryside Review Committee in 1978 and by MAFF's own Advisory Council in the same year, fell on deaf ears. The 1979 White Paper, *Farming and the Nation*, issued by the incoming Conservative government, even went for higher expansion targets (10–20 per cent in five years) than the Labour White Paper, *Food from Our Own Resources 1975*. The policy review of the Agricultural Development and Advisory Service (ADAS) in 1979 stated the prime purpose of the service to be the development and application of advanced technology, without even a sideways glance at its environmental effects.

Although the opposition parties had begun to take some interest in the negative consequences of production-oriented agricultural policies, the environment was not an issue of significance in the 1983 General Election. Nevertheless, uneasiness was growing among Conservative backbenchers, who were concerned more about the waste of money and the failure to apply free-market principles than about the damage to the environment. The NFU was profoundly shocked, however, when this unease manifested itself in the publication of a ferociously critical book, *Agriculture: The Triumph and the Shame*, by Richard Body, who was not only a Tory MP for a large agricultural constituency (Holland-with-Boston) but had also been a farmer himself. Body estimated that since 1946 farmers had been given public support to the value of £40 billion at 1982 prices, and were still getting £3.35 billion a year. This came as a revelation to many who were not tuned in to conservationist sources. In November 1983, Sir Michael Franklin, Permanent Secretary at MAFF, warned farmers that they could not afford to ignore or to minimise 'the tide of public opinion running against the industry'. Governments do, in fact, pick and choose when deciding which trends in public opinion to ignore and which to conciliate. Hindsight suggests that Sir Michael was giving a coded warning that MAFF could not continue for very much longer in its obstinate resistance to change.

It is questionable, however, whether the inertia of MAFF and the farming and landowning lobby could have been broken down without massive external intervention, even if the publication of the UK response to the World Conservation Strategy in 1983 and the NCC's strategy for nature conservation in 1984 had not added to the growing pressure for change. The decisive event, which shifted them from their traditional postures, was clearly the sudden imposition of milk quotas and levies by the EEC in April 1984. It was clear that this emergency action, forced on the Council of Agricultural Ministers by the need to avert the bankruptcy of the EEC, would be followed by further cuts in the money flowing into agriculture. The milk quotas may well aggravate environmental problems, by forcing milk producers to intensify grass production or to develop other forms of production. But the significance of the cuts lies in the immediate perception by the NFU and the CLA that conservation would not only be good for their public image; it could also put money into farmers' pockets to replace that lost, or soon to be lost, as production supports are cut down.

Their reaction demonstrated the point that this chapter has emphasised, that agriculture is not in the grip of unstoppable technology or blind economic forces. On the contrary, the framework of the agricultural economy was constructed by politicians, and politicians can demolish it or change it if the political will to do so is present. The solutions to many of the problems lie within the realm of practical policy, once the political, financial and emotional climate becomes favourable. The proposals for policy changes made in the final chapters would have looked politically 'impossible' until very recently. But it is now politically much easier for politicians and civil servants to look at alternatives with a more open mind.

FURTHER READING

The structure and achievements of British farming have been well documented by agricultural economists. A particularly useful source is Denis Britton, Alison Burrell, Berkley Hill and Derek Ray, *Statistical Handbook of UK Agriculture* (School of Rural Economics, Wye College, Kent, 1980). For a detailed economic analysis of agricultural policy see B. Davey, T.E. Josling and A. McFarquhar, *Agriculture and the State* (Macmillan, 1976).

Concerning EEC policy, the standard reference is

Rosemary Fennel, *The Common Agricultural Policy of the European Community* (Granada, 1979) and a shorter summary of the CAP is to be found in J.S. Marsh and P.J. Swanney, *Agriculture and the European Community* (Allen & Unwin, 1980). An up-to-date economic analysis which also addresses the future is Brian Hill, *The Common Agricultural Policy: Past, Present and Future* (Methuen, 1984).

By comparison, the literature on forestry is rather thin, but a standard text is N.D.G. James, *A History of English Forestry* (Basil Blackwell, 1981).

3. The Impact of Agriculture and Forestry on the Countryside

'Many critics would see the most serious failure of the conservation movement as the sheer scale of loss or damage to wildlife, its habitat and physical features that has taken place since 1949.' So writes Derek Ratcliffe, Chief Scientist of the NCC, in his 1983 report on the future of nature conservation in Great Britain. 'All main types of ecosystem have suffered appreciable loss,' he adds, 'but for some the scale and rate have been catastrophic.'

This is not an overstatement: the present generation is witnessing the most comprehensive and far-reaching change of the natural history and historical landscapes of Britain ever experienced in such a short period of time. What is particularly alarming is that so little is understood about these changes — their magnitude and long-term consequences — yet what is known is simply appalling. The grim chronicle reads as follows: over the past 35 years, the nation has lost 95 per cent of lowland herb-rich grasslands, 80 per cent of chalk and limestone grasslands, 60 per cent of lowland heaths, 45 per cent of limestone pavements, 50 per cent of ancient woodlands, 50 per cent of lowland fens and marshes, over 60 per cent of lowland raised bogs, and a third of all upland grasslands, heaths and mires. As much as one-third of all lowland rivers have been altered by drainage schemes and 'improvement' works, and over half the ecologically most interesting estuaries have been affected by recreational and other developments.

As habitats have been damaged or destroyed, so individual species of flora and fauna have suffered in parallel. Butterflies and dragonflies have been the most blasted victims. The Large Blue butterfly became extinct in 1979, but eight more species are endangered and another twelve have declined so much that they are now officially rare — this out of a total British list of just 55 breeding species. Of 43 species of dragonfly, three or four have become extinct since 1953 and ten have decreased to the point of becoming very rare. As Ratcliffe points out: 'Insect biology is such that these creatures are on the whole less buffered against adversity than the vertebrates and higher plants. The possibility that butterflies and dragonflies may be indicators for wider problems among the less studied groups of invertebrates is worrying.' Birds, though more resilient to habitat alteration, are by no means unaffected. The NCC report concludes that 30 lowland and six upland species have shown appreciable long-term decline during the last 35 years. Loss of hedgerows, copses and open moorland to coniferous plantation are the major causes, although drainage and ground disturbance are also important contributory factors.

Amongst the mammals, the otter has become extremely rare and bats are now legally protected. Of the country's twelve reptiles and amphibians, four are endangered. Botanical losses are also substantial and include ten extinctions since 1930. Of the 1423 native vascular plants, 149 have declined by at least 20 per cent: 69 belonging to wetland habitats, 32 to permanent grassland, 18 to woodland and 14 to sandy or heathland habitats. In addition, 317 plant species are now officially regarded as rare. Of these, 117 have shown a loss of at least 33 per cent: 34 belonging to grasslands, 21 to wetlands, 19 to sandy or heathland habitats and 14 to dry banks or shingle.

WHY AND WHAT SHOULD WE CONSERVE?

These devastating conclusions from Britain's most authoritative conservation source only tell what is known for certain, and from a national perspective. Locally, the losses may be much worse: almost every countrydweller can recite a litany of areas which were full of wild flowers, frog spawn and butterflies in their childhood but are no longer. In his powerfully argued book on the importance of wildlife to everyday life and in everyday places, Richard Mabey emphasises that it is the loss of once common species — bluebells, toads, redshank, grass-snakes — that is bringing home to ordinary people the scale and pace of this savage destruction of the nation's natural history. 'The fact is,' writes Mabey,

> we do not want the natural world preserved as a museum piece. We want the opportunity to experience it face to face, with its qualities of wildness and renewal intact. We want, all of us, to hang on to favourite places and familiar creatures, and to the uniquely private network of meaning and association that attaches to them.

Conservation is, and must remain, a part of everyday experience. For, as Mabey argues, only by being aware of nature in their daily surroundings can people fully appreciate its deeper meanings, since everything they do has consequences for living systems and the availability of resources for their children and grandchildren. Indeed, the morality of conservation transcends generations as well as all living and inanimate objects. The message of conservation is therefore the message of caution against mankind's own enthusiasm for achievement and domination narrowly defined in human-centred terms. Man's ability to unleash the forces of nature has far outstripped his ability to foresee or control the potentially cataclysmic consequences. Such awesome technological power needs to be exercised with proper care and restraint, in full consciousness of the terrible responsibility that man now bears for the fate of the natural world on which all life ultimately depends.

A conservation ethic has other purposes too. It can provide a sense of identity with one's surroundings and with the past, which may be especially important when people are confronted with change. We need to feel some association with the past, a sense of where we came from. When objects or symbols rich in the meanings and associations which give people their attachment to place are lost

same for racial identity?

or altered, they become confused and disoriented. These reactions can breed a pathetic sense of helplessness in some, anger and frustration in others. Hence the outcry in almost every small community over proposals to remove or alter the landmarks which give a locality its distinct identity. Hence, too, the particular resentment over the loss of hedgerows, some of which have acted as parish boundaries since pre-Norman times, or the cutting-down of 200-year-old trees which have witnessed generations of parish history. The historian Keith Thomas, in a comprehensive study of changing attitudes to nature in England between 1500 and 1800, described the eighteenth-century passion for trees as a profound expression of a sense of local identity. 'England had no forests on the North American scale to act as a focus for such feelings,' he writes. 'But she did have individual trees which played a crucial part in her social life. From Anglo-Saxon times trees have been an essential landmark, demarcating local boundaries or indicating the meeting place for assemblies.'

Admittedly, a commitment to conservation is invariably, in part, an expression of nostalgia for times past. The poet John Clare, for instance, in his 'Village Minstrel' written in 1821 after most of the enclosures had taken place, lamented the loss of his 'countryside' with more eloquence than is found today, but with similar sentiments:

There once were brooks sweet wimpering down the vale;
The brook's no more — Kingcup and daisy fled;
Their last fall'n tree the naked moors bewail,
And scarce a bush is left to tell the mournful tale.

So far we have built up a picture of conservation as part of an ecological ethic and a psychological need to retain a sense of association and continuity linking past, present and future. But conservation has inspirational and educational purposes as well, both in terms of revealing what is beautiful and in helping people to become aware of the workings of nature. In British culture, unfortunately, these two aspects tend to be divorced. Scenery is perceived solely in visual and aesthetic terms and as quite distinct from the physical and natural characteristics of the land. This is not true of other countries. In Germany, for example, the beauty of landscape is seen as integral to scientifically sensible management — management that takes into account the opportunities and the impediments created yet imposed by soils, water, wildlife, climate and relief. This Germanic approach to landscape design apprehends the physical, biological and cultural processes of an area in order to integrate agricultural and forestry management with building design and location into a harmonious landscape whole.

There is no equivalent tradition in the British Isles. A split developed in the 1940s between the ecological or scientific interests, which were pressing for legislation to protect wildlife and natural systems, and the recreation and landscape preservation interests that were pressing for access to open country and the establishment of national parks. The division was institutionalised by the passage of the National Parks and Access to the Countryside Act 1949, and in the separate creation of the Nature Conservancy (as it then was) and the National Parks Commission (now the Countryside Commission). The division at official level was paralleled by the growth of voluntary bodies whose concern lay primarily, and sometimes exclusively, with nature or with landscape and access. Although the voluntary bodies have become more aware of the commonality of interest between landscape and nature conservation, the official agencies remain as far apart as ever. Nor is there any equivalent to the European landscape tradition in the British planning and landscape architecture professions. The former is mostly devoted to the built environment, while the latter is primarily concerned with form and appearance rather than the fundamental laws of the earth and ecological sciences. More devastating, of course, has been the separation of nature and landscape conservation from the promotion of the economic exploitation of rural resources. This reflects in part the extent to which these resources are privately owned or controlled, and the extent to which their exploitation is promoted by powerful sectional interests each organised around a single resource and narrowly oriented to maximising output and profit with little regard for the integrity of the rural environment or other interests in the countryside.

In the practice of 'conservation' there should be scope

for protecting both the wildlife and landscape 'jewels' — the representative sites of habitat and scenery — and attending to the 'everyday' surroundings — both rural and urban — that are the context of our day-to-day life. Urban man should not be isolated from wildlife, even though it is unrealistic to provide him with the richness and diversity of nature still found in many rural areas. It is, therefore, unwise to concentrate attention and effort on the losses of habitat and scenery in the 'choice' areas, some of which are rarely visited by ordinary people. Yet current countryside protection policies, in so far as they exist, direct most of the limited public funds to the remoter sites and the spectacular landscapes of the national parks, and neglect the commonplace environments.

Emphasising wildlife management in cities might help to assuage, although it could never extinguish, the powerful emotions and images invoked in British people when thinking about 'the countryside'. Over 74 per cent of the population walk in the countryside at least once a year, and 54 per cent at least once a month, mostly as day-trippers. About 82 million visits to the countryside were made in England and Wales in 1977 (the last year for which comprehensive statistics were compiled), with a further 6 million in Scotland.

A survey of public opinion on resource and environmental issues, conducted by the MORI organisation in 1983, confirmed that the British people do care about their countryside, though not in a very coherent way. As is so often the case, answers are tremendously influenced by the context of the question. For example, 53 per cent stated that 'attractive countryside' made a valuable contribution to the overall quality of their lives, and 37 per cent noted that 'wildlife in gardens and the countryside' was similarly important. Nevertheless, in the setting of all issues regarded as important, wildlife conservation ranks only 9th in a list of 16 items. The impression gained from these and other responses is that a majority do not see a connection between wildlife losses and landscape change on the one hand, and their immediate lives and worries on the other, even if they do express a vague sense of shared loss over changes to landscapes and depletion of species in the 'remote landscapes' that are not part of their daily lives. There is a great need for people to come to appreciate the relationship between their desire for an affluent material existence and conservation principles. For our long-term well-being is crucially dependent on environmentally sensitive policies.

WHO ARE THE CULPRITS?

Because the rate and scale of habitat losses and landscape changes are not fully known, it is difficult to be too precise about who is at fault. It is hardly surprising that the representatives of farmers and landowners like to shift attention away from what is happening on farmed and forested landscapes and blame the loss of countryside on urban sprawl, new factory sites, motorways, power stations, power lines and mineral workings. These are easy targets, for they are subject to planning regulations and are much more tangible than the subtle but more widespread changes which have occurred in the management of rural land. However, according to the late Robin Best, the acknowledged authority on these matters, the amount of land taken out of agricultural production for development is declining. Generally, too, British towns are remarkably compact and well-contained compared with most developed countries. Less than 12 per cent of England and Wales is given over to urban uses, the smallest proportion in Western Europe.

In the main, planning policies to constrain urban sprawl have proved effective, despite some unwelcome side-effects on the pattern of development in outer suburbs and on suburban land values. Green-belts have a special place in the British imagination. For better or worse they are regarded as the lungs of the city (even though they are mostly used by affluent suburbanites for recreational purposes) and a vital barrier against the depredations of builders. The recent furore over proposals to redefine the boundaries of green-belts and to relax development controls unleashed these emotions, forcing the government to back down. However, this does not dispense with the need for some basic re-thinking concerning the size and purpose of the green-belts. Much of the land within them is poorly managed and under-used, its landscape blighted or vandalised and its recreational potential not fully realised. Any reformulation of the objectives of green-belt policy should ensure that this land is not merely preserved from concrete and tarmac but is put to worthwhile and attractive use, in order to enhance the surroundings of our major conurbations.

Concerning the wider countryside, Best's work reveals that the rate of loss of agricultural land to urban sprawl reached a peak in the 1930s, when land was cheap and planning controls rudimentary. In those days, about 25,000 ha. of farmland were lost each year in England and Wales. This compared with an average annual rate of 16,000 ha. in the post-war years, following the introduction of planning controls and the policy of urban containment; although by 1978, as the economic recession deepened, the figure had fallen even further to about 8000 ha. Much of the recent loss, curiously enough, has not been in the rapidly populating South and East but in the older industrial towns of the North and West and around metropolitan London. Most of the important agricultural land in the shire counties remains intact.

Professor Best concludes that the removal of agricultural land was, in the past, not only a matter of relatively little concern but was easily compensated for by the vast improvements in agricultural productivity described in the previous chapter. He warns, nevertheless, of the dangers of complacency: recent relaxations in development-control procedures, together with the devolution of planning powers to district level, where willingness to concede to developmental pressures is arguably greater than at the more 'detached' county level, may well result in an increased loss of agricultural land if the economy picks up. Since the late 1970s, through its advice to local planning authorities and ministerial decisions on planning appeals, the government has fostered a more sympathetic climate for developers. The Council for the Protection of Rural England has warned that 'Quite new economic and political pressures are building up for the extensive use of virgin countryside sites for industrial, commercial and housing developments.' Certainly, some of the locational trends for new private housing, for hypermarkets and warehouses and for foot-loose, high-technology industries would seem to favour rural and urban-fringe sites accessible to the motorway network.

Industrial pollution also affects wildlife, though again nobody knows how seriously. Both the North York Moors National Park Committee and the Peak District National Park Planning Board have conducted extensive surveys of the degraded moorlands and have found nineteenth- and early twentieth-century industrial pollution an important cause of damage to plant communities. However, such other factors as overgrazing, fires, erosion caused by walkers and picnickers, plus the influence of frost and rain, are much more dominant. More recently, there has been much publicity regarding the possible effects of acid rain — wet and dry deposition of pollutants derived from the combustion of coal, oil and gas and motor vehicle fumes — on the ecology of freshwater fish, invertebrate and plant life. According to a recent review by the Royal Commission on Environmental Pollution, there has been an increase in the acidity of Britain's rainfall over the past ten years, mostly due to emissions from coal-burning power stations. This may be creating chemical changes in soils and run-off waters with serious long-term consequences for the aquatic wildlife of many of Britain's ponds and rivers, notably in the less fertile igneous mountainous areas of the North and West. The Royal Commission has rightly urged that more funds be allocated for research into the ecological effects of acid deposition, but at present the main research institutes are starved of funds.

Urban encroachment, thoughtless development and pollution damage, though causes for legitimate concern, account for but a modest proportion of contemporary landscape and habitat changes. Undoubtedly, the main pressures arise from agricultural intensification and afforestation.

HABITAT LOSS AND LANDSCAPE CHANGE

Chapter 2 illustrated the changing nature of farming in contemporary Britain. Most of the trends identified there are inimical to rural conservation. Gerald Wibberley has expressed the conflict in stark terms: 'Conservationists want essentially the products that low fertility brings. Modern British agriculture stresses all that goes with high fertility.' The maintenance of wildlife, attractive landscapes and public access to rural land all depend upon extensive farming systems: much land maintained in a low state of fertility (usually by intermittent grazing), to yield a diversity of plants and animals; other, marginal, land out of active farming use altogether, and plenty of cover to provide a range of natural and semi-natural habitats and much scenic interest. Modern agriculture, in contrast, aims to push up production through high inputs of chemical and mechanical energy and a heavily regulated and artificial environment, in which constant attention is given to the elimination of physical constraints, natural diversity and competing fauna and flora.

Farming and heritage protection are by no means necessarily in conflict. In many cases they must work hand-in-hand. For example, the rich aquatic plant communities found in the drainage ditches of Broadland and the Somerset Levels are heavily dependent upon dredging, clearing and water-level management that are part of traditional marsh husbandry (see Chapters 10 and 11). Moorland, heathland and upland meadows all depend upon certain approaches to farming (notably the kind and number of stock being grazed, and fertilisation practices) for their appearance and for their species' diversity. The problem is that most of the technological, managerial and economic influences behind modern farming and forestry are incompatible with the kind of husbandry most suitable for maintaining the nation's wildlife habitats and traditional landscapes. The prime causes are the simplification of ecosystems following upon monoculture or reduced crop rotations, and the widespread application of chemicals which destroy soil biota and which tend to eliminate all plants and animals unnecessary for the crop being produced.

As mentioned earlier, the scale and rate of habitat damage and species loss are without parallel. The pattern of habitat alteration, though, has been immensely varied in terms of both ecology and location. Losses of landscape features, it should be appreciated, only have meaning when quality is related to quantity. Not all hedgerows are important either for ecological or for landscape reasons; a derelict hedge may be ecologically interesting but unattractive, while a mismanaged hedge may be worthless. Similarly an even-aged heather moor may be as visually pleasing as a multiple-aged moor with its variety of microhabitats, but they cannot be compared for their ecological interest. In the welter of change and destruction, therefore, some losses are more keenly felt than others, and some are beyond reckoning. There is a very real danger, for example, that most of the ecologically specialised remnants of bogs, heath, lowland calcareous grassland and herb-rich hay meadows will only exist, through legal protection and careful management, as living but unvisited museums. Such an outcome, though tragic, would be a poignant monument to the gross negligence, mismanagement and greed that had brought it to pass.

Hedgerows and amenity trees

In 1962 there were approximately 1 million km of hedgerows in Britain covering over 200,000 ha. — an area greater than that of all the nature reserves. It is estimated that between 1945 and 1970 about 1 per cent of hedgerows (some 8000 km) were removed annually, amounting to a cumulative loss of 225,000 km. Since then, it is believed (but not proven) that the rate of loss has slowed down. The greatest losses have occurred and are still occurring in the predominantly arable areas, with over half the Norfolk hedges having been removed between 1946 and 1970, and with rapid increases in grubbing in Midlands counties as intensive arable cultivation marches westward.

Loss of hedgerows, depending upon their state of maintenance and the amount of woodland in the locality, can result in the loss of an important wildlife sanctuary at the field margin. Max Hooper, a senior scientist at the Institute of Terrestrial Ecology, calculates that about 250 plant species are basically hedgerow plants. Further hedgerow removal would affect about 20 of them very seriously, another 20 species quite seriously and a further 30–50 species to a marked extent, possibly leading to extinctions in some counties. Norman Moore, another distinguished ecologist, estimates that 21 of 28 species of mammals, 65 of 91 species of birds and 23 of 54 species of butterflies breed in hedges, though none is confined exclusively to this habitat. However, if both the woodlands and a large proportion of hedgerows in an area are removed, the consequences for these fauna can be devastating.

Many 'amenity trees' — the characteristic hardwoods associated with hedgerows and fields that contribute so much to the gracefulness of the farmed landscape — date back to the enclosure period and are now overmature. Partly for this reason and partly through neglect, hedgerow trees were lost twice as fast as hedgerows between 1947 and 1970. Again, the most severely affected areas were those associated with arable farming: some areas lost nearly 90 per cent of their trees. During the 1970s, Dutch elm disease added its toll, virtually wiping out this most majestic of indigenous trees. Until the mid-1970s the rate of planting of amenity trees was far below the rate of removal. Although more saplings are now being planted, there are worries that many do not receive adequate attention, that some are unsuitable for the locality, and that others are susceptible to diseases and chemical sprays.

Wetlands

Wetlands range from estuaries, saltmarsh and freshwater meadows (where the water-table is at or above ground level) to peat bogs and raised bogs (where water-tables vary but are usually at ground level) to drained grazing marshes (where water-tables are held around 50–75 cm below ground level). Some are of great ornithological interest if flooded in the winter; others can be of considerable botanical and entomological interest where there has been a long unbroken record of traditional management.

Since 1949, about 50 per cent of lowland fens, mires and valleys have been destroyed or significantly damaged, mostly due to drainage and reclamation. About 60 per cent of lowland raised bogs have been lost to afforestation, peat-winning, reclamation and repeated burning during the same 35-year period. In some counties, the losses have been much higher: in Lancashire, for example, 99.5 per cent of the lowland bogs have been reclaimed.

The amount of land where drainage is grant-aided by MAFF has increased from 25,000 ha. annually in 1970 to over 100,000 ha. and remains the second largest component of grant aid (after the construction of farm buildings), absorbing £44.4 million in 1980/81. A recent survey by the RSPB has shown that land drainage and the consequent 'improvement' of grazing areas are catastrophic for breeding and wintering wetland birds. The endangered field-nesting birds are snipe, shoveler, redshank, lapwing and yellow wagtail: nesting pairs can be reduced by well over half following even partial drainage improvement. Dyke-nesting birds such as coot, moorhen, reed warbler and grebe may be even more seriously affected. Overwintering birds such as teal, wigeon, pochard and Bewick's swan are also vulnerable, though judicious release of water at critical times and in critical areas can alleviate population decline.

Drainage also involves the artificial channelling of rivers and streams, destroying nesting sites and bankside vegetation and changing water chemistry. So it is hardly surprising that the Nature Conservancy Council has become alarmed at the cumulative effects of river 'improvements' which turn rivers into lifeless, featureless canals. Eleven species of dragonfly flourish in permanent ponds and ditches; none occurs in temporary ditches, modern, steep-sided drainage channels or piped water courses. An interim analysis of the effects of river 'improvements' on waders carried out by the British Trust for Ornithology demonstrates that breeding populations in England and Wales are much smaller than previously thought; that the number of available breeding sites is severely restricted; and that when breeding is attempted it is often unsuccessful. As a result, many river valleys have lost their breeding populations of waterfowl — notably wildfowl, snipe and redshank. The consequences of land drainage are so widespread that the Nature Conservancy Council is beginning to accept that conservation of wetland birds, plants and insects may have to be confined to protected sites. At present only 13 per cent of all remaining wetlands are SSSIs; at least three times this area should be officially protected if a range of representative habitats is to be safeguarded.

Chalk Grassland

Until the late eighteenth century, vast areas of chalk downland were used for sheep pasturage: the close-cropping animals encouraged a remarkably varied mixture of grasses and herbs and associated insects. Nowadays much of this land has either reverted to scrub because sheep grazing at traditional stocking levels is less economic and rabbit populations have declined, or it has been fertilised and reseeded for more productive grazing, or it has been ploughed. Since 1949, over 80 per cent of chalk grassland has disappeared. Many downland SSSIs have been ruined botanically through the application of artificial fertilisers sprayed from the ground and the air. In Wiltshire, 29 of the 50 SSSIs were lost in this way before 1980; one of the features of the Wildlife and Countryside Act is that the NCC must now be informed before such operations can take place.

Heathland

Heathland, like bogs, is a biotype that does not have to be eliminated to be ecologically destroyed: fragmentation is as much a harbinger of death as total destruction. It is also a major recreational resource, a patch of semi-wild open country to which the public has access, often in counties that are thickly populated or intensively farmed. The NCC estimate that nearly 60 per cent of heathland has been destroyed since 1949, largely by conversion to arable or improved grassland, afforestation and building. Some have also been invaded by scrub, owing to lack of grazing. The most vulnerable species are reptiles — notably lizards and snakes. In Dorset the sand lizard and the smooth snake are particularly endangered. Once again, it seems that only protection through purchase or designation can guarantee the survival of the remaining heathland, and even then the ecological viability of much of this may be in doubt. Because neglect, vandalism and fire are all serious threats, careful management is usually necessary if serious damage is to be avoided.

Moorland

The ecological and scenic importance of moorland is considerable, especially as moorland habitats are so very different throughout upland Britain, varying with climate, altitude, topography and management practices. With new drainage and reseeding techniques, much of this land is convertible into coniferous forest or improved pasture. This may involve losses not only in landscape and wildlife terms but also of public access and recreational opportunities. Chapters 8 and 9 examine the history of efforts to protect the scenically and recreationally important moorlands of the Exmoor National Park from agricultural reclamation, and the ecologically rich moorlands of the Berwyn Mountains from afforestation. Over 46,000 ha. or about 10 per cent of all moorland in national parks have been reclaimed since 1950, and each year about 5000 ha. of moorland throughout England and Wales are altered ecologically and scenically.

Moorland loss is not entirely due to reclamation and afforestation. Industrial pollution, damage by fires, excessive trampling, and overgrazing are all taking their toll. To add to a complex picture, there is the question of grouse management and moorland conservation. Needless to say, opinions vary greatly both as to the ethics and ecological value of grouse shooting. But the peculiarities of the various moorland habitats need to be very carefully managed through controlled stocking and burning, and if the economics of game enable such practices to be guaranteed, then successful moorland management may be possible, though never assured.

Afforestation of open moorland is also a highly controversial issue. Forestry interests, for example, are proud of the fact that coniferous stands provide habitat for a variety of birds which would otherwise not be found — goldcrest, crossbill, black grouse and siskin — though other upland birds such as greenshank, golden plover, dunlin, raven and golden eagle are adversely affected. The net effect is very much more complicated, however, because numbers and species both vary with forest age and management, and there continues to be dispute between the RSPB and the Forestry Commission. With sensitive forest management, including multiple species, trees of various ages and the provision of forest glades, much can be done to satisfy mutual interests (so long as it is accepted that forestry is not merely a matter of producing timber). However, government policies and financial support for forestry which mean that afforestation is only profitable with large economies of scale, minimal labour costs and shortened rotations militate against the integration of conservation management. The need to protect fairly large areas of open moorland for landscape purposes and to preserve the hunting grounds of birds of prey remains a matter of considerable controversy between conservation interests and the forestry lobby. Moreover, afforestation can restrict public access to the very areas that people particularly enjoy — the wide open expanses of fells and moors. Afforestation also affects water supply and quality, for afforested catchments retain run-off by up to 20 per cent and, because the trees trap pollutants, considerably worsen the acidification problem.

Limestone Pavements

Limestone is used for established rural activities such as the building of drystone-walls and, increasingly, for such modern urban needs as rock gardening. Damage to the limestone pavements of northern England is serious, since they support a rich but almost irreplaceable plant life. The NCC estimate that nearly half are ecologically worthless and only 3 per cent or so remain completely undamaged. Under Section 34 of the Wildlife and Countryside Act 1981, relevant ministers may issue limestone pavement protection orders where the conservation value of such areas is seriously threatened. Despite their precarious state, however, by mid-1984, $2\frac{1}{2}$ years after the passage of the Act, no such order had been issued.

Ancient Deciduous Woodland

One of the pre-eminent conservation issues is the need to retain broadleaved woodland in lowland Britain, some of which has occupied the given site for nearly 10,000 years. One problem here is that of definition. The Forestry

Commission, when undertaking woodland surveys, do not distinguish between *ancient deciduous woodland* (mostly undisturbed for at least 300 years) and *broadleaved woodland*, some of which may be extensively managed for game, and most of which, having been replanted with indigenous and exotic species, is termed 'secondary' woodland. The NCC estimates that in Britain as a whole there are 300,000 ha. of ancient woodland and 320,000 ha. of secondary woodland.

The NCC also calculate that 30–50 per cent of ancient woodland has been lost since 1950. This is mostly due to changes in agriculture or to a switch to the higher yielding and economically more attractive conifers. The remaining woodlands are of immense conservation value, since many of the rarer vascular plants mostly found in primary woodlands have no colonising ability. Unless they appeared with the forest they could not have become established. This is true too for a number of insects, notably butterflies. Ancient woodlands also contain a much greater variety of birds than planted woods with introduced tree species. In addition, ancient woodlands provide a vital 'gene pool', a storage for plant species which cannot otherwise be created. As such, they are both a control by which to gauge the diminution in the flora and fauna of surrounding areas and a breeding stock from which any losses can be replenished.

The amenity value of small woodlands should also be emphasised. A recent Countryside Commission survey suggests that there may be as much as 340,000 ha. of small woodland (i.e. woods below 10 ha. in extent) in England and Wales. They play a vital part in breaking up and framing the landscape, softening the edges of scarps and bluffs and filling out hollows. No upland or lowland landscape could ever be truly British if these woodlands were to disappear. Yet their survival is by no means assured.

Any further loss of ancient broadleaved woodland would be a serious matter. The highly artificial economics of modern forestry are not friendly to owners of broadleaved woodland, however, so the future of ancient woodland may depend almost entirely upon special designation and grant aid to encourage informed and careful management. Much secondary broadleaved woodland can be maintained through the economics of hunting, but increased planting grants and better markets for small wood products are also required. The survival of the 100,000 very small woods (i.e. those below 2 ha.) cannot be guaranteed otherwise: at present less than a quarter of them are in a reproducible state; over half are hopelessly over-mature and exposed to grazing. The chief woodland specialist at the NCC, George Peterken, believes that the only hope is to establish a heritage wood dedication scheme, possibly run jointly by the NCC and the Forestry Commission, which would channel money into specialised management of these woodlands primarily for conservation purposes. At present, though, the Commission refuses to grant aid for a range of low-input systems of silviculture which have lower outputs but are beneficial to conservation.

THE EFFECTS OF AGRICULTURE AND FORESTRY ON THE SUSTAINABLE PRODUCTIVITY OF ECOSYSTEMS

The integrity of the natural environment should be a matter of concern to everyone, and not least to farmers and foresters, because food and timber production involve the management and harvesting of natural systems. Some modern agricultural and forestry practices, however, are undermining the ability of soil, water and wildlife to sustain production. We shall use the term 'sustainable productivity' to characterise the management of resources so that they continue indefinitely to be ecologically healthy and productive. This precludes by definition any activity that is so seriously damaging to the life-supporting capabilities of soils, water or wildlife as to render them incapable of supporting crops or trees. What is more problematic are the efforts of scientists and managers to upgrade productivity through highly specialised and artificial means — such as plant and animal genetics, chemicals designed for specific purposes, sophisticated tillage and the prodigal use of fossil fuels. All this may increase output in the short term, but only with expensive and resource-demanding requirements, and vigilant management. Indeed, most modern farming and forestry depends upon large amounts of chemicals and energy, and will collapse when these are no longer available on the present scale.

Jennifer Rees, an agricultural consultant, notes that it is possible to grow wheat yielding 15–16 tonnes per ha. compared with the current national average of about 6 tonnes and the average for 1950 of only 3.5 tonnes. However, to do so requires 456 kg of potash per ha., 308 kg of phosphate, 123 kg of magnesium, a total of 642 kg of nitrogen applied at critical points in the growing cycle, plus three applications of growth regulator and 'extravagant' use of fungicides. The modern crop is heavily dependent on sophisticated and expensive chemical inputs. The annual growth in the use of fungicides is over 10 per cent; and of herbicides over 20 per cent. Pesticide use must be increased simply to keep the chemically-resistant pests at bay. Ms Rees comments:

> one of the most alarming consequences of high-tech arable farming is that land which is intensively cropped for corn year after year becomes barren. The basic soil infrastructure is destroyed so that there is little inherent fertility remaining. It is no longer capable of supporting crops without large doses of fertiliser. In another 20 years a large acreage of British farmland will be unable to support traditional crops, yet research into organic farming methods is underfunded.

Soil treated in this way also becomes more susceptible to water and wind erosion.

The Soil Survey of England and Wales has published a number of studies which show that soil erosion is a more serious problem than was once thought. In East Anglia, annual erosion rates are averaging as high as 18 tonnes per ha. (compared with 0.1 tonnes per ha. from undisturbed woodland or heathland), but in parts of Bedfordshire they exceed 40 tonnes per ha. The Soil Survey concludes that some 27,000 sq. km of soil (about 44 per cent of all arable land) are now unstable, and that at known rates of soil loss, much of this land could be unproductive within 30 years.

In similar vein, there is a danger that the genetic

manipulation of cattle breeding will produce cows unable to survive — let alone produce milk — on the low-cost feeding (i.e. grass or straw) that may have to be the staple diet again in years to come. It seems that the modern 'bionic dairy cow' does not have the stomach capacity to process a traditional diet. Its counterpart, the modern 'bionic beef cow', also requires increased amounts of high-energy specialised feeds to survive. Recent developments in sheep breeding suggest that in 25 years free-range sheep grazing, vital for the maintenance of upland landscapes, may be a rare sight. Trends in modern agriculture not only require enormously expensive inputs, but a dangerous dependence on resources, most of which have to be imported, certainly from outside the farm, and in many cases from abroad.

In the past, such fears have been treated dismissively by the agricultural research and advisory establishment, but there are signs that opinions are changing. As Professor Frank Raymond, Chief Scientist at MAFF, admitted in April 1984: 'We know extremely little about lower input systems, because virtually the whole of our research and advisory effort has been geared to high input/high output systems of farming.' He was speaking at the second annual conference of the Society for the Responsible Use of Resources in Agriculture and on the Land (RURAL). The society was set up by leading farmers, landowners and agriculturalists. Its aims include 'exploring profitable alternatives to high input/high output systems of farming, particularly those which reduce dependence on fossil fuels and on inputs which might adversely affect the environment'. It has begun to mount various practical demonstrations and projects to show how farming can become more environmentally sensitive and resource-conserving.

Likewise the Soil Survey is beginning to develop the concept of land 'suitability' rather than that of land-use 'capability' formerly used by the Survey. The latter incorporated the features of topography, drainage and soil type, and provided only a general guide for management. The new system is far more comprehensive, embracing soil conditions, climate, relief, farm size and farming operations, and is far more specific regarding the scope for sound management and sustained production. The suitability concept is already part of a new series of soil maps, and experimental maps of land suitability for both afforestation and agriculture are currently being prepared. These should form guides for future land-use planning, including the setting aside of some lands primarily for habitat and landscape purposes.

There are also worries about the growing use of fertilisers and pesticides on water quality and on 'benign' insects and fungi, some of which are natural predators to troublesome pests. Excessive use of pesticides has also encouraged the evolution of resistant strains of pests. These matters were reviewed by the Royal Commission on Environmental Pollution in its 1979 report on agriculture and pollution. The Commission recommended that the use of chemical fertilisers and pesticides should be curtailed, with much greater attention given to integrated fertilisation and pest control. It expressed particular concern about 'the scale of pesticide use', identifying a number of reasons for unnecessary pesticide applications: poor training of operators; inefficient spraying methods; 'insurance' spraying by farmers to forestall a pest attack that may not, in fact, occur; poor decisions by farmers about when to spray; and 'cosmetic' applications merely to make the crop look good in the shops. The Commission called for much tighter controls over pesticide usage.

The Royal Commission gave particular attention to the pollution associated with intensive animal husbandry. In traditional mixed farming, the manure produced is part of a self-sustaining cycle in which nutrients are returned to the land. In contrast, intensive livestock units may be operated as isolated enterprises, having no necessary relationship with other farming activities, with their feedstuff bought in and the area of land available for the disposal of excreta quite insufficient to exploit its nutrient value. In these circumstances, the excreta is regarded as waste, to be disposed of as cheaply as possible. The Commission estimated that the pollution load of excreta produced by farm animals in the United Kingdom is equivalent to that of 150 million people, but found that methods of disposal and treatment were usually crude and primitive, causing problems of smell, risks to public health and pollution of water courses. Farm discharges now account for a fifth of all reported cases of water pollution in England and Wales. The Royal Commission concluded that farmers must 'accept the costs of pollution control' just as other industries had. In its most recent (tenth) report, issued in 1984, the Royal Commission returned to the issue as part of a general review of the extent of pollution in Britain. It found that in most sectors there had been considerable progress in tackling the grosser forms of pollution during the last 20 years, with one notable exception — agriculture — where the Commission observed steadily increasing incidents of farm wastes.

At present, far too little is known about the long-term effects of liberally applied agricultural chemicals on ecosystems, though there is growing alarm over nitrogen levels in groundwater supplies and nutrient-enrichment of many rivers and lakes. A recent Royal Society study on the nitrogen cycle in the United Kingdom reports that both surface and underground water supplies are now severely contaminated with nitrates derived mainly from agricultural soils. It warns that, owing to slow transit times, the nitrate concentration in many supply wells will rise over the next 20 or 30 years to well above the maximum acceptable level specified by both the European Commission and the World Health Organisation. Already average nitrate levels exceed this limit in nearly a fifth of groundwater sources in East Anglia. Studies of groundwaters most at risk have indicated annual leaching of applied nitrogen of 30–80 kg/ha. from arable land — losses with a manufactured value equivalent to £10–25 per ha.

The official response to these various authoritative reports has been complacent. Farming continues to enjoy privileged exemptions from planning controls and many aspects of pollution control. In its investigations, the Royal Commission 'formed the view that the MAFF approach to pollution questions has been unduly defensive and protective towards agricultural interests'.

The House of Lords Select Committee on Science and Technology has looked at the environmental effects of afforestation, especially conifer plantations on soils, water supplies and wildlife. It was concerned that far too little is known about the long-term effects of softwoods on upland soils which have not been cropped for trees for many hundreds of years. When a soil is drained and supports trees utilising a low-nutrient budget, it may be difficult to restore its original structure and nutrient status. Single-stand conifers are also prone to pests and pathogens which can result in extensive applications of pesticides (e.g. fenitrothion) which can be seriously damaging to insects. The Forestry Commission is anxious to diversify its tree ages and species to overcome this problem, but will have to be more conciliatory towards conservation interests if a satisfactory compromise is to be reached.

The same Select Committee has also examined the relationship between agricultural and environmental research in a report published in 1984. It criticised not only the paucity of research on the long-term environmental implications of contemporary farming and forestry practices, but the lack of coordination and sustained financial commitment (vital to this kind of work) by all the relevant research councils and funding departments. In particular, the Agricultural and Food Research Council, it was suggested, was too oriented towards research designed to increase agricultural productivity to the neglect of other legitimate public concerns. A cause of this was said to be 'the closed loop between the Agriculture Departments and agricultural research', whereby research priorities were dominated by the interests of the farming and food industries: 'The opportunities for outside interests to contribute are heavily circumscribed — environmental interests are conspicuously absent from agricultural research committees'. Major research gaps identified by the Select Committee included farmland ecology, monitoring the long-term effects of agricultural practices on wildlife populations and the productive sustainability of soils, alternative patterns of land use and farming systems, and the socio-economic impact of changes in agricultural policy and technology. The solution proposed by the Committee was to make the agriculture departments responsible for promoting research on the environmental effects of agricultural practices — a recommendation which the Committee had to defend from the obvious charge that this amounted to putting the polluter in charge of identifying and policing his own pollution.

Straw and Stubble Burning

In many respects the issue of straw burning epitomises the wastefulness and irresponsibility of modern agriculture. On 8 August 1983, David Dixon and Joanna Titford pulled up behind a heavy goods tanker on the A19 in North Yorkshire. Dense smoke was billowing across the road, making driving impossible. A heavy articulated lorry drove blindly into them from behind. Both were killed instantly. The smoke came from straw being burnt on an adjacent field: the hedge and the verge adjacent to the road were also ablaze. In all, nine vehicles were damaged in the subsequent pile-up and a number of people sustained minor injuries. Subsequently, the farmer involved, Lieutenant-Colonel Montagu Charles Warcup Peter Consett, was fined a total of £2500 on three charges brought by the local district council: burning straw without a fire break, not giving the fire brigade any notice, and failing to provide supervision by a responsible person throughout the period of the burn. Each of these three violations (the first two of which the defendant admitted) broke the voluntary NFU code on straw burning.

That particular tragedy was the most serious of a long summer of public discontent over the whole issue of straw and stubble burning. To the modern arable farmer, the 'waste straw' is a nuisance: he rarely has the livestock to use the straw as food and bedding; chemically impregnated straw does not mulch easily; and fields must be drilled quickly after reaping to ensure maximum production for the winter cereal crop. Straw is therefore an 'uneconomic' resource. Burning is by far the least expensive method of disposal. The 'costs' are passed on to the public in the form of smoke-stained skies, smutty washing and house furnishings, increased breathing problems for those with respiratory ailments, and the destruction of trees, hedges, heathland and other wildlife habitats.

Nowadays some 7.5 million tonnes of straw are burnt in Britain each year, mostly between July and September. Because good straw-burning days are relatively infrequent, there is a tremendous conflagration when they do come. In 1983, the fire brigades reported more than 2500 fires as a direct consequence of burning, involving nearly

1800 call-outs. Since farmers do not pay rates on their fields and farm buildings, they do not contribute anything like their fair share to the costs of the county fire services.

The political controversy that followed the straw-burning season of 1983 focused on the adequacy of the 'voluntary burning codes' — formulated by the NFU/CLA with MAFF support — and on whether an outright ban would force farmers to recognise that straw must be used as a resource rather than regarded as waste. The NFU/CLA, backed by the Agriculture Departments, are desperate to avoid a ban: for one thing, it would be difficult to dispose of 7.5 million tonnes of straw! In March 1984 the government announced much tougher guidelines and district councils were encouraged to adopt them as bye-laws, along with a £2000 fine for non-compliance. These guidelines insist on: no burning at night, or on weekends and Bank Holidays; a 5-metre ploughed boundary and 25-metre strip around all hedges, trees, buildings, and nature reserves; a maximum burn of 25 ha. at any one time, with two people permanently in supervision and adequate water supplies nearby; plus, in some areas, one hour's notice to the local fire brigade.

These are stringent conditions, but not sufficient to assuage public opinion. Already, both the Countryside Commission and the Royal Commission on Environmental Pollution (in its tenth report) have called for an outright ban, phased in over five years. The Royal Commission was anxious to emphasise that only a ban would enable the technology necessary to utilise whole straw to be developed. This technology includes chemical decomposition to convert straw to a satisfactory mulch or to a useful synthetic food, the production of straw briquettes for burning in closed stoves, paper and board manufacture, and improved forms of cominution to return straw to the land. Much of this technology is already patented: it only requires some investment capital and the incentive of enforcement. In addition, that technology has export potential.

The straw-burning question typifies the dilemma of modern agriculture. Waste straw is a product of the bias towards cereals and arable monoculture. It also reflects the modern chemical age, when cereals are so heavily treated that their waste products are not capable of breaking down naturally. In addition, the issue shows how the farming community seeks to 'get away with it' at the public expense. The outcome of the argument over bans or voluntary codes will indicate whether public anger over agricultural irresponsibility will force politicians to take a firmer line, both to stop the nuisance and to insist that straw be treated as the valuable resource that it is. The long-term solution lies, however, in a shift back towards mixed farming, using more organic techniques, so that farms no longer generate unusable surpluses of slurry or straw.

The British countryside tries to serve four masters. The public want it to provide adequate food and timber, to be a setting for active and passive recreation, to harbour wildlife and to look inspiringly beautiful. The farmers and foresters want it to be productive and wealth-creating. Developers expect it to be ready for engineering projects and buildings, and politicians want it to meet all of these objectives. The classic British way out is to compromise — to fudge and nudge over almost every hectare. This is no longer possible. The time has come to be clear about priorities and to guide land-use decisions accordingly. How this will be done will depend crucially on the manner in which the various pressure groups influence political judgement and shape legislation. These matters are addressed in the next section.

FURTHER READING

The most comprehensive recent statement of habitat losses can be found in *Nature Conservation in Great Britain* (Nature Conservancy Council, 1984), though Charlie Pye-Smith and Chris Rose, *Crisis in Conservation: Conflict in the British Countryside* (Pelican, 1984) is also a good reference.

Both the Nature Conservancy Council and the Countryside Commission submitted valuable documentary evidence to the House of Lords Select Committee on the European Communities, *Agriculture and the Environment* (HMSO, 1984). Changes to the countryside are also documented in *Agricultural Landscapes: A Second Look* (Countryside Commission, 1984).

There are two useful references on the sustainability theme. Andrew Warren and Barry Goldsmith (eds), *Conservation in Perspective* (Wiley, 1983) is an excellent review of conservation and management issues for various ecosystems. The House of Lords Select Committee on Science and Technology recently reported on *Agricultural and Environmental Research* (HMSO, 1984), and this provides a powerful statement on the future of research in relation to maintaining the productive sustainability of agriculture. The Forestry Commission, in its report on *Broadleaved Woodlands* (1984) also addresses this theme, though the document covers wider social, economic and management aspects of this important ecosystem.

Section 2
The Political Background

4. The Farming, Landowning and Timber-Growing Lobby

In November 1979 Mr Charles Jarvis, an Essex farmer and Chairman of the British Farm Produce Council, delivered a lecture to the Royal Society of Arts with the title 'The Infinite Resource', in which he sought to justify the proposition that agriculture is the original and fundamental source of all true wealth, and consequently that the nation must foster and encourage it so that all may be wealthier. The immediate pretext for delivering the address was the omission by the then Chairman of ICI of any mention of farming in a lecture presented the previous year on 'Industry — The Provider'.

Agriculture is, after all, Britain's biggest single industry, and this particular example of a farming spokesman's assiduity in ensuring that the fact was not overlooked shows the thoroughness with which the National Farmers' Union and the Country Landowners' Association work to advance the concerns of their members in every relevant forum of debate and influence. These are the two organisations which dominate the agricultural lobby — the one, a trade association representing farmers; and the other, a group which defends and promotes the interests of owners of rural land.

The themes emphasised by the NFU and CLA have been so consistent that it is no surprise to find many of the points presented by Jarvis repeated in a glossy brochure published by the NFU in 1982. 'Farming — The Backbone of Britain' amply demonstrates how, at a time of relentless gloom and despondency in economic affairs, the agricultural industry can present itself as one of Britain's more convincing post-war successes.

The brochure's impressive array of statistics show that the total output of British agriculture is greater than that of the entire UK motor industry and double the combined turn-over of British Rail and British Airways. Since the war, wheat yields have nearly trebled and milk yields more than doubled. Such spectacular increases, moreover, have been matched by impressive improvements in labour productivity — an area in which, by common consent, the general experience of British industry has been disappointing. Thus an increase in output per person of 43 per cent between 1976 and 1981 compares with a figure of 3 per cent for manufacturing industry. Between 1970 and 1980 Britain's self-sufficiency in all food increased from 47 to 60 per cent, and in the types of food we can grow in our climate, from 59 to 75 per cent. This general improvement in our degree of self-sufficiency has been accompanied, it is claimed, by movements in price and income relativities which overwhelmingly favour the consumer.

With whatever justification the statistics may be questioned, this record of economic success is certainly enviable. But the agricultural industry is distinctive in other ways too, about which the NFU and the CLA are typically less forthcoming. As we have seen (Chapter 2), farmers receive more state aid than any other industry. Agriculture is, moreover, the only industry in Britain that is wholly exempt from paying rates, and that has a government ministry specifically concerned with its needs and which provides a sophisticated advisory service (ADAS) at no cost to the individual farmer. In addition, agricultural activities and developments are peculiarly free from the sorts of planning control and regulation which are accepted as appropriate in other industries. So although government commitment to a secure and prosperous agriculture has until recently remained virtually unquestioned for over 40 years, the massive resources which have been directed into agriculture to underpin this commitment have not been accompanied by any attempt to curtail the autonomy of the individual producer. It is not difficult to demonstrate, then, that in terms of both its remarkable achievements and its equally remarkable autonomy agriculture is an exceptional industry. Just as the emergence and persistence of this 'exceptionalism' presents a complex story (see Chaper 2), so there is no simple explanation for the ways in which it has been sustained, though analysis of the power of the farming and landowning lobby has to be central to any explanation.

A UNIQUE PARTNERSHIP

Given a statutory role in the annual round of decision-making on farm prices by the Agriculture Act 1947, agricultural interests developed and consolidated their governmental links, particularly with the Ministry of Agriculture. Already by the early 1960s, the relationship between the NFU and government was, according to Self and Storing, 'unique in its range and intensity'. Later commentators have tended only to confirm and amplify that judgement. Indeed, in recent analyses of British politics, agriculture has been cited as perhaps the one unequivocal example of an economic sector where an interest group has been officially recognised by the state and incorporated into the process of decision-making, not merely to represent its members but to play a joint role in the political management of the sector.

The NFU has derived considerable political advantage from its symbiotic relationship with MAFF — through the ministry's single-minded commitment to the farmers' cause, through the NFU's entrenched role in policy-making and through its privileged access on a routine basis to centres of decision-making, including the highest levels of government. This is the key to the NFU's influence and it is significant that, in the inter-war years, before it achieved this intimate relationship with the ministry — indeed, before the ministry became so closely involved in the management of the agricultural sector — the NFU was a relatively weak and marginal interest group. Nowadays, the ministry and the union are in constant contact at all levels over the myriad of issues, large

and small, that arise in the development and implementation of agricultural policy.

The NFU's working partnership with the state has
enabled it to exert an influence which has been disproportionate, given that its membership is too small directly to
determine the outcome of elections and that it does not
have at its disposal the direct economic sanctions available
to some other key business organisations or trade unions.
But the partnership has also placed constraints on the
NFU. As Self and Storing noted, 'the tendency of the close
concordat has been as much to debilitate the union as to
hamper the government'. The constraints on MAFF from
other government departments concerned at the financial
and other implications of developments in agricultural
policy have also been significant. The NFU does not have
such a close relationship with these other departments
and, far from being in a position to dictate terms, it has in
fact been highly dependent upon the goodwill of successive governments. It has been the sheer reluctance of
governments to change farm policy in any fundamental
way which has most obviously benefited agricultural
interests, particularly the large farmers who dominate the
NFU, and has been the most significant of the factors
conferring power on the NFU. Throughout the post-war
period, the farming and landowning lobby and the state
have been moving in tandem with a powerful momentum
in pursuit of the same broad priorities.

Although their most important channel of access to
decision-makers is through MAFF, the NFU and the CLA
have not neglected other political channels, including
other government departments, the European Commission, local government, Parliament and the mass
media. The agricultural interest enjoys an in-built bias in
most representative assemblies, which they have been
able to exploit. Through their traditional social and political leadership of rural areas, farmers and landowners tend
to be disproportionately represented on parish, district
and county councils and in the British and European
Parliaments. They are a sizeable minority in the Commons,
particularly on the Conservative side; and a majority of the
Lords. Most members of Tory Cabinets are landowners or
have agricultural connections, and even Labour Cabinets

usually have a few. At the very least, this ensures an informed hearing for the farming lobby. The NFU has developed particularly effective links with Parliament — so much so that when the CBI, of which it is an influential member, decided to improve its lobbying arrangements in the late 1970s, it modelled its new system on the NFU's, adopting in particular that organisation's practice of central coordination and encouragement of contacts between its members and MPs in the constituencies.

An important corollary of the partnership between the farming lobby and the state has been a reluctance to resort to legislative control of the activities of farmers. In any case, the relatively modest legislative base — much of it very dated — on which MAFF operates has meant that much policy-making has been accompanied by considerable latitude and discretion for producers. Understandably, therefore, a 'what we have we hold' mentality has prevailed in relation to many of the issues of public concern discussed in Section 1, and much of the apparent power of the lobby has derived from its ability to resist fundamental changes on matters such as planning controls and de-rating by working to bolster and sustain an already engineered consensus with government.

During the past decade, however, various factors have ensured greater prominence and contention for questions of agricultural policy. These include the excesses of the Common Agricultural Policy; the shift of the burden for agricultural support from the taxpayer to the consumer which followed EEC entry; rising unease over animal welfare; and political interest in the welfare of rural communities. But the most serious challenge to the privileges of farmers arises from conservationists. As the Society for the Responsible Use of Resources in Agriculture and on the Land (RURAL) notes in the report of its inaugural meeting held in April 1983, 'farmers are becoming increasingly aware that they are under threat to their freedom of action because of the strength of public opinion about the way land is being managed'.

Indeed, so concerned have the NFU and the CLA become with the drift of public opinion that they have recently sought funds for an unprecedented £27,000 study to be conducted by the Centre for Agricultural Strategy,

Reading University, and designed to counter criticism of the farming community and improve agriculture's public image. This was also the specific objective of 'The Backbone of Britain' campaign. The ministry meanwhile has acknowledged concern: in May 1984 it appointed as special adviser a farmer prominent in both the NFU and the CLA; and in July it established an Environment Co-ordination Unit with a staff of six, to be headed by a food scientist with the rank of Assistant Secretary, the fourth highest in Whitehall.

The struggle to counter the increasingly articulate voices of the industry's critics presents the farming and land-owning lobby with perhaps its sternest task to date. The lobby's unique partnership with the state depends upon its ability to discipline its own members such that they voluntarily comply with agreements reached with government and cooperate with the implementation of policy. Thus the struggle is at the same time a critical internal process of education and inducement in which the NFU and the CLA cannot afford to be unsuccessful, though the authority of their leadership is much less strong than it once was. This broader struggle is especially challenging because it takes them beyond the somewhat circumscribed channels of political influence in which they have been so effective during the post-war period.

THE ORGANISATION AND WORKINGS OF THE LOBBY

The NFU and the CLA, both studiously non-party-political organisations, have their origins in the years of agricultural depression at the turn of the century. Formed in 1908 the NFU had, by 1912, established a national network of county groups with the membership of 290 contributing a subscription income of just £29. Today, 140,000 farmers and growers throughout England and Wales representing over 80 per cent of full-time farmers pay over £7 million towards the cost of running a union whose net assets to October 1983 were £9.1 million. Separate unions exist for Scotland and Ulster, and in the mid-1970s the breakaway Farmers' Union of Wales achieved formal government recognition, having been formed 20 years earlier following frustration at what was felt to be persistent indifference to Welsh problems. A small number of tenant-farmers, similarly feeling that the NFU was failing to represent their interests adequately, especially in their dealing with landlords, formed an association in 1981. Not surprisingly it was the effective representational monopoly granted to the NFU under the terms of the 1947 Act which was both a culmination of and basis for the largest growth in the NFU's membership that occurred during and after the second world war. The subsequent efforts at establishing rival farmers' organisations have not posed any major challenge to the ability of the NFU to speak for the industry with total authority.

Internal strains within the NFU may present a greater potential threat. The increased specialisation which has followed EEC membership has had a profound impact on the NFU's internal politics. At the 1984 annual meeting, for instance, the appearance of unity so carefully nurtured in recent years was exposed as spurious when the growing rift between arable farmers and livestock producers — popularly characterised as 'corn vs. horn' — erupted in acrimonious discontent. The internal consensus, so essential to a working partnership with the state and achieved relatively easily in the days when mixed farming predominated, is currently in some disarray.

The NFU, though, is so structured as to absorb many internal differences. It is a federation of 49 county branches (themselves derived from 860 local branches) which have a tradition of considerable autonomy deriving from both an inability and a lack of will to impose greater central direction. The membership is inclined to insist on the right to criticise even in specialist areas where it may have no real competence. There is an obvious strength in local autonomy, but at a time when agricultural activity is being ever more closely examined it can, as the case studies in Section 3 demonstrate, be a source of acute embarrassment as well. Moreover, such centripetal tendencies can make decision-making tortuous, stifling initiative in the process and engendering a 'safety first' mentality. County branches send delegates to the national council; and for obvious reasons richer farmers tend to be heavily over-represented.

With its 135 members it can be an unwieldy assembly achieving a clear sense of direction only with difficulty. There are, in addition, other powerful factors channelling policy making initiative towards the NFU's elected and appointed full-time officials.

Council elects the president, deputy president and vice-president, who allocate work amongst themselves. Invariably one of the deputies will cover livestock, the other cereals. The work of furthering members' interests and the NFU's internal decision-making centre on a network of commodity committees, supplemented by a few task-specific committees such as the economic committee and the parliamentary committee. Chairmen of the commodity committees work closely with the NFU's senior economic staff and commodity advisers. In addition, its combined staff of around 840 — a third of them based at Agriculture House, Knightsbridge — provide members with a whole series of professional services ranging from legal, taxation and insurance matters to advice on commercial contracts and assistance with complaints relating to defective machinery, farm buildings, chemicals and feedstuffs.

The CLA, formed one year earlier in 1907, and now elegantly housed just a short step from Agriculture House in Belgrave Square, has a similarly strong basis in its network of 47 county branches. Its 50,000 or so members together own the bulk of England and Wales and, like the NFU, it has a Scottish counterpart in the Scottish Landowners' Federation. There is considerable membership overlap with the NFU and, just as the NFU emphasises that it is largely an organisation of small businessmen (although nearly 50 per cent of agricultural output is produced by just one tenth of all farms), the CLA makes great play of the fact that 50 per cent of its members own less than 40 ha., and only 20 per cent more than 100 ha. But there are good reasons why it has been unable to shake off the image of being dominated by the larger landowners with holdings of 1000 ha. and more. There is close co-operation between the two organisations, though on matters of agricultural policy the CLA is usually overshadowed by the NFU, whose lead it usually follows. As the CLA Secretary commented in conversation, 'The only thing we fight about with the NFU is landlord/tenant relationships.' But even here the frustration of the two organisations recently has been mutual and directed at government for its dilatoriness in responding to a painstakingly negotiated NFU/CLA package of proposed amendments to the relevant legislation.

In the CLA, policies are settled by a council which is composed of representatives from every branch. Council elects an executive committee from its own membership, and the legal and parliamentary, agriculture and land-use, taxation, water, minerals and finance committees are chosen from candidates nominated by the branches. Council and the policy committees are supported by small teams of professional staff who are involved in both advisory and political action. The technical advice they can offer, particularly on legal and taxation problems, provides a valued return for membership subscriptions. An active publications department makes available an extensive range of documents and advisory memoranda on every aspect of taxation, employment, housing, way leaves, game, land tenure, public access and conservation.

As with the NFU, lobbying activities are dependent on nurturing an extensive range of contacts with whom information and opinion can be exchanged, as well as participation on working parties and the provision of evidence for official committees and formal meetings. But such activities can only bear fruit if a climate of mutual respect between the CLA and the various ministries and statutory bodies with which it deals is sustained. And if the CLA does not have quite the relationship with MAFF which gives the NFU the appearance of having a hand in almost everything the ministry does, it has, through its quiet, behind-the-scenes diplomacy, been tenacious in its defence of the rights of private property. Amongst other priorities its perennial rearguard actions to deny any credibility for such ideas as land nationalisation and a wealth tax link it ideologically and practically with the Conservative Party and it has always been well represented in the House of Lords. The few Conservative peers who voted for amendments opposed by the CLA during the passage of the Wildlife and Countryside Bill in 1981 provided a rare spectacle. Whilst it is, perhaps, only natural that the main emphasis of its activities should have given it a fundamentally defensive image, its lobbying activities have helped secure for members more tangible benefits than merely the prevention of unwanted measures.

Apportioning credit for the success of lobbying activities is notoriously difficult because it entails projecting what might have happened had no effort been expended at all. (The impact of the lobby on the Wildlife and Countryside Act is given detailed attention in Chapter 6.) But that impressive success aside, the CLA can point to the rewards of painstaking application in relation to recent taxation policies and such new measures as the Agricultural Holdings Act and the Occupiers' Liability Act. At the NFU, economists have calculated that the NFU's efforts during 1983 (for example, in preventing the rating of agricultural land and buildings, and stopping the revaluation of the green pound) helped members retain £600 million of their profits that might otherwise have been lost — a return, they claim, of 8000 per cent on the investment of a subscription. It is much harder, of course, to put a figure on benefits from representations on such contentious issues as straw burning and pesticide control. Not unnaturally, the promotional publicity makes no mention of the defeats which have become more prevalent following the greater politicisation of agricultural questions consequent upon EEC membership. Occasionally, farming interests can now look weak, even in relation to quite modest aims and, on matters of great weight such as the recent imposition of milk quotas, utterly impotent.

In the changed environment created by EEC membership the farming and landowning lobby still deploys its skills and abilities in familiar ways, albeit in more varied directions. Although the old-style annual price review has been replaced by up to a dozen individual decisions in the course of a year, the NFU considers that the CAP 'follows the same basic principles as the 1947 Agriculture Act', and the UK government is, in any case, still responsible for many commodity guarantees and prices. Contrary to expectations before EEC entry, lobbying continues much as before, but is now directed additionally through COPA (the European farmers' organisation), which is the officially recognised channel of contact between national farming organisations and the European Commission.

Efforts are made to maintain contact with MEPs and their researchers, but more work continues to be based in London than was thought likely. That the positions adopted by the NFU and COPA often diverge has certainly increased the uncertainty of the NFU's political environment. Its most effective response, nevertheless, is still to persuade the British government to adopt NFU-preferred policies and to encourage it to advocate them in the Council of Agricultural Ministers and other Community fora. Given that it deals through a ministry which is so committed to the farmers' cause, this is a strategy which has served the NFU well for 40 years.

THE TIMBER-GROWING LOBBY

Also based behind the imposing Georgian façade of Agriculture House are the staff of an influential pressure group whose principal role is to represent private timber-growers and woodland-owners in dealings with government departments and other national bodies. Like the farming and landowning lobby with which it liaises closely, the timber-growing lobby has pressed for an expansionist and profitable industry and argued the compatibility of such aims with environmental and amenity considerations. Just as the NFU and CLA have been forced to become more image-conscious, the timber-growing lobby has recently sought to increase its effectiveness by merging the interests of Timber Growers Scotland and Timber Growers England and Wales to form a body whose 3700 members manage over 800,000 ha. of woodland. Before their unification as Timber Growers UK Ltd (formally accomplished on 1 October 1983) the two organisations had been linked through the umbrella Forestry Commission of Great Britain. This had been replaced because it was felt not to be clearly enough distinguished from the Forestry Commission.

Innocent observers could, indeed, be forgiven for some confusion given the ways in which the priorities and concerns of public and private forestry interests have become so closely enmeshed. The Forestry Commission, as well as raising, managing and selling timber from its own estate

of 840,000 ha., also regulates the activities of the private
forestry sector through a combination of legal and financial instruments (see Chapter 2). There is a 60 per cent
state/40 per cent private mix in Scotland, and in England
and Wales the figures are 34 per cent state and 66 per cent
private. The timber-growing lobby is represented on the
Home-Grown Timber Advisory Committee, the Forestry
Commission's main statutory advisory body. Moreover,
Timber Growers England and Wales was formed in 1960
with financial assistance not only from the CLA but also
from the Forestry Commission; and the new Timber
Growers UK, like the Forestry Commission, has its administrative headquarters in Edinburgh. Just three private
forestry management companies tend three-eighths of the
woodland in private ownership. The most commercially
aggressive (see Chapter 9) of them, the Economic Forestry
Group, was formed in 1958. In the 25th anniversary
edition of its newsletter, Lord Taylor of Gryfe, the Group's
chairman from 1976–81, commented:

> The great thing about Forestry is that it is a partnership.
> The dreary debates between Public and Private sectors
> which bedevil other areas of our national economic life do
> not apply in the rational world of men and women who
> grow trees. It was therefore an easy transition when I
> ceased to be Chairman of the Forestry Commission and
> became Chairman of the Economic Forestry Group.

Decisions in this 'rational world' are in fact taken in the
light of an often unplanned interaction between a system
of public subsidies and tax concessions so elaborate as
more or less to obliterate any public/private distinction.
Thus the Economic Forestry Group, a public company
with part or full ownership of 12 operating companies,
and an annual turnover of £27 million in 1982, acts on
behalf of investment companies and other clients who are
able to offset all the start-up costs of buying land and
planting against income (see Chapter 2). Indeed, so essential are concessions and grants as the lifeblood of forestry
that there is strong justification for Chris Hall's characterisation of it as 'the artificial offspring of two world wars'.
   The other factor which has fuelled criticism of the
forestry lobby's ambitions has been the overwhelming

concentration — for obvious economic reasons — on fast-maturing softwoods. Thus, although the Forestry Commission *Census of Trees* (November 1983) emphasises that the total area of woodland in England has increased by about 14 per cent since the war and in Wales by more than 40 per cent, the increases have been largely in conifer plantations — from 165,000 to 380,000 ha. in England, and from 42,000 to 168,000 ha. in Wales. Much of the substantial increase in conifer acreage has occurred in environmentally sensitive upland areas; and concern over the forestry lobby's projections and preferred production targets is heightened by the fact that about half of the technically plantable area lies within national parks or areas with AONB designation.

Moreover, with the rapid decline of labour-extensive woodland management, the pattern of economic pressures and incentives can even encourage landowners to convert mature broadleaved woodlands to coniferous plantations. There has been understandable concern, therefore, about the future of this type of woodland. This has only deepened contemplation of the possible implications of the requirement, following the Forestry Act 1981, for the Forestry Commission to raise £82 million from asset sales by 1986. The Commission claims there has been no decline in the extent of English broadleaved woodlands since the war, omitting to mention that that was a low point for British forestry, and that much of the acreage now consists of new plantings. The prospects for the irreplaceable fragments of our ancient forests and semi-natural woodland are more uncertain. At least some of the woodland that the Commission is selling is of this character, and the buyers will almost inevitably be those for whom woods are most profitable when newly planted, or grubbed out for agriculture. Although the Forestry Commission remains the controlling authority responsible for issuing felling licences, and is statutorily charged with taking account of ecological and recreational interests, there is understandable disquiet given the overwhelming commitment of both public and private sectors of the forestry lobby to increased production.

So manifest was the impact of conifer planting that conflict between forestry and preservation interests was

evident long before the last decade's more general growth
of awareness in environmental issues and now the most
recent policy developments have done much to place
forestry at the centre of the wider crisis in the developing
relationship between agriculture and conservation as well.
So, having identified the main organisations of the farming, landowning and timber-growing lobbies and indicated the nature of their resources and advantages of
access, it is necessary to consider their evolving attitudes
towards conservation.

ATTITUDES TOWARDS CONSERVATION

The close and continuous relationship between the NFU
and CLA and relevant ministries, and their involvement
with numerous pieces of legislation, has provided the
lobby with recurrent opportunities to present a coherent
philosophy to civil servants and politicians. Especially in
the wake of the Wildlife and Countryside Act, the NFU
and CLA have presented farmers as custodians of the
countryside, and have sought to emphasise the moral
obligations of responsible stewardship inherent to landownership. The NFU is clearly the senior partner of the
lobby in relation to agricultural policy, but the CLA has
retained a long-established priority on thinking about conservation matters, often adopting a more progressive or
conciliatory line than its sister organisation. As the leader
in the October 1983 issue of *Country Landowner* concluded,
'in accommodating agriculture and the other productive
uses of the countryside with the legitimate interests of
conservation there should be scope for the CLA to take a
lead'.

The relative urgency and manner of response to a recent
disturbing lapse from the stewardship ethic was symbolically indicative of this. As we have seen, the long-term
viability of the farming and landowning lobby's partnership with the state depends on its ability to control its own
members to ensure that agreements are honoured and
policy effectively implemented. Accordingly, no sooner
had the Wildlife and Countryside Act, with its philosophy
of voluntary cooperation and goodwill, been passed, than

the CLA council found itself considering a proposal that 'mavericks be ostracised and asked to leave the association'. The general view of the council on that occasion, though, was that malefactors should be kept within the association so that it could educate them. However, in July 1983, for the first time in the CLA's 76-year history, the council did decide to expel a member. The man who achieved this dubious distinction had recently been gaoled, amidst much publicity, for felling trees on his land in Kent in flagrant defiance of tree preservation orders and a High Court injunction. The NFU subsequently contemplated expelling him as well, but concluded in the manner of that earlier CLA council meeting that to do so would diminish the possibility of influencing his future conduct. The contrasting responses of the two organisations reveal the acute dilemmas they face following the dramatic politicisation of land-use issues, and the consequent opprobrium for any behaviour which discredits the voluntary approach.

Ideas of 'stewardship' remain potent both as an ideology which can legitimate the private ownership of land and as an educative ethic which influences the behaviour of individual landowners. As the foreword to a 1984 handbook issued jointly by the NFU, the CLA and the Royal Institution of Chartered Surveyors on *Management Agreements in the Countryside* maintains, the people best placed to conserve the countryside are 'landowners and farmers who have a moral responsibility for the sensible stewardship of their property'. Such sentiments draw strength from that persistent strain in our national culture which has seen dependable gentlemanly virtues as rooted in the countryside. The myth of the rural idyll and its associated 'gentry' sentiments has continued to be vibrant in postwar political life: but the resonance of sets of ideas such as those embodied in the notion of 'stewardship' can suffer depletion if a gap between the claims of the ideology and perceived reality becomes apparent. The mounting evidence of habitat loss chronicled in Chapter 3 has certainly forced the CLA and NFU to work harder than ever to sustain such beliefs. Commenting in 1981 on the results of a CLA survey of its members' contribution to conservation, Lord Middleton, the then president, suggested that a sense of responsibility was the main influence on landowners in their management of the countryside: 'The long-term view of their duties to the land', he claimed, 'is something which is innate' (*The Field*, 18 November 1981). It is precisely because such ideas no longer seem untendentious, that is a measure of the difficulties now faced by the farming and landowning lobby.

In an earlier period things were less problematic for them. The priorities in their emerging position on conservation issues are already apparent in the submission made by the CLA to the first of the 'Countryside in 1970' conferences organised by the Nature Conservancy and the Council for Nature in 1963 (see Chapter 5). George Howard, the then president of the CLA, prepared a paper as a basis for the formulation of CLA policy in relation to the theme of the conference — 'Human Impacts on the Countryside'. In it he emphasised the ability of the CLA to take a broader and longer-term view than the many bodies with sectional interests in the countryside, whilst recognising the difficulties posed by the fact that such a 'broader spectrum of interest is principally confined to those who may be defined as estate owners [defined as those with holdings in excess of 300 ha.] rather than owner-occupiers', noting in passing that though these owners 'may be a small minority numerically in the membership of the CLA [8 per cent] their acreage is vastly important [66 per cent]'. The paper, and the CLA's final submission for the 1963 conference, 'Landowners and the Future', point to a basic identity of interest between the concerns of agriculture and amenity interests. Not only is the countryside man-made, but change in its appearance is not necessarily harmful, for 'If land ceased to be used agriculturally, much of its current attraction for the town-dweller would disappear. Scrub, thorn and tussocky grass are not such a pleasant sight for the townsman as waving corn'. Much exercised by questions relating to access, the submission emphasises that it must be paid for and that, 'If the Nation wills the end, it should will the means'. A separate circulated note reiterates the point, adding that 'Conservation demands greater Exchequer assistance', and calling specifically for additional finance for national parks. The main paper refers to an extensive range of topics, expressing disquiet, for example, at the possible long-term effects of the increasing use of chemical sprays and dressings. These and other land-use changes, such as drainage and afforestation, are presented as of vital concern to the landowner, not least because of their possible impact on the long-term capital value of holdings. Reflecting the CLA's basic concern with the need to strengthen the capital base of private landownership and promote the long-term prosperity of agriculture there is, in 'Landowners and the Future', a sense of the responsible recognition of a wide range of problems being perennially tempered by precisely those priorities and, of course, a fundamental belief that public ownership of itself can resolve none of the conflicting claims on land-use.

Thirteen years later, in its 1976 response to the Countryside Review Committee's discussion paper 'The Countryside — Problems and Policies', the tone is more strident. The committee had been set up to review the range of government policies affecting the countryside and comprised senior civil servants from relevant government departments and agencies. Noting that wider discussion earlier might have helped avoid some of the 'detrimental consequences' of 'so much recent regulatory legislation', the CLA response makes its familiar points about the long-term interests of the countryside being best served if as many decisions as possible are left in the hands of the individual owner. In the CLA's view, neither the fact that it is the landowner who is responsible for most important decisions affecting land-use nor agriculture's position as the foremost rural industry is given sufficient recognition. It does applaud, however, the decision of the committee to reject any proposals for further legislation concerned with the management of the countryside since 'Land management requires a positive and sensitive hand and can only be restricted by further planning control legislation.'

Some indication of the effectiveness of CLA/NFU lobbying is provided two years later in a 1978 response to another Countryside Review Committee paper. On this occasion the CLA was able to welcome the CRC statement that 'the first objective of a rural community is to produce food and timber', but the committee's characterisation of the second objective as being to 'conserve natural beauty and amenity' provides an opportunity to reiterate the claim that 'The countryside is the visual expression of farming and timber production' — the reassertion of a claimed identity of interests which has been a persistent feature of the farming and landowning lobby's case since the early 1960s and before. In this and other position papers from the CLA, a wholly proper emphasis on the economic viability of the countryside is accompanied by the view — increasingly seen as unwarranted by non-farming interests — that the resolution of other problems will be achieved if this prior commitment is accorded sufficient recognition.

A similar orientation is evident in the development of NFU thinking on conservation during the period. Formerly, it has shown little interest in matters which, though a suitable avocation for relatively leisured land-owners, seemed marginal to the interests of the working farmer. However, since the passage of the Countryside Act 1968, when the first sustained attempts were made to introduce some statutory regulation of agricultural development in environmentally sensitive areas, the NFU has joined the CLA in emphasising its concern for conservation and has ensured the representation of the farming viewpoint in conservation debates. Concern about environmental issues is given attention, for instance, in its newsletter *Insight* with three 1971 reports from the NFU's countryside working party: *Looking at the Landscape, Wildlife Conservation and the Farmer* and *Access, Recreation and the Farmer*. Of the three reports, the second is the shortest and its claim that 'intensive modern agriculture and wildlife conservation are not incompatible' reflects a concern apparent in the preamble to all the reports to cast doubt on claims 'that no one is caring for the land in the way that the 18th- and 19th-century landowners did'. Overall, there is the same emphasis on access and landscape issues that we have noted in CLA documents, and a similar concern to sustain a voluntary non-legislative approach buttressed by financial incentives if farmers are to add wider social and environmental objectives to their primary, food-producing role.

Already by the early 1970s though, the stance of the

farming and landowning lobby in relation to many issues of environmental concern had the general tenor of a rearguard action, particularly in the face of mounting pressures for greater powers to regulate the environmental impact of agricultural development. The farming and landowning lobby, not unnaturally, has resisted any such curbs. Always ready to discuss specific conservation problems in a positive manner, the CLA and NFU have stressed the need to retain the goodwill and voluntary cooperation of the farming community if practical remedies are to be found. Together they have responded to the charges of conservationists by presenting farmers as stewards of the countryside. While staunchly resisting any form of planning constraint or encroachment on a farmer's eligibility for government improvement grants, they have pressed for payments and tax incentives for farmers to pursue conservation objectives and, in particular, to compensate for any potential income forgone through farming so as to preserve the landscape and wildlife of an area.

Two particular initiatives stand out: in 1970 the two organisations joined with MAFF, the Nature Conservancy Council, the RSPB and the Royal Society for Nature Conservation in supporting the formation of the Farming and Wildlife Advisory Group (FWAG). Its aim was to bring together agriculturalists and conservationists to promote mutual understanding and cooperation. FWAG's avowed principle is that wildlife conservation and profitable farming need not be incompatible and that loss of wildlife habitat through agricultural intensification can best be ameliorated by encouraging farmers to modify their practices and providing necessary advice. Though not mentioned by name, the FWAG ethos is clearly evident in the NFU countryside working party report on *Wildlife Conservation and the Farmer*, discussed earlier, when it calls for advice and information for farmers 'if they are to take account of wildlife when planning changes on their farms'. FWAG has, in fact, appeared remarkably influential, not least because it has enjoyed the patronage of MAFF, and the ministry certainly encouraged its regional advisers to cooperate as closely as possible with the county FWAGs which began to be established in the 1970s.

The second initiative of note by the CLA and NFU was the publication of the leaflet *Caring for the Countryside* (1977). This joint statement of intent acknowledged that farmers have an important part to play, not only in the production of food and timber, but also in the conservation of scenery and wildlife; and it presented a basic conservation guide for their members' use as well as encouraging them to seek appropriate advice. The statement was very much a response to overtures, seeking an accommodation between conservation and agriculture, from the Countryside Commission following its *New Agricultural Landscapes* study, and from the Nature Conservancy Council following its *Nature Conservation and Agriculture* report (see Chapter 1). Significantly, the Countryside Review Committee, on which both bodies were represented along with senior civil servants from the DoE and MAFF, declared in its paper, *Food Production in the Countryside* (1978) that, 'The goodwill inherent in this statement should be one of the cornerstones of future government policy for conservation.' On the premise that 'any new policy must have the broad support of the farming community', it roundly rejected any imposition of controls over agriculture, arguing that they would be cumbersome, costly and unconstructive. Instead, it called — with words which were surely mellifluous to the CLA and the NFU — for a 'voluntary and flexible policy, based on advice, encouragement, education and financial inducements'. The rearguard action had successfully denied those seeking fundamental reform any sort of bridgehead in official circles.

The CLA and NFU, of course, have worked to consolidate this advantage. For example, in its response to the Countryside Review Committee's paper *Conservation and the Countryside Heritage* (1979) the CLA reiterated its commitment to the paramountcy of the interests of local communities if the countryside is to be 'a living reality'; the interdependence of agriculture and conservation; the need to assess the costs of preservation in terms of loss of production for the country and loss of income for the farmer and landowner; the need for the NCC to put more resources into management agreements and to inform owners of SSSIs of their valued characteristics; and the general undesirability of any further proliferation of designations in the countryside. These were all points it had also been able to make in its response to the six consultation papers published in the autumn of 1979 in preparation for the introduction of the Wildlife and Countryside Bill.

STEWARDSHIP: THE MYTH AND THE REALITY

In this way the requirements of the farming and landowning lobby in relation to any potential countryside legislation were effectively established in official thinking during the 1970s when mounting evidence of destruction was prompting both a greater scepticism about stewardship claims than ever before, and an increasingly convincing case for intervention to moderate the impact of agricultural development and protect valued aspects of the countryside heritage. Inevitably, many of the arguments presented by the farming and landowning lobby seem defensive. After all, it is seeking to safeguard privileges which its members have taken for granted as integral to the post-war reality within which they have been operating. Nevertheless, the concern of landowners and their representatives over matters relating to conservation is genuine, long-standing and significant. So far only major initiatives relating to the policy context have been discussed, but to respond to demands from sceptics who regard the stewardship ideology as a form of crass special pleading, that evidence be presented of its practical impact, there is much that the CLA can draw upon, not least the contribution of game preservation to the ecology of the countryside.

As the NCC acknowledges in its publication *Nature Conservation in Great Britain* (1984), 'The traditional landowners' enthusiasm for fieldsports is closely linked to the conservation of habitat important to wildlife on farmland.' Much of the credit for establishing a scientific basis for recognising this is due to the Game Conservancy, an independent charitable trust, whose research on reducing the impact of new farming operations on game has received much financial support from the CLA. A concern with the fortunes of game, for example, has been instrumental in leading some farmers and landowners to rethink their crop-spraying policies, and currently a project set up with a substantial grant from a group of conservation-minded farmers is examining the impact of agrochemical sprays on farmland wildlife.

In 1958 the annual CLA Game Fair was instituted with the object, in the words of the then President, Sir John Ruggles-Brise, 'to attract keen shooting men and particularly farmers and small landowners to see something of modern methods of rearing and managing game birds in order to improve small shoots and how things can be fitted into good farming and forestry practice'. It was hoped that 2000 people might attend that initial fair. In the event, the fair attracted 8500, and today it extends over three days and is held in a different location each year, providing an opportunity to emphasise a conservation ethic to over 100,000 people — an opportunity which is not wasted.

Irrespective of an interest in fieldsports, as the CLA membership survey conducted in 1981 shows, landowners have contributed to conservation in many ways and with greater resolve since such matters have received greater publicity. But whilst it is important to acknowledge the worth of individual contributions in relation to tree-planting, hedgerow care, the creation of ponds and new habitats, and so forth the survey is, perhaps, more interesting for the insight it offers into the dilemma faced by the farming and landowning lobby in its efforts to counter adverse publicity. CLA regional secretaries covering the counties of England and Wales distributed a 14-point questionnaire to about a third of the membership but the total number of replies represented a response rate of only 13 per cent of the 18,000 surveyed. Since the survey was conducted in the highly charged atmosphere of 1981, it is reasonable to suppose that those who responded did so because they were able to react positively to the questions, but this must cast doubt on the appropriateness of generalising the results for the whole membership as CLA spokesmen subsequently tended to do. More damaging, certainly, to the credibility of the study was the absence of any attempt to discover what actions, if any, members had explicitly refrained from for conservation reasons. Conservation interests can be forgiven for suspecting that, in relation to the overall scale of the problems they are highlighting, the efforts disclosed by the survey can only constitute a token gesture, however sincere and doubtless effective in some local contexts.

This is the nub of the problem now faced by the NFU and the CLA. In terms of the often sterile war of words in which they are now necessarily engaged, their best efforts can so easily be presented as a sort of ineffectual 'tokenism'. Over the years the CLA in particular, has made a number of positive initiatives related to the spheres of land-use and the viability of local communities. Co-operating with the Council for Small Industries in Rural Areas (COSIRA) and the Countryside Commission it has recently instituted awards for landowners who have done most to create jobs outside agriculture and who have made the biggest contribution in the urban fringe towards bringing the 'townsman' and 'countryman' closer together; and these supplement the Farm Buildings Award Scheme which has existed for some time. Early in 1984 it launched a campaign to encourage its members to use small areas, such as awkward field corners, rough woodland and river banks to re-establish and encourage many of the wild flowers and grasses whose numbers have been reduced by post-war agricultural change. In its monthly journal the *Country Landowner* features relating to conservation issues and matters relating to access have proliferated reflecting a concerted public relations effort which is, at the same time, an attempt to ensure that members do justice to the highest ideals of stewardship.

Such issues are no less matters of concern to the NFU but discussion of them is accorded a comparatively lower profile in their publications, whilst in the *Timber Grower*, the journal of Timber Growers UK, they have at last been given more detailed attention since the establishment of a new environmental subcommittee in 1978. Sometimes, though, these efforts betray the siege mentality which has too often characterised the thinking of the farming, landowning and forestry communities. Although there has been an admirable willingness to encourage piecemeal initiatives and conservation measures to a far greater extent than it has been possible to indicate here, there has been an equally tenacious — albeit understandable — defence of the wholly exceptional position of agriculture throughout the post-war period. By the same token, this has effectively precluded the reforms seen as necessary by those most alarmed at the accelerating impact of the 'second agricultural revolution'. The farming, landowning and timber-growing lobby has hung on to privilege, acquiesced in and connived at the massive, state-funded expansion in agricultural production and has, as a consequence, reaped a harvest of adverse publicity in which no amount of presenting the positive efforts of individual landowners and farmers can hope to redress any sense of balance for what has been lost. The gains and losses simply are not commensurate.

Farmers and landowners have a sense of injustice at this state of affairs. Their highly efficient and well-integrated organisations are by no means so powerful as to have been solely responsible for the situation in which they find themselves. As we have emphasised earlier, there is no warrant for such a crude conspiratorial theory: rather we must look to the relation between the increasingly entrenched and inflexible concerns of the Ministry of Agriculture and the system into which farmers (some with huge capital debts) have increasingly become locked so that their interests and concerns cannot but be at one with their ministry.

The Director-General of the CLA, writing in the October 1983 *Country Landowner*, hinted at the problem: 'Relations with the Ministry have perhaps been at their smoothest', he wrote,

> when there has been a clear identity of interest between the Ministry's chief objective of promoting food production and some matter of particular importance to CLA members such as, for example, land drainage. Things are not quite so straightforward when discussion centres on how best to deal with new constraints on agricultural progress.

At a time of 'external' threat the unnaturally close relationship between the ministry and the farming lobby has suffocated any prospect of a radical rethinking whether of the grant-aid system or any other fundamental feature of present agricultural policy. The ministry is patently resistant to change, and the NFU is equally reluctant to rock the boat which has been sailing so sweetly on the strong tide it worked hard to generate. On more than one occasion in the past, and again recently, the CLA has proposed that the Ministry of Agriculture should extend its functions to embrace a general duty for the well-being of rural areas. The idea, included in the response to the Countryside Review Committee's 1976 discussion paper *The Countryside — Problems and Policies*, was supported by the Timber Growers, among others, but made little progress in ministry circles. The NFU was always opposed to any such change and took care to reiterate its opposition in its response to a Countryside Commission report on the uplands which, among other things, claimed to have found a unanimous desire for better coordination of all government activities. Whilst not of great significance in itself, perhaps, the ill-fated career of that idea is indicative of the more general tendency of the NFU and MAFF to resist change from whatever direction it might come.

But there are now mighty forces ranged against the immovable object. An Oxford conference speaker early in 1984 won applause when he described Agriculture House as 'fast becoming a mausoleum of democratic bureaucracy', but as we have seen, the emerging cracks in the internal NFU consensus may prompt change — particularly if the taken-for-granted power of the NFU turns out to be contingent on a policy commitment which is currently being assailed from many quarters. In May 1984, following a stormy annual general meeting and in the wake of the imposition of quotas on milk production and the acceptance, at least in principle, by the Council of Ministers of financial ceilings in most areas of CAP expenditure, the NFU initiated a wide-ranging review of its own policies. The statement announcing the review acknowledged that,

Over recent years there has been a significant (and perhaps accelerating) change in the British political, economic and social scene which affects the public acceptance of agricultural support. There has been a particularly important public reaction to the impact of agriculture on the environment. Against this background it seems right to conclude that we are now at a watershed and that the era when agricultural expansion was widely accepted as a desirable goal has passed.

From MAFF too there are signs of movement. In November 1983, for example, a number of changes to the system of capital grants were announced: withdrawing grant for land reclamation in the lowlands and for hedgerow removal; reducing the rate of grant for drainage works; and increasing the rate in the Less Favoured Areas for planting or improving hedges, planting trees as shelter belts and for drystone-walls. Though welcomed by conservationists, the measures were considered to be too little and too late, and were in any case counteracted by massive extensions of the Less Favoured Areas which made more hill and marginal land eligible for ecologically destructive grants for land improvement and drainage. A year later, though, grants were cut for drainage and were withdrawn altogether for land reclamation, and the capital limit for any grant was halved from £100,000 to £50,000. However, MAFF's position is increasingly being compromised by developments essentially beyond its control which could decisively alter the balance of power between it and the DoE. For the first time since conservation issues moved to the centre stage of politics pressure has accumulated in a way which makes a fundamental policy change possible. There is even alarmist speculation in the farming press that the current Minister of Agriculture may be the last (*Big Farm Weekly*, 17 May 1984).

William Wilkinson, Chairman of the NCC, speaking at the launch of *Nature Conservation in Britain* on 26 June 1984, was uncompromising: 'We cannot agree to more land being brought into cultivation, or cultivation on the lower grades of land being intensified', he argued, adding that, 'as long as present policies in agriculture aimed at maximising production persist, we are rowing against the tide.' The ministry and the NFU, which together worked to stimulate that tide, are looking less able, by the day, to prevent its being turned to some degree however effectively they may conspire to sustain it. As Laski pointed out many years ago, 'The *status quo* does not abdicate in the face of logic', but on this occasion the accumulating pressures are amounting to more than mere argument. The repertoires of resistance are looking increasingly threadbare as the hitherto dominant ideology of stewardship is progressively depleted by forces beyond the control of the community fighting to sustain its credibility.

FURTHER READING

Although now somewhat dated, Peter Self and Herbert Storing, *The State and the Farmer* (Allen & Unwin, 1962) remains a good starting point for consideration of the NFU and the CLA. Graham Wilson's *Special Interests and Policy-Making: Agricultural Policy and Politics in Britain and the USA 1956–70* (Wiley, 1977) provides a provocative account of the relationship between the NFU and the Ministry of Agriculture, Fisheries and Food. Howard Newby's works contain many astute observations about the representation of farming and landowning interests, and his study, conducted with Colin Bell, David Rose and Peter Saunders, *Property, Paternalism and Power: Class and Control in Rural England* (Hutchinson, 1978), includes important insights into NFU and CLA activity at the local level.

A number of articles also provide valuable assessments of the lobbying strength and recent policy priorities of the farming and landowning lobby. Principal amongst them are Wyn Grant, 'The National Farmers' Union: The Classic Case of Incorporation', in *Pressure Politics*, ed. David Marsh (Junction Books, 1983); J.J. Richardson, A.G. Jordan and R.H. Kimber, 'Lobbying, Administrative Reform and Policy Styles: The Case of Land Drainage', in *Political Studies*, Vol. 26 (1978); and Graham Cox and Philip Lowe, 'Agricultural Corporatism and Conservation Politics', in *Locality and Rurality*, ed. Tony Bradley and Philip Lowe (Geo-Books, 1984).

The present chapter is most obviously indebted, though, to the many working reports, advisory leaflets, press releases and policy statements issued by the NFU and the CLA. Their annual reports are an invaluable source, as are the CLA's magazine *Country Landowner*, the NFU's *British Farmer and Stockbreeder* and *Insight*, and the quarterly journal of the Timber Growers UK, *Timber Grower*. In addition the farming press, such as *Farmer's Weekly* and *Big Farm Weekly*, and magazines such as *The Field* and *Country Life* provide useful coverage of farming and countryside politics.

5. The Conservation Movement

The past 20 years have seen the emergence of conservation as a large and diverse movement enjoying extensive popular support. Its concerns range from issues to do with the future of industrial society, the extinction of species and even human survival, to the preservation of the aesthetics and inspirational quality of our natural surroundings. These concerns have been taken into the political arena too. Since the 1960s, conservation groups have emerged as a significant force, enjoying contacts with local government, Parliament and the civil service, and using the media to mount campaigns. Not only have they influenced legislation and official policy, but they have also gained considerable public support. Indeed, it seems that conservation groups are part of a broadly-based change in the way people perceive and evaluate their relationship to the natural world.

ORGANISATION OF THE CONSERVATION LOBBY

There are close on 50 national voluntary groups concerned with rural and nature conservation. They vary considerably in structure and resources, and in their objectives and significance. Many are small, specialist groups, such as the Botanical Society, the Marine Conservation Society and the Joint Committee for the Conservation of British Insects, each with no more than a few hundred members, and dependent for their vitality on the spare-time efforts of a handful of enthusiasts. Usually their influence is limited, though they may be important sources of expertise in their particular field.

In contrast is that slumbering giant, the National Trust, which controls immense resources. It is, for example, the largest private landowner, owning more than 1 per cent of the land surface of England and Wales. It is also the biggest voluntary organisation with over 1,100,000 members, and the charity with the highest national income. Not surprisingly, the conduct of its affairs requires a considerable bureaucracy of some 1400 staff.

The dominant group in the field of nature conservation is the Royal Society for the Protection of Birds (RSPB). With a membership close on 400,000, a permanent staff of 350, and responsibility for about 100 bird reserves, the RSPB has won international renown for its work and expertise in the field of wild bird conservation. Another key group is the Royal Society for Nature Conservation, which derives its importance from its role as the national coordinating body for the country trusts for nature conservation. There are 46 trusts and their combined membership stands at 150,000. They are the leading local groups concerned with conservation and have extensive practical commitments. Together they manage 1400 nature reserves covering about 45,000 ha. They are also, perhaps, the largest reservoir of local knowledge on wildlife, giving advice to farmers, landowners and local authorities.

The two important groups concerned with landscape and amenity protection are the Council for the Protection of Rural England (and its Scottish and Welsh equivalents) and the Ramblers' Association. Each has London headquarters with a small staff, but the members are organised into local branches which act as environmental watchdogs within their localities. The CPRE has 30,000 members, and the Ramblers' Association 40,000.

The sheer variety and multiplicity of groups often bewilders observers and is not infrequently a cause of frustration for the groups themselves. It is partly a product of history. New groups are set up as people perceive new problems, but the older groups seldom fade away. By and large, they do fulfil distinct functions. For example, in the nature conservation field, the World Wildlife Fund is the fund-raiser and banker; the British Trust for Conservation Volunteers provides voluntary manpower; the Field Studies Council is the educational arm; the county trusts for nature conservation are the landowners, reserve managers and local watchdogs; the Fauna and Flora Preservation Society specialise in international issues; and the British Association of Nature Conservationists is the radical ginger-group and think-tank.

The diversity of the groups also maximises the popular appeal of the conservation lobby. If all the groups were amalgamated into one super-group it is unlikely that it would attract as much support as the combined strength of the separate groups. This is partly because many people belong to more than one, but also because the groups' different styles and objectives attract people of different ages and social background. Thus the British Trust for Conservation Volunteers attracts teenagers; Friends of the Earth, people in their twenties and thirties; the National Trust, the middle-aged; and the CPRE, the retired. Similarly, whereas the memberships of the National Trust, the CPRE and the county trusts for nature conservation are strongly upper-middle-class, those of the RSPB and the Ramblers' Association are more lower-middle- and working-class.

It must be added that there are political costs involved in the division of the lobby into so many groups. There is rivalry between the groups, and competition for external sources of funds, media attention and popular support. A unified stance or combined action across the whole lobby is uncommon. This is not necessarily because there are conflicts — though conflicts do arise, particularly between the objectives of preserving the countryside and pro-moting access to it. It is more because of the sheer logistics of orchestrating so many separate voices. A lot of effort is expended maintaining communications amongst the groups themselves. An official of the RSPB commented in discussion: 'We put a lot of time and resources into keep-ing good relationships and preventing others doing silly things which might affect us detrimentally. Liaison itself could be a full-time task.'

However, as the Secretary of the Ramblers' Association remarked in conversation, 'To make any impact on decision-makers you have to speak in concert with other bodies with similar interests.' When a number of conservation groups do cooperate on a campaign, they can present an impressive show of strength, with each mobilising its own supporters and contacts, and each making its own tactical contributions. One group's letter to *The Times*, circular to MPs, or representation to a minister, may be followed up by other groups making a similar point, thereby adding to the sense of a weight of opinion behind an issue. Pressure can be applied at many points to influence or induce government action.

Cooperation between conservation groups is fostered by the multitude of links between them. Most groups exchange literature, and a few even share staff or premises. Routine contact between officers, however, is by far the most usual link between them. This is often supplemented by cross-membership ties, whereby a leading member of one group occupies a leading position in another. Thus the conservation lobby is knitted together by overlapping networks of contacts. Through these networks, a range of groups can be quickly alerted to an issue, political intelligence can be exchanged, and tactics can be informally coordinated.

In an effort to present a more united front to government and the media, a number of umbrella groups have been established with federal constitutions, such as the Council for Environmental Conservation (CoEnCo), the Council for National Parks, Wildlife Link, Countryside Link and the Tree Council. Their achievements have been limited, although the Council for National Parks made a major contribution to the Countryside Commission's uplands debate in 1983 and Wildlife Link has played a key role in coordinating the lobbying of nature conservation groups. A major difficulty for some umbrella groups is that they are starved of resources and granted only limited autonomy by their constituent groups who are naturally jealous of their own authority and resources. Therefore, they are unable fully to develop their functions and thus to demonstrate their worth. A former director of Friends of the Earth (FoE), explaining why it avoided joining formal coordinating bodies, characterised them as 'mere talking-shops'. This may be a fair comment, though FoE does have the reputation for mounting its own campaigns in the media often with a cavalier disregard for the work being done by other groups in the same field.

POPULAR SUPPORT FOR CONSERVATION

The combined membership of nature and rural conservation groups is about 1 million, and this figure does not include the 1,140,000 people who belong to the National Trust. This makes conservation a sizeable social movement. Even so, it is important to know whether the values it promotes command support beyond those who are active in voluntary groups, particularly as the membership of conservation groups is unrepresentative of the general public in terms of social composition.

The vast majority of members of conservation groups are middle-class. The RSPB's membership is mainly lower-middle-class, attracting those employed particularly in technical and clerical occupations. Most other groups are strongly upper-middle-class, drawing the bulk of their support from those in professional and managerial occupations. The more radical groups do not deviate from this picture. Surveys of FoE and the Conservation Society have shown them to be solidly middle-class, with their memberships strongly concentrated in the personal service professions, such as medicine, teaching, social work, academia and the arts. The distinctive characteristics of radical environmentalists are that they tend to be younger (in their twenties and thirties, unlike the predominantly middle-aged membership of the more conservative groups) and highly educated — a majority of the members of FoE and the Conservation Society have degrees.

Does the fact that membership of environmental groups is predominantly middle-class mean that the environment is basically a middle-class concern? This need not be so. It could be that environmental groups are merely reflecting a general characteristic of voluntary organisations — that they tend to be formed and supported mainly by the middle-class. In this respect, environmental groups are in such company as Oxfam, the RSPCA, the NSPCC, Shelter and the National Council for Civil Liberties. The critical question is whether the values expressed by environmental groups are more widely shared. Here we must rely on indirect evidence. There have been few systematic surveys of public opinion on environmental matters in Britain. Those that have been made, however, do suggest that the environmental movement enjoys very extensive sympathy throughout the general public; and that this passive sympathy is socially much more broadly based than membership of environmental groups. What distinguishes conservationists, therefore, is not so much their concern for the environment, as the degree of importance they attach to such concern. The widespread latent concern is revealed in the protest groups which emerge when local beauty spots or areas of wildlife interest are threatened. In such circumstances, conservation becomes a central rather than a peripheral concern for local residents who are prepared to organise and fight for their local amenities.

Other evidence of general concern for wildlife and the countryside comes from mass culture. Wildlife programmes on television and radio have perennial appeal: some 9 million people regularly watch 'Wildlife on One'. Wildlife programmes also register the highest levels of audience satisfaction. Television has been responsible for establishing nature as a central feature of popular culture. Sentimental attachment to wildlife is exploited by advertisers in selling anything from cosmetics to confectionery. The fact that trips to the countryside are the most prevalent form of out-of-the-home recreation would suggest that this attachment is not just sedentary or mawkish.

More specific evidence of attitudes towards conservation comes from a public opinion survey conducted in 1982 by MORI. Some 53 per cent of the 1991 respondents said they would support an increase in income tax of one penny in the pound to pay for measures to protect wildlife and the environment compared to 26 per cent who said they would oppose such a move. As many as 31 per cent claimed that within the last year or so they themselves had donated money to a charity concerned with conservation, and 4 per cent claimed to belong to a conservation organisation. The respondents were also asked, 'Which of a number of amenities make a valuable contribution to the overall quality of your life?' Apart from 'streets safe to walk in', 'attractive countryside' was mentioned most (by 53 per cent of respondents) and much more frequently than other amenities, such as good public transport, parks, access to a car, libraries, sports facilities, leisure centres and theatres. Only 2 per cent of respondents said that attractive countryside did not make a valuable contribution to the quality of their life.

This all suggests very widespread support for the objectives of the conservation lobby. On the specific issue of the conflict between agriculture and conservation, however, opinions were more divided and ambivalent. When respondents were asked which of 13 possible functions are the most important ones for farmers to fulfil from a national standpoint, 'ensuring that activities are not harmful to the environment' was mentioned with the fourth highest frequency. The functions which achieved even greater support were, in descending order, 'providing high quality food', 'buying British machinery and raw materials', and 'increasing production each year'. Evidently, many people perceive no contradiction between increased agricultural output and a conserved environment — or at least they expect British farmers to encompass both functions.

When the respondents were asked which functions farmers are particularly poor at, 'looking after wildlife' was mentioned with the third highest frequency, surpassed only by the negative evaluation of farmers' performance in remunerating their employees and providing jobs. Even so, a critical view of farmers' contribution to conservation is still only a minority opinion, albeit held by a sizeable minority. This became apparent when respondents were asked their opinions as to whether, on balance, places for wildlife and attractive countryside are being needlessly damaged by farmers, or whether farmers are making new wildlife habitats and a different but just as attractive countryside. Some 49 per cent of respondents held the latter view — the traditional view of farming — but 36 per cent were of the opinion that there is needless destruction by farmers. It would seem that the popular image of farming is undergoing a fundamental change, and that a sizeable and growing body of opinion — though still a minority of the populace — shares the concern expressed by conservationists about the impact of agriculture on the countryside.

POLITICAL RESOURCES AND ACCESS

The political challenge facing conservation groups has been to translate their evident popular support into political influence. Pressure groups seeking to influence legislation and policy-making bring differing skills and levels of competence to the process of negotiation and they also vary in their ease of access to the different parts of the political system. Most conservation groups run their political activities on a shoe-string, paying their staff low wages and relying on a lot of voluntary assistance from sympathetic specialists and free publicity via media coverage of their stances. Thus, when confronting a large company, a statutory body or a major interest group, conservation groups can seldom match their opponents in terms of financial resources, and it is quite beyond their means to engage in the sort of slick lobbying and PR which some private interests do.

The vogue for conservation during the past decade, however, has meant that groups have been able to recruit energetic, idealistic staff of high calibre, although relatively low wages tend to favour enthusiasm over experience. Most groups can now draw on considerable expertise amongst their staff and honorary officers, particularly in the fields of natural history, nature conservation and land-use planning. This may be important in contributing to effective argument and in establishing a group's authority in its dealings with politicians and civil servants. MPs, for example, are typically understaffed and overworked, and often rely on pressure groups with which they are in broad sympathy to keep them briefed. Similarly, if a group's special competence is recognised by a government department, it is likely to be drawn into close consultation over relevant issues.

Shortcomings have arisen as conservation groups have tackled ever more complex technological projects requiring highly specialised knowledge, and as they have moved out of their traditional preserves to combat the environmental effects of other aspects of public policy. To penetrate energy, transport or industrial policy demands additional skills. Lacking sufficient technical back-up, conservation groups may be unable to overcome administrative 'stonewalling', or match the sheer weight of expertise of industrial or commercial lobbies.

Agricultural policy is perhaps even more impenetrable than other sectors. According to one commentator, Wyn Grant, a unique combination of practical, technical and political knowledge often seems necessary: namely, 'mud on one's boots, a degree in agricultural economics, and an understanding of the international manoeuvrings that lie behind the Common Agricultural Policy'. Conservation groups have had to extend their expertise as they have taken on agricultural issues, but major gaps remain. For example, no group employs an economist, which is a serious drawback when many of the projects they are tackling — such as the reclamation of wetlands and moorlands, land drainage schemes, and the expansion of domestic forestry — may, in the final analysis, make dubious economic (as well as environmental) sense. Some academic economists though have lent a hand, most notably J.K. Bowers whose evidence has forcefully challenged the economic rationale of various drainage and afforestation projects. Recently also, both the CPRE and the RSPB have begun to produce authoritative critiques of aspects of agricultural support.

In the main, conservation groups have less influence with government than the major economic interest groups. They have fewer political resources and lack powerful sanctions. Unlike the NFU, for example, they are not of central importance to the effective performance of government or the economy, and consequently do not have the same close, symbiotic relationship with senior civil servants. They tend, therefore, to be excluded from the formative stages of policy-making.

Most conservation groups do have reasonable access to the Department of the Environment but it does not play a role on behalf of environmental interests equivalent to that played by MAFF which promotes agricultural interests and is committed to the farmers' cause. Partly, this is because it has many other functions, some of which, such as promotion of the construction industry and mineral extraction, are at odds with the function of environmental protection. It deals, therefore, with many interest groups. Indeed, the NFU has more extensive dealings with the DoE than most conservation groups on matters such as the protection of agricultural land, town and country planning, minerals, pollution control and water management.

In the past, conservation groups have looked to two Quangos within the tutelage of the DoE — the Nature Conservancy Council and the Countryside Commission — to act as advocates of the cause of rural conservation within government, and there are very strong though informal links between these agencies and the lobby. But their circumscribed authority limits the usefulness of such links. Despite their very broad responsibilities for the protection of wildlife and landscape and the realisation of recreational opportunities these agencies have few real powers.

The Nature Conservancy Council declares national nature reserves which it owns, leases or manages by agreement. These now number around 200, but cover well under 1 per cent of the land surface. More generally it must achieve its purposes by education, persuasion and voluntary agreement backed when funds permit by financial inducement. Its success in persuading owners and managers of the 4000 SSSIs that it has designated to desist from damaging change has not been great. In 1981 the NCC estimated that each year between 10 and 15 per cent of SSSIs suffer some damage to their wildlife interest. The Wildlife and Countryside Act 1981, however, requires owners and occupiers of SSSIs to consult the NCC before undertaking any potentially damaging operations. (The effectiveness of this new provision is assessed in Chapter 7.)

The NCC's strategy for *Nature Conservation in Great Britain*, published in 1984, drew attention to the statutory and financial limitations that prevent it from exercising any responsibility for integrated resource conservation, and confine it to what it termed 'cultural conservation' — 'the conservation of wild flora and fauna, geological and physiographic features of Britain for their scientific, educational, recreational, aesthetic and inspirational value'. Listing 'the alarming losses in the national natural heritage' in recent years, the strategy called in effect for a halt to compromises at the expense of nature, and defined its major preoccupation as 'to save what is left'. It identified the major obstacles to effective action as the 'derisory' allocation of resources, 'unsympathetic land-use policies and inadequate statutory measures for nature conservation'.

Similarly, the Countryside Commission may grant aid to local authorities and others to purchase or manage land to protect valuable landscape features or to establish country parks of which there are now around 190. But most of its funding and effort again go on education, inducement and advice; and in opposing, sometimes at public inquiry, particularly damaging change. It also operates as the agency for central government funding of the ten national park authorities.

The Commission has measured its own performance as recently as 1984, when it published *Second Look* by the landscape architects Richard Westmacott and Richard Worthington, who re-surveyed the seven areas they had studied for the Commission eleven years earlier for their report *New Agricultural Landscapes*. They found that, although the rate of deterioration had slowed significantly, in none of the areas could the countryside be said to be safe from the threat of sudden and devastating change. They detected no noticeable swing to conservation among farmers and landowners, and found that even where interesting and valuable landscape had survived it was often badly cared for. Although the rich landscapes were generally getting richer, the poor ones were becoming poorer; local landscapes were being steadily eroded and the essential variety of the countryside was being lost. The survey, in short, confirmed the failure of current policies to achieve even the Commission's modest aims.

Not only do the conservation agencies have few powers, but their resources are also limited, and are certainly no

match for those which encourage agricultural intensification and afforestation. The combined annual expenditure of the Nature Conservancy Council, the Countryside
Commission and the national park authorities for 1980/81
was about £27 million, and this included their administrative expenditures. Together they employ a total of
about 1300 staff. The comparable figures for the Forestry
Commission are £103 million and 7200 staff. In 1980/81,
just the capital grants to farmers from MAFF amounted to
about £200 million, and this is quite apart from the costs of
the price supports, the research, technical, credit and advisory services, and the taxation and rating concessions
which support the farming industry. The ministry's
Agricultural Development and Advisory Service (ADAS)
alone employs 4800 staff. The total annual cost to the
consumer and the taxpayer of state support for agriculture
has been estimated at £5 billion. State support for conservation is puny by comparison. At present, government
allocates 0.01 per cent of public expenditure (0.005 per
cent of GDP) to support nature conservation — an amount
which the NCC has calculated as the equivalent per capita
of the price of a cup of tea.

It should be clear that the major decisions affecting the
British countryside are not made within the Countryside
Commission and the Nature Conservancy Council, but
within the Ministry of Agriculture, the Treasury and the
European Commission. Even so, conservation lobbying
tends to be channelled towards these agencies. This suits
government very well, because the agencies thereby
deflect pressure away from the government departments
and other centres where the critical decisions are made
about the economy, the legislative programme and the
allocation of resources. Indeed, in contrast to the agencies'
accessibility and receptiveness, environmental groups
find MAFF the least accessible and the least receptive of all
government departments.

It has been argued by Wyn Grant that the conservation
agencies, with their limited scope for making policy initiatives and their political marginality, 'create a kind of
phoney "insider" status for some groups in order to
reassure them that they have a sympathetic point of
access within the government machine'. To a considerable

extent, in fact, the agencies act as negative filters on conservation matters. Proposals emanating from the conservation lobby are processed through the agencies, but whereas demands opposed by the agencies are unlikely to be taken seriously by government, it does not follow that initiatives supported by them will command government attention. Indeed, ministers and senior civil servants are inclined to regard the conservation agencies — despite their status as statutory advisers to government — as pressure groups whose views should be treated with scepticism and whose involvement in central policy-making should be carefully circumscribed. The agencies tend, therefore, to filter out of the political process all proposals that they believe to be politically unacceptable — which is precisely what the NCC did in 1984 in its strategy for nature conservation, and the Countryside Commission in its proposals in *A Better Future for the Uplands* of the same year.

Failure to be closely involved with policy-formulation in the crucial initial stages within the central departments of government often means that conservation groups are later faced with an uphill campaign against a course of action to which officials, ministers and major interests have become committed. This was certainly the case with the Wildlife and Countryside Bill (see Chapter 6). Good media and parliamentary relations can compensate to a certain extent by enabling groups to raise issues for government attention and by ensuring considerable opprobrium for any official initiatives with blatant and damaging environmental implications. Many MPs and peers are sympathetic to conservation issues, and most groups have good contacts with the mass media and can count on a ready and usually favourable treatment for their views. As a result, a combination of parliamentary pressure and public censure has occasionally proved an effective weapon, enabling conservation groups to take the offensive against recalcitrant government departments and win important concessions.

Certainly the style and tempo of conservation politics are changing. Previously, groups used to be much more discreet and reserved in their political activities, avoiding the limelight and political strife. A shift of tactics has come

about in response to the great increase in public concern
and media attention, and to the belated recognition that
the limited influence conservationists have enjoyed
through established channels is quite insufficient to
achieve major reforms. The new style of lobbying depends
less on the censure of educated taste, more on direct
appeals to popular opinion through the mass media;
less on personal influence and string-pulling behind the
scenes, more on an open, adversarial approach demanding proficiency in technical debate. The newer groups,
particularly Friends of the Earth and Greenpeace, have led
the way in this direction. Some of the older groups are
following gingerly behind, taking care not to disrupt their
established relationships with government or to alienate
the sympathy of their more conservative members.

Another constraint that many of them face is their charitable status. Under British charity law the price paid for
tax-exempt status is that an organisation must not overtly
campaign for changes in laws or policies. A charity may,
for example, feed the hungry or treat the sick, but it must
not offer an explicit political challenge to the laws or interests
that cause the evils it attempts to mitigate. What this means
in practice is that a voluntary body which enjoys charitable
status must be very discreet and restrained in any lobbying,
and its efforts to inform opinion must be carefully presented
as public education and not as propaganda. The law, in
short, powerfully reinforces the *status quo*.

EVOLVING ATTITUDES TOWARDS AGRICULTURE

As we have seen, few people anticipated the rapid transformation in agricultural practices which would occur in
the post-war period. As a consequence, the measures intended to safeguard the countryside, introduced in the
late 1940s, have proved quite inadequate in relation to the
forces of agricultural intensification and afforestation.
These shortcomings and many of the incipient environmental problems of modern agriculture, were first aired
publicly at 'The Countryside in 1970' conferences, organised by the Nature Conservancy, the Royal Society of Arts
and the Council for Nature in 1963, 1965 and 1970.

The conferences were intended to consider the major underlying trends in the development of the countryside with a view to formulating 'a common policy for the future'. The participants included the leaders of nearly all national environmental groups, representatives of farming, forestry and landowning interests, and key industrialists and government officials. By enabling all interests to put forward and debate their views, the conferences presented in sharp relief the disagreements and common ground. It was clear that there no longer existed an identity of interests and harmony of purpose between farming and rural preservation. Yet by bringing together for the first time farming, landowning and conservation leaders, in a working relationship, the conferences created an atmosphere of cooperation, a commitment to mutual understanding and a spirit of compromise. The Duke of Edinburgh, who presided, summed up the mood at the first conference when he spoke of the 'enormous problem that is going to confront us over the next few years', and urged the various interests to come to terms with their differences for 'if we don't swim together, we will most certainly sink separately'.

As well as being a vast exercise in bridge-building, the conferences may claim some solid achievements, not least in paving the way for the Countryside (Scotland) Act 1967 and the Countryside Act 1968. There was also a strong emphasis on environmental education and various initiatives were launched to alert schools, colleges and teachers to this important topic. Many of the conferences' recommendations were for institutional change, including proposals to replace the National Parks Commission with a Countryside Commission with a broader remit, to establish a Countryside Commission for Scotland, to set up country parks, and to introduce new development plans. These and other recommendations were implemented by government, but because of the emphasis on consensus and agreed reforms the conferences dodged or at best glossed over some of the basic conflicts and fundamental problems, giving the impression that, with goodwill all round, all would be well.

The conciliatory approach of the 'Countryside in 1970' conferences was embodied in a number of intiatives by

public authorities. The most significant of these was
the development of countryside management. It was
pioneered by the Countryside Commission in recognition
of the inability of conventional land-use planning to deal
with contemporary countryside problems. What was
needed, it seemed, was some more positive and flexible
means of intervention than planning controls, that would
promote desirable land-uses and management practices,
and be sensitive to the varied pressures and constraints on
rural land. The philosophy of countryside management
was that farmers and public and private landowners
should be persuaded to collaborate in positive works for
the care of the landscape and provision for access and
recreation.

The Commission pursued and refined this approach in
various selected areas — in heritage coasts, in the uplands,
on the urban fringe, and in the intensively-farmed lowlands. In each, a number of conservation and recreation
projects were promoted by a project officer liaising with
groups and organisations interested in the use of the area.
The cooperation of local farmers and landowners was
achieved through the provision of advice, small grants
and practical assistance. National Park Management
Plans, introduced by the Local Government Act 1972, extended the approach, at least within the national parks, by
creating a formal procedure for elaborating management
objectives for the park authorities and for liaison with
relevant government bodies and interest groups. Implementation of these plans — as well as countryside projects
elsewhere — has in some cases relied on management
agreements; that is, formal written agreements, whereby a
landowner or occupier undertakes to manage the land in a
specified manner in order to satisfy a particular public
need, usually in return for some form of consideration.

Area management, and management projects, plans
and agreements together represent a set of tools for public
authorities pursuing conservation policies. However,
since the mid-1970s the limitations as well as the strengths
of countryside management have steadily become apparent. On the one hand, it has proved particularly effective
in tackling tactical problems, such as small-scale landscape
improvements, the provision of minor recreational works,

and easing of the friction between farmers and visitors. On the other hand, it has not been able to deal with fundamental conflicts between land-users nor to hold out in the face of economic pressures or structural changes in the rural economy. Moreover, because most farmers and landowners are unwilling to relinquish their right to improve or develop land for any considerable length of time, management agreements tend to offer only short-term security for the public interest or public investment, and can prove very expensive. Indeed, countryside management has had little demonstrable impact on agricultural practices or agricultural management.

Recognition of these shortcomings has fuelled demands for fundamental reform of agricultural policy and statutory control of farming and forestry development. Accompanying this change in the perception of the problem has been a near reversal of some groups' attitudes towards agriculture. Originally, for example, the CPRE regarded farmers as the guardians of the countryside and it was closely allied with farming and landed interests in opposing urban encroachment. Its approach to the problems that arose in the 1950s and 1960s was to persuade farmers not to undertake activities damaging to the landscape. Extra powers were only needed, it believed, to protect certain designated areas such as national parks. With the evident failure of this strategy and the continuing pace of agricultural change, the CPRE responded to the *New Agricultural Landscapes* study with a proposal for a comprehensive notification system whereby a farmer would have to give notice to the local planning authority of any intention substantially to alter the landscape. Failing agreement with the farmer on how the land was to be managed, the local authority could, as a last resort, serve a preservation order on him, restricting his actions.

The farming lobby has, not unnaturally, resisted any such curbs. The NFU and the CLA have been quite prepared to discuss specific conservation problems, but have stressed the need to retain the goodwill and voluntary cooperation of the farming community if practical remedies are to be found. Together the two organisations have responded to the charges of conservationists by presenting the farming community as stewards of the

countryside. While staunchly resisting any form of planning constraint or encroachment on a farmer's eligibility
for government improvement grants they have pressed
for payments and tax incentives for farmers to pursue
conservation objectives and, in particular, to compensate
for any potential income forgone through farming so as to
preserve the landscape and wildlife of an area.

The first sustained attempts to introduce some statutory
regulation of agricultural development in environmentally
sensitive areas were made in the 1960s. In 1963, the
Society for the Promotion of Nature Reserves (now the
Royal Society for Nature Conservation) supported a
Private Member's Bill which would have obliged farmers
to notify the Nature Conservancy of their intention to
undertake operations detrimental to the scientific interest
of an SSSI. This was unsuccessful, as were efforts by
conservation groups to include a similar safeguard in the
Countryside Act 1968. As we shall see in Chapter 6, the
measure was eventually included as an amendment to the
Wildlife and Countryside Act 1981, but only after intensive lobbying by conservationists in the face of staunch
opposition from the NFU and the CLA and resistance by
MAFF and the Department of the Environment. Though
this success after previous failures may be taken as an
indication of the growing strength of the conservation
lobby, the measure itself is a very modest reform, allowing
damaging changes to be monitored but not controlled; and
it took almost 20 years to achieve, during which time large
numbers of SSSIs were destroyed, and the evidence of
widespread destruction became incontrovertible.

Similarly, attention had first been drawn to the ploughing-
up of open moorland on Exmoor in the early 1960s, and an
unsuccessful attempt was made to amend the Countryside
Act 1968 during its passage through Parliament to give the
national park authority powers to control moorland conversion in designated areas. Losses of moorland continued, so that by the mid-1970s a fifth of the open land on
Exmoor had been enclosed and 'improved' since its designation as a national park in 1954. Eventually, pressure
from the CPRE and the Countryside Commission led the
government to appoint Lord Porchester to inquire into the
issue in 1977 (see Chapter 8). It was largely to implement

his recommendations that the Labour government introduced a Countryside Bill in 1978. This Bill proposed that ministers should have the power to designate specific areas of open moor or heath within which national park authorities would have been able to make moorland conservation orders to prevent ploughing or other agricultural 'improvements' considered likely to be detrimental.

The NFU and the CLA opposed the Bill, as did the Conservative opposition, which rejected any form of compulsion or regulation in favour of reliance on the voluntary cooperation of farmers, arguing that more generous compensation would lead to suitable voluntary agreements. Though the Bill had completed its committee stage when the minority Labour government fell and had been amended to make management agreements the main instrument of reconciliation, the Conservative Whips would not agree to rush through its remaining stages 'on the nod' as they did with other legislation, and so it was lost. Once in office, the Conservatives introduced their own Bill, which eventually became the Wildlife and Countryside Act 1981, and which finally brought to a head the argument of controls vs. voluntary cooperation.

FURTHER READING

There is a multitude of groups and organisations in the rural conservation movement. A guide to the national bodies and their publications is included in *The Countryside Handbook* (Croom Helm, 1985). A practical guide to local conservation activities is Angela King and Susan Clifford, *Holding Your Ground: An Action Guide to Local Conservation* (Maurice Temple Smith, 1985).

The organisation of the conservation lobby and its links with Parliament, government and the mass media are analysed by Philip Lowe and Jane Goyder, *Environmental Groups in Politics* (Allen & Unwin, 1983). A pertinent discussion of pressure-group tactics, which is drawn upon in this chapter, is Wyn Grant, *Insider Groups, Outsider Groups and Interest Group Strategies* (University of Warwick, Department of Politics, Working Paper 19, 1978).

The best source of discussion and information on

current issues and debates in the field of conservation is *Ecos*, the quarterly journal of the British Association of Nature Conservationists. Other useful magazines include the CPRE's *Countryside Campaigner*, the RSPB's *Birds*, and the Royal Society for Nature Conservation's *Natural World*, while the annual reports and specialised publications of the Countryside Commission and the Nature Conservancy Council detail the progress of official conservation efforts.

6. The Wildlife and Countryside Act

The disparities between the farming, landowning and timber-growing lobby and the conservation movement described in the preceding two chapters are well illustrated in the political contest that surrounded the genesis and implementation of the Wildlife and Countryside Act 1981 — an Act whose passage did more than anything to highlight the issues and polarise the conflict between agriculture and conservation. The intention to introduce a Wildlife and Countryside Bill was announced on 20 June 1979. But the previous month, within days of the Conservatives taking office, both the CLA and NFU had separate meetings with agriculture and environment ministers to discuss their legislative proposals. Broad agreement on the Bill was reached and from this point through to the enactment of the legislation the government, the CLA and the NFU remained in essential accord on the philosophy of the Bill and their approach to its more contentious aspects.

The government's proposals were set out in six consultation papers, published between August and October 1979. Significantly, they were drafted by civil servants in the DoE's rural directorate and not by the government's statutory advisers, the Countryside Commission and the NCC. Indeed, the views of these two bodies were not formally sought until the public consultation stage — surely an indication of political marginality.

In one area only — bird protection — was there qualified approval from environmental groups of the government's proposals. The relevant measures followed from
the requirements of EEC Directive 79/409 on the Conservation of Wild Birds which the government was
obliged to enact by April 1981. The Directive arose out of
public disquiet at the annual slaughter of migratory birds
that was common in Southern Europe, but goes further
in providing a general system of protection for all species
of wild birds found in Europe. The RSPB had been closely
involved in the formulation of the EEC Directive, and its
advice had been sought by the European Commission as
early as 1974. Moreover, the Society's European officer
was appointed to the Commission's expert committee
which would oversee the implementation of the Directive. Its adoption by the Council of Ministers had involved the RSPB in protracted consultations with both
the DoE and Commission officials and, in the process,
the RSPB had established good working relations with
DoE civil servants.

When it came to enacting the Directive in Britain there
was clearly considerable correspondence between the
views of the DoE and the RSPB, and it is therefore significant — though hardly surprising — that the RSPB was
the only environmental group to be consulted *before* the
consultation papers were issued. The expertise of the
RSPB in the complexities of both bird protection and
European legislation had been acknowledged and most
of the Society's objectives were achieved before the Bill's
public and parliamentary stages. At least in the field of
bird protection the RSPB is clearly more influential than
the government's own statutory adviser, the NCC and,
as we shall see, such apparent discrepancies of authority
and status were to be crucial to the subsequent lobbying
process.

THE PUBLIC CONSULTATION PERIOD:
AUGUST 1979–OCTOBER 1980

The consultation papers proposed a whole series of
minor reforms, but the proposals for conserving natural

habitats and open moorland in national parks attracted greatest attention. They embodied the view that control of farming operations was unnecessary and potentially counter-productive. Conservation objectives should be secured instead through the voluntary cooperation of farmers and landowners, encouraged where necessary by management agreements drafted and financed by con-servation agencies or local planning authorities. The only elements of compulsion proposed were reserve powers to require landowners or tenants to give up to 12 months' notice of any intention to convert moor or heath to agri-cultural land in specified parts of national parks (this became the basis of Section 42 of the Act); or of any intention to undertake operations which could be detri-mental to the scientific interest of selected SSSIs (the basis of Section 29 nature conservation orders). In either in-stance the powers would be activated by ministers and applied to specific areas. Ministers assured the NFU and the CLA that there was no intention to use the reserve powers for national parks (a similar reserve power in the 1968 Act providing for six months' notice had only been used twice on small parcels of land in Exmoor) and that only a few especially important SSSIs would be given this extra safeguard (a maximum of about 40 was suggested out of a total of some 3500 SSSIs).

Environmental groups responded unfavourably and a few, including the Ramblers' Association and the CPRE, were unreservedly hostile, but the impact of their res-ponse was blunted by the diversity of their prescriptions and the lack of a concerted approach. Lord Melchett, the Labour peer, convened a Wildlife Link Committee which sought to coordinate the response of nature conservation groups. Legislative safeguards for wildlife habitats were central to their counter-proposals since government pro-posals to protect a small number of SSSIs seemed inade-quate in the face of the threats posed by agricultural intensification and afforestation. Rather than select a few 'super-SSSIs' (and by implication downgrade the re-mainder), voluntary conservation groups urged safe-guards for all 3500 sites. Owners of SSSIs, they suggested, should be obliged to notify proposed changes of agricul-tural practice to give the NCC opportunity to negotiate a management agreement and, where a reasonable agreement could not be reached, the Secretary of State should have powers to make an order preventing harmful change to the site.

The NCC, however, took a different view. Ever since calls for improved safeguards for SSSIs were first made in the early 1960s it had been markedly less enthusiastic than voluntary conservation groups in seeking controls which might overstretch its staff and resources and draw it into confrontation with farmers and landowners. Thus, a few minor reservations aside, it broadly accepted the government's proposal and expressed itself fully satisfied once assurances had been given that the criteria for special protection would be broadened and the NCC consulted before the selection of any site. This accommodation set the NCC on a collision course with the voluntary conservation groups. Inevitably, much of their lobbying during the public consultation period was directed at shifting the NCC's position before the Bill reached Parliament, as it was unlikely that the government would contemplate a change of mind while still enjoying the backing of its official conservation advisers.

Eventually, the NCC council was pressed to re-open the issue following approval by Parliament of new procedures for farm capital grants in August 1980. After a review by Sir Derek Rayner, and in an effort to cut civil service staff, the government had sought to remove the requirement that farmers should seek prior approval from ADAS to carry out work for which they intended to claim grant. As this would also remove the possibility of any official persuasion or advice being brought to bear to safeguard natural features or wildlife threatened by improvement schemes, the proposed change in procedures had elicited strong protests from conservation organisations. The government had responded with a concession requiring farmers wishing to carry out work in national parks or SSSIs to consult respectively the national park authorities or the NCC.

This was an important departure. It introduced the principle that a farmer contemplating certain agricultural changes should first be obliged to consult a conservation or planning authority. In an unusual move, Lord Melchett, as Chairman of the Wildlife Link Committee, was allowed to address the November council meeting of the NCC. The council was persuaded to press for the new principle to be extended to include *all* intended changes of land use on SSSIs that might be detrimental to their conservation interest, not just grant-aided changes. The NCC's chairman accordingly asked that an appropriate amendment be made to the Bill. Finally, on 12 December 1980, and after publication of the Bill, the NCC made public its concern that the proposals to protect only a selection of SSSIs did not go far enough. Thus just four days before the Bill's second reading in the House of Lords the nature conservation interests had achieved at least a semblance of unity.

Landscape and amenity interests, with the CPRE, the Council for National Parks and the Ramblers' Association taking the lead, continued the coordination they had developed for the Labour government's Countryside Bill, and quickly achieved a common stance. In November 1979 they held a joint press conference with the Countryside Commission to stress the need for order-making powers to protect landscape and wildlife. A comprehensive system was drawn up by the Commission whereby together with the NCC it would be authorised to designate small areas of significance for landscape or nature conservation in which such powers would operate. A new system of agricultural grants and subsidies was also advocated to encourage farm enterprises which might contribute to conservation as well as to food production. The same month, the Countryside Commission met the NCC to seek agreement for such a package, but the NCC regarded conservation orders as unenforceable and unnecessary given the NCC's existing compulsory purchase powers. The Commission's proposals were felt to be too sweeping to be politically practicable. This failure to agree meant that there was no strategic consensus on the Bill across the conservation lobby.

Whereas conservation groups had not begun to prepare their positions on the Bill until the consultation period, the NFU and the CLA had already discussed their concerns in private consultation with MAFF and the DoE in the early summer of 1979. They were, in any case, articulating principles to which they had committed themselves during discussions of other legislation. Nevertheless, they responded to the consultation papers with great care, making many detailed points and proposing specific amendments and, being already in broad agreement with the government, the consultation period provided an opportunity to marshal arguments for the parliamentary debates.

Since the critics of the government's proposals had the authoritative backing of the Porchester Report (as well as the support of local government interests, including the Association of County Councils) it was crucial for the NFU, the CLA and the government to demonstrate that Lord Porchester may have been premature in his judgement that a purely voluntary approach had failed on Exmoor. Indeed, they argued that the voluntary approach was capable of achieving far more than the compulsory powers he recommended. In addition, the NFU and the CLA were concerned to safeguard their members' interests in determining the ground-rules for conservation payments. November 1979 saw negotiations begin between the Exmoor national park authority, the CLA and the NFU to draw up financial guidelines for management agreements (see Chapter 8). The DoE, MAFF and the Countryside Commission sent observers to these highly significant negotiations and, whereas Porchester had proposed a once-and-for-all compensation for the permanent loss of rights to reclaim equal to the loss in land value, the NFU and CLA insisted that those who voluntarily set aside this option should have the right to choose to be compensated by annual payments related to loss of profit. The guidelines, finally signed on 7 April 1981 (at the time of the Wildlife and Countryside Bill's second reading in the Commons), in effect treat these two schemes as alternatives by allowing farmers to choose between them. The success of the Exmoor negotiations was important for the government: its speakers in the second reading debates in both Houses referred to them as indicating a new spirit of compromise which confounded Porchester's worst fears and vindicated the voluntary approach. The NFU and the CLA, meanwhile, viewed the Exmoor agreement as providing a model for similar agreements elsewhere, and in their parliamentary briefings they made many references to the Exmoor solution as indicating the soundness of a voluntary approach. That such arguments were effective is indicated by the statutory guidelines for compensation relating to management agreements drawn up following the passage of the Bill which do, indeed, follow the principles established in the Exmoor agreement.

A number of minor changes were made to the Bill arising from the consultation period and some of these were announced in the summer and autumn of 1980. They included technical modifications to the provisions for species protection, extension of protection for the otter to Scotland, and alteration of the status of the Countryside Commission to become an autonomous, grant-aided body outside the civil service.

The Bill, introduced in Parliament on 25 November 1980, elicited some predictable responses. The CLA's magazine commented that it 'held no surprises' and was generally acceptable to landowners because, as their chief legal adviser noted, 'the CLA had won most of its points in the pre-Bill discussions'. Similarly, the NFU, in the first of many parliamentary briefing papers on the Bill, welcomed 'the government's good intentions of striking a fair and reasonable balance between agricultural interests and other interests where these may come into conflict'. The RSPB, however, in its magazine, greeted the Bill with 'mixed feelings', describing it as 'good in parts but disturbingly bad in others'. The Countryside Commission meanwhile in its 13th annual report noted that 'Government had not been able to accommodate many of our suggestions', and the director of the CPRE, in a letter to *The Times* on 10 December 1980, declared, 'the Bill has no teeth'.

The Bill was to be scrutinised first in the Lords. Though this was unusual for a measure of such size and importance, and was largely the result of pressure on the parliamentary timetable, it is not at all exceptional for conservation legislation to be first introduced in the Upper House, reflecting the traditional absence of political contention in this field. If that was the government's expectation, however, it was to be rudely shattered.

THE PARLIAMENTARY PHASE:
NOVEMBER 1980–OCTOBER 1981

The passage of the Bill generated considerable debate. The NFU's lobbying activities, closely coordinated with those of the CLA, were by far the most extensive. With three representatives from its land-use division working full-time on the Bill, it was the only group with the resources to be present at all stages. Leading conservation groups typically had a member of staff with prime responsibility for the Bill whilst a host of other groups lobbied on specific clauses. A staggering 2300 amendments were tabled — an indication of the intensity of this lobbying and the personal interest taken by many MPs and peers.

The parliamentary briefs prepared by the NFU and CLA reveal a singleness of purpose and coherence of philosophy which was never lost in the presentation of a mass of detailed argument relating to particular clauses. In line with the government's declared preferences, both groups continually emphasised their commitment to 'goodwill and voluntary means' with reserve control powers and formal constraints invariably characterised as wholly negative and a threat to efficiency. In advocating their preferred response to the problems identified in public debate, prominence was given to the need to develop a partnership between farmers and the relevant countryside agencies and voluntary bodies. The corollary of this emphasis was a concern lest insufficient money be available to implement the legislation and that a breakdown in the voluntary scheme caused by lack of finance might be misconstrued as a lack of cooperation on the part of the farming community.

This sustained argument was, of course, appropriate to the relatively privileged position the NFU and CLA had secured in the drafting of the Bill. 'Voluntary means' and 'goodwill' were presented as principles allowing of no compromise: a fitting presentational strategy for a philosophy whose notional 'ideal world' seems to be defined precisely in terms of the absence of controls. As the NFU's parliamentary secretary put it in conversation, 'planning controls are only the ultimate, there are various degrees of nastiness between nothing and everything'.

Conservation groups, in contrast, were confronted by more perplexing considerations of lobbying strategy and their reactions to the Bill's progress reveal three distinct positions. The first of these, 'pure pragmatism', was — not surprisingly given the pressures to which it was subjected – most obviously espoused by the NCC. It found its expression in adjustments of position and demand according to perceptions of administrative feasibility and 'the politics of the possible' and, given the philosophy so firmly embedded in the Bill, it necessarily conceded most of the arguments of the farming and land-owning community. A 'cooperation plus safeguards' position underpinned the thinking of the Countryside Commission and most conservation groups. Whilst broadly accepting the 'voluntary goodwill' arguments presenting farmers as guardians of the countryside, it recognised the existence of farming 'mavericks', and hence argued a need for reserve powers. Moreover, conscious that farmers can be pulled in other directions by powerful incentives they suggested reform of the agricultural support system, and a need for conserva-tion incentives, although this did not entail arguing a fundamental conflict of interest between agriculture and conservation.

Just such a claim, however, typified the third 'rejec-tionist position' espoused by Friends of the Earth (FoE), some of the Labour opposition, and Marion Shoard, a former staff member of the CPRE, whose book *The Theft of the Countryside* did so much to galvanise and polarise debate following its publication in October 1980. Rather than focusing on individual motivations, this view pointed to two sets of opposed values, institutions and interests, and argued that farming operations should be brought within the ambit of planning controls.

All sides found informed support in the Lords, though three-quarters of those who spoke in the second reading debate were landowners, knowledgeable about, and not unsympathetic towards, farming. The majority were also office-holders in conservation groups and this in-formed interest combined with the looser party disci-pline in the Lords gave peers the opportunity to discuss the Bill's provisions at length and make a succession of amendments. Most were of a technical nature and readily accepted by ministers, but with considerable cross-bench voting seven amendments were also successfully moved against the government, including legal protection for the curlew, redshank and bar-tailed godwit; powers to establish marine nature reserves; and retention of a right of appeal to the Secretary of State when a local authority proposed closing a public footpath. These successes reflected the extent to which committed peers and conservation groups were influencing several backbench Conservatives — characterised by one Conservative MP as 'a posse of maverick peers'.

Significantly, however, none of the amendments won by the conservation lobby against government advice was opposed by the farming lobby, whereas all major amendments opposed by the NFU and CLA were defeated, and these included powers to make moorland conservation orders and to protect all SSSIs. Conservation groups had worked hard to rally support for these two measures but they were narrowly defeated in an unusually full House amidst strong suspicion that an unofficial government Whip was in operation, with even Lord Carrington, the then Foreign Secretary (himself, a former president of the CLA), being mobilised for the divisions.

The most far-reaching amendment won by the conservationists empowered MAFF to pay capital grants to farmers in national parks for schemes to promote conservation, maintenance of rural population and diversification of the rural economy. Moved by the influential Conservative peer and former minister, Lord Sandford, this amendment was slipped into the Bill by a margin of two votes in a thinly-attended House during the report stage. It is clear from the debate that the government and the NFU were caught unawares, having not fully appreciated the significance of the amendment and having assumed that it would be withdrawn. This may have been Sandford's intention, but Lord Melchett indicated his willingness to press it to a vote if Sandford did not. In the event, the government's defeat was regarded as a major tactical victory for the conservationists, but MAFF ministers and officials saw the new clause as a totally unacceptable intrusion upon agricultural policy and resolved to emasculate it later in the passage of the Bill.

The government introduced several amendments of its own in the Lords. Some were concessions seemingly intended to placate conservation groups and defuse the increasingly unfavourable publicity that the Bill was attracting as journalists latched onto the conservationists' criticisms. An NCC survey of the rate of damage to SSSIs – details of which were released in January and February 1981 — had particular impact on the media and parliamentary debates, causing ministers some obvious embarrassment. The survey indicated that the annual rate of damage was more than three times the previous estimate made in 1976, of 4 per cent.

The government maintained that any damage arose from a lack of knowledge or understanding by individual farmers of the wildlife importance of their land, rather than from any wilfulness or inexorable pressures. Its response, therefore, was to introduce a requirement for the NCC to serve a notice on all owners or occupiers of SSSIs telling them why their site was of interest (though this was already done as a matter of course) and the operations which would damage it. The government also added a new clause allowing ministers to issue a code of guidance which would encourage owners and occupiers to cooperate in the conservation of SSSIs. Both the NFU and the CLA welcomed these new provisions, subject to the inevitable proviso that adequate funds be made available for management agreements to ensure the success of the code. Conservation groups, however, did not regard a voluntary code as an acceptable substitute for powers to prevent the destruction of an SSSI. In a letter to the Secretary of State, the chairman of the NCC argued that no voluntary code could be 'effective in restraining either that small minority of farmers who care nothing for conservation or those who feel, in present economic circumstances, that they have no option but to maximise production'. But the government persisted in the view that losses to SSSIs could be stemmed through appealing to the goodwill of farmers.

Another government concession was provision for the compulsory reclamation of a 'super-SSSI' illegally damaged or destroyed, though this was to be invoked only when practicable, and was considered by conservationists to be a token gesture. The government also introduced a clause which extended to internal drainage boards the duties of water authorities to take account of nature conservation, and to require both to consult the NCC before carrying out operations likely to damage SSSIs. These provisions were in response to the criticisms that had been expressed of drainage schemes in areas such as the Halvergate Marshes and West Sedgemoor, and of the unaccountable nature of internal drainage boards (see Chapters 10 and 11).

Lobbying tactics changed in the Commons. Relegated to a standing committee of 21 MPs, the committee stage offered restricted scope for publicity and cross-party lobbying. Moreover, with the government intending to reverse some of the changes made in the Lords, conservation groups were disappointed that backbench Conservatives who had expressed support for the conservation case in the second reading debate were not selected for the committee. Its voting on critical issues was, inevitably, along party lines and conservation groups seeking to consolidate their gains were therefore obliged to channel their lobbying efforts through the opposition, who willingly responded.

By this stage, conservationists had redefined their objectives to those changes which they considered the minimum necessary to make the Bill acceptable. The opposition threatened to talk the Bill out if the government were not prepared to make concessions, and environmental groups expressed themselves prepared to see the Bill lost if their earlier gains were reversed and no corresponding improvements made. With much important business to get through before the parliamentary recess and no scope for extending the session because of the forthcoming Royal Wedding, the government was more than usually vulnerable to threats of all-night sittings. Under this pressure it made a number of tactical concessions. These included the registration of an SSSI as a land-charge so that, if a site changed hands, the new owner or occupier was to be made aware of its status; the extension of protection for limestone pavements to

Scotland; and the provision for marine nature reserves, as inserted by the Lords, after persistent efforts by MAFF and commercial fishery interests to weaken the measure.

By far the most important gain for the conservationists came in the amendment to what became Section 28 of the Act, requiring owners or occupiers of SSSIs to give the NCC three months' notice of any intention to carry out potentially damaging operations. This became known as 'reciprocal notification' — reciprocal, that is, to the duty that the NCC had been given of informing owners or occupiers of those operations which could cause damage. The Chairman of the NCC had written to Tom King, the then Under-Secretary of State at the DoE responsible for the Bill, urging that 'statutory notification to NCC is the minimum necessary to make the government's proposed code of practice effective'. This promised to give the NCC the opportunity to persuade farmers to modify their plans or to negotiate a management agreement or, as a last resort, to effect a nature conservation order. The context in which these orders might be used was thus modified: the NCC and conservation groups now envisaged their being applied in the event of an irretrievable breakdown of voluntary negotiations on *any* SSSI and not just to safeguard a strictly limited number of sites as the government had intended. At the very least, reciprocal notification would provide a much-needed mechanism to monitor SSSI losses. More importantly, it gave the NCC a say for the first time in agricultural land-use planning.

Perhaps the best gauge of the way in which the bounds of unacceptable controls were so tightly drawn by the CLA and the NFU is the dismay with which they responded to the government's decision to table this amendment. In its parliamentary briefing, the CLA declared, 'the government has now abandoned the voluntary approach'; whereas the NFU, somewhat less stridently, felt that it must 'state its disappointment that the government has appeared to have withdrawn its previous commitment to a voluntary procedure'. In the light of such reactions it is perhaps not surprising that the amendment proved sufficient to appease nature conservation groups.

The farming lobby was compensated for this setback by a number of gains, the most significant of which was the requirement that the NCC should give three months' notice to the owner or occupier of a site which it intended designating as an SSSI, thus allowing time for representations or objections to be made. The NFU and the CLA had pressed for this right of appeal, though they were unhappy that the appellate body was to be the NCC and not an impartial body. Another major gain was a provision for an owner to claim compensation from the NCC for any depreciation in land value due to the imposition of a nature conservation order, as well as for losses incurred as a result of being prohibited from undertaking specific farming operations (Section 30).

Amenity groups achieved much less satisfaction than the nature conservationists — predictably so, given the background of Conservative opposition to the landscape protection measures embodied in Labour's abortive Countryside Bill. The CPRE and the Council for National Parks brought forward the preliminary findings of the University of Birmingham's moorland study, which indicated extensive and continuing losses of open moorland to agricultural reclamation and afforestation not just on Exmoor, but nationally. Despite being urged to keep options open until these findings could be evaluated, ministers reiterated their belief in a voluntary approach and used their parliamentary majority to defeat amendments aimed at establishing reserve powers for moorland protection. They did, however, accept the need to monitor moorland change and inserted a clause requiring national park authorities to prepare and review annually a map of 'particularly important' moor and heath (Section 43).

It was the government's response to the Sandford amendment, however, which aroused the greatest contention. The main pressure to delete this amendment came from MAFF. The government substituted clauses which, instead of enabling MAFF funds to be used for wider purposes than agricultural production, simply exhorted the Minister of Agriculture, when considering grant applications in national parks, SSSIs and other specified areas, to further the aims of conservation, but only so far as may be consistent with the agricultural purposes of a scheme. Two of the lobbyists behind the original amendment, Tony Jones of CPRE and Fiona Reynolds of the Council for National Parks, commented bitterly:

> Having promised to retain the spirit and purpose of the Sandford amendment, government presented the House of Commons with a treacherously emasculated version. The MAFF grant remains restricted to the narrow profit-oriented purposes of agricultural business. (*Countryside Campaigner*, January 1982)

Disappointment amongst the environmentalists turned to consternation as they reflected on the other part of the government's response to the Sandford amendment. This required that where an agricultural grant was refused by the minister on conservation grounds, the objecting authority (the NCC in SSSIs and the county planning authority in national parks) would be required to offer a compensation payment to the farmer (Sections 32 and 41). The CLA and NFU, which all along had taken care to emphasise the resource implications of retaining goodwill, welcomed the new measure as providing the necessary financial safeguards and recompense for farmers affected by conservation objections. Robin Grove-White, Director of the CPRE, summarised the objections of environmentalists in a letter to *The Times*:

> It gives legal expression to the surprising notion that a farmer has a right to grant aid from the tax-payer: if he is denied it in the wider public interest, he *must* be compensated for the resulting, entirely hypothetical 'losses'.... There is, however, even greater cause for concern. The Bill requires compensation to farmers to be paid not by the Ministry of Agriculture, whose relentless promotion of new farming methods through the grant system is now the source of many conflicts, but from the meagre budgets of conservation agencies such as the NCC and the National Park Authorities.

The new measure was subjected to a torrent of criticism by conservationists in letters and articles in the press and representations to ministers and politicians. When the Bill returned to the Lords for the consideration of Commons amendments, in October 1981, environmental groups focused all their efforts on an attempt to restore the *status quo*, making it discretionary rather than obligatory for conservation agencies to offer payments should they object to a proposed agricultural development. An amendment to this effect was tabled by two Conservative peers, Lords Buxton and Onslow, and was supported by all the major environmental groups as well as by the Association of County Councils, the Countryside Commission, the Association of National Park Officers and the Royal Town Planning Institute. Intensive lobbying preceded the vote. The CPRE, the RSPB, the Council for National Parks and the Royal Society for Nature Conservation called a joint press conference and sought to marshal the fullest support in the Lords. The secretary of the Ramblers' Association wrote to the Secretary of State for the Environment describing the government's new clause as 'lunatic', and warned that if it was not amended, 'national park and local authorities will be afraid to object to harmful agricultural schemes for fear of having to pay the cost'.

The NCC, however, remained out of line, and in the debate on the amendment, Earl Ferrers, a MAFF junior minister, replying for the government, made much of this, quoting extensively from a letter from the NCC which stated that:

> The NCC has given the government its support for the present wording of the clause because it removes the uncertainty which has bedevilled negotiations between the conservation agencies and farmers and landowners in the past. It also places a firm commitment on government to make adequate resources available to deal with those agreements resulting from the new measures over the years and we are working on the assumption that they will do so.

The NCC's support for the government was critical. The amendment (to replace the duty to offer a management agreement with a discretionary power) was defeated by 57 votes to 59, with Lord Arbuthnott, former president of the Scottish Landowners' Federation and deputy chairman of the NCC, voting with the government. In the judgement of the CLA's magazine, it had been 'the tensest cliffhanger of all': the time when 'our hero [the farmer] was finally rescued by only two votes'.

The closeness of the vote and the fact that the original Sandford amendment had seemed such a triumph for the conservation lobby made its defeat on this issue particularly galling. Disappointed conservationists rounded on the NCC accusing it of treachery and of caving in to political pressure. There is strong circumstantial evidence for this interpretation of events — the chairman of the NCC was a former president of the CLA. Yet a logic of action, barely discernible at the time, can appear compellingly coherent in *post-hoc* rationalisation. As a spokesman for the NCC, Alan Vittery, subsequently explained in conversation:

> We saw the government's proposals as an opportunity to reveal the true cost of conservation. ... Now it is the Government's responsibility to provide the necessary funds, not ours. ... Before we were in a 'no-win situation', now we can't lose. Either we get sufficient money or the Government will have to come up with a better arrangement to safeguard threatened sites.

POST-ACT POLITICS

On 30 October 1981 the Wildlife and Countryside Act received the Royal Assent after several hundred hours of parliamentary debate stretching over 11 months. Its fundamental character represented a success for the astute and carefully sustained lobbying of the NFU and CLA. Although the government had conceded a statutory three months' notification of operations for SSSIs, the CLA, in its annual report, admitted that this constituted but 'a relatively minor infraction of the voluntary principle'. As against this minimal setback the CLA could point with satisfaction to a number of gains made in Parliament: a legal right for owners to be informed of the existence of an SSSI; a statutory duty on the NCC to consult owners before new designations are made; an arbitration procedure for management agreements and compensation for diminution of the capital value of land in respect of nature conservation orders. Moreover, the NFU and CLA had successfully resisted any move towards broadening the purposes of agricultural grants or towards the extension of planning controls to agricultural operations. They had also seen the voluntary arrangements developed on Exmoor, including annual payments for loss of grant and profit, endorsed as a model for dealing with similar problems elsewhere. The Somerset and South Avon branch of the NFU, in a letter to farmers on West Sedgemoor, described the Act as a 'less bad piece of legislation than we dared hope for', and urged them to help make it work because the alternative would not be 'no system of conservation at all, but much greater State intervention ... something which must be avoided at all costs' (26 April 1982).

The passage of the Act in no sense marked the end of political conflict over the legislation. Lobbying and consultation continued on a number of contentious issues, including the code of guidance for owners of SSSIs and the financial guidelines for compensating farmers denied an agricultural grant. The NFU and CLA were drawn into drafting both of these and thus continued to have a tactical advantage over conservation groups who were not consulted until after drafts had been published. The final version of the financial guidelines was published on 2 February 1983. These significantly extended the operation of the principles of the Act. The NCC agreed to treat forestry applications in SSSIs on a par with agricultural proposals for compensation even though under no statutory obligation to do so, thereby overturning its earlier practice which involved no compensation. A circular accompanying the guidelines encouraged local planning authorities to consider applying their provisions to management agreements not just in national parks but in other parts of the countryside, such as AONBs and heritage coasts.

With a will born of necessity, the NFU and the CLA embarked on the task of creating a consensus around the Act. Concerned to ensure that the stewardship practices of farmers and landowners more than matched the rhetoric of the voluntary case, the CLA was at pains to emphasise the moral obligations attaching to ownership of an SSSI. It produced its own version of the code of guidance, and urged its members to comply 'in both the letter and spirit'. The NFU likewise circularised its members warning them that

> the government, with NFU support, had a very tough task in maintaining this largely voluntary code as opposed to the range of compulsory restrictions proposed by conservation groups. *It must be stressed* that if farmers are not prepared to be conciliatory on SSSIs, for example by modifying schemes where possible and seeking management agreements (with payments) where appropriate, then there can be no question that a future Government of any party would consider more punitive controls for SSSIs and possibly elsewhere. (NFU, 6 November 1981)

Both organisations had been keenly aware that the crucial battle for public opinion could be lost by default. In one parliamentary briefing the CLA complained that

> Tales of destruction in the countryside catch the headlines and are easily digested by the public mind. The quiet efforts of owners working on good conservation policies, perhaps over many years, are much less sensational. ...
> The imbalance in the reporting of good conservation news leads to an unwarranted readiness by many people to accept the need for greater control. (CLA, 22 April 1981)

To combat such 'tales of destruction', the CLA sought to publicise the results of its own surveys which pointed to considerable positive conservation action — planting trees, managing hedges, and so forth — on the part of CLA members. The NFU, for its part, initiated a publicity campaign with the title 'The Backbone of Britain' through which it hoped to 'repair damage where it has been caused between the two main sections of society — those who live and work in the town, and those who work in the country' (NFU press release, 29 June 1982).

For both organisations, the main thrust of their efforts to highlight and reinforce a conservation ethic and cooperative spirit amongst farmers and landowners has been through their encouragement of and publicity for the farming and wildlife advisory groups (FWAGs). Twenty-seven county FWAGs had been formed by May 1979, 36 by November 1981 and, in the wake of the Wildlife and Countryside Act, complete national coverage was achieved by early 1984 when, in what represented a major triumph for FWAG, a Farming and Wildlife Trust was launched principally to raise the money needed to fund the employment of 'farm conservation officers' in the counties. The patrons of this registered charity read like a 'Who's Who' of the countryside. Since 1981 the farming and landowning community has mobilised the resource provided by the existence of FWAG to try to ensure that the Act — with its philosophy of goodwill and voluntary cooperation — is seen to succeed.

But whilst the CLA, the NFU and the government are committed to the success of the Act, environmentalists have remained sceptical. From the start, some considered that it was bound to fail to halt the decline of rural habitats and landscapes and the sooner it was discredited the better. Thus groups such as FoE, CPRE, the Council for National Parks and the Ramblers' Association have looked to medium-term campaigns to achieve some controls over agricultural development and the reform of agricultural policy. Gradually, these groups have been joined by the mainstream nature conservation groups who, though recognising benefits in the Act, have become more and more aware of its shortcomings as experience of its operations has accumulated. The general politicisation of countryside issues has had a radicalising effect on the whole conservation movement and individual groups are now presenting a much more aggressive and confrontational style in their lobbying than before the Act.

Previously, conservation groups had regarded themselves as above or beyond party politics; however, the experience of the Act's passage drew them willy-nilly into the party arena. A number of milestones in this process can be identified. The first was Conservative opposition to Labour's Countryside Bill (see Chapter 5): previous countryside legislation had enjoyed bipartisan support. The second was the introduction of legislation by a Conservative government which seemed to environmentalists to be overtly biased in favour of the farming lobby and indifferent to their own reasoned views. The third arose from the coincidence that the man who played the key role in coordinating the conservation response to the Bill, Lord Melchett, was also Labour's spokesman on the Bill in the Lords. The fourth was the strict party discipline maintained by the government throughout the Commons proceedings which obliged environmental groups to channel their lobbying through a willing opposition.

Labour MPs who embraced many of the conservationists' concerns and preferred remedies made various undertakings to introduce appropriate amending legislation when next in office. This initiated debate within the Labour Party culminating in the formation of the Socialist Countryside Group in March 1983 and the commitment of the party to make all agricultural aid subject to environmental criteria and to extend development control to farming. Conservation groups, for their part, have maintained and strengthened the links with MPs and peers forged during the Bill, and some have begun to reassess their traditional apolitical stance. Leading members of FoE and the Ramblers' Association, for example, are working within the Liberal and Labour Parties to establish a firm commitment to conservation and agricultural reforms.

Even the more conservative environmental groups, though unlikely to identify with a particular party, have been provoked into a more demonstrative and adversarial stance. The RSPB, for example, has become much more openly critical of official policy, on more than one occasion threatening legal action where the government seemed to be failing in its duties to conservation. The EEC Birds Directive on which parts of the Wildlife and Countryside Act are based opens up new opportunities in this respect, allowing appeal to the European Commission and ultimately the European Court if the government seems not to be honouring its commitment to the general principles of bird and habitat protection enunciated in the Directive.

Conversely, Lord Melchett has suggested that conservationists are justified in breaking the civil law to defend threatened wildlife habitats (*The Guardian*, 16 July 1984). In Halvergate (see Chapter 11) and elsewhere, direct action has begun, as protestors have sought physically to block the destruction of particular conservation sites. Farmers, though, are more than a match for such tactics and on West Sedgemoor (see Chapter 10) and throughout the Scottish Highlands and Islands the NCC has been confronted with incidents of agrarian protest in its attempts to implement the Act.

The polarisation of debate has made the position and future of the two conservation agencies particularly problematic. For some years both the Countryside Commission and the NCC have pursued policies based on the notion of a consensus between agriculture and conservation and the Act propels them further in this direction. As the Bill progressed through Parliament, this produced a widening rift between voluntary groups and the conservation agencies as the former grew frustrated at the government's intransigence, and the latter acquiesced in the government's intention.

Suspicions of the agencies amongst environmentalists has been heightened by the trend of political appointments to their governing councils and national advisory committees. A majority of the new appointments made by the Conservative administration of 1979–83 had farming, forestry or landowning interests, and most of them had served or were still serving in an official capacity with the NFU, the CLA or their Scottish or Welsh equivalents. Appointments to the NCC even included Sir Hector Monro, the junior minister responsible for preparing the Bill and a member of the Area Executive Committee of the Scottish NFU. A similar trend occurred amongst the ministerial appointees to national park authorities. The central purpose can only have been to press the conservation authorities into line behind the implementation of the Act.

FURTHER READING

Stimulating introductions to the underlying issues in the conflict between modern agriculture and conservation are Bryn Green, *Countryside Conservation* (Allen & Unwin, 1981); Ann and Malcolm MacEwen, *National Parks: Conservation or Cosmetics* (Allen & Unwin, 1982); and John Blunden and Nigel Curry, *The Changing Countryside* (Croom Helm, 1985). A detailed account of the genesis and passage of the Wildlife and Countryside Bill is Graham Cox and Philip Lowe, 'A Battle not the War: The Politics of the Wildlife and Countryside Act', in *The Countryside Planning Yearbook*, Vol. 4 (Geo-Books, 1983). The standard legal guide to the Act is Barry Denyer-Green, *Wildlife and Countryside Act 1981: The Practitioner's Companion* (Royal Institution of Chartered Surveyors, 1983).

7. The Implementation of the Act

By raising expectations and heightening awareness of the issues, the passing of the Wildlife and Countryside Act has resulted in a marked shift in the terms of the conservation debate. Whereas previously the onus had been on the conservationists to demonstrate the harmful effects of changing farming and forestry practices, the onus is now on the agricultural community and the government to demonstrate that the Act is being effective in halting the destruction of wildlife habitats and landscapes. In this context, conservationists have presented any threat or damage to an SSSI as a failure or inadequacy of Part II of the Act.

The requirement for owners or occupiers of SSSIs to give notice of potentially damaging operations and for national park authorities to monitor the loss of open moorland have ensured that disputes between agriculture and conservation have continued to attract attention. Similarly, provision for consultation before new SSSI designations has meant more publicity for the process of designation itself, as witnessed most spectacularly by the case of West Sedgemoor (see Chapter 10). It is hardly surprising, then, that reports of damaging operations being carried out during the three months' consultation period, both in West Sedgemoor and elsewhere, have caused alarm in conservationist circles.

THE COST OF THE ACT

The greatest controversy surrounding the Act has focused on the amount of money needed or available for its implementation, and the related issue of how the conservation agencies discharge their new powers and duties. The verdict of the CPRE and the Council for National Parks when the financial guidelines were published was that 'they will prove impossibly expensive for conservation authorities, as well as hugely and expensively burdensome in administrative terms', and that they 'will be prejudicial to effective safeguarding of valued landscapes and wildlife species and habitats'. Lacking the resources to finance more than a few management agreements, conservation agencies would be reluctant, it was feared, to press their objections to harmful agricultural and forestry schemes, which would therefore proceed unchecked. During the Bill's passage, ministers had given assurances that adequate resources would be made available. Significantly, both the Countryside Commission and the NCC recalled these assurances in their subsequent annual reports, expressing their trust in them, though the NCC acknowledged that 'in future the cost of nature conservation will be more closely related to normal market prices determined by current agricultural grant and price support systems . . . we can no longer rely on securing land for conservation at minimal cost to the exchequer'.

The CLA and NFU, too, were concerned that sufficient funds should be made available to finance management agreements, but they were also anxious to dispel any notions that farmers stood to make a killing. The CLA's legal department maintained that, because of the provisions for consultation between MAFF and the NCC, it would be 'unlikely that there will be a flood of unmeritorious schemes for agricultural improvement on SSSIs so that they can be turned town and a conservation grant applied for' (*The Field*, 16 June 1982). In a circular to its county branches, the NFU stressed that 'If farmers are seen to abuse the system by "trying on" dubious schemes the credibility of both the NFU and the farming community will be placed at risk, and there is every possibility that government would withdraw the provision as legislative time permitted' (6 November 1981).

It was over SSSIs that some of these issues first came to a head. Sir Ralph Verney, then chairman of the NCC, had assured conservation groups that limited finances would not prevent it from objecting to potentially damaging proposals. However, in the first case to arise — a proposal to improve the drainage of wet meadows on part of Walland Marsh, Kent to allow conversion to arable use — the NCC withdrew its objection when the DoE refused to fund a management agreement with the owner. Though the NCC had sufficient money at the time, it was concerned that even more important sites might be at risk later during the same financial year for which finance would then be unavailable. The NCC's inaction created a storm of protest, with Ian Prestt, Director of the RSPB, demanding that the NCC

> must object loudly when any site is at risk, whether or not it has the money to pay compensation. Only then will the public and Parliament understand that it is the government's failure to produce the cash that is the real cause of the destruction of our wildlife heritage. (Quoted in the *Observer*, 21 March 1982)

A related concern was that the NCC's wariness of antagonising local farmers was leading to considerable delay and even reluctance in the designation of new SSSIs, particularly in areas such as the Berwyns and West Sedgemoor (Chapters 9 and 10) where forestry or agricultural development was in prospect. First FoE and then the RSPB threatened the NCC with legal action if it failed to fulfil its statutory duty of designating land which met its scientific criteria. In reaction to such criticisms and 'to remove misunderstandings about how it intends to implement the SSSI provisions', the NCC issued a formal statement on 10 August 1982 which detailed its commitment to using the powers of the Act to the full to safeguard SSSIs, whilst ensuring that owners and occupiers were not 'unreasonably disadvantaged by any constraints resulting from the notification of their land as an SSSI'. Inevitably, the decision, announced three months later, to designate 1000 ha. in West Sedgemoor was widely seen by interests opposed to such an extensive designation as a political sop to 'buy off' conservationist discontent.

Fears that the costs of management agreements would rapidly render the Act unworkable have proven premature: 'We haven't yet lost a site for want of finance', commented Alan Vittery, a spokesman for the NCC, in conversation in August 1984. So far, all agreements have been within budget, and that budget has been increasing. The money going to site-acquisition and safeguards by the NCC rose from £756,000 in 1980/81 to £1.2 million in 1982/83. For 1984/85, £1.895 million was budgeted for, but in July 1984 the government announced that it was providing an additional £2.55 million, making a total of £4.445 million for that year. Furthermore, it is always open for the NCC to ask government for additional money if an important site cannot be safeguarded within its prevailing budget. Since 1977 no such request has been refused, though, as W.M. Adams commented, 'this may say more for the NCC's care and extreme caution in selecting cases than the government's generosity or future enthusiasm for paying'.

By August 1984, the NCC had entered into 154 management agreements since the passing of the Act, covering 12,591 ha. and costing £382,721 in lump-sum payments, and £79,577 per annum in recurring payments. At that time, the NCC was discussing with owners and occupiers nearly 600 further agreements, covering over 60,000 ha. The estimated costs of concluding all these agreements was about £1.4 million in capital payments and arrears, and an annual commitment of about the same amount. The Countryside Commission, by comparison, paid £57,000 towards the cost of six management agreements entered into by national park authorities in 1983/84 at a cost of £77,000. Two more agreements involved initial annual payments of £12,000, while the annual costs of 40 additional agreements being negotiated by the park authorities in May 1984 were estimated at £85,000. The NFU was able to conclude, in a briefing note for a House of Lords debate on the workings of the Act, in June 1984, that 'the cost of funding conservation agreements is modest and represents good value for money to the nation'.

The figures for existing agreements, however, give a misleading impression of the eventual recurrent costs of implementing the Act's compensation requirements. This is in part because the 'going rate' for management agreements rose rapidly in this period, and in part because there are many more agreements in the pipeline than have been finalised. The full cost of management agreements to protect the wildlife interest of West Sedgemoor, for instance, is likely to be about £150,000 per annum (see Chapter 10). Increasingly, acquisition of threatened sites appears preferable to paying out considerable annual compensations with no absolute guarantee of permanent protection. Indeed, the RSPB has ruefully contrasted the NCC's likely annual bill for conserving two-thirds of West Sedgemoor with its own expenditure of £1 million in acquiring the other third, to which the NCC contributed just £67,000 in grant aid.

West Sedgemoor is only the first of a number of SSSIs to be designated on the Somerset Levels. There are ten areas on the Levels, including West Sedgemoor, totalling well over 6000 ha. that the NCC considers of exceptional wildlife value. If it were to designate all of these in keeping with its statutory obligations, the eventual cost of management agreements could well exceed £1 million per annum. The Somerset Levels, moreover, are only one of a number of important wetlands under threat of major drainage schemes; others include the Whittlesey Washes, the Amberley Wild Brooks, the Idle Washlands, the Cambridgeshire fens, the Derwent Ings and the Halvergate Marshes. And wetlands are only one of a number of types of habitat that are currently under intense pressures (see Chapter 3). No expenditure is currently contemplated to protect landscapes and habitats outside SSSIs or national parks.

It can be expected that as the 'going rate' for management agreements rises, and as farmers become aware of the money to be made by securing agreements to conserve their marginal lands, so demands for compensation will grow dramatically. In its 1982/83 annual report, the National Heritage Memorial Fund, to which official and voluntary conservation bodies have increasingly turned for financial assistance to secure sites, expressed its concern that heritage land is 'at severe risk of undesirable development because of the potentially very high cost of compensation under management agreements provided for in that Act'.

In a detailed study for the British Association of Nature

Conservationists and the World Wildlife Fund of the Act's effectiveness in habitat protection, W.M. Adams has estimated that the full potential cost of management agreements for the SSSI system alone could be up to £40 million per annum — more than $2\frac{1}{2}$ times the NCC's total grant-in-aid for 1984/85. The NCC, whose previous estimates have proved very conservative, is anticipating that eventually a third of SSSIs will need management agreements, and that compensation will be running at £15 million per annum (*The Times*, 13 November 1984). These estimates should be compared with those originally made by the government in the Financial Memorandum to the Wildlife and Countryside Bill, which suggested that the Bill's habitat protection measures might involve the NCC in additional expenditure 'of the order of £600,000 or £700,000 on average per year, depending on financial and other circumstances'.

ADMINISTERING THE ACT

The main reason why current costs are only a fraction of what they may be in the future is that the Act is still far from being fully implemented. Some of the national park authorities, including Snowdonia and the Yorkshire Dales, seem to be markedly reluctant to use the Act's provisions because they fear the financial implications. Park authorities are still using earlier legislation facilitating management agreements or Section 39 of the 1981 Act to which the financial guidelines do not necessarily apply. Both the Brecon Beacons and Northumberland national park authorities, for example, have negotiated long-term arrangements for woodland management under this Section 39 which involve no financial payments, although increasingly the guidelines are encouraging farmers and landowners to expect the 'going rate' for compensation, even in cases where statutory application does not apply. By May 1984, not a single mandatory agreement arising from Section 41 of the Act (see Chapter 6) had been negotiated by any of the park authorities, nor were any under negotiation.

Whereas the Act has been cautiously, if not coolly,

received by some national park authorities, at least one local authority — Suffolk County Council — has resolved that it cannot justify offering management agreements with the payment of compensation as provided for in the guidelines, having calculated that it could cost at least £6–8 million per annum to safeguard the county's remnants of marginal land with scenic or ecological value. The Countryside Commission is able to cover three-quarters of the costs of management agreements in national parks and the Broads, but only half the costs elsewhere. Financially hard-pressed county and district councils are thus in no position to use the Act to safeguard cherished areas of countryside outside the national parks and SSSIs. Indeed, apart from the Broads Authority (see Chapter 11), only one local authority, Hampshire County Council, had, by April 1984, negotiated a management agreement under the Act involving compensatory payments.

The NCC, in contrast, after its initial equivocation over costs, has shown every commitment to the new legislation, though it has faced other difficulties in implementing its new responsibilities. In their desire to appease the landowning and farming interests, ministers devised a bureaucratic nightmare and failed totally to anticipate the time and the manpower that would be needed to implement the new procedures imposed on the NCC, although their complexity and ineffectiveness are obvious enough.

Under Section 28, the NCC has to re-notify some 30,000 owners and occupiers of some 4000 SSSIs. To win their understanding and sympathy the regional staff of the NCC try to contact them personally before formal notifications are sent. As the case-study chapters reveal, the task of explaining the workings of the new Act to farmers and landowners can be very time-consuming and is rife with opportunities for misunderstanding, both genuine and disingenuous.

The NCC has had to up-date and standardise its procedures of site appraisal, listing and protection. All sites have had to be reappraised before they can be renotified, because many have been damaged or have simply changed through natural succession since the previous revision of SSSI schedules (which in some counties was more than ten years ago). Some sites have had to be

deleted and most have needed boundary revisions. Formal re-notification, then, involves sending a detailed site
description and map as well as a site-specific list of potentially damaging operations to each owner or occupier, and
in addition to local planning authorities, water authorities
and the Secretary of State for the Environment. Finally,
the site has to be registered as a land charge.

A major proportion of the time of the NCC's regional
staff has been taken up with re-notification. Initially, the
NCC intended to complete the task by the end of 1983, but
it underestimated the operational problems, and its most
recent estimate is that re-notification will not be completed
before 1990. At the end of August 1984, only 1070 sites —
about a quarter of the total number — had been re-notified.

Until a site is re-notified it is without even the Act's
modest safeguards, and only then do the long-term financial and administrative implications begin to be apparent.
In many cases, the farmer's reply is that he does wish to
carry out one or more of the potentially damaging operations specified by the NCC. The NCC then has three
months to respond, although under the code of guidance
it has undertaken to make an initial response within a
month. If the operation is unacceptable, the NCC can
either try to persuade the farmer to modify it, offer a
management agreement, offer to lease or buy the land, or
ultimately purchase the land compulsorily. Any of these
options necessarily involves NCC staff in detailed discussion and negotiation, which inevitably consumes the
time available for re-notification. W.M. Adams concludes:

> The Act is maybe workable, but the cost in financial, logis-
> tical and bureaucratic terms is enormous. As the flow of
> casework resulting from renotification increases, the pace
> of renotification is likely to slow. Far from being a short
> administrative putsch, the task is likely to become part of
> life in the NCC for a distressingly large number of years.

Inevitably, the NCC's other responsibilities must suffer,
and the designation of new sites has been put back for
years.

Proposed SSSIs have to undergo a similar procedure
before they can enjoy any protection. However, the procedure is even lengthier and more complicated, involving

the following stages: personal approaches, pre-notification of owners, occupiers and relevant authorities; a three-months' consultation period; the consideration of any objections; and formal confirmation of the notification to the same parties. As the case studies of the Berwyns and West Sedgemoor (Chapters 9 and 10) illustrate, obstructive farmers opposed to SSSI designation can tie up key NCC staff in protracted discussions. In the meantime the site has no safeguards whatsoever.

Indeed the consultation period invites pre-emptive destructive action on the part of farmers or landowners determined to frustrate the designation of their land. It is no wonder that the consultation period has come to be known as the three months' loophole. Although it is likely to be closed very soon by amending legislation, it illustrates the failings of most of the Act's provisions for habitat protection. It confers very limited powers on the NCC, which is rendered all the more impotent by the cumbersome procedures it is required to observe. By the end of August 1984, only 311 new sites had been notified, but nearly 1000 sites known to be of wildlife or geological importance awaited designation. Many were being left 'on ice' because the NCC feared they might be destroyed if formally notified. Most, however, just became part of the NCC's huge backlog of work. The Act, in effect, has forced the NCC to dishonour its statutory duty to notify sites which meet its criteria.

The 1981 Act gave the NCC onerous new responsibilities in other fields, notably in species protection and marine nature conservation. However, instead of increasing its manpower to match these additional demands, the government sought to cut the NCC's staff. On 26 May 1982, the then Secretary of State, Michael Heseltine, met the NCC's chairman and director-general to express his concern that staff reductions within the NCC did not match those of other agencies funded by the Department of the Environment. Overriding their objections, Heseltine insisted on subjecting the NCC to a Rayner review in order to find scope for economies and for hiving-off functions. When the review was completed in March 1983, it found that many of the staff were overworked and — exceptionally for such an exercise — even proposed a small *increase* in staff. The NCC remains, however, grossly understaffed. One of the most worrying consequences has been the neglect of its general advisory role and responsibility for the wider countryside. As the Peak Park Joint Planning Board complained in its annual report for 1983/84:

> Ironically, whilst the Wildlife and Countryside Act gave us extra conservation duties and opportunities, the same Act gave the NCC so much extra work that it had to withdraw from giving such general advice as we had previously received so that they could concentrate on their own reserves and SSSIs.

FAILINGS AND ACHIEVEMENTS

Severe staff constraints have resulted in inadequate monitoring of the Act's effectiveness in safeguarding landscapes and habitats. Information from the NCC's regional offices revealed that during the year April 1983 to March 1984 damage was known to have occurred on 156 existing and proposed SSSIs. This was 3.7 per cent of the total number of sites. The figure is bound to underestimate the true extent of damage because information was patchy on sites awaiting re-notification — which are the majority. Of the 156 known damaged sites, 81 were awaiting re-notification and this figure too is almost certainly a gross underestimate. A further 34 were proposed SSSIs, of which seven were in the statutory consultation process (and therefore were casualties of the three months' loophole). These figures are disturbingly high in relation to the 183 new sites notified during the period. At least a further 23 sites were damaged after notification or re-notification. In most of these cases the damage was accidental, though in October 1984 a Leicestershire farmer was fined £200 with £50 costs for having limed an area of acidic wet grassland without consulting the NCC, and other prosecutions were being considered.

Damage varied from the very minor to total loss (three sites). In over half the cases damage was caused by agricultural activities such as ploughing, drainage, re-seeding and the use of fertilisers and chemical sprays. A further 10 per cent involved the felling of trees — in some instances as a means to agricultural conversion. Motorcycle scrambling, fire and the dumping of waste together accounted for over a quarter of incidents. The NCC concluded, somewhat wishfully, that 'since the new Act our impression is that damage to SSSIs has diminished' (press release, 2 February 1984). But whether damage has been reduced to an acceptable level and at an acceptable cost are the central questions on which the Act will be judged.

No equivalent statistics are yet available on threats to the landscape of national parks, although figures are available from a survey conducted by Ian Brotherton for the Countryside Commission of the number of proposals for grant-aided agricultural operations notified to national park authorities under the agricultural capital grants regulations that came into force in October 1980. These notifications can trigger the provision of Section 41 of the Act, which requires the park authority to offer a compensatory management agreement if the Minister of Agriculture upholds its objection to the operation. Some 2757 notifications were processed by the park authorities between April and September 1983. They had no comment on 86 per cent of these, and their conditional agreement was given to a further 9 per cent. For the remaining 5 per cent (151 notifications), the park authorities anticipated adverse environmental consequences — mainly to the landscape — and sought modifications.

In 145 of these cases modifications were agreed between the farmers and the park authorities, including 18 cases (involving mainly cladding and roofing material) in which the park authorities undertook to make a financial contribution to the additional costs. During the six-months period there were only six cases over which agreement could not be reached, and in three of these the farmer proceeded without a grant. These involved the erection of a conspicuous modern farm building in unspoilt countryside, and the 'improvement' of small, though prominent areas of wet heath and maritime grassland. In the three other cases — involving proposals for land clearance and drainage — consultations between the farmers, the national park authorities and ADAS were still in progress at the end of the period.

William Waldegrave, the Parliamentary Under-Secretary of State for the Environment, having reported these results to the Commons on 31 July 1984, commented that he found them 'reassuring as [they] demonstrate that the vast majority of farmers are willing to modify farm improvement schemes, where necessary, for conservation reasons'. Closer study, however, does not confirm this complacent interpretation. First of all, in an estimated 20 per cent of cases, the work had been started or even completed before the park authorities had been notified. These cases are in addition to the unknown number which are not notified at all. Apparently, MAFF does not regard the failure to notify a park authority as grounds for refusing a grant, thereby signalling to farmers that they lose nothing by doing the work first and notifying afterwards.

There is also circumstantial evidence that the park authorities are allowing many development schemes to go through unchallenged even though they may harm the environment. The Dartmoor Preservation Association, for example, has kept a record of all the applications for grant aid approved by the national park authority that would result in the loss of open country. Such operations generally include spraying with fertiliser, liming and slagging, re-seeding and, less frequently, ploughing. According to the Association's calculations, the areas of open country affected in the three years since October 1980 totalled over 400 ha.

There are several reasons why park authorities may be taking an excessively lenient line. First, many of their members have a background in farming or forestry and may be inclined to look favourably on the needs of local farmers, while the park authorities are reluctant to upset their powerful local farming communities. Second, there are strong reasons for believing that the vetting of grant proposals is being skimped for lack of time and staff. There have been considerable pressures on the park authorities to handle the task smoothly and quickly, but with little or no additional staff. On average, each park is having to handle over 500 notifications a year, and the average time taken to deal with a notification is 15 days. Inevitably, many must go by 'on the nod'. Third, if the park authority insists on its objection to a grant-aided operation it has to compensate the farmer for loss of grant and the additional net income which would have ensued.

Fourth, because the park authority has no power to stop the proposed development, it is in a very weak bargaining position: at any time, the farmer may choose to proceed with his plans, and the authority usually has little choice but to accept whatever concessions a farmer is willing to make. Farmers may even refuse the offer of compensation under a management agreement. By April 1984, in the North York Moors, for example, eight such agreements had been offered *and rejected*, and not one management agreement had been concluded with a farmer. The national park officer there commented that, 'The general reaction of farmers seems to be a resistance to any interference with their freedom to farm as they wish' (*Rucksack*, October 1983).

Finally, the park authorities can only act as advisers to MAFF or the Welsh Office agriculture department, neither of which regards their views as decisive in determining whether grant should be paid: park officers are therefore put in a position of guessing what the agricultural departments will 'wear'. Thus the Dartmoor national park authority decided *not* to object to a proposal to clear, plough and reseed 3 ha. of registered common land on Dartmoor, despite strong opposition, because it felt that 'an objection was unlikely to command MAFF support' (Park committee minutes, 2 December 1983). In the main, the park authorities seem to confine their objections to the cases where the environmental objections seem incontrovertible and overwhelming: and even then they may not prevail.

If agreement cannot be reached between the park authority and a farmer, ADAS steps in to try to resolve the issue. Significantly, ADAS sees its role as honest broker, and exerts pressure on both the farmer and the park authority to compromise. If the authority remains dissatisfied, it may formally object to the minister. In four of the eight cases that went to ministers in 1982 and 1983, the strong objections of the national park authorities or the NCC were over-ruled, and in the fifth the minister granted part-payment. Only in three of the eight cases did the minister support the objections. This miserable record of failure to back conservation even in the tiny minority of cases taken to them on appeal does not inspire confidence that the agriculture ministers are discharging their statutory duty under Sections 32 and 41 to further conservation in awarding grants in designated areas. The North York Moors national park committee, which has had the experience of trying to make the Act work, has concluded that:

> The national park authorities are given an impossible task without proper powers and safeguards when seeking to protect moorland and other valuable habitats from damaging operations. Management agreements are not the answer in this conflict situation. (Minutes, 5 September 1984)

REFORM OF THE ACT

A series of local conflicts in 1982 and 1983, some of which are covered in the case studies in Chapters 8–11, exposed in practice the shortcomings in the Act that its critics had identified during and after the parliamentary debates. These conflicts presented successively bigger challenges to the Act's procedures and their underlying philosophy, and each assumed national significance as the national lobbies seized on them as test cases.

From late 1983, as evidence accumulated of the costs, difficulties and complexities of the Act, pressure began to build up to remedy its most obvious defects. On 30 October, the CPRE and the Council for National Parks marked the Act's second anniversary by issuing a statement declaring that experience had proved it to be 'toothless'. Indeed, far from protecting the rural environment, the Act was charged with 'stimulating new pressures on the countryside because of the rights it gives to farmers of large compensation payments'. The following month, Wildlife Link published a report criticising the slow progress with the implementation of the Act and calling as a matter of urgency for the NCC to be given much more resources and manpower to complete re-notification and to fund management agreements. The report detailed the damage to 22 SSSIs and proposed SSSIs since the passage of the Act, but these statistics were superseded only eight months later, in July 1984, by a report by FoE which gave 133 cases of damage or destruction in SSSIs since the Act had become law. Likening the Act's safeguards to a 'leaky sieve', and its compensation arrangements to 'legalised bribery', the report roundly declared, 'the Act is failing miserably, and must be overhauled'.

On 15 March 1984, the new chairman of the NCC, William Wilkinson, wrote to the junior minister, William Walde-grave, requesting that steps be taken to close the three months' loophole and to overcome two other difficulties. The NCC had found that the three months allowed for negotiation after it had objected to a proposed operation were quite inadequate, and it wished to see the notifi-cation period for potentially damaging operations ex-tended to six months. In addition, it was concerned that it was taking up to three weeks to prepare, and for the DoE to process, a nature conservation order. A number of sites had been damaged because of this delay in providing the urgent protection supposedly offered by the Act, includ-ing the proposed SSSI of Tealham and Tadham Moors on the Somerset Levels. The NCC, therefore, proposed that it should have an emergency 28-day 'stop' power to cover the period in which the Secretary of State reached his decision on a nature conservation order.

It was no longer possible, in the light of these glaring deficiencies, for ministers to maintain the line that the Act must be given time to prove itself. The Treasury was also beginning to express unease at the escalating cost of management agreements. In March 1984, in the context of the Halvergate controversy (Chapter 11), William Walde-grave announced that he was asking MAFF to come up with ways of protecting valuable sites without invoking those sections of the Act which obliged conservation agencies to make substantial compensation payments to landowners. 'It is proving a rather expensive beast to water', admitted Michael Jopling, the Minister of Agricul-ture (*Farmers' Weekly*, 18 May 1984).

A Private Member's Bill introduced by the Labour MP, Peter Hardy, to close the three months' loophole forced the government's hand on this issue. The effect of the Bill, which had its second reading on 6 July 1984, would have been to make an SSSI effective from the moment when a proposed notification was served, but subject to rights of objection and the obligation on the NCC to reply to objections within six months. The measure enjoyed the support of conservation groups, and qualified backing from the CLA and the NFU. Though the Bill stood no chance in the parliamentary timetable, it elicited a commitment from ministers to introduce or support a similar measure in the autumn session.

Ministers and their advisers now directed their efforts towards devising ways of patching up the Act that would appease its conservationist critics and curb the runaway costs, but without setting in train a wide-ranging debate that might propel the government into committing much greater resources or conceding stronger statutory powers. Ministers' hopes of containing the debate seemed doomed, however, when the Commons Select Committee on the Environment announced that it would conduct a review of the Act in the autumn.

The reaction of the farming lobby to the welter of criticism of the Act was to argue, somewhat contradictorily, both that it was premature to reach a final judgement on its effectiveness and (to quote an NFU parliamentary briefing of 7 June 1984) that 'the evidence to-date demonstrates that the Act is achieving considerable success as a mechanism for conserving SSSIs'. The NFU, whilst arguing that the number of sites which had been damaged was small, had to concede that the three months' loophole should be closed, and offenders prosecuted. But it clung with customary tenacity to its established stance that,

Whilst legislation may assist in providing a framework for implementing conservation measures, ultimately the long-term diversity and interests of the countryside can only be maintained and enhanced through cooperation and voluntary means.

Condemnation of the Act by conservationists also provoked the NFU leadership into more exasperated responses. Sir Richard Butler, President of the NFU, denounced what he termed 'mindless and naive' criticism of farmers by 'braying do-gooders'. Such criticism, he asserted, would be counter-productive and had already caused the destruction of features by farmers alarmed at the possibility of planning constraints. 'Push farmers into a corner with nowhere else to go and they will go for your throat', he warned. 'Rest assured that a significant proportion will get their tractors out and rip up perhaps a grove of orchids, meadowland and hedgerows out of sheer frustration and annoyance' (*Daily Telegraph*, 26 March 1984; *Farming News*, 30 March 1984). Such intemperate outbursts may have pleased farmers, but they fuelled claims by critics that a rather crude form of blackmail lurked behind the commitment to goodwill and voluntary cooperation. The following month, though, Sir Richard began to change his tune.

By early 1984, the European Council of Ministers, faced with the imminent bankruptcy of the EEC brought about by agricultural profligacy and the need to shore up the farmers of Greece, and shortly Spain and Portugal, had accepted in principle financial ceilings in most areas of CAP expenditure. The moment of truth for the NFU came in April with the imposition of quotas to cut milk production. The NFU correctly interpreted this development as heralding the end of an era during which increased production was the be-all and end-all of agricultural policy, and immediately set about devising a new strategy. It began seriously considering whether the 'braying' of the critics did not, in fact, suggest ways in which farmers, through subsidised conservation practices, could regain some of the income they were clearly going to lose as production incentives were cut. A wide-ranging debate on agricultural policy had been opened up.

BEYOND THE ACT

As political concern about the overall costs of agricultural policy mounted, so the operation of the Act began to highlight the specific workings and consequences of agricultural support. In particular, the requirement for conservation agencies to compensate farmers for loss of grants and subsidies revealed the scale of such payments. The leaked details of individual management agreements served to dramatise the excesses and iniquities of open-ended agricultural subsidies as much as revelations about butter mountains and wine lakes. The £500 per ha., index-linked annual payment that the NCC agreed to give a farmer not to drain and plough some 40 ha. of the Halvergate Marshes SSSI was, after all, equivalent to the profits he could have expected to make from grants and protected prices for producing surplus cereals. Likewise, the NCC's opposition to Fountain Forestry's scheme to plant conifers on 1000 ha. on the slopes of Creag Meagaidh SSSI highlighted both the large grants and considerable tax relief (in excess of £600,000) that a private forestry investment company could exact from such a scheme, and the huge cost of compensation that faced the NCC if grant were refused.

The disparities of compensation payments also pointed up the inequalities in the distribution of agricultural support. The £280,000 paid to Lord Thurso for a 99-year lease to safeguard a blanket bog in Caithness from peat-cutting and conifer-planting contrasted with annual payments of less than £10 per ha. being offered to crofters in neighbouring Sutherland not to improve their hill pasture. Just as it is the wealthy farmers and landowners who gain the lion's share of agricultural and forestry subsidies, so it is they who stand to gain the most in compensation if they own improvable or afforestable land in SSSIs or national parks.

Two influential books published in 1982 and 1983, respectively, fused together the economic and the environmental critiques of agricultural policy. The first *Agriculture: The Triumph and the Shame*, was by Richard Body, Conservative MP for Holland-with-Boston, an agricultural constituency which has felt the full effects of recent policies in concentrating farming in a handful of large, highly capitalised units. It would be hard to exaggerate the sense of shock experienced in Conservative, farming and landowning circles at the vehemence of Body's attack on the agricultural support system, based as it was on a thoroughly Thatcherite belief in monetarism and free trade. Though his free-market solution found few supporters, Body's criticism of the destructive pressures on the physical and social environment of rural areas signalled to conservationists an unsuspected impatience with current policies in the heart of the Conservative Party.

The second, *Agriculture, the Countryside and Land Use*, was a more objective, though equally trenchant, critique of agricultural policy written by two academic economists, J.K. Bowers and Paul Cheshire, who argued that the high cost of the support system created inefficiency, injustice, over-production and environmental damage. A substantial scaling-down of the enormous burden of direct and indirect support for agriculture was justified not only on social and economic grounds but also as 'the single most important change in agricultural policy from the viewpoint of conservation'. This would decrease the intensity of exploitation of land and lower capital investment in farming with beneficial effects for the environment and other users of the countryside. 'There is', they said, 'a hard-nosed economic argument for conservation', which only seemed expensive because it had to compensate for an expensive system of agricultural protection.

The response of the farming lobby has been simply to assert repeatedly that conservation depends upon a prosperous agriculture. Thus Sir Richard Butler told a meeting of the Suffolk Trust for Nature Conservation that 'Conservation costs money which can only come from a profitable agriculture. It is naive to believe that measures to cut agricultural expenditure and production in the EEC will benefit the environment if they mean a sharp drop in farm income' (*East Anglian Daily Times*, 24 March 1984). Or as Lord Stanley, a spokesman for the NFU, put it in a debate in the House of Lords on 23 July 1984: 'the first priority of any farmer is to make profits in order to support his family, his staff and his village – in that order. Butterflies must inevitably come last – not disregarded, but last'. The implication being, apparently, that the butterflies will only survive if profits are very healthy! This message was relayed by so many farming spokesmen on so many platforms during 1983 and 1984 as to suggest that the strictures of Body and Bowers and Cheshire had touched a nerve in Agriculture House.

Another significant political development was a shift of attitude within the Conservative Party itself towards both agricultural and environmental issues, presaged in part by Body's book. According to leaked Cabinet papers, Mrs Thatcher's first administration had been anxious to 'reduce over-sensitivity to environmental considerations' (*Sunday Times*, 18 November 1979). However, by 1984 her second administration was beset by industrial and economic problems and had attracted much adverse publicity over issues such as acid rain and nuclear wastes. The influential Royal Commission on Environmental Polution had accused it of being complacent, and it was widely reported that the prime minister was revising her opinion of the political significance of environmental concern, particularly in the light of the electoral successes of Green parties in Western Europe. 'Tories seek to win environmentalist vote' ran the headline in the *Financial Times* (16 July 1984), following a series of ministerial meetings examining Britain's environmental policy. Ensuing developments included the establishment of environmental coordination units in both the DoE and MAFF, and the appointment of a countryside research officer by Conservative Central Office. At the same time, agricultural subsidies had become a target for the monetarists in the Cabinet and at the Treasury, and when the prime minister launched a campaign against middle-class monopolies, she was credited with the belief that 'an attack on farmers' privileges is long overdue' (*Sunday Times*, 19 February 1984). One outcome has been a marked reduction in grants to farmers: in 1982/83, £205 million was available under the agriculture and horticulture grant scheme, but in 1984/85 only £130 million was allocated.

An important development occurred in the autumn of 1983 when more than 60 (mainly Shire) Tory MPs supported a campaign successfully orchestrated by the CPRE against two draft circulars on *Green-Belts* and *Land for Housing* which would have relaxed green-belt controls. The episode served to arouse concern on the backbenches over the government's attitude towards countryside protection and its bad public image. By early July 1984, 166 MPs — mostly Conservatives — had signed an early day motion put down by the Conservative MP, Andrew Hunter (but inspired by the CPRE) expressing alarm at the continued threats to Britain's heritage of landscape and wildlife and calling on the government 'to ensure that agricultural policy, and the structure of public funding, is widened so as to take full account of the need to protect and enhance the environment'. Similar views appeared in two pamphlets, *Conserving the Countryside: A Tory View*, published by Conservative Central Office in May 1984 and written by Kenneth Carlisle, a Suffolk farmer and MP for Lincoln; and *Conservation and the Conservatives*, published in October and written by Tony Paterson, the parliamentary liaison officer of the Conservative Bow Group. These detailed the continuing losses of wildlife and habitats and called for the balance to be restored between agriculture and the countryside, including a major overhaul of farming policies and the strengthening of safeguards in the Wildlife and Countryside Act. The Conservative Party, it seemed, was readjusting its historic attitude towards the land in a way that balanced the old Tory paternalism and the new monetarism: preparing on the one hand to give greater priority to countryside conservation; and on the other, to subject agriculture to the rigours of greater competition and less state aid.

In this changing climate, examples of the failings of the Act, of exorbitant management agreements or of the intransigence of MAFF assumed new prominence and political significance. Seizing their opportunity, conservation groups launched new campaigns with objectives which went beyond merely remedying the faults of the Act. In November 1983, FoE published their *Proposals for a Natural Heritage Bill*, with the intention to 'update the Wildlife and Countryside Act by applying selective controls and incentives which are known to work in other spheres [in order to] restore the balance between agrarian development and conservation equitably'. The measures proposed included bringing under development control such intensive agricultural and forestry operations as the construction of farm buildings, commercial afforestation, wetland drainage and the improvement of moorland, heathland and permanent pasture; safeguarding SSSIs from damaging development in a similar manner to listed buildings; and subjecting MAFF grant aid to conservation criteria.

In January 1984, the CPRE launched a 'Campaign for the Countryside' aimed at securing 'fresh government agricultural policies more sensitive to conservation'. Representations were made to the Ministers of Agriculture and the

Environment and to the European Council of Environment Ministers. Support was also canvassed amongst MPs and peers. Writing to its county branches asking them to button-hole their local MPs ('particularly Conservative backbenchers'), the CPRE's director advised them to stress that the initiative was 'thoroughly constructive ... not "farmer-bashing" in any way, but placing the responsibility for desirable changes in the relationship between landscape/wildlife conservation and agriculture where it belongs — with the government's agricultural grant-aid policies' (6 April 1984). Talks were also initiated with the CLA and the NFU to seek common ground.

A remarkable feature of the CPRE's campaign was its links with the parallel one launched in April 1984 by *The Observer* 'to preserve our natural heritage and save Britain's countryside from further depredation'. The newspaper specifically urged that loopholes in the Wildlife and Countryside Act be closed and that the Minister of Agriculture should adapt farm grants so as to promote conservation. Throughout the summer and autumn there followed a series of articles by their environment correspondent, Geoffrey Lean, highlighting specific threats to the natural heritage. *The Observer* used the CPRE as its consultant and as a clearing-house for the readers' letters it solicited describing damaging developments, as well as examples of constructive conservation. Other newspapers, too, sensed a quickly ripening issue. The *Sunday Times*, for example, began campaigns in August 1984 to safeguard ancient woodlands and to control the use of pesticides.

The conservation agencies also felt emboldened to take a more public and sceptical stance towards government policies. In June 1984, the Countryside Commission issued a revised policy statement on *Agricultural Landscapes*, following consultants' reports demonstrating the marginal effect on the general deterioration of the farmed landscape of the Commission's efforts during the previous ten years. Sir Derek Barber, the Commission's chairman, acknowledged that 'in a number of English counties, particularly in eastern England and the Midlands, the landscape is now only a shadow of its former character and beauty'. The statement shifted the emphasis of the

Commission's policy in the lowlands from the development of new landscapes, towards the management and protection of those features which remained. Despite this apparent admission of failure, the Commission continued to express its firm commitment to the voluntary approach of the 1981 Act, whilst urging that, to be given the chance to succeed, agricultural policy would have to be amended to discriminate in favour of activities which benefit the environment and against those which are detrimental. Sir Derek followed this up in September by calling upon the government to publish a White Paper on the 'Management of the Rural Estate', with a new priority for the countryside and 'sensitive revision of policies for agricultural support so that they favour, rather than thwart, conservation'.

The NCC was more forthright. Its report, *Nature Conservation in Great Britain* (26 June 1984), detailed 'the overwhelmingly adverse impact of modern agriculture on wildlife and its habitat in Britain'. Speaking at the launch of the report and its accompanying strategy, William Wilkinson commented forcibly, 'Conservationists are regularly pressed to compromise. The answer in most cases must be no. As the review shows, there is little left with which to compromise. The salami-slicer has been at work too long.' Then with remarks clearly addressed to the Secretary of State for the Environment, Patrick Jenkin, who was present at the launch, and his Cabinet colleagues, Wilkinson urged that 'nature conservation needs a higher place in national priorities and a stronger claim on the nation's resources'. It was characteristic of the government's ambivalence that Jenkin, while welcoming the NCC's new strategy, asserted that '*A miniscule part* of the sums of money that go to the support of agriculture and forestry diverted to the ends of conservation would work wonders' (emphasis added). However feebly, this response did at least concede in principle the major point on which there was agreement across the whole conservation movement, from the Countryside Commission to FoE — that part at least of the agricultural budget should be redirected to support conservation-oriented husbandry.

An inquiry by a House of Lords select committee into draft regulations from the European Commission on

improving the efficiency of agricultural structures provided an unexpected platform for conservationists to
publicise their arguments for reform of agricultural policy.
The draft regulations did little but tinker with the existing
framework for agricultural grants, even though the EEC's
Third Action Programme on the Environment, agreed by
the Council of Ministers in 1982, stated the need to

Promote the creation of an overall strategy making environmental policy a part of economic and social development,
[resulting] in a greater awareness of the environmental
dimension, notably in the field of agriculture [and]
Enhance the positive and reduce the negative effects on the
environment of agriculture.

Some 24 conservation organisations presented written
evidence to the Lords select committee on the environmental costs of agricultural policy, and throughout the
winter and spring of 1983/84 a string of conservation
witnesses, representing both the official agencies and the
voluntary bodies, paraded their arguments before it.

With unprecedented unanimity the Countryside Commission, NCC, RSPB, CPRE, the Council for National
Parks and others argued the case for drastic changes in
agricultural support, away from maximising production
and towards the integration of food production with wildlife and landscape conservation. In response, MAFF's civil
servants emphasised the regard they already showed
environmental considerations, but they stuck firmly to the
traditional MAFF line that environmental benefits must
always be incidental to the central purpose of agricultural
aid — namely, farming 'efficiency'. They claimed that this
was also the correct legal interpretation of the Treaty of
Rome. Brian Peart, Under-Secretary at MAFF, argued that
unless government schemes for agriculture and for
environmental improvement were kept separate, 'you are
in danger of having confused objectives and . . . expensive
administration'. DoE officials echoed the same sentiments.

In the event, the select committee accepted neither of
these points in its final report published in July. Legal
opinion sought by the CPRE was that 'it would be proper
. . . if it were regarded as desirable . . . to require that
agricultural and environmental considerations be taken

together in the assessment of eligibility' for farm support under the Treaty of Rome (see Chapter 11). The select committee agreed that MAFF and the DoE adopted 'an unnecessarily narrow attitude to the Treaty of Rome'. Contrary to their representations, the committee proposed that 'care of the environment should have comparable status with the production of food' in the promotion of farming improvement. Far from endorsing a sharp demarcation between environmental and agricultural policy, the select committee called for 'the revision of existing priorities and greater coordination and cooperation' between MAFF and the DoE. 'In the past', it complained, 'the DoE have been largely subordinate to MAFF, and have not been active enough in promoting care for the environment.' The DoE was urged 'to revise their role in relation to agriculture generally', and MAFF was berated for being 'backward-looking' and too 'production-oriented'. Both departments were roundly upbraided for being insufficiently responsive to the strength of public opinion on the countryside. An equally critical report on agricultural research and the environment was published by the House of Lords science and technology committee in the same month (see Chapter 3).

Such swingeing reports indicated the extent to which conservation groups had captured the high ground in the conflict with the farming lobby. When the House of Lords debated the reports on 23 July 1984, Lord Belstead, the Minister of State for MAFF, announced that the government had decided to seek a completely new title in the EEC structures regulation 'conveying powers which would enable us in environmentally sensitive areas to encourage farming practices which are consonant with conservation'. He claimed that this would 'herald a totally new policy for balancing agricultural and conservation objectives'. However, conservationists noted that the proposed amendment would only extend the principle to 4 per cent of the land area of the UK, at the most. And they were uncertain whether it heralded a genuine conversion or (as seemed more likely) was a typical MAFF ploy designed to enable it to shelter behind the failure of the EEC to reach unanimity on the amendment, for Belstead had emphatically rejected the committee's view that the British government should take the lead rather than waiting for Europe.

The different responses of the NFU and the CLA to this development are instructive, and highlight the different styles of the two organisations described in Chapter 4. The NFU briefing for the Lords debate warned that 'British producers must not be placed at a competitive disadvantage *vis-à-vis* their continental counterparts', and concluded: 'Although there is scope for taking more account of environmental objectives in the regulations, the encouragement of a thriving agriculture must remain paramount.' In October, the NFU issued its *New Directions for Agricultural Policy* which gave priority to ensuring the financial position of the industry, while calling for 'new integrated policies ... to cover the whole complex of farming, rural development and environmental needs' in the uplands and, more generally, for encouragement to farmers 'to take proper account of environmental needs'.

In contrast, on the eve of the Lords debate, the CLA joined with the CPRE for the first time in calling for 'changes in policy which would help end the unfortunate and damaging conflicts over the effect of modern agricultural practices on the countryside'. The joint statement continued:

> we are determined to work urgently together to obtain adjustments to agricultural support policies, which will establish a better balance between efficient agriculture, private landownership and the public interest in conservation and enjoyment of the countryside.

The CLA then set up a working party to formulate policies for integrating agriculture and conservation. As its report made clear when published in September, the rationale was to ensure that the money being lost to farming was not lost to the countryside. The CLA's report went much further than the NFU's in recognising the desirability of redirecting public funds where they were most needed in both social and environmental terms, and in accepting the case for planning controls over farm buildings and roads. Once more the CLA had staked its claim for constructive leadership of the agricultural lobby.

A sense that conservationists might be on the threshold of an important victory was sharpened by other events. The imposition by the Secretary of State for the Environment of an Article 4 Directive to prevent the drainage of one of the holdings on the Halvergate Marshes (see Chapter 11) was a body-blow to the argument that planning controls were totally inappropriate in regulating agricultural development. The Secretary of State's decision in this case seemed to signal a new assertiveness on the part of the DoE in its dealings with the agriculture departments. Against this had to be set the fact that, although Patrick Jenkin insisted on referring to a Cabinet committee the decision of the Secretary of State for Scotland to favour the private forestry scheme on Creag Meagaidh SSSI despite the NCC's strenuous objections, the result was a shoddy compromise by which grant would be paid to Fountain Forestry for afforesting half the proposed area. The summer and autumn of 1984 were punctuated by these and other unusual developments which seemed to signal the government's difficulty in adapting to the sea-change that was taking place in the relationship between agriculture and conservation.

THE CONTINUING STRUGGLE

Though ministers were committed to closing the glaring loopholes in the Wildlife and Countryside Act, no mention of conservation of the environment was made in the Queen's Speech which opened the 1984/85 parliamentary session. The government continued to drag its feet on this matter, pleading lack of parliamentary time. It seemed also that there was some reluctance to introduce a modest amending Bill for fear of giving MPs and conservation groups an opportunity to press for more wide-ranging reforms. In the event, a Wildlife and Countryside Amendment Bill was introduced by Dr David Clark, the Labour spokesman on the environment. Dr Clark had consulted widely, and the measure enjoyed the support of the NFU, CLA, the Ramblers' Association, CPRE, the Council for National Parks, FoE, RSPB and the Royal Society for

Nature Conservation. The Bill, which had its second reading on 8 February 1985, would close the three months' loophole and would extend from three months to four the period of notification for potentially damaging operations in SSSIs. A few other specific amendments were also included, the most far-reaching being to place an additional duty on agriculture ministers and the Forestry Commission to further conservation. The government, while anxious to see the three months' loophole closed, did not support the latter measure and, therefore, there was some uncertainty whether sufficient parliamentary time would be made available to ensure the Bill's passage. However, to sink or emasculate it would undoubtedly cause the government much political embarrassment; and the government's position, that minor adjustments to the legislation were all that was needed, was, in any case, being overtaken by other events.

A few days before Dr Clark introduced his Bill, the House of Commons select committee on the environment reported on its investigations of the operation and effectiveness of the Wildlife and Countryside Act. Throughout the autumn the committee had received a stream of evidence from agricultural and conservation interests. In its report, the committee welcomed what it perceived as 'a new mood' amongst farmers and their representatives, and reasoned that, with appropriate amendments to the Act and to agricultural policy, which went well beyond the necessarily limited measures of Clark's Bill, the voluntary approach could prove effective. These included the extension of prior notification for farm grants to the whole countryside, backed up by a change in MAFF rules to allow grants to be refused for operations notified retrospectively; provision to be made for national park authorities to be able to apply for landscape conservation orders analogous to nature conservation orders; greatly increased priority for conservation in the training and work of ADAS staff; and greater recourse to, and more resources for, the negotiated purchase of threatened sites as an alternative to compensatory management agreements. The committee prefaced these and other recommendations with the following warning:

Our underlying concern is that, even if the changes we recommend are made to the Act and its administration, the wider agricultural structure will fuel the 'engine of destruction'. . . . Without fundamental changes in the structure of agricultural finance, conservation will continue to be set in weak opposition to the forces of intensive and, paradoxically, frequently unwanted production, instead of being an integral part of good husbandry, as it should be. MAFF must reappraise its attitudes.

With pressure continuing to mount for a major review of agricultural policy, the publication of this report and the Amendment Bill placed the ball firmly back into the government's court. In the event their response on both counts was to prove overwhelmingly defensive. David Clark's bill suffered a depressing, if predictable, fate: emasculated in Committee, only the clauses extending Maps in National Parks and closing the Section 28 and 29 'loopholes' survived in recognisable form and further evidence of the government's apparent determination to 'dig in' was provided by the tone of the *Reply to First Report from the Environment Committee*, published in May 1985. This was given White Paper status and its emphasis was predominantly on consolidation. Thus, whilst it welcomed the Committee's endorsement of the Act and their support for its voluntary philosophy; welcomed the new mood abroad in the land, manifested, for instance, in the work of the Farming and Wildlife Advisory Groups; pointed to new initiatives such as the Countryside Commission/MAFF experimental scheme for the Broads (see Chapter 11) and welcomed the possibilities opened up by the newly agreed EC Agricultural Structures Regulation, it generally rebuffed the Committee's recommendations emphasising the extent to which MAFF already sees conservation objectives as a major part of its overall responsibilities.

In response to the specific recommendation that the government should urgently undertake a review of the whole use of the rural estate and produce a White Paper the government cited its response to the Countryside Commission's report *A Better Future for the Uplands* (see Chapter 13) and the new Broads scheme as evidence that conflicts between departmental policies could be resolved using existing machinery and blandly commented that it would continue to respond appropriately to other current issues of public debate affecting agriculture and the rural environment.

Meanwhile pressure was sustained by a critical National Audit Office report on the CAP presented to Parliament in August 1985 by the Comptroller and Auditor General. Sir Gordon Downey criticised the EEC bureaucracy for its failure to make any regular assessment of the CAP's consequences, pointing in particular to its vague aims and heavy costs. His strictures were succeeded, in the following month, by the 17th report of the House of Lords European Committee on reform of the CAP which warned that if the CAP were left unreformed 'the existence of the EEC itself would be put in jeopardy'.

FURTHER READING

There has been considerable comment on the workings of the Wildlife and Countryside Act. The most thorough assessment of the implications for habitat protection is W.M. Adams, *Implementing the Act* (British Association of Nature Conservationists and World Wildlife Fund, 1984); while controversies surrounding the implementation of the Act can be found in his *Conservation and Agriculture: The Debate 1981–1984* (Packard, 1985). A special issue of *Ecos* (Vol. 6, No. 1, Winter 1985) was devoted to a review of the failings and achievements of the Act. The House of Commons select committee on the environment investigated the workings of the Act in the autumn of 1984 and its report and minutes of evidence are an unequalled source of comment and information; see *Operation and Effectiveness of Part II of the Wildlife and Countryside Act* (HMSO, 1985).

Section 3
Case Studies in Conflict and Compromise

Case Studies: Foreword

During 1982 and 1983 the focus of debate and controversy over the conflict between agriculture and conservation moved from the national level to a series of local issues involving the new machinery of the Act. The most prominent of these issues — Exmoor, the Berwyns, West Sedgemoor and Halvergate — are covered in chronological sequence in the following four chapters. They presented successively bigger challenges to the Act's procedures for rural conservation. Each assumed national significance as the national lobbies seized upon them as test-cases for the Act, and sought thereby to establish or resist the creation of important precedents.

With most legislation, the period after the parliamentary phase, like that before, is more important in determining the extent and nature of what has been enacted. This is partly because much legislation is enabling rather than mandatory, and allows considerable discretion to ministers, civil servants and statutory bodies but also, importantly, because the implementation requires new administrative procedures to be worked out. In the process, those closely involved may seek substantially to enlarge or diminish the spirit of the legislation.

Each of the cases chronicled here established precedents for the implementation of the Act, progressively straining its mechanisms and policy premises. Exmoor was effectively the starting point for the new Act, the place where previous countryside policies had come to grief and where the principles and procedures later embodied in Part II of the Act were forged. With Halvergate, the cycle from policy breakdown to legislative reform to policy breakdown appeared to be coming full circle. Certainly by 1983, the controversy over the drainage and ploughing up of the Halvergate Marshes seemed set to assume the position that moorland reclamation on Exmoor occupied during the 1970s — namely, the quagmire in which official conservation policies and procedures got bogged down. Just as Exmoor had been the place where a series of *ad hoc* responses to a succession of crises eventually established a major new policy departure, so in relation to Halvergate ministers have been forced to fly by the seat of their pants in an effort to salvage the Act, and in the process have made decisions with potentially major policy implications.

The case studies draw on personal experience, extensive interviews and discussions with those closely involved and the statements and records of relevant organisations. There is, therefore, no general literature closely related to the issues covered in these chapters.

8. Moorland Preservation in Exmoor

The controversy over the reclamation of moorland in Exmoor has raged with varying degrees of intensity for more than 20 years. Its landscape has acquired a symbolic significance because all parties to the conflict have seen Exmoor as creating (or threatening) precedents that could be applied in other parts of the country where the interests of landowners or farmers are in conflict with those of others. Indeed, the compensation terms negotiated by the NFU and CLA with the Exmoor national park committee in 1981 proved to be the blueprint for the national guidelines on management agreements issued by the Department of the Environment two years later.

THE DISAPPEARING MOORLAND

It was inevitable, given the conditions in Exmoor, that it would become the scene of a conflict between those for whom the national park purposes of conserving natural beauty and promoting recreation were primary, and those for whom the moorland was an agricultural resource, a source of livelihood, of profit or of capital gain.

With Dartmoor, whose moorland is more than twice as extensive, Exmoor forms one of only two large areas of more or less wild, open country in southern England. It is

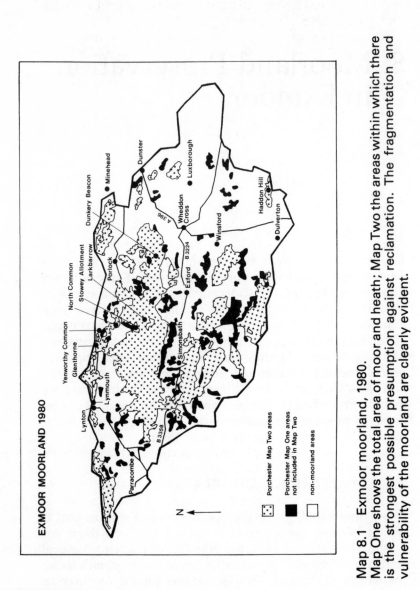

Map 8.1   Exmoor moorland, 1980.
Map One shows the total area of moor and heath; Map Two the areas within which there is the strongest possible presumption against reclamation. The fragmentation and vulnerability of the moorland are clearly evident.

a precious but fragile resource. When the national park was designated in 1954 the moorland was about a third of the park's area. Today it is about a quarter, and is so fragmented (as can be seen from Map 8.1) that any further encroachment of reclaimed pasture, however small, may destroy the sense of limitless space that is already largely a visual illusion. The Nature Conservancy Council has argued consistently since 1977 that there should be no further significant reduction or fragmentation of the remaining areas of moorland if viable wildlife populations are to be maintained.

The mild climate, the lowish altitudes, the flattish tops of the moorland plateau, some relatively good soils and the lowest rainfall of the western national parks provide favourable conditions for reclamation — indeed, so favourable that when hill farming subsidies were introduced in 1949 strong pressure had to be exerted by the NFU to persuade the Ministry of Agriculture to include the Exmoor upland within the hill-line. Conflict arose in the 1960s because modern technology gave a new impetus to reclamation at the time when the rapidly shrinking remnants of the moor had been recognised as a wildlife, scenic and recreational resource of national significance. The introduction of tractors followed by new techniques for converting moorland to agricultural land led to the reversion of the steeper slopes to bracken, gorse and scrub, and encouraged the cultivation of the flatter tops. But the tops constitute the moorland plateau that is the heart of the national park — Exmoor's main open space. The Ministry of Agriculture encouraged reclamation and new technology through ADAS, and offered both capital grants of 50 per cent or more for reclamation or other improvements and headage payments on the additional stock that could be carried on the improved land.

When it was proposed in 1962 to reclaim 90 ha. of heather moorland at Countisbury on the coastal ridge where the moor stands 1000 feet above the Bristol Channel, the three national park committees (from 1954 to 1974 Exmoor was administered by two national park committees of the Devon and Somerset County Councils with a joint advisory committee) were alarmed to discover that they were without the financial resources or powers to deal with the proposal. At that time there was no notification system and the NFU denied that there was any serious threat to the moorland.

In an attempt to establish the facts, the Exmoor Society commissioned a scientific study of land-use and vegetation from Geoffrey Sinclair, who had surveyed the area for the second Land Utilisation Survey of Great Britain. His map and his report, *Can Exmoor Survive?*, showed that the moorland had shrunk from 23,800 ha. in 1957/58 to 20,100 ha. in 1966, mainly through agricultural reclamation. By contrast, the NFU and CLA estimated the loss of moorland to agriculture at less than 40 ha. per annum. But officials of MAFF and the Devon and Somerset county councils accepted Sinclair's figures as being accurate to within 3 per cent.

In 1969, on the basis of the survey, officers of the national park committees prepared a map of the areas of moorland 'critical to amenity' extending to 17,700 ha. The NFU and CLA refused to recognise the map as a definition of areas in which there should be any presumption against reclamation and thereby delayed its publication until 1974. In a document entitled *The Reclamation of Exmoor* (1966), they asserted that 'where conflicts of interest do arise, agriculture should be accorded first place in the order of priorities'. It was the right and the duty of farmers, they said, 'to expand their enterprises and to improve their productive capacity to a maximum'.

The first phase of the conflict ended with the passage of the Countryside Act 1968. The NFU and CLA lobbied successfully to persuade the government to ignore the requests from the Exmoor national park committees, the Devon and Somerset county councils and the Exmoor Society for powers and resources to control the moorland. At the last moment the government introduced two new clauses which empowered the Secretary of State for Housing and Local Government (later for the Environment) to make orders requiring farmers to give six months' notice of their intention to convert moor or heath to agricultural land. Lord Kennet, the minister responsible, argued that if it proved to be impossible to negotiate an agreement before the six months' notice had expired, the county councils could make compulsory purchase orders (CPOs) or access orders. But he resisted an amendment moved by Lord Foot to make it unequivocally clear that CPOs would in fact be available if negotiations failed. Lord Kennet objected on 20 May 1968 that 'this would not be accepted by the other side of the deal, by the landowning and farming interests, without a good deal of bad blood and sourness'. Thirteen years later, on 16 March 1981, Lord Kennet had the good grace to tell the House of Lords that the 1968 Act had not worked, and was 'an error of judgement on our part'.

To avoid compulsory notification under the new Act, the NFU and CLA proposed a 'gentleman's agreement' under which they would advise their members to notify the national park committees of their intention to reclaim moorland within a revised critical amenity area. The Ministry of Agriculture also agreed to advise farmers that they should notify the committees voluntarily. No funds were provided to smooth the path to agreement. The national park committees struck a bargain on these terms and no blanket Section 14 orders requiring notification of moorland conversion were ever made. As a device to control reclamation, the voluntary notification system was a complete failure. Nineteen proposals were notified between 1969 and 1973, but notification did not lead to a single agreement. MAFF interpreted in the most narrow and formal way its obligation under the 1968 Act to 'have regard to the desirability of conserving the natural beauty and amenity of the countryside'. It treated all applications as confidential and argued that it was statutorily obliged to pay grant for any proposal that satisfied agricultural criteria. MAFF never advised a farmer against reclamation on grounds of amenity or conservation, nor was it ever asked by the national park committee to withhold grant.

In 1974 a new Exmoor national park authority was created as a single committee of the Somerset county council. It assumed responsibility for the whole park and was equipped with new resources of money and staff. But the new committee was strongly imbued with the philosophy that it wanted no more powers; indeed, Lord Porchester later pointed out that it would probably not use them even if they were available. In 1976 the committee commissioned a report on moorland management from

John Phillips, an expert on heather management. He urged the long-term desirability of retaining low-input/low-output farming systems, and strongly urged the committee to identify those areas of high-quality moorland which should not be enclosed or reclaimed under any circumstances. He concluded, 'unless strong and constructive steps are taken along these lines, Exmoor as it is today will go on being eroded, until one day people will wake up to the fact that it has disappeared except as a name on the map'. The Phillips Report was withheld from the committee until discussions on the draft national park plan had been concluded. The plan's policies for agriculture, finally adopted in 1977, gave first priority to maintaining and strengthening liaison with farming and landowning interests. It relied on voluntary management agreements and, as a secondary course, on land acquisition by agreement to protect the critical amenity area.

The suppression of the report, and attempts to censure Malcolm MacEwen, a ministerially-appointed member of the committee, for publishing its 'confidential' conclusions, coincided with six months' notice being given to the committee of proposals to reclaim two very sensitive areas of moorland. The first was made by Ben Halliday, the vice-chairman and an appointed member of the committee, until his resignation in 1977. His Glenthorne Estate (Map 8.1) lies on the coastal ridge between the Oare valley and the Bristol Channel, sloping precipitately for 1000 ft from the last remaining strip of heather moorland to the sea. Halliday proposed a comprehensive management agreement to embrace farming, woodland, nature conservation and public access, but insisted on reclaiming moorland, although stating that his initial proposal to reclaim the entire 101 ha. of moorland on Yenworthy Common and North Common (Map 8.1) was negotiable. The second proposal, by one of Halliday's neighbours, was to reclaim 121 of 142 ha. on Stowey Allotment, in the heart of Exmoor, which the park committee had bid for unsuccessfully at auction in the hope of protecting it.

THE PORCHESTER INQUIRY

When five months had passed without Stowey Allotment even being discussed by the committee, Sir John Cripps, the chairman of the Countryside Commission, asked the committee to take no decision on either proposal until a joint site meeting had been arranged. This and other requests from the Commission were rebuffed by the committee, which eventually agreed by a very large majority to make no objection to the reclamation of the whole of Stowey Allotment, and approved in principle the reclamation of a substantial area of moorland in the Glenthorne Estate.

In May 1977 the Countryside Commission submitted an adverse report on the committee's handling of these matters to the Secretary of State for the Environment. But already the nationwide publicity had persuaded the Conservative leader of Somerset County Council to ask the Secretary of State to intervene. This led in April to the appointment, jointly by the Secretary of State for the Environment and the Minister of Agriculture, of Lord Porchester to study 'land use in Exmoor'.

The fact that Lord Porchester was a landowner and a former chairman of the County Councils' Association added greatly to the force of his conclusions. First of all he established the facts. Relying on studies by MAFF, he found that 64 per cent of the hill land within the critical amenity area was physically improvable. After excluding land in public or National Trust ownership or subject to common rights, he arrived at a figure of 5200 ha. theoretically at risk. Using aerial surveys dating from 1947, Porchester found that the area of moorland (which in 1947 was just under 23,900 ha.) had been reduced to 19,000 ha. in 1976. Four-fifths of this loss had been to agricultural conversion — an average of 128 ha. a year. These findings substantially vindicated Sinclair's earlier survey.

Porchester concluded that the moorland was fragile and that serious inroads had been made into it by a sequence of operations by individual farmers, each of which could be defended on agricultural grounds. In their evidence to him representatives of the farming and landowning interests had accepted the principle of restricting certain farming activities on the moorland if the price paid was sufficient. Porchester, therefore, recommended giving statutory force to the notification system and giving the national park committee the power to make moorland conservation orders binding in perpetuity. In addition, he proposed that farmers should be able to enter into conservation agreements, by which they would be paid annual sums for any management operations required to conserve the character of the moor.

The Report advised the park committee to define those moorland areas of exceptional value that should be made, for all time, as safe from reclamation as the uncertainties of both human and natural affairs might allow. It advocated a 'virtually rigid regime of conservation' for the heartland of Exmoor and for other areas of exceptional value, including the coastal heaths. Outside these areas some improvement was allowable without harm to the characteristic scenery; but even these areas, Porchester warned, were not expendable.

This analysis led Lord Porchester to recommend the preparation of two maps (see Map 8.1) to replace the critical amenity area map. Map 1 would identify the total area of heath and moorland; Map 2 would define 'those particular tracts of land whose traditional *appearance* the national park authority would want to see conserved, so far as possible for all time', and within which there would be the 'strongest possible presumption against agricultural conversion' (emphasis added). The 'exceptional values' that Lord Porchester wished to conserve appeared to be largely, if not exclusively, scenic.

Perhaps the most valuable contribution made by Porchester at the national level was to be found in his criticism of the Ministry of Agriculture's handling of conservation. He urged that 'the Ministry should recognise and support the policy of conservation . . . and feel obliged to withhold grant for the reclamation of *any* moorland shown on Map 2' (emphasis added), pointing out that any resulting loss in meat production would be negligible (0.003 per cent of UK lamb and 0.0005 per cent of UK beef production).

The NFU had insisted that 'fair compensation' for forgoing moorland reclamation must take the form of an annual sum equivalent to the loss of potential profit from reclamation, to be renegotiated periodically to take account of inflation. But Porchester objected that this basis would neither protect the moorland 'for ever', nor be 'fair' to the paying authority, which would come to the negotiating table armed with nothing but its powers of persuasion and the offer of an agreement or purchase. For these and other reasons he advised that the ground-rules for compensation be statutory and that, for the permanent loss of the right to reclaim, it should be a once-and-for-all payment equal to the depreciation in the capital value of the asset, which had been the statutory basis for compensation for compulsory purchase of land for nearly a century and a half.

The national park committee endorsed Porchester's recommendations on 6 December 1977 — albeit with reservations about compensation; the voting was 19 to 0, with one abstention. The reason for this remarkable *volte-face* is not hard to find. The Labour government had already indicated that it was embarking on speedy consultations with a view to early legislation. The chief executive of Somerset county council advised the committee that if it did not accept the main recommendation to introduce moorland conservation orders, either the government would reorganise the committee as an autonomous board or it would take these matters out of the hands of the committee altogether and entrust them to the Countryside Commission. Nevertheless, the committee's split personality was revealed by its decision at the same meeting to approve by 11 to 5 the Glenthorne management agreement, which provided for the reclamation of 40 ha. of moorland on the coastal ridge at East Yenworthy Common that Porchester had identified as part of the area to be rigorously protected.

The outcome of the Porchester Report was settled in May 1979 by the election of a Conservative government closely identified with farming and landowning interests. The NFU, and its leaders in Exmoor in particular, had objected vehemently both to moorland conservation orders and to the once-and-for-all compensation payments recommended by Porchester which the Labour government had accepted, in spite of a hostile motion adopted by the NFU annual general meeting in 1978. Faced with NFU opposition and the new government's refusal to consider any controls over land management, the Exmoor national park committee beat a retreat. In November 1979, while recording in its minutes the 'brute fact' that the government's proposals left it powerless to prevent the destruction of areas of natural beauty, it agreed not to press 'at this juncture' for powers to make moorland conservation orders. But the fact that two far- mers had recently reclaimed 27 ha. of moorland without the committee's consent persuaded it to make a last attempt to secure some powers. In February 1980 the com- mittee voted unanimously for a resolution urging the gov- ernment to include in the Wildlife and Countryside Bill a reserve power, to be activated by ministers, that would enable the park authority to make moorland conservation orders should the need arise. The government rejected even this modest request. An all-party amendment to the Bill, although supported by the Conservative-controlled Association of County Councils, was defeated in the House of Lords on 16 March 1981 by 97 to 91.

Work went ahead on other aspects of the Porchester Report. Map 1 had been completed in 1979. It found the total area of moor and heath to be 19,600 ha., or 28 per cent of the area of the national park, of which about 1900 ha. were intermediate or fragmented areas where semi- natural vegetation was less dominant. Map 2, as finally agreed at the end of 1980, included 16,000 ha. or about 82 per cent of the total area of moor and heath shown on Map 1 (Figure 8.1). Although Map 2 was based entirely on scenic criteria, the NCC and the voluntary conservation bodies argued that over 90 per cent of it was of exceptional value for nature conservation as well. But the committee rejected the NCC's request that 1400 ha. should be added to the map on the ground that moorland and woodland were a single ecosystem, and that the integrity of all the remaining blocks where semi-natural vegetation was dominant should be protected. In 1984, the NCC prepared a separate map of areas of nature conservation value, but the fundamental inconsistencies remained. One part of the semi-natural vegetation — the moorland — enjoys a special status (including a unique commitment by central government to provide 90 per cent of the finance for its conservation) whereas other parts — the woodlands, coast and riverine systems — do not.

The policies adopted on 4 November 1980 for Maps 1 and 2 (and later incorporated in the revised national park plan) contrast sharply with the flabby statements incorporated in 1977 in the original national park plan. The new policies embody 'the strongest possible presumption in favour of the conservation of natural flora, fauna and landscape . . . the strongest possible resumption in favour of traditional rough grazing compatible with conservation' and 'support, financial and otherwise, for management schemes that conserve natural flora, fauna and landscape features'. Proposals to reclaim moor and heath on Map 1 but not on Map 2 were to be considered on their merits, but the exclusion of areas from Map 2 'does not mean that they are expendable'. Even so, Porchester's recommendation that reclamation grants be withheld in Map 2 was ignored by the government, although it has been revived in the Countryside Commission's 1984 report, *A Better Future for the Uplands*.

The Porchester Report also led to the introduction of a systematic, business-like, and ultimately public, procedure for dealing with reclamation proposals under the voluntary system. It dealt a death-blow to MAFF's traditional stance that the confidentiality of grant applications precluded publicity for reclamation proposals and any discussion of them between MAFF and the committee. From 1978, the committee received formal assessments of reclamation proposals from MAFF, the NCC, the Countryside Commission and the national park officer. The NFU encouraged its members to notify all proposals voluntarily and agreed to the extension of notification from the critical amenity area to the more extensive area of Map 1. Moreover, it extended the voluntary period of notice from 6 to 12 months. The Wildlife and Countryside Act later amended Section 14 of the Countryside Act 1968 to give the minister a reserve power to impose a compulsory 12-months' notification period — although ministers have said they do not intend to activate this power unless some emergency arises.

The Conservative government made it clear from the outset that it rejected moorland conservation orders, planning controls or any other form of compulsion to back up conservation policies. But when this position came under severe pressure during the passage of the Wildlife and Countryside Bill, and the government had to devise some machinery for making its 'voluntary approach' work, it turned to the Exmoor 'voluntary system' and transformed it into a statutory system. Under Sections 32 and 41 of the Act, if the Minister of Agriculture withholds grant in response to objections by the conservation authorities in national parks or SSSIs, the latter must offer the farmer a management agreement. This must restrain the proposed operation, and pay compensation under Section 50 in accordance with guidelines issued in 1983 by the Secretary of State for the Environment and the Minister of Agriculture, and based on those agreed two years earlier between the NFU, the CLA and the Exmoor National Park Committee.

MANAGEMENT AGREEMENTS

The Exmoor guidelines incorporated the NFU/CLA principle, referred to earlier, that farmers should be entitled to compensation by annual payments equal to the profit (including loss of grant) the farmer has forgone. Although the guidelines allow farmers to claim lump-sums, in every case so far they have preferred to take the annuities offered for 20-year agreements for the very good reason that the annuity varies every year in line with an index of profitability for Exmoor hill farms prepared by the agricultural economics department of Exeter University. The 'standard sum' has fluctuated violently, rising from a low initial figure of £23.66/ha. in 1979 to £90.52/ha. in 1981, and falling to £62.90/ha. in 1982. In the long run it can be expected to keep pace with inflation and with farm profits. There are variations in the standard sum to reflect the degree of restraint imposed by the agreement. The farmer who believes that his rate of profit exceeds the standard sum can claim whatever rate he can substantiate from his books; but the farmer whose rate of profit is below the standard can claim compensation at the standard rate. Either way, the farmer cannot lose.

Although the national guidelines issued under the Wildlife and Countryside Act endorse the idea of determining standard sums, none is specified — for the simple reason that standard compensation sums can only be worked out locally, and in areas with relatively uniform conditions. Very few authorities seem likely to offer standard sums. The Broads Authority, for instance, found that no credible standard could be devised in the Halvergate Marshes (see Chapter 11), though one has been agreed for the Berwyn (see Chapter 9).

But the standard sum is only one of three keys to the success achieved by the Exmoor system. It guarantees compensation that will probably exceed the profit that farmers would have made, and it eliminates most of the costly negotiations. Another key to the success of the Exmoor system is the government's decision to pay 90 per cent grant towards a special moorland conservation fund in Exmoor. This compares with 75 per cent grants in other national parks, which have no such special fund, and for other purposes, and with 50 per cent grants for local authorities entering into management agreements elsewhere. The sum specifically earmarked for management agreements by the DoE and the Countryside Commission for 1983/84 was only £300,000, all of it apparently for national parks.

A third factor that has to be borne in mind when assessing the success of the Exmoor system is that the Exmoor farmers have been on the receiving-end of complaints and protests by conservation and recreation interests for 20 years. This movement led to the Porchester Inquiry and to legislative proposals in one Bill and three Acts of Parliament, all in a period of 13 years. Ministers in the present government have stated plainly that the present voluntary arrangement is the last chance that Exmoor farmers are likely to have of averting planning controls or conservation orders. This continuous pressure has undoubtedly persuaded most Exmoor farmers that it is very much in their interest to make the voluntary system work. In the North York Moors National Park, where there have been no comparable pressures (although the scale of the problem is the same), five of the first seven farmers who were offered management agreements after the Wildlife and Countryside Act was passed rejected them, and went ahead with reclamation without grant. On Exmoor, in contrast, agreements have been concluded; others are under negotiation; and not one farmer has gone ahead with reclamation in defiance of the national park committee's wishes since 1979.

The Porchester Report can now be seen as marking a clear watershed. The process of moorland conservation or destruction has virtually been halted. Only 88 ha. have been 'improved' since 1979, all of them outside Map 2, and all with the approval of the national park committee. By September 1984 nine agreements had been signed, under which compensation would be paid to protect 692 ha. of moorland for 20 years. A further 1056 ha. have been permanently protected by purchase, and 101 ha. by purchase and resale subject to a permanent restrictive covenant. In all, just over a third of the area that Lord Porchester found to be 'theoretically at risk' has been protected — although it should be added that Porchester underestimated this area by excluding common land (which can be de-registered) and steeply sloping land (which can be reclaimed by modern techniques, such as aerial spraying). Increasing knowledge of the effects of moorland management techniques on soils, vegetation and wildlife has made it possible progressively to introduce more precise clauses into the agreements to regulate stocking rates and periods, locations for winter feeding, cutting and burning regimes and (where permitted) the use of fertilisers. The agreements have also secured or enhanced public access.

The success in the short term of management agreements in Exmoor should blind nobody to the inherent drawbacks of the system. In a paper given to the Agricultural Economics Society in March 1983, the national park officer warned that 'trivial and spurious claims' might abuse the goodwill on which the entire scheme depends. Every farmer in Exmoor now knows that the Ministry of Agriculture is very unlikely to pay grant for reclaiming any substantial area of moorland. But, as the national park officer also said, the government guidelines and notification procedures 'make it well-nigh impossible to question the wisdom, or indeed the financial soundness, of a farmer's schemes for improvement'.

We question whether any proposals now to reclaim moorland within Map 2 are seriously intended to lead to reclamation; they are clearly devices to obtain the yearly compensation cheque. MAFF officials have pointed out in

their appraisals that some farmers who are claiming compensation have neglected the possibility of raising the
productivity of their existing inbye fields — to do so
would, of course, entail continuous work as well as an
element of risk.

Other major drawbacks are the limited protection
afforded by 20-year agreements, and the open-ended
nature of the financial commitment. The ultimate cost is
unpredictable, and at the end of 20 years the authority
may have to face the fact that the money it has spent will
have been wasted unless it agrees to pay a lump-sum,
should one be demanded, or to enter into further commitments. Should the farmer decide not to renew the agreement the authority has no power under existing legislation
to prevent reclamation. Significantly, land purchase has
proved to be the more important for moorland conservation — it is more effective and, in the long run, cheaper.
The cost of the first eight agreements concluded in Exmoor
was £45,000 in 1983/84, to which should be added the
substantial administrative costs of about £9000. But this is
only the beginning. To protect all of Exmoor's privately-
owned moorland and common land by management
agreements would add perhaps £360,000 a year at current
rates. The park committee asked for a budget of £214,000
for management agreements in 1983/84, to allow it to pay
lump-sums in compensation should they be demanded,
to buy land if the opportunity arose, and to build up
the capital reserve which successive purchases had almost exhausted. The government cut the budget back to
£60,000, and told the committee that it should look to the
Countryside Commission's £300,000 fund if it wanted any
more. But the Commission has made it clear that it cannot
guarantee that money will, in fact, be available when it is
needed to buy land or pay lump-sums. The Warren Farm
and Larkbarrow purchases in 1980 and 1982 alone cost
over £1 million.

The growing cost of management agreements over the
years is bound to exert pressure for economies in other
directions out of an already inadequate budget. Two
examples illustrate this problem. In March 1983 the park
committee decided not to accept responsibility for operating Part III of the Wildlife and Countryside Act, which

requires local authorities to keep the public right of way system under 'continuous review'. Although the government asserted, in DoE Circular 1/83, that there would be no need for additional manpower or expenditure, the officers advised the park committee that considerably more resources would be required. The committee resolved to leave the job to the Devon and Somerset county councils, which have neither the staff to do the work nor the familiarity with the national park that the park authority's staff have acquired. Another example of this trend is the park committee's decision that it could only provide £8000 in 1983/84 towards an urgently needed programme — estimated to cost £23,000 annually over 50 years — to rehabilitate the woodlands which the park committee has acquired over the years. Although the committee bought the woodlands to protect them, it has never allocated sufficient resources to ensure their long-term survival. Despairing of an adequate allocation of public funds it is now appealing to private sources to fund its woodland programme.

THE FUTURE

It seems unlikely that the Conservative government's so-called 'voluntary approach' — the key to which is the payment of escalating compensation — will survive a future change of government. None of the opposition parties seems to be attached to the idea of keeping the conservation balloon aloft by the simple expedient of burning money. By extending the Exmoor principles to the national scene the government has raised the cost of conservation to prohibitive heights. In the long run the only sensible solution is to tackle the problem at source: by stopping the flow of public money, in the form of grants, subsidies and tax reliefs, which encourage land 'improvement', monocultural afforestation and the concentration of farms into ever fewer, larger units. As we go to press we learn that the government has withdrawn all grants for land reclamation, whether in national parks or elsewhere, while offering grants to intensify production on grassland and to improve the management of grass and heather moorland. The introduction of a range of incentives designed to promote resource management, and giving the authorities the ultimate power to control land-use and management, would make it possible to remove a major weakness in the Exmoor management agreements. Because the agreements can only be triggered off by proposals to reclaim or to afforest moorland, they are confined to moorland management. But the moorland is only one element in the Exmoor landscape and its ecology. Management agreements or management plans should be designed to conserve the entire resources of a farm or an estate.

This alternative approach is discussed in Section 4. If adopted by government and Parliament it would not, of course, imply the premature termination of any agreements already concluded on Exmoor. They should be honoured, although the elimination of capital grants for land reclamation would inevitably reduce the compensation to be paid under the agreements. It should be possible to secure the goodwill of Exmoor farmers by emphasising the benefits that would accrue to most of them under the new arrangements, and particularly to those on the margin of survival who are threatened with extinction if the support system is not changed. Exmoor farmers have already demonstrated their readiness to accept a mandatory notification system for grant-aided operations. They now recognise that conservation is of major public interest. Their leaders no longer speak, as they did before 1977, of their right and duty to maximise production (at the taxpayer's expense). They have entered into agreements that enable them to practise conservation management. And they now have an intimate relationship with the national park staff as a direct result of the obligation placed on them to notify all grant-aided operations.

In principle, it should not be a very big additional step for farmers to recognise the absurdity of grants for destructive practices being offered on the one hand, and compensation for forgoing the grants on the other. The real problem is that any change in support policy which sharply reduces the profits of the biggest farmers and the value of their land (which has been grossly inflated by the support system) is bound to incur stiff political resistance.

The issue is whether the nation's interest in conserving Exmoor, and the interest of the majority of farmers in survival on reasonable terms, should be frustrated by those who benefit from the *status quo*.

The future of the Exmoor settlement is uncertain. There are signs of uneasiness among the farmers, three of whom — one the chairman of the NFU hill farming committee — rejected the management agreements offered to them at the end of 1983. Proposals made by the Countryside Commission in its *Uplands Report* (March 1984) would, if adopted, re-open the Exmoor settlement. The Commission asks the government to withdraw all capital grants for land improvement and drainage within the area of Porchester's Map 2 and similar areas in the rest of the uplands. It would compensate some farmers by increasing the level of headage payments in these areas, but only where stocking limits were imposed to prevent overgrazing. These proposals would save the Exchequer money and remove a major incentive for reclamation. But they would also reduce the compensation payable under management agreements.

The consequences of such changes are not easy to predict. The farming and landowning interests are sure to resist any withdrawal of grant. But the Commission, while sowing the seeds of another conflict, has rejected all suggestions that the national park authority should be given the power to control reclamation. This could have serious consequences. Even the Prince of Wales, who cannot be suspected of radical tendencies, has strongly affirmed the need for such controls. In launching the UK response to the World Conservation Strategy in 1983 he used words which he repeated in the Duchy of Cornwall's report on the management of its Dartmoor estate: 'it would seem highly desirable, that in protecting the heritage and the environment of the Park, the National Park Authority should be in a sufficiently strong position to have the final say where matters of public concern are involved'. By interfering with the settlement, but without giving the 'final say' to the national park authority, the Countryside Commission could be jeopardising what has been achieved.

9. Afforestation and SSSI Designation of the Berwyn Mountains

The Berwyn range of mountains is one of the least well-known stretches of upland Wales, running from Llanbryn-mair Moors in the south to Bala, Corwen and Llangollen in the north (see Map 9.1). It covers 62,000 ha., including some of the wildest and most inaccessible country in southern Britain. Most of the land is above 450 metres and rises to over 800 metres. Its wildlife importance has long been recognised, and an SSSI of 3900 ha., Moel Sych, was designated for its botanical interest as long ago as 1957. Its landscape value was recognised in the 1947 Hobhouse Report, which identified it as one of a number of potential conservation areas (later to be renamed Areas of Outstanding National Beauty — AONBs). However, in common with most of the upland areas similarly selected by Hobhouse, the Berwyn has not yet acquired AONB status. Nor was it until the late 1970s that moves were made to extend the SSSI to take into account the ornithological, as well as the previously identified botanical, merits of the area.

This dual significance was recognised by Derek Ratcliffe in his national review of nature conservation sites produced for the Nature Conservancy Council in 1977; the botanical interest of Moel Sych is described in some detail but it is also noted as 'one of the few present-day breeding haunts of the golden plover in Wales', and as having

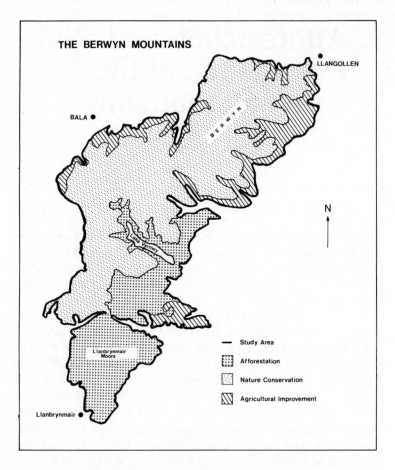

THE BERWYN MOUNTAINS

LLANGOLLEN

BALA

BERWYN

LAKE VYRNWY

N

Llanbrynmair
Moors

Llanbrynmair

— Study Area

Afforestation

Nature Conservation

Agricultural Improvement

Map 9.1   The Berwyn Mountains

'other moorland birds such as the merlin and the ring ouzel'. The wider expanse of the Berwyn is also important for red grouse, raven, peregrine and hen harrier, and Greenland whitefronted geese overwinter on Llanbrynmair. It was the knowledge that the Nature Conservation review would not mention any of the latter species that prompted the Royal Society for the Protection of Birds (RSPB) to embark on a large-scale survey of bird populations throughout upland Wales.

In September 1977 the RSPB presented to the NCC details from the survey of nine upland sites. It is notable that it was a private voluntary organisation that assembled this information even though it is the NCC which has the statutory duty to designate scientifically important sites and to establish the relevant scientific criteria. As will be seen the distinctions between private and public, voluntary and statutory were blurred in the Berwyn case, and informal influence and authority often proved more significant than formal powers. The RSPB study concluded that the retention of these nine sites was 'vital if viable populations of upland birds are to be maintained in upland Wales'. Three of them were to be found in the Berwyn, and were virtually contiguous: North Berwyn, South Berwyn and Llanbrynmair Moors. Officers of the NCC agreed that, on the evidence presented, the sites appeared to be of sufficient importance for scheduling. The RSPB urged the NCC to proceed with designation and to discuss with the relevant authorities how any afforestation or agricultural improvement might affect the scientific interest of the sites. The NCC opened discussions with the Forestry Commission, the Welsh Office Agriculture Department (WOAD) and the Agricultural Development and Advisory Service (ADAS) — discussions which soon revealed radically different assessments of the area's potential.

AN INDEPENDENT APPRAISAL

It was agreed amongst these bodies that an impartial study of the area was needed, and in December 1978 Reggie Lofthouse, a former chief surveyor with ADAS, was approached to conduct it. Two months earlier the NCC and RSPB had prepared a confidential document, 'The Berwyn Mountains Feasibility Study — Assessment of Biological Interest', and another on the Llanbrynmair Moors. These, together with data on plantable land supplied by the Forestry Commission and on improvable land by WOAD and ADAS, formed the basis of the Lofthouse appraisal. With this evidence he was to examine and weigh each of the three competing land-uses so that they might be 'accommodated to the least detriment of each'. Moreover, Lofthouse undertook that

> a clear indication should be given of areas where each one of the three interests should take priority over the other two; and where the technical arguments were equally balanced, to take into account any social or economic reasons [which] should not be ignored in arriving at a decision in the national as opposed to a local or individual interest.

Lofthouse completed his report in November 1979. Its tone was conciliatory and accommodating. It suggested guidelines whereby WOAD, ADAS, the Forestry Commission and the NCC might attempt to harmonise their interests through the limited leeway available to them in the administration of their duties. Instead of a detailed land-use strategy, it presented a broad zoning of the area indicating where particular uses should be given priority (see Map 9.1).

Though the report was well received by the commissioning agencies, events had already overtaken it. What was particularly unfortunate was that, during its preparation, proposals were made by the Economic Forestry Group for a major afforestation scheme in the Llanbrynmair Moors. As rumours leaked out about these proposals and the NCC's interest in the area, the issue became more public and politically charged. Inevitably it was absorbed into the wider debate and uncertainties that preceded the Wildlife and Countryside Bill. The decision was taken to release the Lofthouse Report — contrary to the original intention — but its publication in September 1980 simply served to fuel the controversy. Whereas the Secretary of State for Wales, speaking in the House of Commons, welcomed it 'as a most valuable fresh approach' that could be 'turned into an exciting new strategy model', the farming press generally denounced it as a 'carve up'. Doubtless, if it had retained its confidential status the Lofthouse Report would have provided useful baseline data and sensible guidelines for subsequent negotiations between the statutory bodies. As a public document, however, it created confusion and dissent.

The farming unions and the Timber Growers' organisation complained about being excluded from the study. To have involved them might have been politically expedient but it would not have been in accord with the limited objectives of the Lofthouse appraisal. It was not intended to address the specific problems or prospects of individual landowners, nor to provide a field-by-field guide to appropriate land-use. In his introduction to the published version of the study, Lofthouse emphasised:

> It is a strictly limited study. It is not an attempt to indicate the future use of land in the study area. Owners and occupiers, by making their own land management and farming decisions, are the main arbiters of improvement or change.

However, the appraisal was essentially a mapping exercise, and it is not surprising that the graphic representation of an extensive zone indicating nature conservation as the priority land use made more of an impact on the farming population than the stated aims of the study with its careful assurances and conciliatory tone.

If such a large zoning for conservation inevitably aroused the suspicion and opposition of the farming community, it also placed the conservation interests in a considerable dilemma over the means by which such an extensive area could be safeguarded. In reality, the Lofthouse appraisal could only be taken by the NCC as an indication of the need to designate a large area of the Berwyn as an SSSI. The quandary for the NCC remained at what point to designate. Under the 1949 legislation, the NCC was not obliged to consult the Forestry Commission or WOAD prior to designation — indeed, the Forestry Commission and WOAD's own complex consultative procedures on contentious grant applications need only come into play *after* designation. Yet the tenor of the Lofthouse Report predetermined that negotiation — rather than any action which could be considered as precipitate or unilateral — was the appropriate way to proceed. The appraisal scrupulously avoided commenting on whether all or any part of the conservation priority zone should be designated as an SSSI.

The legal situation regarding SSSI designation is very clear. As stated by the NCC in its first annual report in 1975, the Council is *required* by Section 23 of the National Parks and Access to the Countryside Act 1949 to notify any area of land, 'not for the time being managed as a nature reserve', which it considers to be 'of special interest by reason of its flora, fauna, or geological or physiographic features'. This requirement is restated in Section 28 of the Wildlife and Countryside Act 1981. In addition, the new Act sets out consultation procedures which did not apply prior to 1981 and therefore were not operable in the Berwyn case. Under both Acts, the basis for designation is an evaluation of an area's scientific interest. Objections and representations *under the 1981 Act* have only to be 'considered' by the NCC, which, as the statutory body established to advise and to conduct research on the relevant scientific issues and criteria, has the legal authority to designate where scientific interest is clearly established. Thus, a proposed SSSI designation, even under the 1981 Act, is only contestable on the basis of contrary scientific evidence. Otherwise it is not negotiable; and before 1981 there was no legal basis whatsoever for challenging the NCC's judgement.

Yet running throughout the Lofthouse Report is the question of whether SSSI designation is negotiable. In the aftermath of the Berwyn case this became a matter of bitter contention, creating in the case of West Sedgemoor considerable confusion and controversy (see Chapter 10). It is particularly disturbing therefore to discover that government departments were a source of the sophism. It is remarkable, for example, that the Forestry Commission maps and overlays prepared for Lofthouse were accompanied by a paper entitled 'The Forestry Case against Designation as NNR or SSSI of Extensive Areas of the Berwyns', which discussed the effect of designation on the potential for afforestation. Though WOAD and ADAS did not formally make out a comparable case, limiting themselves to the presentation of technical material on land classification, Lofthouse does record 'apprehension' on their part.

It is evident that the Forestry Commission, WOAD and ADAS regarded the designation of an SSSI as essentially contestable. As Lofthouse remarked:

> I have observed that when FC, WOAD/ADAS and NCC officers meet together the FC's view on what land is plantable is not questioned. WOAD/ADAS opinion as to what is or is not improvable agriculturally is accepted. Yet NCC views on what land should be notified as SSSI seems to be more critically examined by the other two.

This reveals much about the relative political standing of the bodies concerned. Indeed, it could be argued that the NCC assessment based on plainly observable plant and animal communities has greater scientific validity and accuracy than notions of plantable and improvable land. As we have already emphasised, political and economic considerations are usually of far greater significance in determining what happens to land than purely technical or ecological factors, or national conservation considerations.

Though Lofthouse rightly asserts that the scientific case put forward by the NCC must be accepted, he too slips into treating designation as contestable. There is a need, he says, 'for special consideration of such large areas before notification and perhaps this appraisal suggests a technique of examination so other interests can be given proper due before any formal step is taken'. We shall return to the question of 'large' sites below, but it should be stated here that there is nothing in the legislation to imply different procedures for different sizes of site. Negotiations over land management should commence after designation not before, and it is the unwillingness of Lofthouse to commit himself fully on this point that is one of our major criticisms of his appraisal.

A second criticism concerns the zoning of Llanbrynmair Moors for afforestation, which largely accommodated the interests of the Economic Forestry Group in the Area. The latter put forward its afforestation scheme while the appraisal was being conducted. It is unclear whether knowledge of the scheme affected the zoning exercise, but the question arises whether, in the absence of the proposal, Lofthouse would have chosen for afforestation the site reckoned by many to be the most important of the three Berwyn sites under consideration for their special ornithological interest. The RSPB had first asked the NCC to designate Llanbrynmair Moors in the mid-1960s. Had it been designated it is unlikely that the forestry proposal would have arisen. In the event, Lofthouse records only the botanical interest of the site and then addresses the afforestation proposal in terms that effectively preclude conservation from serious consideration:

> We have in the Llanbrynmair Moors area suitable land for forestry, no official objection from agriculture, social and economic advantages to the community including the farmers, a private initiative from skilled foresters to plant, a desire on the part of the owners and occupiers to accommodate them and thus, from the point of view of the Berwyn Mountains areas as a whole, the spontaneous occurrence of conditions which allow considerable forestry in a locality suitable for it to the relief of pressure on other parts of the study area. This coincidence of national, local and individual interests points to a recommendation in favour of forestry.

A few small sites, it is suggested, should be retained for their botanic interest but Lofthouse does not mention the ornithological losses that would be associated with a major afforestation scheme.

LLANBRYNMAIR MOORS

The part of the Llanbrynmair Moors in question is an estate of 5265 ha. For 150 years the hill land had been managed as a grouse and sheep moor. This together with the lower land was let to tenant-farmers. When the owners decided to sell the estate in 1979, the 13 tenant-farmers were given the option of purchase, but faced problems raising sufficient capital to buy *all* of the land on each of their farms. One of the farmers approached the Economic Forestry Group to do a deal on the top land suitable for afforestation. Subsequently nine of the tenant-farmers with top land became involved in a scheme by which the Economic Forestry Group would purchase and afforest the land on behalf of clients interested in the tax concessions available to forestry investors. It was proposed to plant 1780 ha., grant-aided by the Forestry Commission at a cost to the public purse of approximately £409,400 (quite apart from the tax concessions on the money invested in the scheme). As well as releasing capital for the farmers which enabled them to buy the remainder of their holdings, the scheme promised them the added benefits of provision of fencing, roads and shelterbelts and by the end of 1983 some 60 miles of fencing and 20 miles of road had been constructed.

The NCC was informed of the proposal in June 1979 and lodged an objection in August, only to withdraw the objection three months later. The scheme was given the go-ahead by the Forestry Commission with the proviso that 40 ha. of botanical importance should not be planted. The NCC's decision not to press its objections seems to have been based on a number of pragmatic considerations. In particular, it did not have the necessary cash to purchase — or even rent — the area. Moreover, by November it had received copies of the Lofthouse appraisal and, having initiated it, could not easily disown its recommendations. In any case, Lofthouse had zoned a large area elsewhere for nature conservation, and so the NCC decided to cut its losses in relation to the Llanbrynmair Moors. However, the decision was greeted with dismay by the RSPB. In the words of its director, Ian Prestt, in the spring 1980 issue of *Birds*:

> More than any other recent case, Llanbrynmair Moors exemplifies the vigour and determination with which forestry interests pursue their objectives and the relative weakness and uncertainty of the NCC attempts to defend important ornithological sites from harmful land use change.

Roger Lovegrove, the RSPB's Wales officer was more explicit: 'gone is one of the finest moors in Wales, home of 15 per cent of Welsh golden plover population, as

well as dunlin, hen harrier, merlin and greenland white-
fronts in winter'.

Apart from the loss itself, what is so disturbing about
the Llanbrynmair case is the failure of the organisations
involved to agree, or communicate effectively, on the basic
ecological characteristics of the site and the consequences
of change. Indeed, it does not seem to be clearly understood precisely how damaging afforestation will prove.
The NCC, it is apparent, had scant information on the
botanical nature of the site and, having been refused
access to survey the area, was dependent upon the RSPB
for ornithological data. As far as the RSPB was concerned,
it was the leading site on the Berwyn. Species such as the
merlin, of which there is now one pair on Llanbrynmair
Moors, are dependent on a particular combination of habitats — the close proximity of heather moor flanks and
traditional hedged farmland. Thus, like other such highly
selective species, it is vulnerable to both afforestation and
moorland improvement, and has deserted most of its former haunts in south-west England, the South Pennines
and Wales. Yet at least one prominent member of the
private forestry sector expressed the opinion that 'there's
never any danger of things becoming extinct as there's
plenty of ground for them'. Small wonder that the conflict
over Llanbrynmair was not marked by a high level of
constructive dialogue!

With the fate of Llanbrynmair decided attention shifted
to the ramifications of the Lofthouse Report. Initially the
NCC planned to designate a new Berwyn SSSI — an
expansion of the original Moel Sych site — of an additional
21,000 ha., but hopes of a conciliatory attitude from the
farming and forestry lobbies following the NCC's concessions over Llanbrynmair were quickly dispelled. In June
1980 the NCC agreed to postpone designation for a further
three months, and a month after that it made the Lofthouse Report available. This led to a lively public meeting
convened by the Welsh Office in Aberystwyth, a meeting
that heralded an intensive campaign against designation
that went on all summer. Any scruples that the Forestry
Commission, WOAD and ADAS might have felt about
challenging the validity of the NCC's attempt to fulfil
its statutory duties were as nothing to the extraordinary

Dunkery Beacon and the Horner Valley woods, one of the largest Sites of Special Scientific Interest on Exmoor, owned by the National Trust. The extensive ancient woods are degenerating through overgrazing by sheep and deer and insufficient management.

Photo: M. MacEwen

In the foreground, unreclaimed heather moorland on Exmoor overlooking the Chalk Water; beyond, the featureless fields of Stowey Allotment, the reclamation of which (with the consent of the national park authority) sparked off an explosion of protest in 1977.

Photo: M. MacEwen

Hawkridge Combe, Exmoor, with heather moorland in the foreground, showing how reclamation in the 1960s cut broad swathes of enclosed pasture to the very top of the moorland plateau.

Photo: M. MacEwen

campaign that was now unleashed. It is worth looking at the nature of this campaign in some detail because it illustrates the ferocity which even moderate NCC proposals can elicit.

The word 'moderate' to describe SSSI designation under the 1949 Act is used advisedly because it involved negligible restraint on a farmer's freedom of action or eligibility for government support. That Act placed upon the NCC the duty to inform the *local planning authority* of areas of special scientific interest, so that the authority could take this into account in exercising its development control functions from which farming activities were specifically exempt. The Countryside Act 1968 nominally broadened the responsibility for rural conservation to include all other public authorities. Section 11 reads as follows:

> In the exercise of their functions relating to land under any enactment every Minister, government department and public body shall have regard to the desirability of conserving the natural beauty and amenity of the countryside.

Conversely, Section 37 of the 1968 Act requires planning and conservation authorities to take into account the needs of agriculture and forestry. In addition, Section 15 empowers the NCC to enter into financial agreements with the occupiers of SSSIs.

Any misunderstandings that farmers might have had of the implications of SSSI designation were compounded, at the time of the Berwyn case, by uncertainty and apprehension over the outcome of the mounting national controversy between agriculture and conservation. Changes in the procedures for farm grants introduced in October 1980 seemed to herald a greater say for conservation interests: the new procedures required farmers in SSSIs to consult the NCC on proposed agricultural improvements for which grant aid was being sought. Some conservationists were pressing for tougher measures, including planning controls, to be included in the forthcoming Wildlife and Countryside Bill. Naturally enough, the dismay of the Berwyn farmers at the prospect of SSSI designation was fuelled by these wider political developments.

At the forefront of the local opposition was the Farmers' Union of Wales, always eager to steal a march on its rival, the National Farmers' Union. The Montgomery branch secretary of the FUW, John A. Jones, decried designation as holding in prospect 'grave social and economic effects on farming communities and . . . the imposition of intolerable restrictions'. Julian Fenwick, chairman of the Montgomery branch, was equally strident in his condemnation:

> The area — it cannot be called a site — is so huge and so typical of much of mid-Wales and North Wales, let alone of England and Wales, that this area seems to be unfairly discriminated against. . . . farms will become, effectively, nature reserves and subject to Conservancy Council control. . . . If the presence of a pair of merlins or hen harriers on a farm carries the threat of an SSSI designation, followed by the loss of grant aid, many people will have little mercy on these birds.

The NFU offered less hyperbolic but equally firm criticism, as did the CLA, and the Timber Growers' organisation. The four organisations sent a joint letter to the Secretary of State for Wales criticising the lack of consultation over the Lofthouse appraisal, and stressing the need for consultation over land-use decisions, particularly where the interests or livelihood of individual landowners were affected. This, of course, is the correct position *after* designation. But the letter contested the NCC's case, calling on it to publish its scientific evidence and sources, and went on to argue that

> any genuine consultation on future land-use strategy should not be pre-empted by designation either by the Nature Conservancy Council or indeed by the Countryside Commission. In this case the NCC's proposal to designate 53,000 acres as an SSSI within the study area is seen as an attempt to pre-empt an approved land use strategy.

Once again this conveniently ignores the NCC's statutory duty to designate irrespective of any land-use strategy or other arrangements that might be negotiated to improve land management within or without an SSSI. Indeed, far from pre-empting a rational land-use strategy, designation represents the only formal means of registering the wildlife value of an area and thus facilitating more balanced decision-making, taking into account the full range of public and private interests in land use.

Meanwhile the local and national press waded into the dispute. The Liverpool *Daily Post* derided the NCC as a 'non-consulting bureaucratic dictatorship', 'locked up in their ivory academic-tower', and acting in a 'draconian' and 'presumptuous' manner. The politicians, ever anxious to impress in a farming constituency, also entered the fray. Beata Brookes, the Conservative MEP for North Wales, deplored what she called 'blanket designation'. In the House of Commons local Conservative MP, Delwyn Williams, talked of an 'indiscriminate blanket conservation order', and proceeded to take the NCC to task on its scientific evidence. Of the hen harrier he said, 'I do not accept that 20 pairs need 53,000 acres to support them' — at a stroke dismissing the scientific judgement of the NCC and RSPB. Of the plant communities he declared, 'I cannot think that they are entirely rare or absolutely unique to this area.' Repeatedly the anti-designation lobby criticised the extent of the proposed SSSI, arguing that the word 'site' implied a very limited area, and thereby accused the NCC of over-stepping its authority. However, neither the 1949 nor the 1981 Act uses this term; both refer to 'any area of land' to signify what has come to be known, somewhat misleadingly, as a Site of Special Scientific Interest.

On 18 September, in the face of such a tirade, the NCC announced deferment of designation for another six months so that further talks could be held with farmers in the Berwyn. The next few months saw a quite remarkable thaw in attitudes and relations between the two sides, starting with the NCC showing a more 'diplomatic' posture and greater determination to get alongside the local farmers and discuss their specific concerns. In October an NCC spokesman announced:

> In the near future the Council plans to visit all owners and occupiers of land in the proposed area. The intention is to discuss with each farmer his current and future plans for the development of the enterprise, particularly as far as reclamation and grant-aided improvements are concerned. In the light of these discussions, the NCC will look into the possibility of entering into conservation management agreements. If agreement can be reached we will then assess the rates and amount of compensation which the Council is prepared to pay for any loss of livelihood involved.

For their part, the NFU, FUW and CLA organised a meeting in Bala which proposed a deal whereby the farmers would promise good conservation practices in return for the NCC not designating such a large area. The meeting was chaired by Alun Evans, a vice-chairman of the NFU in Wales and a member of its hill farming committee. He was a man with something of a vision: the Berwyn Society.

THE BERWYN SOCIETY

The Berwyn Society was formed following the Bala meeting. The professed aim of the society, which comprised the local farmers and landowners, was not only to safeguard their interests, but also to provide adequate assurances to secure the nature conservation interest of the area. In December 1980 the society held its first meeting with officers of the NCC, and so started a series of discussions which culminated in the pruning of the SSSI and the forging of a unique relationship between the NCC and the Berwyn Society. But this took over a year, and was not concluded before the NCC and the Berwyn Society had publicly clashed over the vexed issue of notification. On this occasion, in April 1981, the NCC again indicated its desire, indeed its duty, to notify. It acknowledged the agreements and understanding that were being reached with the Berwyn Society but stressed that designation was a separate issue. The Berwyn Society's reaction was publicly to offer to be the responsible conservation body. This put the NCC on the spot. On the one hand it had committed itself to fulfil its *legal* duty to designate and was under increasing pressure from the RSPB to do just that. On the other hand, the society's offer of active cooperation was conditional on designation being dropped or greatly diminished. The NCC was acutely aware of the need to secure this promised goodwill which would be vital in conserving the area. Moreover, the Berwyn Society had the full backing of the farming lobby. The NFU's annual report for 1982 described it as 'a constructive and forward thinking body of land occupiers and users'.

In the long months that followed — the NCC having again agreed to postpone designation — further difficult negotiations were held with the society. What emerged in February 1982 was a unique compromise. A joint statement by the NCC and the Berwyn Society announced that an agreement had been reached on the designation of a smaller SSSI of 15,300 ha. A further 4860 ha. around the edge of this site has subsequently come to be known as a consultation zone, and it is this area which is now the focus of most attention. The SSSI occupies the higher land, nearly all of it being above 500 metres, and much of it common land. The consultation zone occupies the lower, potentially 'improvable' land. Conservationists argue forcibly that it is just such land that it is imperative to protect through designation, otherwise there is nothing to inhibit a farmer in the consultation zone from carrying out whatever improvements he wishes, although, through the Berwyn Society, the farmers have undertaken to approach the NCC if contemplating any changes and to seek management agreements where appropriate in much the same way as within an SSSI. Government, for its part, has given assurances that money for such agreements will be made available. So far the arrangements seem to have been largely effective and compromise seems to be the order of the day. From the farmers' point of view the Berwyn Society offers a skilled and efficient local negotiating service, one which is both knowledgeable about local farming conditions and commands the respect of the NCC. In return, the society has demonstrated the will to deliver the cooperation of local farmers (who number over 100), and with designation always a possibility — especially if the voluntary consultative arrangements manifestly break down — the NCC can maintain the pressure on the society.

Nevertheless, conservationists are sceptical of the deal. Voluntary consultation without statutory back-up has been tried elsewhere, most notably between 1968 and 1977 on Exmoor (see Chapter 8), and has failed. The question also arises: if the farmers are so willing to submit to the joint 'supervision' of the Berwyn Society and the NCC, why did they object so strongly to the extended SSSI which would have given them a legal guarantee of compensation under the Wildlife and Countryside Act 1981 in return for acceptance of the statutory constraints of an

SSSI? Part of the answer seems to be the Berwyn farmers' suspicion of any government order or imposition, almost irrespective of its content. There is a strong tradition of resistance amongst Welsh hill farmers to any initiative which smacks of meddling by London-based bureaucrats. The designation procedure and the lack of established means of consultation or a facility for involving the local farmers was at the heart of much of the opposition. In principle, the procedural reforms introduced in the 1981 Act were intended to meet such criticisms, though, as the case of West Sedgemoor illustrates (see Chapter 10), there is still ample scope for misunderstanding and contention. The judgement of Welsh farmers was summarised in the following motion which was passed unanimously at the 1983 annual general meeting of the Farmers' Union of Wales:

> The Farmers' Union of Wales being deeply concerned about the effect that the Wildlife and Countryside Act 1981 is having and will have in the future on farming in Wales, and the absence of any machinery to allow a democratic appeal to be made to an independent authority such as the Secretary of State for Wales against any proposal by the Nature Conservancy Council to designate land used for agriculture as a Site of Special Scientific Interest ... , consider that the Act should be amended to provide the necessary appeal machinery thereby safeguarding individuals against the unilateral decisions of the Council which is empowered ... to be prosecutor, judge, jury, and executioner in the field of site designations.

Undoubtedly some of the initial suspicion of Berwyn farmers also derived from ignorance of the precise implications of an SSSI, a state of affairs for which neither the NCC nor the farming press and the farming establishment can escape blame. In retrospect, the protracted period of dispute and discussion between 1979 and 1982 may be seen as a necessary episode in which the fears and suspicions of the local farmers were allayed and they were gradually won round. In the process, the farmers also achieved major concessions. Most of the land with prospects for improvement or afforestation was excluded from designation and procedures were established whereby the

NCC consults with them about its intentions. The farmers retain their autonomy within the consultation zone, while the NCC is committed to compensate farmers if they forgo any opportunities for agricultural improvement, either in the zone or in the SSSI.

The Berwyn Society must be regarded as something more than a defensive front to protect the farmers' interests and autonomy. From the NCC's point of view, it holds out the prospect of facilitating genuine conciliation, and representatives from the NCC now sit on its managing committee. From the farmers' point of view, the Berwyn Society is an imaginative and resourceful stratagem: its establishment was a bold step which enabled them to seize the political initiative, which they still hold. In May 1982, the chairman of the Berwyn Society, Alun Evans, was appointed to the NCC's Advisory Committee for Wales where he now helps to formulate official conservation policy for the whole Principality.

The astuteness of local farmers' leaders was not always matched by the other protagonists. The NCC in particular, perhaps through a genuine uncertainty over how best to act, gave the appearance both to its supporters and its opponents of weakness and lack of purpose. Its avowed wish to avoid conflict had just the opposite effect, inviting recalcitrance and stonewalling from its opponents (including other branches of government), which simply served to make the resolution of the issue more intractable. The NCC gave the impression of being unable or unwilling to fulfil its statutory duty and this allowed the general status of SSSI designation to be called into question. For several months after the notification of the compromise SSSI, the RSPB was close to taking the NCC to court over the matter, but held back. This was partly because it was persuaded by the NCC to give the consultation zone a chance to work, but more importantly it was reassured by the NCC's more vigorous approach to the scheduling of West Sedgemoor (Chapter 10) and other sites, which seemed to indicate that the NCC had learnt certain lessons from the Berwyn case.

Needless to say, the sequence of events and the outcome were viewed differently within the NCC. Contrasting the handling of West Sedgemoor and the Berwyn

Mountains, Sir Ralph Verney (who was chairman of the NCC at the time) commented of the latter: 'This is a striking success story because we took enough time, in spite of pressures from the RSPB, to get the farmers on our side' (personal communication, 25 March 1984). Even so, the NCC Report for 1982/83 states unequivocally, 'if the NCC fails to notify a site which in its opinion is of sufficient interest to merit SSSI status it is in breach of its statutory duty'. While this puts beyond doubt the NCC's obligations, it leaves the Berwyn consultation zone in an indeterminate position.

The consultation zone has no status in law, and the NCC and WOAD are not required to justify their decisions in relation to it. Anyone can buy maps showing SSSIs and observe for themselves the nature of the sites and the activities taking place within them, but that is not the case with the consultation zone. The legitimate interest of other parties in the working of the arrangements is denied. The NCC, for instance, were not prepared to release maps showing the extent of the zone for the purposes of our research; nor have the NCC, WOAD or the Berwyn Society stated publicly what is a notifiable agricultural operation within the zone. It is difficult, therefore, to reach an objective assessment of how effectively the new arrangements are operating. We have been informed that few grant-aided improvements have yet been considered by the society and that no major problems have arisen, although there has already been an instance of unauthorised improvement within the consultation zone.

In March 1984 the Berwyn Society and the NCC agreed on a formula for determining payments for management agreements. This includes a standard figure for 'the additional gross income achieved from carrying out a typical upland improvement', from which must be deducted the costs involved in carrying out the improvement, for example, for fencing, draining and re-seeding. Both the standard gross income and the standard unit costs will be reviewed and agreed annually by a panel of the Berwyn Society representing the farmers, WOAD and the NCC, and will form the basis of the automatic recalculation of annual payments to individual farmers. A farmer can choose to opt for the standard assessment or an individual assessment. Either way, he cannot lose. The less efficient farmer should make more from the standard sum than from his proposed improvements; whereas the more efficient farmer and the farmer with the more improvable land have the opportunity to claim compensation over and above the standard payment.

These arrangements still have to prove themselves over the years ahead, in which the technical and economic pressures to intensify hill farm production may continue to mount. But this is only one of a number of question-marks hanging over the future of the Berwyn.

THE PROSPECTS FOR THE BERWYN

Crystal ball-gazing is a notoriously hazardous business even when firm factual indicators are available. In the case of the Berwyn a number of possible future developments remain purely speculative and yet need to be mentioned if a full picture of the prospects for the Berwyn is to be presented. Two particular developments which cannot be ruled out would sharply re-focus the dispute. A major afforestation scheme in the North Berwyn, if proposed, would re-open many of the conflicts of Llanbrynmair Moors. Though the Forestry Commission is no longer so extensively involved in new planting, the private sector continues to have an aggressive approach to upland plant-ing as an attractive tax haven for those on very high incomes. The possibility is given added weight by recent questioning of the future of common land in the uplands. It would be open to the NCC to offer a management agreement to counter the financial gains (including the government grants and tax concessions) which would accrue to any afforestation scheme, though the cost could be enormous.

Whereas a major afforestation scheme would be certain to arouse the opposition of the conservation lobby, a firm proposal from the Countryside Commission for a Berwyn AONB would undoubtedly provoke the farming and land-owning lobbies. The Commission has long had an interest in the area; and in a policy statement issued in 1983 it reconfirmed its commitment to seek AONB designation

for the Berwyn Mountains (which would have to be confirmed by the Secretary of State) 'as soon as the resources
of the Commission and the local authorities allow'. The
Farmers' Union of Wales, however, has promised that any
attempt to designate an AONB on top of the SSSI would
make Halvergate and Sedgemoor look like 'minor skirmishes'. It is difficult to see why it should engender such
implacable opposition, for AONBs are even more toothless than SSSIs. Once again the very act of designation is
taken by farmers' groups as meddling by bureaucratic
outsiders intent on restricting farming practices and opening the countryside to recreational pressure. The issue is
likely to remain dormant for some time, if only because
the Countryside Commission in Wales is small and seeking to establish itself as an honest broker in Welsh rural
affairs, particularly through the Wales Countryside Forum
which it recently initiated. It is hardly likely to prejudice
these wider initiatives by a sudden move to promote
AONB designation of the Berwyn.

If a major new afforestation proposal or AONB designation could be discounted there would still remain some
uncertainty over the future of the SSSI and more especially
the consultation zone. Indeed, the most serious concern
over the Berwyn 'solution' is its fragility and the fact that
the future has not been secured to the satisfaction of
nature conservationists. This is partly a reflection of the
legislation and partly the peculiar local arrangements in
the Berwyn. SSSI designation in itself cannot prevent a
farmer from doing anything he wishes with his land:
under the 1981 Act, it simply provides a framework for
notification and negotiation. Within the consultation zone
the position is even more precarious. It only needs one
maverick farmer to act without using the proffered offices
of the Berwyn Society for the NCC to find itself in the
extraordinary dilemma of having to designate either the
whole of the zone as an SSSI or the small island site of the
disputed action. Nor is it clear that WOAD would take as
strong a line in refusing grant aid for agricultural
'improvements' as MAFF appears to do in the Exmoor
Map 2 area.

Whether pressures for agricultural improvement continue is largely a function of the operation of policy in the

uplands, particularly the future of the Less Favoured Areas Directive (see Chapter 13). It is ironic for conservation that if the pressure slackens and the relative 'boom' in hill farming ends, then afforestation pressures are likely to increase. Either way, under present legislation, conservation is likely to remain a secondary consideration in terms of positive policy. The pressures will not easily be dispelled, nor will a strategy to integrate conservation with agriculture and forestry be easy to come by. The Berwyn Society approach offers a number of hopeful aspects, but a long-term solution with general application would have to be worked out in the context of reforms of agricultural, forestry and conservation policies.

10. Wetland Reclamation in West Sedgemoor

Guy Fawkes aside, effigy-burning is not a prevalent feature of British political culture. Hardly surprising, then, that those farmers who gathered at Stathe in Somerset on 22 February 1983 to set fire to the hanging figures of the outgoing NCC chairman, Sir Ralph Verney, the NCC regional officer, Peter Nicholson, and the RSPB regional officer, Stan Davies, ensured that the newly-designated West Sedgemoor SSSI would become the most widely reported instance of mistrust between agricultural and conservation interests. That anger and frustration should have reached such a pitch was in many ways a consequence of the uncertainties associated with its being a test-case under the 1981 Act.

RECLAMATION IN THE SOMERSET LEVELS

Oddly enough, the incident was not without precedent. Between 1750 and 1770 Richard Locke carried out a series of experiments to improve the meadows of the Somerset Levels: those 68,000 ha. of marshland, bounded by the Mendip Ridge to the north and east, the limestone hills of Dorset to the south and the Blackdown Hills to the west, where eight rivers meander and converge towards the Bristol Channel. When he turned his attention from the

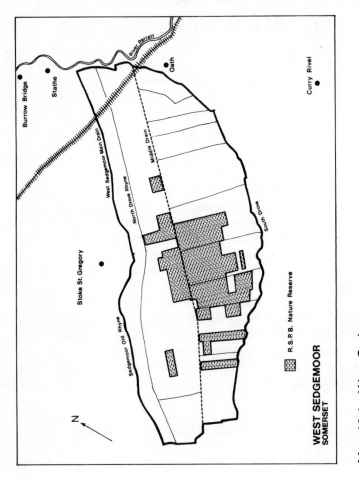

Map 10.1   West Sedgemoor

coastal clay belt to the peat moors of the inland valleys, however, his enthusiasm for agricultural improvement and 'inclosing' met with such spirited resistance from the commoners that he was 'stoned, bruised and beaten by the mob till the blood had issue from my nose, mouth and ears' and his effigy was burnt 'by the owners of Geese'.

The recent pretext for anger is so exactly the converse of its basis 200 years ago that the anecdote highlights the underlying causes of conflict in West Sedgemoor with dramatic irony. Moreover, just as the wider response to the recent incident showed it to have been an ill-judged and intemperate affair (seven Labour MPs tabled a Commons motion expressing their distaste and *The Guardian*, in a self-consciously tendentious Leader, accused the farmers of displaying an 'insolent ingratitude typical of their community'), Locke's troubles seem merely to have roused interest in his projects for reclamation. Other factors also stimulated a change in attitudes throughout the Levels in that period. In a context of general agricultural expansion and improvement the long-prevalent problem of over-stocking became more pressing and with increased prosperity many graziers and farmers in the fertile clay belt had the resources to pursue schemes for reclamation of the peat moors. Moreover, in addition to demand and available capital, there was a new mechanism, the Parliamentary Enclosure Act, which could be used to effect drainage improvements.

The pace of reclamation within the Levels varied considerably. Of the five relatively distinct regions — each corresponding to the catchment area of a major river — the Southern Levels (including the valley of the winding, narrow and shallow River Parrett) were barely affected by any improvements until after 1810. West Sedgemoor is one of a number of isolated moorland basins within the Southern Levels, and prints dating from 1791 show it as an open, treeless landscape with no ditches.

Described as one of the most improvable tracts of wasteland remaining within the county just prior to its reclamation, West Sedgemoor was the subject of an enclosure award in 1816, and by 1822 the moor's 1000 ha. had been allotted to almost 900 people living in its 15 parishes who could claim grazing or other rights. Two major open, parallel drains — the Middle and North Drove rhynes — fed by a network of ditches were established but reclamation did little to stop flooding and in 1850 West Sedgemoor was described as grazeable only in the driest of seasons.

In fact the draining of the Southern Levels as a whole steadily deteriorated. The main river channels of the Parrett and its tributaries the Tone, Isle and Yeo were much constricted and generally inadequate for the evacuation of surplus water — whether caused by rainfall or the high tides which would surge up the Bristol Channel and break through to the Levels. The Land Drainage Act 1861 provided for the creation of internal drainage districts and when, after two years of particularly severe flooding, the Somerset Drainage Act was passed in 1877 their number was increased by a further 11 to a total of 19 throughout the Levels.

The West Sedgemoor Board undertook responsibility for digging and maintaining the main ditches, and met the cost of such works by levying rates on the landowners. But despite earlier piecemeal experiments with steam-pumping it was not until 1944, when a new pumping station with a diesel engine was installed on the moor's lowest point at Stathe, that really effective drainage became possible. Many of the parcels of land allotted at the time of the enclosure reclamation having proved too small, amalgamations had occurred and the number of owners further declined in the years of unrelieved agricultural depression towards the end of the nineteenth century.

More recently, some capital works and major improvements, over and above the regular work involved in clearing out water courses, have been 50 per cent grant-aided by MAFF, whilst much of the expenditure by the Wessex Water Authority (WWA) has been grant-aided at a rate of 80 per cent. The internal drainage boards are responsible for the water levels in the wide flanking ditches — known locally as rhynes — which take water from field drains whilst also providing a source of water for livestock and acting as stock-proof 'wet-fences'. The WWA, meanwhile, takes responsibility for the main drains and the arterial rivers. IDBs tend to be wholly dominated by farmers and landowners and take a fairly narrow view of their concerns.

Certainly it is significant that the Royal Society for The Protection of Birds (RSPB) — although now the major landowner in West Sedgemoor with a holding of 300 ha. built up since 1978 at a cost of £1 million — is not a member of the IDB. In 1978 there were around 100 owners and occupiers, but following the RSPB's acquisitions the number is now about 70.

That is still a relatively large number of owners and occupiers though, and, together with two related factors, this contributed to the intractability of recent conflicts. In the Commons on 18 April 1980, Hector Munro, Under-Secretary of State for the Environment, assessed the prospects for resolving difficulties on Exmoor favourably because 'the moorland has relatively few owners and occupiers' who, he felt, would respond to voluntary management agreements. In stark contrast the complexities of dealing with a large number of owners and occupiers were to make West Sedgemoor appear dangerously damaging to the voluntary co-operation case enshrined in the 1981 Act.

The first of those additional factors is that most farmsteads in the Levels are on higher land in villages with other land held divided into a number of isolated compartments on the lower ground: a pattern of highly fragmented landholding surviving from the days of the enclosure reclamation. Such fragmentation enormously complicates any attempt to negotiate an agreement about the way in which an area might be farmed since a 40 ha. block could have as many as ten owners. At the time of notification as many as 49 owners had less than 16 ha. on the moor, with 27 having less than 4 ha.

The second additional factor is that many of the farming families are long established in the area. A comparison of the Schedule attached to the 1816 Enclosure Award and the 1982 list of drainage ratepayers shows that nearly half the farm families who now have over 16 ha. on the moor were named on the former list. Understandably, perhaps, a certain resistance to change — from whatever direction it may come — has always been apparent on the moor.

RECENT DRAINAGE DEVELOPMENTS

The new pumping station constructed for West Sedgemoor in 1944 made a vast improvement in drainage operations possible and by the mid-1960s drainage had become well organised. Ditches, which take water from small parcels of land, discharge into rhynes and the pump at Stathe lifts the drainage water into the River Parrett which is tidal at this point. Under normal conditions the pump takes about a week to clear flood water from the Moor. The Moor, with its 4500 ha. catchment area, is a floodable area with a flood frequency of once every five years in summer but once a year in winter. In the summer, water is fed onto the moor from upstream of the Oathe sluice via Wickmoor rhyne. This maintains penning levels but with arable farmers anxious to avoid the waterlogging of their crops the water levels have been progressively reduced in recent years by the IDB.

The piecemeal phasing of improvements since the initial Enclosure Award makes it inappropriate to talk in terms of a 'tradition of farming practice', if that is taken to imply an unbroken and unchanged pattern of land use. However, until recently, certain long-persistent farming practices suited to the drainage condition of the Moor dominated. Most of the land had simply been left to develop 'naturally' following the early drainage improvements. The result was a low-input/low-output system of farming given over to summer livestock grazing and haymaking, with the moor virtually unused in winter. Farm income was augmented by raising beef cattle from the dairy herd. The first critical change came with the post-war drainage schemes which made it worthwhile to improve permanent grass by applying herbicides to 'agriculturally worthless' growth and re-seeding with higher-yielding grass species. But the basic farming regime remained unchanged: rhynes were cleared periodically and limited flooding with a high water-table for the greater part of the year was accepted. In this artificial landscape owing its existence to human contrivance, the approach was broadly compatible with the continued survival of a wide variety of plant and wildlife. Apart from dairying, the only other significant activity on West Sedgemoor was willow-growing for basket-making and charcoal, and there are still five established growers on the eastern end of the Moor. The other major industry in the Levels is peat winning: Somerset supplies about one-fifth of the peat used in the UK. But although output has doubled since the mid-1970s, extraction is largely confined to two extensive zones at Westhay Moor and Meare and Shapwick Heaths.

Michael Williams, the historian and geographer of drainage in the Somerset Levels, noted the 'great changes' which occurred in the brief interval between the completion of his initial studies in 1961 and his return to the Levels in 1966, but concluded his book, *The Draining of the Somerset Levels*, with the observation that the improvements have resulted 'in an intensification of the pastoral economy, rather than its replacement by arable farming'. Indeed, although noting the risks to prosperity in being dependent upon a single commodity, he saw little prospect for the diversification which might bring greater financial security because of the restricted drainage condition of the moors. No change in the agricultural economy of the Levels would mean, he felt, 'a more or less stable landscape'. The Southern Levels would continue to be pervaded by a quiet stillness: a region where the straight droves and rhynes lined with leaning pollarded willows would continue to form a timeless relief powerfully resistant to fundamental change: where a pattern of life linked, as always, to the control of water-levels could be expected to persist like some picturesque tableau. More recently, however, further critical developments have begun to make that assessment of limitations, and image of the future, look rather less compelling. Over the last decade or so the possibilities for more thoroughgoing grassland improvement — and even ploughing for arable cropping — have expanded dramatically. The Southern Levels have lost their serene innocence.

Between a third and a half of the fields on West Sedgemoor have been underdrained since the war. The bulk of this activity followed the development of a pilot scheme of underdrainage by MAFF in 1971. Two years later five farmers arranged a joint pumping scheme which isolated an area of land, making the improvement of 200 ha. possible. It was the use of automatically-operated, electrically-powered pumps to remove water from the drains that effectively established the potential for a new agricultural system. These pumps make it possible to lower the water level in rhynes by 1–1.5 metres which enables the smaller rhynes to be filled in while the remainder are deepened and widened. Pipe drains are laid under the fields to draw water into the rhynes, thereby lowering the water-table which in turn threatens the existence of the typical plants of the natural water meadow. Herbicides are, in any case, invariably used to kill off natural vegetation, and fertiliser is applied as part of the process of drilling in a specially formulated grass monoculture, usually based on Italian rye grass. Such strains, though more nutritious, are far less able to withstand flooding so the pressure to keep main drainage channels free of any vegetation to ensure the free flow of water at times of heavy rainfall is increased. The impact on flora and fauna of these changes can be devastating.

The caution of local farmers has always tempered the speed of change, and some of those who were later to lead the opposition to SSSI designation also vociferously opposed the introduction of the first pump drain on the moor. But by 1977, spurred on by the promotional efforts of a special 'Somerset Moors Panel' established by MAFF, two more grant-aided pump schemes had been installed and another pair were awaiting completion. Nevertheless, the majority of farmers on West Sedgemoor rejected a million-pound drainage scheme, proposed in that year by the IDB and WWA, which would have virtually eliminated serious flooding. No doubt they feared that the drainage rate could become prohibitive. The fragmented pattern of landholding was an additional fetter on such developments. In addition, the poor condition of many unmetalled droves made them unsuitable for heavy vehicles and machinery so that, even where the water-table could be lowered sufficiently to enable an area to be ploughed, the growing of arable crops was confined to parts of the moor adjoining highways.

In the early days of the pump-drainage schemes a variety of crops were grown — peas, beans, carrots, potatoes, as well as cereals — and all yielded well. This strongly confirmed an assessment of the agricultural potential which had been made in 1970 by the Agricultural Advisory Council in its publication *Modern Farming and the Soil* which had pointed to the Fens as a suitable analogy when illustrating the potential productivity of the peaty areas of the Somerset Levels. The comparison became the *leitmotif* of the progressive farmers' case. Their most illustrious representative, Ralph Baker, took care to reiterate his oft-quoted claim that 'when drained the land would be as productive as the Lincolnshire Fens', when he met visiting members of the same council in 1978 who were collecting evidence for their report on *Agriculture and the Countryside*. By that time, however, voices questioning the direction of agricultural policy were sufficiently well articulated for them to note 'a widespread feeling that agriculture can no longer be accounted the prime architect of conservation nor farmers accepted as the natural custodians of the countryside'. But the 1970 Report had clearly envisaged a lowering of water-tables in some areas, and further ditching and draining in others, making three-quarters of the Levels capable of high agricultural productivity.

The soils in the centre of West Sedgemoor itself are made up of Altcar series fen peats classed by MAFF as Grade 2 (defined as land with only some minor limitations on which a wide range of agricultural and horticultural crops can be grown). In contrast the Soil Survey's Land Capability Map classifies large parts of the moor as Vw (where w means wet and V = 5). The discrepancy arises because the MAFF classification relates in this instance to the potential of the land *after draining*, although its official purpose is to classify the quality of the land in its existing state.

This observation is crucial to an understanding of the way in which, in the context of MAFF and EEC-funded *largesse*, the WWA has worked hand-in-glove with MAFF, particularly since the regional water authorities acquired additional functions under the Land Drainage Act 1976. MAFF has been assiduous in proclaiming the benefits of drainage, and has worked to convince sceptical IDBs (who often wish to retain high penning levels) that problems of water supply can be overcome by making cuttings in rhyne banks and installing cow-operated pumps, and that rhynes can still operate as effective stock barriers even when the water level is reduced by as much as 5 feet. Likewise the WWA has seen itself as a protagonist for the virtues of land drainage. In its 1979 Land Drainage Survey

Report, for instance, the authority presented itself as pioneering the way. It argued that innovations only become accepted by the majority over a prolonged period after the courage of the first few has demonstrated their worth; and it affirmed its intention 'to continue to implement capital schemes to improve drainage to enable the agricultural potential of the area to be achieved'. Like MAFF, the authority had a statutory obligation under Section 11 of the Countryside Act 1968 to consider the effects of its activities on flora and fauna, but there is no doubting which consideration is uppermost in its report. For the Somerset local land drainage district alone, it identifies some 500 'problems' of flooding and suggests various works to improve drainage. In view of the ambiguities regarding the area's agricultural capacity and the enthusiastic (if tendentious) interpretation by MAFF and the WWA of their statutory obligations, it is hardly surprising that the voluntary conservation bodies, in their efforts to protect the wildlife heritage of the Somerset Levels, have found themselves questioning the basis of the cost–benefit calculations presented on behalf of farmers seeking grant aid.

The past ecology of West Sedgemoor is little known so, paradoxically, most of the reliable wildlife information dates from the period after 1944 when significant and sustained improvement became possible. In any case, it is probable that the winter water-level would previously have been too deep for wading birds so that much of the area's present ornithological interest would not have been apparent then. Today, following an extensive survey, the RSPB regards it as the most important breeding site in south-west England for waterfowl, especially waders, and there are additionally large populations of snipe, red-shank, lapwing, curlew, black-tailed godwit and yellow wagtail. In some winters there can be up to 10,000 wigeon, and in the cold spring of 1982 the lapwing flock peaked at 20,000. As well as overwintering birds, many passage waterfowl can be present in the spring; and the Levels as a whole support at least 40 per cent of all whimbrel passing through Britain in May. Moreover, the area is rich in insect and other invertebrate life characteristic of a relict fenland habitat, and three of the dragonflies recorded are regarded as vulnerable and requiring wide geographical protection. A high water-table keeps many of the soil invertebrates at or near the surface, thereby providing food for the bird populations, and the unimproved rhynes provide habitat for the otter, a creature now very scarce over large parts of England.

West Sedgemoor is particularly significant for meadows, having the highest number of important fields with high rarity values in the Levels, and of course ecologists normally regard flora as the best general indicator of likely wildlife 'wealth'. Because of their proneness to annual flooding the meadows contain a number of grasslands which are good representative types distinguished by hydrological differences from flood grassland elsewhere. Flowering rush, reeds and sedge grow in the rhynes with yellow flags, water lilies, water violets and loosestrife, and the meadows are studded with cowslips, campion, ragged robin, meadowsweet, marsh marigold and many more.

A gradual lowering of the water-table can only eradicate wetland plants. But the main threat to their existence comes from underdraining operations in specific areas with the associated 'improvement' of natural pasture and conversion to arable cropping patterns. Such changes can also have a profound impact on the waterways them-selves. The more herbicides and fertilisers are used the greater is the chance that chemical run-off will pollute the rhynes. But the greater the range of natural grasses and wild flowers in a field, the more superb nesting sites it has, the less likely it is to contain a high proportion of good grass. In an area where farms and farmers are neither large nor, by recent standards, prosperous, such considerations weigh heavily even when farmers genuinely claim an inborn love of the local flora and fauna. The NCC regional officer, Peter Nicholson, described it in conversation as 'a death of a thousand cuts. Rarely is it one big decision: usually damage is done by an individual farmer on 5–10 acres. But in that way a whole area can change in a matter of years.'

So by the early 1970s, the necessay elements were present for making West Sedgemoor a particularly intract-able instance of conflict between farming and conservation interests. The moor, as a direct result of the persistent problems facing attempts to improve drainage on the Southern Levels, had a high conservation value which could only be effectively preserved by holding in abeyance its similarly high potential for improvements in agricultural productivity — activities for which ample encouragement, advice, technical capability and finance were readily available. Drainage — the begetter of a delicate harmony between man and nature in the Wetlands — now stood poised in West Sedgemoor to become, by a potentially tragic dialectic, the destroyer of what it had earlier nurtured.

THE SOMERSET WETLANDS PROJECT GROUP

Bernard Storer, a local schoolmaster active in the Somerset Trust for Nature Conservation (STNC), was acutely aware of the implications of the new agricultural system ushered in by the coming of the pump-drain. Along with the RSPB, the STNC had for some years been trying to bring the best wildlife areas to the notice of the NCC and the county and district councils and had sought coordinated action between the NCC and MAFF. In 1975 Storer wrote to the NCC detailing the damaging consequences of recent developments and with the approach of the European Wetlands Campaign (an international project launched by the Council of Europe) the communication proved timely. The NCC responded by setting up a Working Party, the Somerset Wetlands Project Group. Eight hundred copies of its consultation paper (published in 1977) were distributed and interested parties were invited to respond thus initiating a new phase in the consideration of West Sedgemoor's future.

Not surprisingly the composition of the Project Group reflected its provenance. With six members from the NCC, five from STNC, Stan Davies of the RSPB, two representatives each from MAFF and the WWA, one from Somerset county council and two advisers from agriculture and the peat industry, it was clearly skewed towards the wildlife conservation interest. The opportunity was not taken at this stage to involve local farmers and landowners further in discussions about the future of the Levels. As Ralph

Baker, the agricultural adviser, identified himself so strongly with the improving farmers' case, lines of communication with the local community were rather less open than they might have been.

For the NCC, conscious of pressures on wetland areas but hitherto relatively inactive because of its limited staff, the work of the Project Group generated for the first time a full awareness of the real wildlife wealth on the Levels and the extent to which improvements had insinuated themselves. So it was not surprising that whereas the consultation paper particularly drew attention to the ornithological interest of West Sedgemoor, the area was not mentioned in the NCC's Nature Conservation Review (also published in 1977) which listed the most important conservation sites in Britain. In 1977 the NCC's case for West Sedgemoor was, to use Peter Nicholson's words, 'being argued from a very weak position'.

Pointing to intensified husbandry and a general lowering of the water-table as the factors likely to have the most profound impact on wildlife, the consultation paper noted with some surprise that 'the Water Authority's existing drainage works are of sufficient capacity to effect a lowering of levels' so that the capacity of the arterial drainage system would not necessarily be a limiting factor when farmers considered implementing the changes made possible by the new pump-drain. Moreover the study pointed to the difficulties faced by the NCC, the STNC and the RSPB in giving advice in a situation where 'most of the work does not require planning consent and is carried out in such a piecemeal fashion that it would be extremely difficult to assemble a case against individual applications'.

The extent of the damaging impact of drainage operations and the new large-scale open excavation of the peat-winning industry impelled the Project Group to preface its outline of options for the future with an uncompromising statement. It could only anticipate extensive deterioration of the conditions for wildlife if present trends were allowed to continue. The options presented ranged from a preparedness to accept the gradual loss of habitats (Option 1), to the possibility of delaying further agricultural improvement until research could provide a fresh direction and allocating no further land for peat-winning (Option 2).

But it was Option 5 which proved the most popular. This proposed the establishment of a land-use strategy, with government departments and local interests agreeing the particular uses for defined areas of land. Of the 33 consultants listed in the Summary of Responses published in 1978, 20 individuals and organisations included it in their preferences whilst Option 3 (protection for key areas) featured 16 times and Option 4 (the improvement of derelict land in worked-out peat areas) featured 12 times. The Community Council for Somerset was alone in selecting Option 2, as were the Lower Axe drainage board in indicating a preference for Option 1. Options 3 and 4 always featured in conjunction with at least one other option, but an agreed land-use strategy was chosen singly by six respondents, including the CLA, the Exmoor Society, Sedgemoor district council and the British Trust for Ornithology. Accordingly, the document concluded that a long-term strategy for the conservation of wildlife on the Somerset Levels should be sought, both for itself and as a framework within which Options 3 and 4 could be implemented. Sedgemoor district council considered that a more detailed report establishing the areas where 'conflicts are most noticeable' should be produced, and both MAFF and the CLA wished to see further work undertaken to identify specific areas and species considered at risk and to formulate detailed proposals to conserve flora and fauna. The view that further work on the study was required was accepted and the Project Group resolved to invite the CLA (who had recommended that a new working party representing a comprehensive range of interests be established) and Sedgemoor district council to help with this phase of the work. The consultants had, almost without exception, offered help, mostly in the form of advice, consultation, participation and negotiation. Indeed, so positive were many of the responses to the consultation paper that the summary concluded: 'the fundamental question is how a meaningful strategy could work on the Somerset Levels without sacrifice of the freedom of the individual owner to farm his land as he wishes'.

Those final lines seem to embody a hope which, in the light of both the real context in which they were made and subsequent events, can only appear naïve because of the very literal interpretation that was to be put upon phrases such as 'farm his land as he wishes' by the farming community. In fact, it might be said that the attainment of an agreed land-use strategy was dependent upon the prior resolution of just those problems relating to the rights of owners of private property which a land-use strategy was *itself* supposed to resolve. Certainly the comments of some of the organisations consulted provided grounds for considerable disquiet on that score: but it was not until the discussions over the Wildlife and Countryside Bill that such issues were really thrust to the forefront of public debate.

Detailed responses to the questionnaire revealed an incipient polarisation of opinion. Twelve of the voluntary conservation bodies and individuals, most of the research-based organisations and three statutory bodies felt that the consultation document presented the land-use picture accurately, but the NFU, the CLA and Fisons Ltd (the company involved in peat-winning on the Levels) all expressed serious reservations. The CLA thought the document 'somewhat alarmist'; the NFU found it 'somewhat biased in favour of the conservation point of view', whilst the RSPB and the STNC considered that it 'veered towards modesty for conservation issues'. MAFF disagreed with the claims advanced regarding the capacity of the arterial drainage system and emphasised that increased agricultural productivity on the 50,000 ha. covered by the Report depended on the construction of the Parrett barrage. Fisons, for their part, took exception to certain sections of the Report which 'could give a misleading impression of the status of our peat operations and of our regard for conservation issues'.

In their 'most helpful detailed reply', the WWA saw the Somerset Moors as 'only a local example of a problem which is national in extent' but took care to emphasise its statutory obligation to provide a service when a need 'which can be shown to be economically viable, is made known by owners or occupiers who have a right to manage their land as they wish'. Similarly MAFF, whilst acknowledging the problems, drew attention to their obligations in the light of the government's White Paper, *Food From Our Own Resources*, which called for increased agricultural production in the interests of the nation. In MAFF's view the pursuit of such a policy was quite reconcilable with environmental protection. The NFU, predictably, also drew attention to the White Paper and suggested that the national wealth generated by a progressive agricultural industry would enable the nation to pay for suitable conservation measures. Given these divergent emphases in the responses the contribution from the south-west chapter of the Landscape Institute seemed the most perceptive: 'The most fundamental observation', they commented, 'concerns the key issue of competing land uses and the unreconciled terms of reference of the various Government Departments and other statutory bodies.'

From fairly informal beginnings the Somerset Wetlands Project had made considerable progress. The views of major interests in the area had been set out and the wildlife wealth of the area — and of West Sedgemoor in particular — had been clearly identified. On this basis the NCC decided that the moor warranted designation as an SSSI and it was treated as such by the NCC and MAFF from 1977 which meant that with the consent of the applicant grant applications were referred to the NCC by MAFF prior to a decision being made. With the concerns of the NCC now beginning to impinge very directly on the interests of farmers the NFU, albeit rather late in the day, became very involved with the area. After discussions with both the CLA and the NFU, and a meeting with IDB ratepayers on 24 August 1978, the NCC decided to send a 'standard consultation letter' to owners and occupiers on West Sedgemoor indicating its intention to designate the Moor as an SSSI. A map was enclosed with the letter which outlined the regulations relating to SSSIs under the 1949 and 1968 Acts, and the NCC offered to talk to individuals about the implications of such a decision. Consequently the period between 1978 and 1981 saw the NCC in frequent confrontation with the ministry over the question of grants, and first Jerry Wiggin, Parliamentary Under-Secretary of State at MAFF, and then his counterpart at the DoE, Hector Monro, were called to the area in the attempt to resolve notably intractable cases. Such episodes marked the beginning of an extended period of intense and continuous pressure for the NCC's South West Regional Office.

Because the conclusions reached by the Project Group had major policy implications, regional NCC and MAFF submitted its findings to Whitehall. In the event, the reaction of central government created further local uncertainty and effectively threw much of the progress made during the deliberations of the Project Group back into the melting-pot. MAFF and the DoE, unable to agree on a response to the results of the Wetlands Project, decided to commission yet another study. In 1979 the DoE, recognising that a problem of national significance attended by considerable public dismay was developing (and encouraged by Penny Phillips, the energetic chairman of Somerset planning committee) requested the county council to undertake a Somerset Levels and Moors Study preparatory to a local subject plan. This seemed to postpone for a while the prospect of attempting effectively to confront the problems on West Sedgemoor itself. But even as the Consultative Report of Survey for the local subject plan was being published in April 1981 the legislative context within which proposals might be made was being transformed. Just as the Enclosure Acts had provided a mechanism for effecting major change in the Southern Levels nearly two centuries before, so the Wildlife and Countryside Act, which received the Royal Assent on 30 October 1981, profoundly altered the situation on West Sedgemoor — not least by catapulting it to a position of prominence in the struggle to determine how the provisions of that Act would be implemented.

The positions advanced by the various interested parties during subsequent, often heated, discussions were to have a significance beyond the immediate issue of West Sedgemoor which became embroiled in a carefully orchestrated struggle over 'the politics of designation'. Fundamentally, the issues most obviously at stake concerned who should decide where SSSIs were to be and how large they were to be. But beyond these were related imponderables: the impact of designation on land values, and the precise form to be taken by the management agreements which would have to be negotiated. Moreover, there was an acute awareness that important precedents were about to be set regarding the amount that would be paid as compensation for 'goodwill and cooperation'.

West Sedgemoor became, after the Berwyns, the first major area earmarked for notification as an SSSI where the NCC invited representations under Section 28 of the 1981 Act. As so often happens when much is at stake, the protagonists in the debate seemed to spend more time talking past each other than actually communicating, with genuine confusion and uncertainty often difficult to distinguish from wilful misunderstandings and mis-representations. The arguments which had been deployed during the passage of the Act provided a ready-made repertoire of responses to be plundered, and some farmers had no difficulty in projecting an image of a farming community rebelling against an unfeeling and heavy-handed bureaucracy. Certainly, the rigidity of the debate — with its standard slogans chanted back and forth — was remarkable. For the farmers and occupiers at the receiving-end of the new legislation there was the obvious implication that they would have to modify the attitude that 'it's my land and no one is telling me what to do with it'. The anger which years of uncertainty had prompted seemed justified by the prospect of such restrictions thwarting ambitions to effect improvements which might raise farm income. The absence of any financial guidelines for compensation at this stage only compounded the sense of frustration felt by many on the Moor. They could only see a future in which they were condemned to be 'second-class' farmers. In such a situation the NCC, forced to act with urgency because of continuing damage to the Moor, was fated to become the focus for their wider resentments and uncertainties about the future. The interpretation put upon its behaviour became the pretext for the alarmist strategy adopted by the relatively small number of farmers who had already underdrained their land and consequently saw little prospect of securing compensation. And, on occasion, tension was further heightened by the disingenuous and opportunist management of the conflict by wider farming interests in pursuit of concerns which went beyond the immediate efforts of local farmers to achieve a secure livelihood.

THE DECISION TO DESIGNATE

Although the very general consultative letter indicating intent had been sent in 1978 it was not until 31 March 1982 that the NCC sent a formal standard letter under Section 28 of the Wildlife and Countryside Act to owners and occupiers announcing that it proposed to designate the whole 1000 ha. of the moor as an SSSI. Its despatch was preceded by a public meeting at Stoke St Gregory at which, it was widely felt, the NCC's attitude had been high-handed. Little real attempt was being made, it was claimed, to win the goodwill of farmers. Indeed, such was the predisposition to see the NCC as the embodiment of rampant bureaucracy that it is easy to explain why the letter itself should have so exacerbated the situation despite its having been widely explained beforehand. The problem centred on a list of potentially damaging operations which — because it had been drawn up by NCC central office to cover all eventualities — was inevitably extensive. Most recipients, ignoring the covering letter to which it was appended, turned immediately to this list and were appalled by its apparent implications. Moreover, the letter itself was arguably ambiguous. Its second paragraph included the statement, 'The list may include operations that are now normal management on your land and therefore may need to be deleted.' Many of the farmers who *did* read the letter took this to mean that any of their current operations appearing on the list would henceforth have to cease. What had been intended as a reassurance had precisely the opposite effect, and many now mistakenly believed that SSSI designation presaged 'a return to the wilderness'.

Nor was this simply the response of a relatively unlettered farming community as the reaction of the CLA's land use advisers, writing in *The Country Landowner* of May 1982, revealed. As well as regretting that insufficient reasons had been given for the notification of all 1000 ha. and expressing disappointment that notification was being made in advance of an agreed land-use policy for the area, they commented that 'If, as appears to be the case, the NCC wish to be informed when fertilisers and sprays are to be applied or grass is to be mown, then this will mean that farmers will continuously need to notify NCC of ordinary day-to-day management practices.' The NFU, meanwhile, objected to the timing of the letter and saw the 'application' as 'ill-conceived and hasty'. But in his letter to owners and occupiers dated 26 April 1982, Anthony Gibson, the county secretary, took care to clarify the ambiguity regarding the list of notifiable operations and reiterated a categoric assurance from the NCC that 'there will be no going back from the *status quo* — in other words in whatever way a piece of land is farmed at the moment it can continue to be farmed after the designation'. Despite such assurances and extensive local press coverage for statements by Peter Nicholson saying that the NCC's only concern would be with new developments and drainage operations, the leader of the militant farmers, David Perrin, could be found a year later still asserting that 'we are all carrying on as we always have' as if this were something other than what was required. Despite the NCC's best efforts to retrieve the situation, by emphasising that they 'would not act to turn back the clock', misunderstandings — both genuine and deliberately contrived — were to remain rife.

During the passage of the Wildlife and Countryside Act, both the NFU and the CLA had taken great exception to the absence of any provision for a right of appeal against designation. Accordingly, they now embarked upon a campaign to reduce substantially the area subject to designation. The CLA wrote to the NCC asking it to reconsider, but polite requests that it act with 'sympathy and tact' in carrying out its duties were effectively coded messages warning it to think again. Similarly the NFU letter to owners and occupiers, while encouraging them to take advantage of offers of help from the NCC, also entreated them to cooperate in the campaign to have already 'improved areas' removed from the SSSI by writing to the NCC setting out, on a field-by-field basis, the presence or absence of scientific interest on their land. Thus a consultation period intended for representations regarding potentially damaging operations became the occasion for a concerted campaign to question the fact of designation itself. It was a campaign which was to be sustained for almost a year. Central to the concerns which fuelled it was a fear that the NCC's budget allocation was barely sufficient to cover the administrative costs of designations under the Act, let alone provide resources for management agreements and the compensation payments for which there were, as yet, no guidelines. Indeed, the NFU was to complain repeatedly about the inappropriateness of the decision's timing on the grounds that it had preceded both the county council's plans and publication of guidelines on compensation. With delay following upon delay, David Perrin commented some months later: 'We want to see cash on the table before we even start talking. I don't see why we should have to sell our livelihoods without any money being talked about. It is nothing short of communism.'

Needless to say, many of the farmers objecting to designation of their land saw themselves as naturalists and conservationists. Bert Betty, for instance, had underdrained 45 of his 54 ha. 'at the suggestion of MAFF', but he had also made a sizeable pond, planted a large number of trees and left hedges in place, and much was to be made of his supposedly enlightened behaviour. But as if to emphasise the precariousness of conservation on West Sedgemoor, even *after* the 1981 Act, three farmers began new drainage operations on 26 ha. in the middle of the proposed SSSI during the three-months' consultation period. With the populations of birds such as the curlew threatened by the way in which isolated improvements tended to 'split the area', the RSPB was alarmed by the NFU's advice to farmers to press for the land to be designated on a field-by-field basis and accused it of going back on its assurances of support for the Act. The RSPB called upon Environment Secretary, Michael Heseltine, to intervene, using the emergency powers available to him. The NFU, in the person of county chairman Brian Rowe, denied that they were trying to clog up the conservation works with correspondence and regretted the precipitate action of the farmers. But with an element of equivocation which was to characterise the response of local NFU throughout, he did not censure them but described their reactions as 'inevitable given the uncertainties of the situation'.

With the course of events evidently deteriorating into bitter conflict, Somerset county council — seeing itself as probably the least engaged and therefore the most open-minded of those directly involved — responded to an initiative by the NCC chairman and invited him to make a 'peace mission' to the Moor. On 11 June 1982 Sir Ralph Verney met Somerset county councillors, local MPs and farmers' representatives at Taunton and agreed to extend the consultation period until the end of August to give the NCC more time for discussions with farmers. The move was welcomed by the NFU, for whom delay was essential if the need for reconsideration was to be pressed upon the NCC. But when the NCC's chairman returned the following month for a public meeting with local landowners and conservation and wildlife groups it was described by *Farmers' Weekly* as 'stormy'. Nevertheless, the NCC felt that the two visits had done much to allay farmers' fears and that early resistance to the proposed designation was now disappearing: a species of 'whistling in the wind' which would be exposed in months to come, even though NFU sources too were reported as claiming that the NCC's whole approach had become much more understanding of farmers' problems. In fact both 'sides' were sure that progress was being made, but their conceptions of what was to count as 'progress' were hardly compatible. For the NCC it meant clarifying its legal duty to notify and the terms of compensation, whilst for the NFU it meant 'softening up' the NCC in the hope that it might reconsider. And such misunderstandings rested ultimately on very different conceptions of what was, or was not, to be regarded as negotiable.

The CLA, in keeping with its more measured approach to such matters, had pursued a rather different strategy in responding to what it certainly saw as an invitation from the NCC to comment on the decision to designate the whole area. With relatively few members on the Moor it had done nothing to encourage a local activism but had, instead, requested Professor Kenneth Mellanby to make what it hoped would be an authoritative assessment of the scientific interest of the Moor as a basis for deciding whether it would be reasonable to reduce the size of the area to be notified. The then President of the British Association of Nature Conservationists visited West Sedgemoor from 5 to 8 June 1982, completed his report on 14

June and, on 21 July, the CLA issued a press release claiming, on the basis of the report, that the Moor's scientific interest could be preserved if designation were restricted to an area of about 500 ha. — much of which was already covered by the existing RSPB reserve. The NCC had not appreciated, argued Mellanby (himself a former senior scientist with the Nature Conservancy), just how much of the Moor had already been 'improved', and he could see no justification for scheduling fields which, having been underdrained, re-seeded and treated with herbicides and fertilisers, have 'very little' botanical interest and 'lack most of the plants listed by the NCC'. The Mellanby Report, though based on a rather minimal familiarity with the area and regarded by many conservationists as a shoddy piece of work (when regional NCC tried to discuss it with him he was 'unavailable'), acted as a firecracker thrown onto a fire whose flames had just been dampened. MAFF's scientific adviser on nature conservation, Dr Way, had also visited the Moor during June and he too recommended a much reduced area for designation, suggesting that about 370 ha. in the centre of the Moor would be appropriate. The clamour for the NCC to reconsider mounted, raising expectations in ways which — given the NCC's statutory obligations — could not possibly be met.

In its formal response of 3 August to the NCC's letter, the Somerset and South Avon branch of the NFU seemed to call for an even greater reduction in the area to be designated. Whilst not claiming the scientific competence to draw lines on a map it too pointed to the areas centred on the land owned by the RSPB as those with the greatest scientific interest, but did not see designation of the whole Moor as necessary to protect them. 'We would contend', it went on, 'that it would be perfectly possible to manage the rhynes and water levels so as to maintain a high watertable in the most important areas and prevent possible pollution of the rhynes in these key areas from agricultural practices carried out elsewhere on the Moor.' With their 'innate predisposition' against formal controls the farming community were seeking a major gesture from the NCC to restore the goodwill which had been forfeited by the manner in which the NCC had presented its untimely proposal.

Although the argument was couched in terms of scientific criteria it is hard not to see the references to a possible 'gesture' from the NCC as an indication of a fundamental and wilful misunderstanding of its position. In conversation Anthony Gibson reiterated his view that, 'so as not to appear intransigent, the NCC should have opened with a "bid" of, say, 1200 ha.' so that they could subsequently appear to be 'giving a little' when coming down to the 1000 ha. they actually wanted to designate. But viewing scientific criteria for designation as essentially negotiable is incompatible with the view the NCC takes of its statutory duties as giving it no scope for 'choice' in the matter — an interpretation confirmed by the separate legal opinions sought by the NCC and the NFU. Nevertheless, the proposed visit by the entire NCC council planned for 18 October 1982, following in the wake of the recommendations in the Mellanby and Way Reports and myriad other forms of pressure, seemed, to the local farming community, to offer the prospect of compromise. In the event sceptics in that community questioned whether a three-hour trip round the area in a minibus could have conveyed a real understanding of the agricultural problems of the area although the 'friendly chat over a cream tea' style seemed to confirm that the NCC might respond to farming pressure. But just for good measure a message, described as 'blackmail' by FoE, was sent by the NFU to Sir Ralph Verney just days before the decision was to be made. 'Beg you to reduce site to essentials', it read. 'Compromise now will guarantee harmony in future.'

The council decided on 17 November that the whole area should be notified. This, according to Brian Rowe, was 'a sad and bad decision which bodes ill for the relationship between farmers and conservationists throughout the whole of the Somerset Levels'. NFU President, Sir Richard Butler, was 'extremely dismayed', whilst the CLA were disappointed that so 'little weight' had obviously been given to Mellanby's findings. *The Somerset Farmer*'s December editorial, meanwhile, declared that 'Détente between farmers and conservationists has been put back maybe five years at a stroke of Sir Ralph Verney's pen'. So far as many local farmers were concerned, months of consultation seemed to have been nothing more than an

expensive charade. 'There are', said Anthony Gibson, 'a
lot of angry people about.'

NCC RESOLVE

In the face of such overwhelming condemnation from the
farming and landowning lobby minimal statements of
scientific rectitude were the only response available to the
NCC. As Peter Nicholson emphasised in statements to the
local press, legal advice had made it clear that 'there was
no way we could meet a compromised solution'. After
years of direct involvement in conservation on the Moor,
the ornithological, botanical and entomological interests
of the site had, in the words of the NCC's chairman,
'been exhaustively assessed and a judgement of scientific
interest had been made'. Moreover, the NCC took the
view that West Sedgemoor constituted a single hydrological regime. To implement the NFU/Mellanby position
by isolating the RSPB reserve as an SSSI would entail large
capital costs for the installation of the sluices and dams
needed to guarantee its long-term viability.

Underpinning the conflicts between the farming and
conservation lobbies, in short, were very different understandings which rested ultimately on incompatible assessments of the significance of scientific evidence. The NCC,
on the basis of its examinations, regarded the area as
essentially indivisible, whilst those opposed to designation of the whole Moor were equally convinced that the
area could be effectively parcelled without compromising
its scientific interest. The NCC is hardly so naïve as to
suppose scientific evidence to be beyond question: but the
rules of the game force it to behave as if its own understanding of the available evidence is. The NCC's decision,
greeted with considerable and surprised relief by the conservation lobby, had demonstrated that it was prepared to
make what Peter Nicholson privately acknowledged to be,
in some ultimate sense, an informed value-judgement —
and make it stick.

But even as the plaudits were resounding around the
NCC's headquarters, its chairman was being put under
extraordinary ministerial pressure through the efforts

of two influential Somerset MPs. Backed by the NFU, Edward Du Cann and John Peyton (then Conservative MPs for Taunton and Yeovil, respectively) made a personal plea to the Environment Secretary to intervene. The NCC had, they suggested, been 'inconsiderate and oppressive', and Sir Ralph Verney was 'quite unable to keep his zealots and minions in any kind of effective check'. The hope was expressed that the minister would 'now set aside the council's decision'. The legal advice sought by the NCC was that the Secretary of State had no such power and Verney warned him that 'an attitude of non-cooperation will provoke greater and possibly irresistible pressure for an extension of planning controls'. Subsequently, a meeting was held at the NCC, where the two were joined by ten council members, the minister's deputy at the DoE, Tom King, and Earl Ferrers, the Minister of State for Agriculture. A joint statement resulted, which noted that the council's decision had been taken on 'carefully considered scientific evidence' and Heseltine, for his part, expressed the hope that the new Act could work effectively and offered to take part in an early local meeting with farmers' representatives, local MPs and the NCC.

Though still an ambition in the minds of some farmers, the possibility of reducing the designated area was effectively foreclosed and the financial issues which had always been central to the conflict now dominated an angry and uncertain debate. The financial guidelines had still not been published and farmers claimed they were in a state of uninformed limbo, although both the CLA and the NFU were engaged in intense discussions with the DoE. Tom King became Environment Secretary on 25 January and one of his first acts as minister was to tell Sir Ralph Verney that he would not be reappointed as NCC chairman. However, the anger of the local farmers was not to be assuaged by this 'scalp', particularly as government at all levels insisted that the decision was unrelated to the West Sedgemoor controversy. Farmers still lacked the financial assurances their action group was seeking and they were further incensed by successive postponements of the planned ministerial visit. With the NFU calling for a one-year truce without any further designations, the 'Battle for Sedgemoor' was to stage its most spectacular media event:

the skirmish in the car park of the Black Smock Inn at Stathe.

Local farmers, it seems, had initially planned to burn in public the letters they had received from the NCC informing them of their new obligations. But having become intensely publicity-conscious over the months of struggle they responded readily to a suggestion that effigies of their 'opponents' should be burnt as well. A *Western Daily Press* reporter helped set up the stunt, which was carefully timed to enable film of the bonfire to feature in the same day's evening TV news. An old Royal Artillery Achilles-Sherman tank carrying a 'Dictatorship Ends Here' banner was driven to the site and, in a welter of anachronistic images, its 17-pounder gun was trained symbolically upon the three hanging figures. National media coverage was assured.

Given the keen appreciation at NFU headquarters of the need to make the Act work, such activities by local 'mavericks' were bound to cause considerable embarrassment. The local branch had, in many ways, played on the fears of local farmers merely by incessantly articulating them whenever the NCC offered fresh assurances. Under strong pressure from both within and outside the area Anthony Gibson, the county secretary of the NFU who is also a regular journalist and broadcaster under various pseudonyms, used his extensive media contacts to mount an effective campaign against the NCC's handling of the affair. *The Western Morning News* and *The Western Daily Press*, in particular, sustained commentaries on the dispute which were as consistently critical of the NCC as they were ill-informed: continual references to the proposed SSSI as a 'nature reserve' indicated misunderstandings which further confused an already complex issue. Faced with the planned 'happening' at Stathe, Gibson could not dissociate himself from a situation he had done so much to create. In response to the RSPB's strong condemnation of the distasteful episode, he argued that 'It is not easy for us to sell a system when the only example we have is a farmer who has been trying unsuccessfully for two and a half years to negotiate a management agreement with the NCC and the most he has been offered in compensation is £35 an acre. Less than he would get on Exmoor.' In fact,

since both he and the farmers knew that this figure was to
be reviewed when the guidelines were published and the
revised figure back-dated, this was yet another instance of
peculiarly special pleading.

CONCILIATORY MOVES

West Sedgemoor was now widely regarded as a test of the
1981 Act, but uncertainty in the area was heightened still
further when details of the Somerset county council consultative plan were leaked prior to the minister's visit. This
politically-sensitive document, which had been kept confidential since May 1982, envisaged specifying 2800 ha. on
the Levels as 'wildlife conservation areas' and a further
3000 ha. as 'areas of exceptional wildlife interest'. In addition, 'areas of high archaeological potential' were to be
identified. News of such novel categories, for which there
was no statutory provision, created further disquiet, and
when Tom King finally attended a highly-charged private
meeting on 5 March 1983 with owners and occupiers, local
MPs and NCC officials at Burrowbridge a great deal was at
stake. Just days before, new drainage operations, which
were to become the subject of the third use by the NCC of
a Section 29 order, had begun on Tadham and Tealham
Moor, with the apparent object of pre-empting another
SSSI designation.

The minister's visit was widely regarded as a great personal success. Not only could he offer, with greater authority, assurances identical to those offered all along by the
NCC but, crucially, could back them with emphatic statements that government money would be available for
compensation. In addition, although all the evidence from
the RSPB suggested that land values in the area were
rising, he assured the farmers that independent research
would be conducted to ascertain the impact of designation
on land values and that 'if it is established that there is a
loss in capital value then that loss will have to be recognised and compensated for'. This remarkable pledge,
going beyond anything the government had previously
said about compensation under the Wildlife and Countryside Act, did much to secure the truce he was looking for

and the way was now clear for him to appeal to the farmers to allow what was 'very much my own Act' to succeed. Moreover, there was enough in his comments about the need for further research on the hydrology of the area and for the appointment of a special liaison officer for Anthony Gibson to suggest to the press in extraordinarily inaccurate fashion that 'Mr King has laid the blame for everything that has gone wrong squarely at the door of the NCC.' This comment was later dubbed with exasperated justification by Regional NCC as a 'sordid lie', for the NCC had itself suggested the research, and had already appointed the liaison officer for the purpose of resolving problems on the ground by 'talking the farmers' language'.

The meeting marked the beginning of a more constructive phase on the Moor. In an attempt to meet the charge that it had not made its evidence for designation available, the NCC circulated a three-page document describing the area's wildlife interest, although it could hardly meet the demands of many farmers who had mistakenly supposed from the Burrowbridge meeting that they were to receive individual, field-by-field evidence. The project officer began work, and with the emphasis very much on bridge-building, the spring and summer months of 1983 saw formative moves towards the negotiation of management agreements. A new district valuer was drafted in, and after seven months some 30 agreements had been initiated. Progress was inevitably slow, as some farmers were reluctant to cooperate too readily lest they appear 'soft' to their fellow activists; and most farmers were reluctant to sign until a 'going rate' had been established. In addition, many of those involved in the negotiations — particularly local solicitors — were working in what was, for them, uncharted territory.

The NCC are, understandably, reticent about the financial details of management agreements, but settlements negotiated were, according to Gibson, on average £70–90 per acre (about £170–220 per ha.). This could entail an upper figure of about £150,000 per annum at 1983 prices for management agreements to ensure the conservation of the whole of West Sedgemoor. By the time the county council's draft *Somerset Levels and Moors Plan* was finally published on 14 September 1983 the NFU was finding the

DoE 'very helpful'. Indeed, the advent of the county council plan was actively resented by the representatives of the farming and landowning community because its extensive proposals seemed likely to disrupt once again the progress which was now being made. Anthony Gibson, who had come round to the view that the farmers should be 'left alone to sort things out quietly on the ground with the NCC' declared, 'There is no way we will talk with them [the county council] about management agreements and we are not going to have any truck with a load of voluntary conservation bodies claiming an executive role in implementing the Plan.'

The *Somerset Levels and Moors Plan* attempts to affirm the place of agricultural improvement in the area whilst also generating mechanisms for protecting the area's wildlife and archaeological values. It emphasises that the county council's own planning powers are limited, and that real protection will therefore depend upon SSSI designation or purchase and lease-back arrangements. To achieve the cooperation needed to implement its proposed strategy the plan suggested that a 'Countryside Forum' should be established. Both the CLA and the NFU expressed doubts about the proposed creation of two new and confusing wildlife conservation classifications which, as the *Somerset Farmer* pointed out, would only be protected if the NCC eventually designated them as SSSIs. Both felt that the Forum and other proposals for working parties would be little more than costly talking-shops, and used the publication of the plan principally as an occasion for symbolic affirmations of the success of the mechanisms provided by the 1981 Act. A workable accord having been painfully achieved with the NCC (which they had earlier described as having been transformed by the Act from 'a well-intentioned conservation organisation to an interfering policeman'), the NFU said it had 'no wish to see "the Battle of Sedgemoor" perpetuated'. The DoE was also wary of disturbing the political settlement and, though it had earlier encouraged the county council's conciliatory efforts, it refused to give the plan statutory approval.

Towards the end of 1983 Richard Cook, an ADAS officer with a personal commitment to conservation, was seconded by MAFF to be the NCC's liaison officer in the

Somerset Levels. This enabled the NCC for the first time to talk to the farmers through an officer whom the farmers trusted. Cook, who describes his function as a 'marriage counsellor', reported at a Royal Town Planning Institute seminar held at Taunton in January 1985 that the mood of the farmers had changed to 'reluctant acceptance' of the SSSIs. Despite the inability of an understaffed NCC to designate more than a small part of the 6070 ha. of proposed SSSIs on the Levels, Cook said that, since his appointment, farmers had not taken advantage of the loopholes in the Wildlife and Countryside Act to go ahead with drainage before designation, despite the fact that conversion to arable farming was profitable even without grants. Of the 800 farmers in the proposed SSSIs, 68 were negotiating management agreements by January 1985 with compensation running at £150–220 per ha. As yet none has been signed, although a number of interim agreements are in operation. His conclusion that the system is proving 'very successful' must be qualified, however, by its inherent limitations. The process of negotiation is laborious and costly in time, money and lawyers' and surveyors' fees. The ultimate cost of conserving all the proposed SSSIs could exceed £1 million. Although Cook thinks it unlikely that agreements will be needed over the entire area, his personal view is that it would be cheaper for the NCC to buy the land. Because it is weak, the NCC has been obliged to accept compromises, particularly where farmers have been unwilling to cease existing damaging practices even when offered compensation. The agreements can do nothing for the remaining 60,000 ha. of the Levels, and although the farmers are gradually learning and modifying their positions, the underlying conflict remains. MAFF's drainage grants are still on offer, and the temptation to convert to arable farming is very strong, threatening the fragile marriages that Cook is arranging — often for no more than three or five years.

However temporarily and uneasily, a tentative peace has now returned to West Sedgemoor, the first SSSI on the Levels. The designation entailed an episode of vitriolic conflict, characterised by remarkable delays, blunders, misunderstandings, arrogance and lack of communication, in the course of which ministries, authorities and agencies hardened in the literal and legalistic interpretation of their statutory obligations. The NCC's regional officers throughout the three-year period were forced to devote virtually the whole of their time to this single issue. Long and complicated discussions about the future of the Levels, conducted amid a wider debate about the relationship between agricultural improvement and conservation, had engendered considerable uncertainty and apprehension on the Moor.

Developments within the wider context were critical in other ways. It is probable that the resolve of the RSPB to bring legal action against the NCC over SSSI designation in the Berwyns (see Chapter 9) contributed to the firm stance which Sir Ralph Verney and his council took to resist the improper pressures exerted over the West Sedgemoor decision. In an area where resistance to change is always a powerful force, there were almost as many opinions amongst the farming community as there were owners and occupiers. Yet a militant action group composed almost wholly of farmers who had already improved their land (and who, therefore, stood to gain little from possible compensation payments) were able to present an impression of unified and implacable opposition. The CLA, with relatively few members in the area, attempted to question authoritatively the NCC decision, but once thwarted gracefully withdrew from that aspect of the struggle. In contrast, the Somerset and Avon branch of the NFU, accorded a local autonomy typical of that organisation, sustained a tenacious, and occasionally irresponsible, pursuit of the rights of private property, acutely aware that the settlement achieved on West Sedgemoor would have far wider implications for the elaboration of procedures under the Wildlife and Countryside Act. As Peter Nicholson of the NCC put it, 'They knew very well what we were saying. They just didn't like it and there were two arguments we could never meet to their satisfaction — compensation and the supposed blighting effect on land values.'

Much to the discomfort of the organisations deeply committed to the success of the Wildlife and Countryside Act, the dispute on West Sedgemoor provided a spectacle of disconcerting brinkmanship which seemed to impel farmers towards civil disobedience, disorder and inevitable legal sanctions. Tom King was only able to appeal successfully for support during the meeting at Burrowbridge because he offered unprecedented financial assurances to the owners and occupiers who confronted him. The dispute had, in the end, come to concern not so much West Sedgemoor, as the authority and viability of the NCC itself, so more than anyone the minister appreciated the full significance of his words when he warned the farmers, 'We are right in the front-line of battle to preserve the voluntary approach to conservation.'

11. Ploughing into the Halvergate Marshes

PART 1: THE BACKGROUND

The term 'Halvergate' has three meanings: first, it refers to a stretch of some 3000 ha. of drained, high water-table marsh that forms a triangle of land between the lower Bure and Yare rivers in eastern Norfolk. This is the heart of the region popularly known as 'The Broads', a network of lakes and rivers meandering through marshes whose water-tables range from surface flooding (fen) to deep arterial drainage. For drainage purposes, the marsh is subdivided into a series of 'levels', or drainage areas. The Halvergate Level is one of five levels in the whole area, the eastern sector of which is known as the Halvergate Marshes (see Map 11.1).

Secondly, the term is used to refer to an area of some 2000 ha. of marsh to the west of the whole area which was subject to three separate but related proposals for improved drainage promoted by the Lower Bure, Acle Marshes and Halvergate Fleet Internal Drainage Board in late 1980. Only part of the Halvergate Level lay within the proposed drainage schemes, and even that was locally referred to as the 'Manor House Level'. So in terms of the story described below, Halvergate is geographically a misnomer; nevertheless, it is this second meaning that now stands as the most widely accepted one and which will be

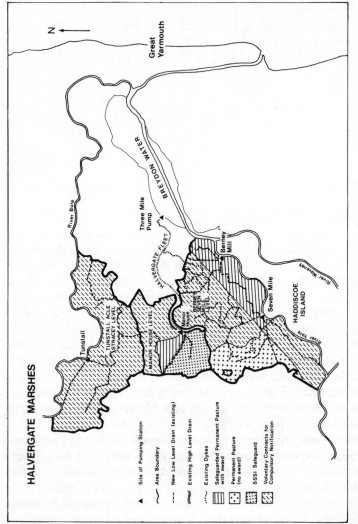

Map 11.1   The Halvergate Marshes Phase 1. 1980–82 showing the three drainage schemes proposed by the Lower Bure Internal Drainage Board and the original suggestions for safeguarding key areas (horizontal hatching) of the marshes put

implied throughout the rest of the chapter. The name itself comes from a nearby village situated on the 'upland' margin of the marsh, adjacent to the Manor House Level. 'Halvergate' also has a third meaning, associated with the dispute between the agricultural and land-drainage interests on the one hand, and the conservation and amenity lobby on the other. It is symbolic of the struggle for political recognition by those lobbies for popular support of their case, and for the redirection of public money to serve what they see as the public interest. 'Halvergate' is a classic environmental *cause célèbre*, the test-case representing the demand for reform of agricultural and conservation policies and expenditures, for reorganising the structure and practices of the land-drainage bodies, and for evening out the balance of political interest between the established influence of the farming and landowning community, and the ever more forceful voice of conservation and heritage protection.

For nine months of the year the Halvergate Marshes are all but inaccessible except to those willing to wade through ankle-deep mud. There are no made-up roads, and walking is discouraged by the myriad of dykes or drainage ditches. On a grey, wintry day the wind cuts through even the thickest clothing. The view is austere and to many uninviting. The marshes are quite flat with few distinguishing features — the odd, derelict wind pump, some clumps of trees, a number of wooden cattle gates. Even in summer, when Broads holiday-boaters moor up at the Berney Inn for a lunchtime drink or step off the local train at Berney Halt, only a handful venture onto the nearby marshes — and few people visit the Halvergate Marshes. Halvergate exists primarily for livestock (mostly young dairy followers, some beef cattle and a few sheep), is almost uninhabited and rarely visited: so why seek to save it?

The simple answer is that Halvergate is the last remaining extensive stretch of open grazing marsh in eastern England. The low-lying valleys of the Broadland rivers used to contain 15,000 ha. of similar marshes, though about two-thirds of these in the middle and upper stretches which were enclosed by nearby 'upland' did not have the peculiar open character of Halvergate. Arable conversion steadily nibbled away at the grazing marshes — so much so that the proposed drainage area contained the only remaining *representative* slice of that landscape. Of about 3000 ha. of truly open marsh in the whole of Broadland, half lay within the proposed Halvergate drainage area with the other half adjacent to it, mostly between the Yare and Waveney rivers. The loss of Halvergate to the plough would have destroyed much of the landscape value of that residual adjacent area even if it had remained in grass. The more enclosed marshes of the upper valleys are also disappearing under the plough: since 1970 about one-third (some 3000 ha.) has gone, of which 2500 ha. has been lost since 1980.

For the landscape conservationists, then, Halvergate was the end of the line: the point at which no further concessions could be made. Its value lies in its total experience — in its sweep of horizon, its characteristic Broadland landscape features, its constantly changing pattern of clouds, its brilliant patchwork of shades of green created by different seeding and grazing practices, its evocative sounds of wind and bird calls, and its varied ecology of drainage dykes containing a fascinating variety of water plants, dragonflies and water beetles. Halvergate is a lowland version of upland moorland: it is wild, open and devoid of settlement. Its expansiveness, its 'naturalness', and its sense of timeless linkage with past agricultural practices and hard-won drainage and flood protection over two centuries make it one of the most precious landscapes in the nation. And, perhaps like moorland, the marshes will come to be appreciated by far larger numbers as a vital component of the nation's landscape heritage.

But there is another reason for saving Halvergate, namely that 'lily-gilded' drainage is simply unnecessary. The additional cereal production is no longer of real economic value to the nation, and in practical and economic terms it will do nothing to reduce world hunger. The crop is too expensive to sell without subvention; and a burden on the taxpayer to grow and to store or dispose of under subsidy. In short, the traditional grazing regimes of the Halvergate Marshes constitute a well-balanced, low-input farming system and no net national gain derives from draining it: any publicly-financed drainage investment would benefit private landowners and tenants at the expense of the public interest. To save Halvergate, therefore, would be to save the nation from wasting its money and to bring politicians to their senses over how to marry agricultural and conservation policies so as to derive maximum public enjoyment at least cost to the taxpayer.

THE *DRAMATIS PERSONAE* OF THE HALVERGATE DRAMA

It is somewhat unfair to describe the two sets of protagonists in the Halvergate drama as camps or choruses, since both sides tried for two years to seek a compromise. Nevertheless, two camps there were — a *conservation* camp, funded primarily or exclusively through the Department of the Environment (DoE), with a remit to protect and manage habitat and landscape amenities; and a *drainage* camp, connected to the agricultural community and linked to MAFF, with a remit to control drainage and to increase agricultural productivity, and with a subsidiary requirement to take into account the interests of conservation and amenity.

In the conservation camp were three organisations: the Broads Authority, the Countryside Commission and the Nature Conservancy Council. The Broads Authority is an autonomous local authority composed of elected representatives of the two county councils (Norfolk and Suffolk) and six district councils, along with coopted members from the Anglian Water Authority (AWA) and the local navigation authority, the Great Yarmouth Port and Haven Commissioners. In addition the Countryside Commission nominates three independent members, and provides half the authority's administration costs plus substantial amounts of grant aid for specific projects. The Broads Authority was established in 1978 as a local authority amalgam, primarily to counter proposals by the Countryside Commission to make the Broads into a national park.

In late 1980, when the Halvergate drama began, the authority was hardly established. It was barely conscious of its national as well as local responsibilities, and was unclear about its duties and powers over conservation as opposed to economic development. Moreover, it was primarily composed of local people who initially reacted to Halvergate as a local problem and who were susceptible to lobbying from agricultural interests. The Authority was therefore vulnerable to manipulation at first, but undoubtedly grew in national standing as the Halvergate issue progressed. But because of its inexperience in such complicated matters, it made a number of negotiating errors during the four-year struggle. As Halvergate dragged on, the Authority became more cohesive in its approach, much more critical and well-informed about the issues raised, and increasingly frustrated by the conflicting cross-purposes of agricultural and conservation policies. In short, the Authority matured politically.

Ideally, the Countryside Commission and the Broads Authority should work hand-in-hand, since they ostensibly have overlapping interests and operational styles (mainly persuasion and financial inducements). However, during the Halvergate episode communications between the two were not always clear, and on three notable occasions they parted company; though in each case they eventually agreed on a common position. At the outset the Commission was pushing the Broads Authority into a tougher policy and negotiating position than most Authority members would have liked. But later their roles were reversed: the Authority attempted to push a somewhat reluctant Countryside Commission into new policy arenas.

The interests of the Nature Conservancy Council (NCC) in the area were literally marginal, since it was primarily concerned with the flora and fauna of the drainage dykes on the western edge of Halvergate. Indeed, the original drainage proposals were only brought to the NCC's attention, and through it to the Broads Authority, because the NCC was in the process of scheduling an SSSI on the western part of the Manor House Level when the drainage schemes were proposed. On landscape matters, the NCC has, unfortunately, little statutory interest. If at times the Broads Authority, the NCC and the Countryside Commission operated at cross-purposes, this was partly due to their different statutory obligations and varying interpretations of their responsibilities.

Behind these three 'front-stage' organisations lay a number of voluntary groups both supporting the conservation camp and pressing it to take firmer positions. Local groups included the Norfolk Naturalists' Trust and the Suffolk Trust for Nature Conservation — both opposed to the proposals but not particularly vociferous or influential — and the Broads Society which, with farmers' voices dominating its executive, was ambivalent throughout. The voluntary organisations played a very minor role, notable for their lack of cohesion, even though they were kept fairly well-informed of developments. The one exception was the Council for the Protection of Rural England (CPRE), which repeatedly demanded a public inquiry where it could present criticisms of existing policies and challenge the economic justification for the drainage schemes. Throughout the two years, it conducted a national campaign against the Halvergate proposals through letters to the press, carefully timed press conferences, and judicious lobbying of MPs and peers. The CPRE's contribution was to maintain a consistent national critique: its influence locally was surprisingly small and, on Broads Authority members, almost negligible. But it was remarkably successful in stirring up parliamentarians and the media at key points, thereby keeping the Halvergate pot boiling.

The drainage camp also consisted of three main organisations: the Lower Bure, Acle Marshes and Halvergate Fleet Internal Drainage Board, the National Farmers' Union and the Country Landowners' Association. The title of the first is a real mouthful so it is shortened here to LBIDB. The LBIDB is one of 217 quasi-autonomous drainage boards in England and Wales. These are remarkable organisations, relics of a semi-feudal age that have long enjoyed having their own way, removed from the spotlight of public attention. They are the only local bodies (apart from local authorities) with powers to levy rates, and they raise about £10 million annually from their ratepayers, in addition to the £2.5 million they receive per year in MAFF grants. Prior to 1980 they were practically accountable to no one except friendly officials within the MAFF. They could raise or lower water-tables, remove sluices, dig ditches or propose expensive arterial drainage

schemes without informing any ecologist, planner or
economist. Indeed, many boards did not even consult
their own members adequately before embarking on expensive capital operations. Under Section 6 of the Land
Drainage Act 1976, IDBs have wide discretionary powers
and can obtain 50 per cent MAFF grants for approved
works. So long as their proposals were technically sound
and economically justifiable grant aid was automatic and
paid out without any public scrutiny. The IDBs grew complacent and somewhat arrogant, and seemed to see their
mission as draining every acre of remaining wetlands.
Shielded by secrecy and confidentiality, and left alone by
an unconcerned public and local authorities, they thought
they were free to get on unmolested with the business of
publicly-subsidised drainage. The Halvergate saga put a
stop to that: nowadays a much brighter light shines on the
operations of IDBs.

The LBIDB was typical. It was nominally run by a board
of elected representatives, but in practice was controlled
by a small executive committee composed almost entirely
of farmers who stood to gain most from improved drainage works. Even the full board was almost totally dominated by farmers, despite the fact that Norfolk County
Council, which contributed to its revenue, had the right to
be represented. Its affairs were handled by a part-time
clerk who managed four other IDBs as well as his real
estate business.

The LBIDB levied two drainage rates — an owner's rate
(£10–18 per ha. in 1982/83) to pay for capital works, and
any AWA precept; and an occupier's rate (£7–12 per ha.)
for annual maintenance and administration. These rates
were based on annual expenditures and were set on land
value. At the opening of the Halvergate dispute IDBs were
not allowed to build up a reserve to help pay for future
capital works that had to be undertaken when pumps
failed or when drainage needed to be improved. They
normally only charged historic capital costs. This artificially depressed owners' rates in the period before a new
capital scheme was proposed. Moreover, agricultural land
values had not been re-rated since 1935. This produced a
serious anomaly in drainage revenue since any urban
property (which has been re-rated many times since 1935)

had to pay far more than surrounding agricultural land and hence subsidised the drainage of that land. In addition, no allowance was made for land improved to yield a higher output through intensive grazing or arable production. Once again those who derived the greatest benefit from drainage were subsidised by their neighbours — in this case, the farmers who did not intensify to the utmost. Under Section 68 of the Land Drainage Act 1976, IDBs can vary drainage rates so long as this is consistent with the purposes of the regional water authority and in keeping with local interests. In fact, IDBs can levy a lower or zero rate on any owner or occupier 'for any reason'. During the Halvergate dispute the Broads Authority estimated that differential drainage rates could have reduced compensation costs by £8000 per annum (about 15 per cent of estimated final compensation costs), but the LBIDB would not entertain the suggestion.

In short, IDBs operate on a very inequitable arrangement of revenue-generation and expenditures are subsidised by substantial amounts of taxpayers' and ratepayers' money, yet are (or certainly were) virtually non-accountable, in the sense that interested parties could not challenge their operations. The absence of any proper accountability angered conservationists and expenditure-conscious politicians alike, and in part lay behind the increasing reluctance by the conservation camp to conclude any kind of 'deal' over Halvergate.

The other two members of the drainage camp were the NFU and the CLA. Throughout the Halvergate drama these bodies were represented by county and national officials. They showed clear unanimity of purpose and cohesiveness of action, and demonstrated their support for both MAFF policies and the drainage interests. Furthermore, they had good connections with both ministers and civil servants in MAFF. In all these respects, the situation of the NFU and the CLA contrasted sharply with that of the conservation groups. Indeed, it is revealing that the former (unlike the latter) were 'front-stage' organisations. The NFU and the CLA purported to represent the individual landowners; but in reality they represented their supposed collective interests, *not* the particular concerns of individual marsh-owners who were as different in their views and responses as pebbles on a beach.

In negotiating terms the drainage camp was far better organised and politically focused than the conservation camp, but as the story unfolded the tables were turned. The effect of the coincidence of the Wildlife and Countryside Bill cannot be underestimated. This not only provided a platform for politicians to draw attention to the ridiculous inconsistency of policy which Halvergate seemed to highlight, but also gave negotiators excuses for delaying crucial decisions while official policy positions were established.

THE PRE-DECISION CONTEXT

The Halvergate problem was created out of policy conditions that advantaged drainage interests over conservation interests. Five factors were involved: (i) traditional marsh management and economics; (ii) MAFF policies towards drainage; (iii) intervention prices under the Common Agricultural Policy, especially the massive incentive offered to cereal over livestock production; (iv) the vested personal interests of the LBIDB executive in improved drainage; and (v) the Broads Authority's strategy for safeguarding landscape. Let us examine each of these factors in turn.

Traditional Marsh Management and the Economics of Grazing

The pattern of marsh-ownership in the Broads is a product of inheritance and acquisition. Over half the landowners in the area of proposed drainage own less than 10 ha. The vast majority are absentee landlords who let their land to local graziers through an annual auction. Unlike agricultural tenancies, grazing licences last only 364 days. This provides flexibility for both landowner and tenant, neither of whom is committed to price or to contract, but is a deterrent to long-term management.

The Halvergate Marshes depend upon a reliable system of drainage for their agricultural and landscape character. In 1980 the whole area was drained by eight pumps, all of which were at least 25 years old, and two of which were over 40 years old. These pumps cannot last forever, and already replacement parts for some of the pumps are very difficult to obtain. The traditional arrangement of a pump supervised by a marshman acting as livestock supervisor and mechanic is no longer popular, especially as three of the existing pumps are not easily accessible by motor vehicle.

These traditions, together with the particular drainage characteristics, combine to create on Halvergate a state of suspended animation in Norfolk marsh agriculture — a delayed stage in the otherwise 'inevitable' transition to intensive cropping. Most of the Halvergate soils are good clays which, when well-drained, are very fertile, capable with large inputs of fertilisers and pesticides of producing at least 5.5 tonnes of wheat per ha. This agricultural an-achronism is a major factor in giving Halvergate its land-scape charm, but it is precisely this anachronistic image which forces 'progressive' farmers to want to change it, and causes many local farmers to judge such landscapes as 'agricultural failures'.

MAFF Policies Towards Drainage

Because IDBs are not allowed to levy rates to build up capital reserves for *future* drainage investments, drainage charges reflect only the historic costs of the existing pumps and annual maintenance. Drainage rates are remarkably low (around £22 per ha.), enabling relatively unprofitable husbandry to survive. But any major new capital investment has to be financed out of *future* drain-age rates — apart, that is, from a 50 per cent MAFF grant. On the Halvergate levels, drainage rates would have risen nearly fourfold to around £80 per ha. had the proposed schemes been implemented, significantly reducing the profitability of livestock letting. Annual grazing rentals on good-quality accessible marshes run at about £200–220 per ha.; and on poor-quality, less accessible marshes, where there is almost no market, rentals range from £80–125 per ha. In addition (although this was never stated in writing) MAFF policies apparently prohibited the grant aiding of replacement pumps to support the existing level of productivity: only modern, more powerful pumps *with*

fully engineered access roads (ostensibly for maintenance
and emergency vehicles but also legally usable by agricultural traffic) were considered eligible for grant aid.

Furthermore MAFF cost–benefit appraisals of new
arterial schemes required that so-called agricultural
'improvements' must justify the expenditure — so the
LBIDB felt it had to go for improved pumps, good access
and plenty of arable conversion. The MAFF evaluation
procedures are internal to the ministry for schemes of
less than £1.5 million but must be approved by the
Treasury when exceeding this threshold. The MAFF
appraisals are essentially financial (i.e. not based on
social cost–benefit analysis) and hence favour a contro-
versially narrow definition of agricultural benefit. The
LBIDB were anxious to separate their application into
three segments, each of which conveniently fell below
the Treasury scrutiny threshold.

In October 1980, alterations to the capital grants and
development schemes ushered in under the CAP established a new, administratively streamlined method of
assessing applications for grant aid. The old arrangement
of prior notification of the applicant to MAFF/ADAS was
replaced by retrospective application, although applicants
in national parks and SSSIs had to show that they had
consulted with the appropriate agencies (the national
park authorities and the NCC, respectively) before
undertaking the work. The Broads Authority were
anxious to be granted *de facto* national park status, and
succeeded in receiving an assurance from MAFF that
applications for *arterial* drainage improvement would
have to be 'acceptable' before MAFF would give grant.
Through procedural changes introduced solely to secure
administrative economies, the principle of prior notification was fortuitously extended to arterial schemes (not
very common in the mostly upland national parks),
thereby giving the Broads Authority a useful delaying
power, and, in effect, making it a requirement that such
schemes be subject to full environmental as well as
financial appraisal. This turned out to be crucial, allowing
the Authority to be fully informed and consulted about
the Halvergate schemes, and granting it a major say in
their fate.

The Common Agricultural Policy (CAP)

As is now well known, but was barely perceived in 1980, the CAP price 'guarantees' have favoured cereals (especially wheat and barley) over livestock through high intervention prices and subsidies for the elimination of small dairy herds. Thus a crude interventionist measure designed for the whole European Community critically influenced decisions at the farm level on the Halvergate Marshes and biased MAFF's financial appraisals by increasing the profits to be secured from improved drainage. These policies also inflated the terms of compensation for loss of profit that had by then been tacitly accepted in principle if the character of the marsh landscape was to be retained. The Halvergate issue emerged just when the wider disadvantages of CAP farm supports were coming under increasing attack.

Put yourself in the position of a Halvergate marsh-owner. If you were an absentee landlord you would merely benefit from the grazing rental (less agent's fees and owner's rates) and in the poorer access areas this would realise no more than £125 per ha. Land values were static. An improved drainage scheme might raise rental income and would certainly increase land values; probably from around £2000 per ha. to about £4000 without improved underdrainage, and to over £5000 with good access and underdrainage. The great temptation would therefore be to sell out: drainage would not greatly increase the returns from grazing, and the hefty rise in occupier drainage rates might well reduce net profits. There would be plenty of eager buyers, anxious to amalgamate parcels of marsh into larger units which could be converted, very lucratively, to arable.

Suppose you were a local farmer with some upland property already in arable production. Improved drainage with grant-aided underdrainage would boost your profits from around £100 per ha. with beef cattle, or £500 per ha. with dairy followers (before the milk quotas imposed in April 1984), to at least £800 per ha. if you converted to winter wheat and used your existing machinery. You could pay off all improvement costs within two years and the rest would be 'gravy'. The financial pressures to switch to improved grazing or into arable production were enormous.

Marsh-ownership and LBIDB Membership

Because of the secrecy surrounding landownership, only the LBIDB knows who owns what in the Halvergate Marshes or how many individual owners or lessees there are. As the Halvergate issue unfolded, however, it became evident that there was disagreement between the 'graziers' (most of whom did not really want a fancy new scheme that would cut into their tight profit margins) and the 'drainers' (who were very anxious to reap the *largesse* of ministerial grants and CAP guarantee prices). But the drainers dominated the executive committee of the LBIDB, and so prevailed. In other Broads marshes, after new arterial schemes have been installed, small parcels of land have been sold to larger owners with the capital and the incentive to convert the amalgamated holdings to arable production. It will never be known how much land would have changed hands had the original Halvergate schemes gone through. Certainly some LBIDB members were poised to make a killing by buying land, thereby benefiting from the estimated £4000 per ha. taxpayer-subsidy (including flood protection from nearby tidal rivers) available to assist them in growing a surplus crop.

The Broads Authority's Strategy for Safeguarding the Landscape

By coincidence, during November 1980, the Broads Authority prepared and committed itself to a strategy designed to safeguard the character of the landscape. The strategy is based on the concept of landscape typicality (i.e. the representativeness of landscape types which are seen to constitute the Broadland landscape heritage). These landscapes include the mature oak/alder woodlands, the immature open reed beds, and the traditional semi-closed and open grazing marshes. The authority agreed to safeguard all the landscapes in grades I and II, so that their present character would be retained. It should be noted that the criteria of selection were (and are) *not* scenic beauty but *typicality and heritage*, as discussed in Chapter 3. It is the association with the unique Broadland ecology and longstanding agricultural practices together with their accessibility for the public, which determined the grade assigned to different landscapes. Most of Halvergate is grade I, and is by far the most representative of the open grazing marshes of eastern Norfolk. But, despite the existence of the Broads Authority's strategy, at the end of 1980 there seemed little chance that the preservation of fairly large tracts of relatively unproductive (and, to many, somewhat scruffy-looking) marsh would command either public support or political credibility.

PART II: THE DIARY OF INDECISION

In the 'diary' that follows, only key points in the various decision sequences will be highlighted. The details are exceedingly complicated, but we are confident that the summary is broadly accurate.

Phase I: LBIDB Case Preparation and Notification (September–December 1980)

The LBIDB prepared their three schemes sequentially, moving from south to north, beginning with the Berney Seven Mile Level scheme, and ending with the Tunstall–Acle proposal. Because the NCC were in the process of notifying an SSSI on the western edge of the Manor House Level, under the new drainage grant arrangements it had to be notified by the LBIDB. The NCC believed that a compromise could be arranged to maintain the high water-tables of the marsh margin, but informed the Broads Authority of the wider implications of the scheme. In accordance with the new MAFF notification policy the LBIDB were asked to consult with the Broads Authority. The LBIDB summarised its views on landscape change in six lines of typescript:

> The Board cannot make any observations on the relative merits of different types of landscape conservation and those which would follow upon the change to mixed arable

and grass management. ... It is considered that the drainage proposals and the consequent change to a mixed pattern of farming will not reduce the *amenity value* of the area as a whole. (Letter from the LBIDB consulting engineers to the Broads Authority, 23 December 1980; emphasis added)

It will be noted that the LBIDB and their consultants did not understand, or feel any sympathy for, the arguments of landscape representativeness or heritage. The gulf of misunderstanding that separated the views of the two camps towards landscape heritage was to widen throughout the three years of the Halvergate dispute, and remains unbridged.

Phase II: Conciliation, not Confrontation (January–February 1981)

In December 1980 representatives of the LBIDB met with the Broads Authority advisory team and agreed that an assessment be prepared of not doing anything beyond replacing the old pumps with new ones of similar capacity. Though the LBIDB argued that this would be economic nonsense and that to take no action would be hydrological nonsense, the Authority had begun negotiations and so the scene was set for talking rather than shouting. In January the Authority's strategy committee walked the marshes with the LBIDB: few members distinguished between the concepts of heritage and amenity. The committee was recommended by its advisers:

(i) to advise MAFF that the change in the distinctive character of Broadland landscape which would result from [the LBIDB scheme] is unacceptable;

(ii) should MAFF decide to support the implementation of the scheme, that the [Authority] would seek an opportunity to express its views at a Public Inquiry;

(iii) notwithstanding the negotiations and the decisions which have been held with the Drainage Board, that the Authority endeavour to examine with the Board and its consultants whether an appropriate proposal may be agreed which retains the distinctive character of the area.

Meanwhile the Countryside Commission resolved a similar set of propositions, beginning with the principle of continuing discussions 'with the aim of finding ways in which extensive grazing might be retained on the Broadland Marshes *and a balance achieved between conservation and farming profitability'* (Countryside Commission press statement, 6 February 1981; emphasis added). The Commission likewise requested a public inquiry should the schemes remain unaltered, under Section 96 of the Land Drainage Act 1976. On 23 January 1981, however, the strategy committee voted to avoid any possibility of a public inquiry and to devise a compromise that would retain 'to the maximum extent practicable the distinctive character of the area'. Authority members (half of whom were farmers with close agricultural connections) did not wish 'to put farmers' backs up'. Additionally, the LBIDB had threatened it would not appear at such an inquiry and would finance its own scheme if denied MAFF grant aid. The conservation lobby was appalled at the committee's pusillanimous attitude, which played into the hands of the drainage camp. In the five weeks before the full authority meeting, hard work by conservationists and pressure from the Countryside Commission succeeded in overturning this recommendation. However, although reverting to the policy originally suggested by its advisers, this decision all but lifted the threat of a public inquiry, for the underlying mood was still for compromise to be achieved through friendly negotiation. Nobody then had any idea that this would prove so difficult, so time-consuming and, eventually, so divisive.

Phase III: Early Negotiations
(March–May 1981)

A series of eleven meetings were held to work out suitable areas for safeguarding landscape, suitable voluntary means of *guaranteeing* safeguards and paying compensation for key areas of marsh, and appropriate notification arrangements for the rest of the proposed drained area. The negotiating teams comprised representatives of the front-stage organisations, and the meetings were chaired by an ADAS official representing MAFF.

The Broads Authority had two categories of marsh protection in mind. The so-called 'red areas' consisted of nearly 450 ha. of marsh in two blocks, one on the Manor House Level and including the proposed SSSI, the other north of the River Yare on the Seven Mile Level. The latter formed a self-contained landscape unit, being bounded to the north by the embankment of a railway-line but with wide open views to the south and east across the river to adjacent grade I grazing marshes. The arrangement for the red areas was a complicated one, but its main purpose was to stop conversion from grazing, with full compensation for profit forgone, backed up by arbitration in the event of dispute. Red-area agreements would be signed voluntarily, but the Authority was prepared to press its objection to any farm-level drainage proposals that might arise.

The rest of the marsh (the 'white areas') was to be subject to voluntary notification agreements or contracts which would bind landowners (or their successors in title) to inform the Authority of any intention to alter landscape character. Under the white-area agreements, however, if the landowner and the Authority could not agree the terms of compensation, the individual would have been free to proceed. In the white areas, therefore, the onus was on the Authority to make all the running and to settle, whereas in the red areas, arbitration would decide the terms and any alteration of the scenic character was ruled out.

Throughout this period the Broads Authority sought to require the LBIDB to share the financial burden of compensation. This involved requests to the LBIDB to re-rate the land and to establish differential drainage rates so that landowners committed to grazing paid lower rates than those who converted to arable. Furthermore, in April 1981 the Authority offered £25,000 to help pay compensation and asked the LBIDB to match this through a special levy. The LBIDB, narrowly interpreting land-drainage legislation, rejected out of hand these initial negotiating positions.

Three options for compensation were discussed: a lump-sum capital payment on signing an agreement with no subsequent payment; an initial lump-sum payment for a 20-year agreement; or an annual payment, reviewed periodically, to run for 20 years. These options were based on the management agreement guidelines already reached for Exmoor (see Chapter 8) but, initially at least, only the annual payments were considered seriously.

Phase IV: First Ministerial Involvement (June–July 1981)

By early June the Countryside Commission had had enough of the prevarication of the LBIDB and were increasingly concerned about the precedents being set of 'double payments' — namely public money being paid out to subsidise drainage schemes, followed by more public money to persuade farmers not to take advantage of the new drainage regimes. The Commission called for a public inquiry, thereby posing a dilemma for the Broads Authority. The Commission was a partner organisation with a remit to consider the national implications of key countryside issues, yet the Authority did not wish to dance to the Commission's tune. The Authority therefore sought to coordinate tactics, and sent its chief executive to the Countryside Commission to formulate a common approach. This proved to be impossible. The Authority rejected the Countryside Commission's call for a public inquiry, which was supported by all the national conservation groups, in the belief that the matter was near to resolution so long as sufficient funds for compensation were available. Accordingly, in mid-July the negotiating teams met in London and agreed an annual compensation figure of £65,000 for the 'red area', equivalent to about £155 per ha. The figure was arrived at largely through horse-trading, and without any detailed study of the agricultural holdings on the protected area itself or any direct negotiations with the landowners or farmers involved. Their interests were 'being handled' by the NFU/CLA and LBIDB. No responsible agricultural economist could have justified the figure.

On 27 July, when the negotiating teams met with ministers from MAFF and DoE, the DoE agreed to pay 75 per cent of the compensation through the Countryside Commission grant-in-aid — an arrangement accepted most reluctantly by the Commission 'as an exception'. Ministerial involvement was unusual but critical at this stage. The Wildlife and Countryside Bill was taking an enormous hammering in Parliament where the conservation lobby was desperately anxious to link MAFF financing of sound agricultural practice with conservation and the social and economic welfare of rural areas (see Chapter 6). In addition, both MAFF and DoE ministers were making it clear in debate that pump replacement was eligible for grant aid (but only so long as some clearly defined agricultural improvement could be justified) and that the IDBs' obligations to conservation and amenity was subordinate to the primary duty to promote agricultural business. Thus Halvergate reached a critical stage at a particularly sensitive period in the stormy passage of the Bill. The £65,000 deal was conjured out of the air in a desperate bid to rid ministers of Halvergate. In fact, the deal merely ushered in a new and even more difficult sequence of events.

Phase V: The Broads Authority Begins To Get Tough (August–December 1981)

In August 1981 the LBIDB pressed hard for the Broads Authority to withdraw its objections to the Acle–Tunstall Level drainage scheme, on the grounds that the Tunstall pump had failed and needed to be replaced, and that no 'red areas' would be affected. The drainage camp offered to get letters of good intent from all the landowners in the area indicating a willingness to sign 'white-area' agreements if the Broads Authority would drop its objection. On 6 August the strategy committee accepted this deal, partly as a gesture of goodwill and partly because the LBIDB were prepared to alter the drainage of the Manor House Level to allow winter flooding which would encourage overwintering birds into the heart of the marsh. The committee believed that this would be good for the public image of both sides.

By mid-August, however, matters had taken a significant turn for the worse. To begin with, it became apparent that the LBIDB was talking to the 18 landowners in the 'red areas' in order to divide the £65,000 per annum into neat packages irrespective of farm profitability or intention to plough. The sheer insensitivity of this approach, so redolent of greed and arrogance, intensely angered the conservation camp. At the same time, the CPRE, along with two prominent peers, Lords Buxton and Onslow, placed enormous pressure on the Broads Authority to delay any deal until amendments to the Wildlife and Countryside Bill that could affect Halvergate had been debated. Lord Buxton conducted a spirited correspondence, in private and in *The Times*, with MAFF ministers in order to stop the 'folly' of double payments and the unnecessary wastage of public expenditure. On 19 October 1981, supported by Lords Onslow and Melchett, he moved amendment 105(A), which was intended to enable water authorities and internal drainage boards to spend MAFF grant aid to mitigate the consequences to amenity and conservation of such grants. Halvergate was a central theme in the ensuing debate. MAFF ministers stood firm, however. IDBs, they maintained, could not spend money on matters which went beyond their land-drainage functions. Agriculture and conservation policies and budgets must remain separate. Lord Buxton withdrew his amendment in the 'confident anticipation' that if the Broads Authority did not agree to the Halvergate arrangements a public inquiry would be convened.

About the same time, the Broads Authority rejected the idea of dropping the objection to the Tunstall Level scheme, despite the fact that letters of intent had been received from landowners representing 75 per cent of the area. The faulty pump parts had been replaced and the Authority's negotiating team felt it would be foolhardy to divide the total scheme in this way when so much had still to be resolved further south. Attitudes subsequently hardened: the negotiating meetings became longer and more strained; mistrust began to creep in. The Broads Authority sought advice on what should constitute terms of compensation from the Department of Land Economy at Cambridge University, and insisted that compensation would only be paid for proven loss. It would not countenance a carve-up. Finally, it renewed its demand that the LBIDB re-rate and establish differential drainage in the safeguarded areas, so as to reduce the burden of compensation and to introduce a modest element of cross-subsidy within the LBIDB.

During this period the Wildlife and Countryside Bill became law, with the consequences described in Chapter 6, including a new positive duty on water authorities and IDBs to further conservation when formulating or considering any proposals. The passage of the Act also plucked the Halvergate SSSI out of the 'red area' and into the new Section 28 responsibilities of the Nature Conservancy Council. Its protection was now no longer a matter for the Broads Authority, and it also reduced the estimated total compensation figure to the Authority and the Countryside Commission by approximately a third. But management agreements were enshrined in the Act despite Lord Buxton's strictures, and were supposed to provide the building-blocks of compromise. The Broads Authority felt cornered by the Act: its room for manoeuvre which it had slowly been expanding, began to contract. Paradoxically, members felt dissatisfied with the political turn of events, yet resigned to follow the spirit of the new legislation.

Phase VI: Second Ministerial Involvement (January–May 1982)

On 29 January 1982 the teams again met with MAFF/DoE ministers to 'sort out' the terms of payment for red-area agreements. The Broads Authority prevailed in its insistence that payments would only be made for proven losses, but it also sought more flexible arrangements for compensation, preferring some form of lump-sum payment. This would involve the Broads Authority buying up marsh and reselling it with a permanent restrictive covenant binding all successive holders in title to grazing. The cost of conservation in perpetuity would be a lump-sum equivalent to the difference in land value. The DoE minister agreed to find the necessary capital to allow this, but although such an arrangement would only apply to the red area outside of the SSSI, it might still cost about £360,000. The reader will note that two kinds of agreement were now being proposed for the red area — the SSSI-type management agreements (under Section 32 of the 1981 Act) with annual payments indexed against inflation; and the Broads

Authority agreements (outside the Act) with once-and-for-all compensation. They were as different as chalk and cheese, a fact that did not help negotiations.

Meanwhile the LBIDB began to get tough. In February it rejected the Broads Authority request for differential rating, although holding out a vague promise to re-rate once the scheme was grant-aided. It also dropped the Manor House scheme by unilaterally deciding to remove a sluice on the Halvergate Fleet and thereby dropping the level of this drain. This decision was taken after the Broads Authority and the NCC had shared half the costs of a consultant's report to assess how the Fleet could be periodically flooded in winter to encourage more water-fowl but before the report could be discussed.

This serious reversal was typical of the arrogance and insensitivity of the executive members of the LBIDB. They had been stung by the Authority's reversal of position over the Acle–Tunstall scheme, which they attributed to 'political' lobbying. But the abandonment of such a crucially important part of the package was a savage blow. Lowering the level of the Fleet meant that surrounding lands could not be kept in good grazing condition, and that the red area along the Yare Bank (which the Broads Authority was considering purchasing) would not be supplied with adequate amounts of fresh water. It also ruined any possibility of creating good conditions for birds to roost. This was the very reverse of 'furthering conservation' as the LBIDB was required to do by Section 48, and measurably widened the gulf that was now increasingly evident between the two negotiating camps.

On the compensation front matters also worsened. The terms for financial compensation under the Wildlife and Countryside Act were still being hotly debated at national level, and negotiators from NFU and CLA headquarters entered the Halvergate discussions to influence any precedents that might be set. There were protracted exchanges with the Cambridge Department of Land Economy over the precise wording and method of calculation for the red-area agreements. It proved impossible to agree on the 'standard sums' that had been one of the keys to success in Exmoor. By May 1982 both sides had reached an impasse. Once again, Halvergate was propelled into centre stage, though the Broads Authority negotiators were not fully prepared for the intensity of the argument.

Phase VII: The 'Rolls Royce' Revised Scheme (July–October 1982)

In June the president of the CLA sought to resolve the deadlock by proposing that *all* the disputed red-area agreements (to which the CLA objected because they were not truly voluntary and were subject to binding arbitration) be replaced by Section 39 agreements (which would not be binding on landowners who refused to accept the terms of a compensation offer). This move showed how much the Act was influential in shaping attitudes, but also how little was understood about the purpose of the red-area agreements. The Broads Authority rejected this suggestion. But, not to be outdone, on 13 July the chairman of the Countryside Commission met with all the landowners involved in the red area (now reduced to 16) to try to break the deadlock. This important meeting revealed that each landowner saw the issues differently, and that they had not been kept properly informed by the NFU/CLA negotiators. The landowners wanted the terms of compensation to be tailored to suit each individual — a principle which should have been accepted 15 months beforehand, *before* the first ministerial meeting. The fact that this was *not* done attests to the way in which the NFU/CLA lobby blocked out the landowners so as to ensure that principles convenient to their national headquarters were established before individual deals were determined. Mistrust was now almost universal, both between the 'camps' and among the marsh-owners and their 'representatives'.

During August 1982 all the landowners were personally contacted by the Broads Authority. The outcome was that not one owner was prepared to negotiate on the Manor House Level as this was no longer the subject of a drainage proposal and hence not technically a matter of a Broads Authority 'objection'. The area of safeguarded marsh therefore had to be contracted by a further 60 ha. with an important loss to the landscape appearance of the western flank. However, all but one landowner on the southern level was willing to sell out to the Broads Authority.

In an attempt to break the deadlock, the NCC regional officer proposed a new drainage scheme involving abandoning the Berney pump and its access road, whilst improving the Breydon pump to the east and beyond the original drainage scheme. This would have kept more of the original red area intact as roadless grazing marsh and reduced total costs, and, with an auxiliary pump, would have provided some fresh water to the all important Berney Level. But the total area of protected marsh would have been reduced even further to about 150 ha. out of the original 450 ha. which were to have been safeguarded.

The deal finally negotiated by October 1982 was a far cry from the original proposal. Only a fragment of the safeguarded marsh was to be protected — and even its vital fresh water supply was insecure. Only purchase by the Broads Authority (with 75 per cent funding by the Countryside Commission) was acceptable to the owners, yet there was no guarantee of any re-sale, certainly not at any definable 'market price'. It was widely believed that there was a 'Halvergate Mafia' at work, prepared to collude to keep repurchase prices very low. Throughout the negotiations the drainage camp constantly complained of 'conservation blight' — the reduction in land value due to the dispute itself — and thereby effectively talked down the re-sale price. The solution adopted was a 'Rolls Royce' model. It would be expensive both in drainage grant, in subsequent on-farm investment, and in compensation, yet would fail to safeguard the overall character of the marsh. It was tailored to the principles of the Wildlife and Countryside Act but was hopelessly out of line with the original intentions of the Broads Authority.

On 22 October 1982, the Countryside Commission refused to accept this deal and once again demanded a public inquiry. This was the second time the two partner organisations had parted company. The Broads Authority strategy committee voted to reject this call and to ask the Commission to 'think again', but on the same day the full Authority rejected this recommendation and also called for a public inquiry. Both the Broads Authority and the Countryside Commission expressed the view that no satisfactory solution to the Halvergate problem could be reached by any form of management agreement if the two schemes were to go ahead as proposed.

Phase VIII: The Ministerial *Volte-face* (November 1982)

On 10 November the teams met with MAFF/DoE ministers for the third time. At that historic meeting the ministers announced a *volte-face*: they agreed to grant aid for the Tunstall pump replacement, but refused the application for grant aid for more powerful replacements for both the Seven Mile and Berney pumps. For MAFF, the Minister of State, Earl Ferrers, indicated that he would consider favourably an application for a replacement pump together with an access road for the Seven Mile pump, but would not consider any new application for the Berney pump. Both ministers noted that these decisions were consistent with Section 48 of the Wildlife and Countryside Act.

A curious silence followed this announcement as both sides analysed its implications. This was only the second occasion that a major arterial drainage scheme had been refused grant aid, and the first time that such a decision had been taken without a public inquiry. It took Section 48 further than the government had originally intended, for the IDB was in effect restrained in the interests of amenity from promoting agricultural business. The favourable Tunstall decision was a gesture of MAFF goodwill to the local drainage interests, who in fact were being differentially treated according to accidents of past land-use history, geography and aesthetic prejudices.

As is so often the case the decision was dressed up as a 'victory for common sense'; in fact, it illustrated how political decisions are taken. Ministers were desperate to find a solution to Halvergate: the matter had dragged on far too long and was an irritating reminder of the problems left unresolved by the passage of the Wildlife and Countryside Act. They had always hoped for a voluntary solution, agreed locally, without any need for ministerial intervention. The last thing they wanted was a public inquiry. It had been acutely annoying and embarrassing to find both the Countryside Commission and the Broads Authority no longer willing to seek a solution on ministerial terms. In addition, one suspects the hidden hand of the Treasury. The final 'Rolls Royce' proposition was so expensive (if the cost of marsh purchase had been included) that no cost–benefit appraisal could have justified it on any sensible interpretation of economic efficiency or social welfare.

The final decision reflected what might well have been the outcome of a public inquiry had one been held. Some form of drainage had to be maintained and the spirit of the Act had to be observed. The aim of the ministerial decision was to maintain the *status quo* — hopefully, by the 'technical' means of not improving drainage or access to part of the Seven Mile and most of the Berney Level. In public at least, ministers hoped that this deal would pull down the curtain on Halvergate. But in subsequent correspondence it was evident that they expected any further marsh safeguarding to be completed locally through Section 39 agreements, triggered where necessary by voluntary early-warning arrangements.

Phase IX: The Lull before the Storm
(January 1983–February 1984)

During the early months of 1983 a little tidying up of the new schemes was required. The LBIDB proposed to remove an existing main dyke and to construct an unusually winding road across the Seven Mile/Berney marshes to the replacement pump. In both cases the Broads Authority succeeded in altering these prior decisions (taken without consultation), first by insisting that the dyke be retained as a landscape feature, and second by ensuring that the drainage access road was designed to run directly to the new pump, with access for the public and an undertaking by the LBIDB that the road would only be used by drainage maintenance vehicles. These skirmishes revealed that the LBIDB was still not prepared to be as forthcoming as the conservation camp wished. They also showed how the Broads Authority was becoming increasingly intransigent over the fine points of detail and was prepared to give very little in compromise.

For a while Halvergate was forgotten. But a number of landowners on the Berney Level felt genuinely cheated by the turn of events. In October 1983 two of them signalled their intention to convert to arable unless the Broads Authority would buy the land. Though not keen on management agreements, they were reluctantly willing to 'consider' Section 39 agreements. Within a month, two more graziers followed suit. The total area involved was 300 ha. — almost as large as the original red area. The ministerial *status quo* was crumbling, yet the only apparent defence open to the Broads Authority was the prohibitively costly Section 39 agreements involving annual payments indexed against inflation.

Meanwhile Suffolk County Council, though a Tory-dominated Shire authority, passed a resolution that it would not enter into any Section 39 agreements even when important grazing marsh was threatened. This line was taken because of concern at the possible cost implications at a time when central government was penalising local authorities which exceeded expenditure targets. But the council was also anxious to reformulate national policy. There is more to Suffolk's resolution than meets the eye — a point not lost on the Broads Authority, five of whose members represent Suffolk constituencies.

Initially, the Broads Authority was not convinced that the owners' intention to plough was genuine, and in any case the Authority took the view that since ministers had accepted a policy of keeping the *status quo*, the Authority should not be expected to pay at least £17,500 annually on management agreements to achieve this end. Although the DoE had conferred quasi-national park status on the Broads by agreeing to let the Countryside Commission pay 75 per cent of the safeguarding costs from its grant-in-aid, the Broads Authority insisted that it would accept nothing less than the 90 per cent rate established in Exmoor where management agreements, at under £75 per ha., were far below the sums being discussed in the Broads. So, when two of the landowners proposed to plough their marshes should agreement not be reached, the Broads Authority requested a fourth meeting with ministers to explain its position.

Phase X: The Fourth Ministerial Meeting and its Aftermath (March–June 1984)

The meeting — which the Countryside Commission also attended — was held on 14 March 1984. The Broads Authority pressed upon the ministers, William Waldegrave of the DoE, and Lord Belstead of MAFF, that the four land-owners in question were the vanguard of what was likely to be a small army notifying an intent to plough. In the light of the dairy quota (imposed that month by the European Commission), declining returns on livestock production and rising drainage rates, the Authority estimated that as much as 2000 ha. of land in landscape grades I and II could be converted over the next five years. Between 400 and 600 ha. of grassland had been ploughed each year during the previous three years.

With compensation costs likely to be £250–400 per ha./per annum, the total annual payment to the four land-owners would be about £90,000 per annum; for 2000 ha. the total annual cost would be not less than £600,000, and could be as high as £1 million. Even if the Authority's grant were raised to the national park rate of 75 per cent, it faced an annual bill of at least £22,000 for the marshes already notified, and over £150,000 for marshland protection in the forseeable future. This would treble the £50,000 allocated for management agreements in its total budget of £734,000, for 1984/85. The Authority calculated that by the end of the decade, about a third of its total expenditure could be committed to paying farmers not to produce a subsidised crop that was already in surplus. Its constituent local authorities were unwilling to increase their contribution; some had even threatened to reduce their allocation should the Authority commit itself to a costly course of landscape protection. The Authority would therefore not pursue management agreements under the Act unless additional financing were made available.

Ministers ruled out a 90 per cent grant, but gradually a package-deal emerged which the Broads Authority enthusiastically dubbed 'partnership payments'. MAFF would consider how far it could go to make livestock production more profitable — possibly through special capital grants (e.g. for access roads, water supply and re-seeding, where acceptable to the conservation agencies) and through headage payments similar to those paid in the Less Favoured Areas. The DoE would consider raising the proportion of its contribution to the Broads Authority's total budget and designating the Broads under Section 41(3). The effect would be to require landowners to notify the Authority of all grant-aided proposals for agricultural development, and to require the Authority, should it object on conservation or amenity grounds, to enter into management agreements with terms of compensation based on the financial guidelines (Section 39 payments are, in contrast, discretionary). A working party was set up to look into all these options with a view to providing ministers with specific proposals by mid-summer.

The working party was not able to agree on any form of LFA scheme for Halvergate. MAFF stuck rigidly to the view that LFA status could only be applied to physically-handicapped land, not to land that was capable of being highly productive. In an ingenious attempt to overcome the deadlock, the Countryside Commission proposed that it would initiate an experimental scheme (under Section 40 of the Wildlife and Countryside Act) whereby it would finance 100 per cent of livestock support payments for an experimental period. These would be paid to any participating landowner, whether or not arable conversion was being considered, for all the grade I and II landscapes of the Broads, not just the Halvergate area. The Commission stipulated, however, that it would not pursue the proposal unless MAFF agreed to take over the payments after three years should the scheme prove successful.

The Commission's proposals were far-reaching. The support payments of about £150 per ha. per annum would be higher than any existing LFA payments, and would be related not to livestock numbers but to area. Payment would only be available to landowners who opted into the scheme. Capital grant from MAFF for eligible work would be raised to LFA levels, but MAFF would be expected not to offer conventional grant aid to non-participating landowners who wished to convert to arable, though such landowners could apply for management agreements. The Commission would also pay for a full-time project coordinator to explain and implement the scheme.

The proposal could cost up to £500,000 per annum depending upon the level of uptake and compensation payments, and the Treasury were extremely wary of the idea. But it is worth pointing out that MAFF and the Exchequer would save up to £250 per ha. in annual subsidies every time a farmer was dissuaded from converting grassland to wheat. (This figure does not include any payments made by the European Commission.) The livestock support scheme could therefore be financed at no additional cost to the British taxpayer at current levels of cereal/livestock subsidy, on the assumption that most of the land would eventually be turned into arable production if existing incentives were retained.

Ministers were optimistic after the March meeting that some solution could be reached. William Waldegrave was advised that all landowners would settle for interim payments, and announced to the Commons on 4 April that he was confident that 'Halvergate was safe for a year'. Ensuing events confounded his optimism.

Phase XI: Diggers, Tractors and Protesters Move In (June–August 1984)

In the meantime the Authority sought to stop the notifying landowners from ploughing for a year by offering a token payment of £50 per ha. Three of the five people in question agreed to this. But two brothers, Michael and David Wright, each of whom owned about 37 ha., rejected the holding payment and gave the Authority notice that they would plough on 10 June 1984 should no satisfactory agreement be reached. To underscore this point they let their marshes only to that date, after which they would receive no grazing revenue.

For payment of a sum reported to be £13,500 Michael Wright agreed to wait a year, but David Wright, whose land was more peripheral to the Halvergate area, wanted a higher compensation figure which the Authority refused to pay. He subsequently received a letter explaining the Authority's position which effectively agreed he could plough. On 10 June he began to prepare the ground by deepening his ditches, with *The Observer* carrying a full story of his intentions. Members of the local FoE branch promptly moved in and sat peacefully on the contractor's equipment. The resulting publicity startled the minister who found that David Wright had made nonsense of his 4 April statement; and it bothered Wright who indicated that he was prepared to settle for compensation on the same terms as his brother. The Broads Authority, however, would not go beyond the holding payment of £50 per ha. which he had already refused. Wright again refused and, despite further peaceful protests by FoE, recommenced ploughing.

Meanwhile, in April, the Broads Authority had been notified by David Archer of his intention to plough 40 ha. of grade II marshes in the middle Yare valley, some distance from Halvergate. The Authority sought an agreement on the same terms that Michael Wright had accepted, but Archer refused to negotiate. He did not appear to be interested in management agreements of any kind, and was anxious only to make more money from his marshes. The voluntary principle so central to the philosophy of the Act was clearly not working.

In something approaching desperation, a new idea emerged more or less simultaneously from the DoE and the CPRE to make a Planning Direction, under Article 4 of the General Development Order (GDO), to prevent drainage works being undertaken. (In effect, an Article 4 Direction brings works normally permitted by the GDO within the development control system.) Directions can be used to control 'engineering operations required ... for the purposes of agriculture' if they constitute 'development' and lead to a material alteration in the use of the land. Once a Direction has been made planning permission must be sought, and should the local authority refuse to grant permission not only would the normal mechanism of appeal and public inquiry apply, but compensation would have to be paid on the basis of the difference in value between the current and the potential use of the land. If a local authority initiated the Direction it would be liable to pay the compensation, but if the DoE acted alone, then the Exchequer would pick up the bill.

On 21 June the Broads Authority decided to ask the DoE to confirm an Article 4 Direction on Archer. This had the startling result of drawing the prime minister into the controversy, for when the DoE and MAFF were unable to reach agreement, Mrs Thatcher called the two ministers, Patrick Jenkin and Michael Jopling, to Downing Street and settled the argument in favour of the DoE, confirming the Planning Direction. This was done on 25 June, but the DoE took care to deny that it was a backdoor device to impose planning controls on agriculture for conservation purposes. The real object, it stressed, was to persuade David Archer to accept a management agreement; and now having no real alternative, he accepted a one-year holding payment pending the outcome of the discussions over the Countryside Commission's experimental scheme. The conservation lobby pressed the Broads Authority to seek a 'blanket' Direction over the whole of the grade I and II landscape areas. Politically this was a non-starter because of the notorious reluctance of ministers to sanction 'blanket' Directions and the enormous resistance of the agricultural lobby to Article 4 Directions for conservation objectives.

Subsequently, FoE peacefully occupied two other farms where drainage had commenced. In neither case was the Broads Authority prepared to offer management agreements, despite the fact that one of those areas was a grade I landscape unit adjacent to a newly-designated national nature reserve. FoE members were playing an important role throughout this period. Their network of dedicated local volunteers kept watch for any new drainage works, and twice they informed the Broads Authority of works which landowners had not notified. They earned the praise of the *Eastern Daily Press* on 18 August 1984 for pursuing their objectives 'in the most direct and peaceful manner'. But the majority of Authority members were becoming tired of the whole issue of drainage and marshland loss and were not keen to spend any more money until a satisfactory long-term solution was agreed.

POST-HALVERGATE: THE POLITICS OF POLICY REFORM

Throughout this period pressure was increasing on MAFF and DoE to coordinate their policies. As we saw in Chapter 7, two Reports published within a week by House of Lords committees in July contained damning criticisms of the failure of the DoE and MAFF to reconcile agricultural and environmental policies. The Lords' European Communities committee was particularly scathing in its condemnation of the two departments.

When the Lords debated the Reports, agriculture ministers announced in both Houses that the government intended proposing an amendment to the revised EEC structures (i.e. grant aid) Directive 'which would not be confined to Less Favoured Areas, and would be designed to allow member-states to pay aids to farmers in suitably designated areas of high conservation value in order to encourage farming practices beneficial to the environment'. Confidence in the seriousness of this proposal was deflated by Lord Belstead's statement that amendments of this nature might not be acceptable to all other member states, adding pessimistically 'we can but try'.

This ingenious proposal was never expected to survive the cross-fire of Brussels political sniping. The British government were seen to be promoting an ill-considered idea on a Community that was less than enthusiastic about landscape conservation and unhappy with the way the government was handling the acid rain issue, notably over reductions in sulphur dioxide emissions and automobile exhaust gases. However, the British negotiators persevered, and on 12 March the new Title was included in the Directive on agricultural structural policy. That Title allowed the UK government to designate up to 2 per cent of land where it would be legally permissible for MAFF to support certain kinds of agriculture in the interest of furthering conservation and amenity. The money, however, would have to come from MAFF: there would be no repayment by the Community.

This is an important initiative though its significance should not be overstressed. A relatively small area of land is eligible, and MAFF may not choose to designate all of it. Over the rest of the countryside MAFF still claims that it cannot provide financial assistance aimed at promoting conservation practices within agriculture. MAFF remains very resistant to any legal moves to force it to further the interests of conservation, as was evident in the way they successfully fought off a proposal in the Wildlife and Countryside (Amendment) Bill that would have placed just such a duty upon them. In the next parliamentary session there will have to be primary agricultural legislation to enable MAFF to operate the new Title and that legislation may provide an opportunity to widen MAFF's conservation responsibilities.

MAFF, it seems, is anxious to change its image. It found a way to cooperate with the Countryside Commission on the Broads Grazing Marsh Conservation Scheme which was officially approved on 30 January 1985 and launched on 15 March 1985. Also on 15 March the Broads were designated under Section 41(3) of the 1981 Act. The Broads Grazing Marsh Conservation Scheme, jointly funded by MAFF and the Commission, is worth £1.7 million over its experimental life of three years. Because only limited funds were made available, the Scheme covers only some 4000 ha. — about 90 per cent of grade I and 40 per cent of grade II landscapes. All of the Halvergate area is included, as is the large block of marshes south of the Yare.

The Scheme is designed to offset some of the economic

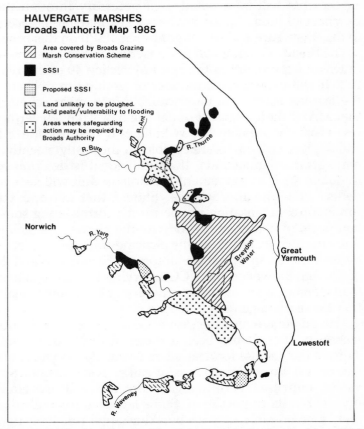

Map 11.2 The Halvergate Marshes Broads Authority Map 1985.

pressures facing traditional livestock graziers in the area. It will pay £123 per ha./per annum (£50 per acre) to all participating farmers. Each will have to agree to inform the Scheme's Project Office (known as the Broads Unit and located in ADAS but run by a Countryside Commission officer with three ADAS colleagues) should he consider any alteration to established and 'acceptable' management practices. Based on a 'bottom-up' approach, the scheme will ensure that each farmer is contacted individually so that specialised management advice can be offered to suit his particular requirements. 'Top-up payments' for positive conservation work will be available, though only in very special circumstances. Wherever possible both Section 39 and Section 41 management agreements will be avoided — if necessary through the purchase of land. About 300 ha. of key marshes adjacent to the River Yare will be bought by the RSPB on this basis.

The Broads Grazing Marsh Conservation Scheme is very much an experiment in the spirit of Section 40 of the 1981 Act. It will experience a number of teething troubles but the lessons learnt will be invaluable for similar schemes that MAFF should launch under the new Title. Nevertheless problems remain: the Wildlife and Countryside Act still applies, so farmers are eligible for the costly 'negative' management agreements. If an individual is determined to obtain such an agreement the Broads Unit will seek to deflect him into the Scheme. Should that fail and the funds for compensation not be readily forthcoming some land may be ploughed. In addition the Halvergate SSSI is not officially included in the Scheme and the six landowners there can utilise the notorious Sections 28 and 29 of the Act. However, the NCC are trying to offer 'positive' management agreements to any farmer anxious to retain traditional management practices.

Halvergate remains the principal case in landscape protection politics. It has been a thorn in the flesh of both sides of the dispute for nearly five years. Halvergate could not be lost for too much was at stake, even though, privately, ministers feel the area is not worth all the effort invested in its preservation. So its legacy is reconciliation and, just possibly, a path-breaking approach to a new attitude to farming the landscape.

Section 4
Proposals for Reform

12. Changing Direction in Agriculture and Forestry

Earlier chapters have shown that it is not possible to treat conservation as a separate, self-contained element in the planning and use of the countryside. This approach, pursued for the past 40 years, has demonstrably failed; indeed, it has been associated with widespread environmental decline, the impoverishment of landscapes and destruction of habitats. A new approach is sorely needed. Conservation should no longer be regarded as a cosmetic frill or a palliative to the damaging impacts of productive and exploitative undertakings. Instead it should be an operative principle infused into all actions and decisions affecting the country's human and natural resources. Living systems should be used and perpetually sustained for the manifold benefit of society.

Relatively little can be done to stop the alarmingly rapid deterioration of the countryside described in Chapter 3 unless there are far-reaching changes to the direction and purpose of British agriculture and forestry. Every subsidy aimed at farmers and landowners — whether it be price-support, development grant, official advice, rate relief, tax concessions on fuel, machinery and chemicals, or even cash-in-hand for conservation — all of them lead to unnecessary capital formation, to excessive borrowing from banks and from nature, to the artificial bidding-up of land values and to ever greater pressures to increase productivity and the rate of profit. All these pressures overwhelm any commitment to conservation, except where the landowner has sufficient spare capital, is aggressively and independently conservation-minded, or is prepared to suffer real or paper losses by jumping off the intensification bandwagon. Unless these pressures and the policies that sustain them are overturned, conservation will continue to be seen as an expensive extra, costed in terms of lost production, focused largely upon key sites, and dependent on public subsidy. Or it will be the prerogative of the landowner with a conscience and a deep pocket.

This and subsequent chapters set out wide-ranging but practical proposals for reform, covering the price-support policies of the EEC, the various grant schemes, and the administration of agriculture and forestry. We lay particular stress on this combination of reforms. There is no simple panacea. Agriculture and forestry are so much the creatures of state support and of complex policy mechanisms that reform must always be sought at a number of different levels. Undue attention to any single mechanism, such as price-support or planning controls, is unlikely to produce the fundamental reorientation that is required and, if pursued in isolation, could have unwelcome side-effects for the well-being of the countryside.

The future of the British countryside depends first and foremost on thriving rural economies and flourishing rural communities. Without a wide mix of people living and working in rural areas, there can be no sustainable agriculture or forestry, few landscapes worth enjoying, and only limited facilities for people to visit and enjoy the countryside. Numerous studies have concluded that rural economies in Britain are inherently weak and unable to capitalise on economic investment, be it in tourism, agriculture, forestry or industry. Much of the financial gain is siphoned off into the cities and to big corporations. The essential task is to create more self-reliant rural economies that capture more of the fruits of local investment and economic activity. Also necessary are greater sympathy and resources from government for the housing and other needs of rural people, including encouragement for voluntary and community services. Though this is not the place to elaborate these issues, it is important that the detailed proposals we make for the reform of agriculture and forestry should be seen in this wider context.

Nor do we provide a blueprint for the resolution of all the problems identified in this book. Indeed two areas are so complex that they merit separate chapters — those dealing with the revitalisation of the uplands and with the issues of planning control and administrative changes (Chapters 13 and 14). This chapter outlines general guidelines for agricultural and forestry reform, and attempts to clarify what different courses of action may or may not realistically achieve.

Constructive reform must satisfy a number of criteria. It should promote the sustainable utilisation of land and resources; it should be cost-effective; it should be fair and just in fulfilling the social needs and interests that attach to the countryside; and it should be politically attainable. Each of these four criteria requires some elaboration.

Sustainable Utilisation

The United Kingdom's response to the world conservation strategy stressed the need to incorporate ecologically sustainable practices into agriculture and forestry and other uses of natural resources. The concept of ecological sustainability has two main strands. The first, productive sustainability, refers to the capacity of soil, water, wildlife and woodlands to sustain production indefinitely. In response to questions posed by the House of Lords select committee on science and technology during their investigation of agricultural and environmental research (1984), one of MAFF's chief scientists stated, 'I suppose that agricultural systems as at present practised are on the whole sustainable', justifying his statement by saying that it had not been established that present systems were not sustainable. This showed remarkable complacency, given that the select committee concluded that MAFF and the Agricultural and Food Research Council neglected the sort of strategic research and monitoring on which such a judgement could be based, and in the light of the contrary evidence marshalled in Chapter 3.

Admittedly, there is a paucity of sound information and research on the long-term consequences of contemporary agricultural and forestry practices; and, even though the productive sustainability of rural resources is self-evidently important, there is much disagreement on what it entails and on how it might be achieved in practice or assessed. However, lack of information and accord on such a vital issue as the maintenance of life-support systems should engender caution, not complacency, and certainly not the rashness evident in the routine and prophylactic use of pesticides and antibiotics, and the cultivation of fragile and exposed soils. Long-term well-being and security should not be gambled for short-term gain.

The other strand in the concept of ecological sustainability concerns the maintenance and enhancement of the cultural value of nature and the countryside. The term 'cultural' is used here in the broadest sense to refer to the whole mental life of a nation. It includes the scientific, educational, aesthetic, inspirational and recreational qualities of wildlife and scenery, together with the historical associations of places and landscapes. These purposes, therefore, encompass the need to conserve wildlife and the physical features of the countryside both as the medium within which natural scientists pursue their quest for knowledge, and for the simple enjoyment and inspiration that can be derived from contact with nature. All of these elements contribute to our emotional attachment to the countryside, an attachment which contributes profoundly to that elusive entity, 'the quality of life'. The immense regional variation of landscapes, reflecting the diverse geology of the British Isles and the successive imprints made by people in history and pre-history wresting a living from the land, amount to a richly varied palimpsest of forms and meanings, which, in its totality, adds to our sense of being 'British' with its unique history and cultural traditions; and, in its diversity, to our keen appreciation of regional distinctiveness and local identity. We have a duty therefore to future generations to preserve and enhance this richness and variety. Yet modern agriculture and forestry are obliterating the relics of the past and of nature, eradicating local and regional differences, and impoverishing these sources of human inspiration and identity.

Economic and Environmental Cost-Effectiveness

The second basis for judging what kind of strategy should be adopted for the future management of the countryside is that of cost-effectiveness. The popular definition of this phrase is 'value for money'. In the light of the principle of sustainability outlined above, 'value' must be understood in terms of social acceptability and environmental suitability, not just lowest money cost. Whatever combination of sticks and carrots is devised, it must be so designed to minimise wastage of both private and public investment; it must ensure that public investment is only directed at socially desirable objectives, and that purely private gains are secured by private, not public, investment, and not at the expense of social and natural assets. The introductory and case-study chapters have illustrated that currently this is not the case: all too frequently, public money is going into well-cushioned private hands, with socially undesirable consequences.

Social Justice in Countryside Management

This leads to the third criterion for reform, namely social justice. Justice, like many themes introduced in this chapter, is an elusive concept. Nevertheless it is of considerable importance. First, there are the rights that people have to a healthy and pleasing environment. Second, is the right of those who live and work in the countryside to a secure livelihood and well-being. Third is the rights and responsibilities of those who own and control land and natural resources. Extensive private rights attach to landownership in our society and these are legitimised in part by the notion that their exercise should be tempered by an ethic of stewardship (see Chapter 4). Equally, though, the state has an obligation to intervene when private interests and actions do not accord with those of society — including future generations. Current financial and technological imperatives in British agriculture and forestry have overwhelmed and in most instances supplanted the stewardship ethic which, in any event, was never dominant in the sense that public benefit took precedence over private benefit. Government policies, admittedly, share much of the blame, and any reform should seek to foster and reinforce a new conservation ethic. In addition, specific procedures should be established which should ensure that private rights do not override the public interest in the use and management of rural land.

Political Attainability

Sustainable utilisation, cost-effectiveness and social justice form the trio of considerations upon which our proposals for the reform of countryside management are based. There is, however, a fourth criterion of a different character, namely political attainability. What is politically attainable will depend first and foremost upon which party is in power. But it is also a function of the relative strengths and conflicting objectives of the different lobbies involved. As Section 2 of this book has indicated, there has been an important shift in the balance of power between the farming and conservation lobbies, with the passage of the Wildlife and Countryside Act representing an important turning-point. There is now a more favourable climate for major reform of agriculture and forestry than for many years.

Political attainability is thus a relative concept. What is attainable today may be unattainable tomorrow; similarly what is unacceptable today may be acceptable tomorrow. This should not be an injunction merely for pragmatism and expediency. Any strategy for reform should adopt both short-term and longer-term dimensions, the first providing conditions favourable to the second. In other words, opportunities should be seized, but attention should also be given to encouraging a climate in which suitable opportunities will arise. No greater opportunity presents itself at the moment than the clamour for the reform of the CAP.

PROSPECTS FOR REFORM OF THE COMMON AGRICULTURAL POLICY

Conservationists have increasingly found cause for cautious optimism in the utterances of European and British politicians about the inevitability of reform of the CAP. Some — most

notably the backbench Conservative MP, Richard Body —
have spiced their case for fiscal reform with conservation
arguments. Measures have already been taken to curb
CAP expenditure (or at least limit its increase) through the
pricing mechanism, and to restrict milk output through
quotas and penal levies on excess production. In spite of
the resistance of some EEC countries, not to mention the
powerful European agricultural lobby, it is difficult to see
how farming can avoid a sustained squeeze over the next
few years.

The measures taken in 1984, however, fall far short of a
major reform of the CAP. In fact they amount to little more
than an attempt to check its worst financial excesses — for
example, freezing milk production at 1 per cent above 1981
levels (which is still about 20 per cent in excess of the
Community's annual requirements) — and to redress some
of the gross disparities in national contributions to the
EEC budget. The popular and media interest in the conservation implications of agricultural support has not been
reflected in the actual political haggling which has been
preoccupied with the financial costs to the Community
and individual governments of an over-protective CAP.
European agricultural ministers no longer have a free
hand in dispensing *largesse* to the Community's farmers,
but in Britain at least it is the Treasury and the Foreign
Office that have been tying the hands: the Department of
the Environment has not been involved. Some conservationists have too readily assumed that curbs on agricultural spending will automatically benefit conservation.
Proposals to cut support to farmers and eliminate surplus
production fall under four headings: reduction of commodity prices, quotas, levies and direct income transfers.

At first sight, *reduction of the prices paid to farmers* would
seem the obvious way forward and, with annual price
revisions being lower than the rate of inflation, this has
been the Community's approach for several years. According to the simple law of supply and demand, farmers
should decrease production of those commodities most
affected by price cuts, and demand for them should rise as
consumers also respond to the lower prices. Unfortunately,
this may not work out in practice. Demand for food-stuffs
is fairly stable, and little affected by price variations. In

any case farmers have other options besides cutting production. Indeed, even under the generous CAP regime of
the 1970s and early 1980s, agricultural prices steadily
declined in real terms, falling on average 2–3 per cent
behind the annual growth of consumer prices. Nevertheless, agricultural surpluses continued to mount. To maintain their incomes, farmers have taken extra land into
cultivation (either through purchase or reclamation); or
have sought to boost output while holding their costs
down by improving their technical efficiency; or have
switched to more remunerative crops. Family enterprises
with no other alternatives for earning money have typically responded by working harder and producing more.
The ability of farmers continuously to produce more at
lower financial cost is also a testimony to the considerable
research, development and promotional effort carried out
by the agricultural research establishment and the agri-
business industry. Their priorities are beginning to change
but only slowly, and the legacy of thirty years' investment
in capital-intensive R & D will continue to influence farming practice for years to come.

Squeezing commodity prices thus serves to intensify
production. To achieve a significant cut back would require a drastic drop in prices so that any increased output
at whatever marginal costs would be quite uneconomic.
This would amount to an agricultural recession. It is
not what the EEC is proposing. John Bowers and Paul
Cheshire, however, in *Agriculture, the Countryside and
Land-Use* do suggest that EEC farm prices should rapidly
be brought into line with those prevailing on the world
market. They persuasively argue that this would be by far
the most important means of reducing the intensity of
exploitation of land, and therefore the damage to the
environment and conflict with other users of the countryside. Within a much reduced level of protection, they also
advocate a readjustment of price-support to favour dairying and livestock-rearing over tillage cropping, in order to
induce a shift from high-fertility arable farming to low-
fertility grassland farming.

Bowers and Cheshire envisage a lean and frugal agricultural industry, less reliant on expensive chemicals and
machinery. They do not mince their words: 'decreased

prosperity in agriculture would lead to decreased land prices and consequently to decreased intensity of exploitation of land and lower capital investment in agriculture'. The discrepancy between world and EEC prices for most agricultural commodities is now so large that a sharp reversal of pressures to increase production would be likely if British farming were subjected to world market conditions. Few wetland SSSIs would be worth reclaiming with prices of less than £80 a ton for wheat and barley. Similarly, the destruction of mixed grassland swards with massive doses of nitrogenous fertiliser would not be profitable if world prices for dairy produce prevailed.

But the problems with the 'market solution' are manifold. First, it would be bound to meet staunch resistance from the farming lobby — not only from big, arable farmers who have grown prosperous under the existing regime, but also from small farmers for whom the sudden removal of support could mean real hardship. Moreover, though the present government has taken steps to curb agricultural spending, it remains committed to maintaining a prosperous farming sector. In any case, while Britain remains a member of the CAP in its present form, any major price-cutting or manipulation of price relativities would have to go through Brussels. Fundamental price reforms, however, are not on the EEC's agenda and are unlikely to be. Indeed, the most formidable political obstacle is the sheer complexity of orchestrating any major reform of the CAP involving as it would all the member governments, the European Commission, the European Parliament and various national and transnational lobbies, such as consumer interests and food manufacturers and retailers, as well as farmers and conservationists.

Apart from questions of political feasibility, a major concern with any scheme to effect a sharp reduction in farm incomes and profits would be the implications for rural communities. Many jobs would be lost in agriculture and its supporting industries; small farms would become unviable; and rural services would be adversely affected. The overall impact, if remedial measures were not adopted, would be to depress rural economies and incomes generally and not just the agricultural sector.

There are plenty of other reasons why agriculture

should enjoy some protection — to even out the vagaries of climate, to counteract cyclical fluctuations in output and competition, to encourage investment and research, and to stabilise supplies and prices. In most of the major food-exporting countries, agriculture is protected to a greater or lesser extent. Thus there is no equilibrium 'world market' price for agricultural commodities, and even if Britain pulled out of the EEC, the government would almost certainly find it expedient to maintain a policy of agricultural price support.

The case for a steady diminution of current price supports, to reduce the financial burden on taxpayers and consumers and to put a brake on agricultural expansion, remains overwhelming. But if the experience of several years of cost-price squeeze in farming is anything to go by, it will be insufficient to secure threatened habitats and landscapes. Nor will it do anything specific to ensure that features or areas of conservation interest are actively cared for and managed.

It is essential that additional measures be employed to curb over-production and to initiate a transition towards a lower input/output agriculture. The main alternatives or complements to price reductions currently being used by the European Commission in the dairy sector are *quotas* and *levies*. Both mechanisms are intended to limit production. Dairy farmers can only expect the guaranteed price for their milk up to a certain annual quota of production which is specific to each farmer. Any excess output attracts a penal levy to cover the costs of storage and disposal, and to make the production of excess milk uneconomic.

The imposition and administration of milk quotas have been matters of great controversy in the farming community, not least because of the speed with which EEC ministers required implementation: the decision to cut back on production, taken in March 1984, was to take effect the following month. The Milk Marketing Board found itself in the unenviable position of having to write to farmers to inform them of the forthcoming cuts without being able to provide the full facts necessary for them to make informed management decisions, including what their specific quotas would be. Hurried discussions took place between the Milk Marketing Board and MAFF on how to achieve the national production quota of 1 per cent above 1981 levels. In the event, the ministry decided, in calculating quotas for each farm, to use 1983 as the base-line year, with farmers being instructed to reduce their output to 9 per cent below their production for that year.

This represents a major drop in production for dairy farmers and there is more to come, for farm quotas will be reduced by a further 1 per cent in 1985/86. To ease the problems for smaller producers the Minister of Agriculture announced in May 1984 an 'Out-Goers Scheme'. MAFF is to pay 13p for every litre of quota given up by a producer quitting milk production up to a maximum of £50 million. The quota thus released will be distributed to farms with sales of less than 200,000 litres (about 40 cows) in 1983, to help restore them to 1983 levels of production. In addition farmers have been able to apply for special dispensations if they have recently made major capital investments or if their 1983 output was badly affected by disease or poor weather.

These attempts to ease the plight of certain producers have done much to prolong the uncertainty over the final allocation of quotas. Meanwhile the handling of the issue has been fiercely criticised by the Farmers' Union of Wales and by action groups set up all over the country to fight for the interests of dairy farmers, particularly the hard-pressed smaller producers. Demands have been made for better representation for them on the Milk Marketing Board. But the Board's voting procedures are heavily biased towards larger producers. Only time will tell whether the politics or the economics of the imposition of quotas turns out to be of greater lasting significance to the industry. What is clear is that milk producers are facing the most severe economic constraints for over 40 years. Other sectors of agriculture are anxious lest they become the next victims, especially if production is boosted by the contributions of dairy 'out-goers'.

For a number of reasons milk quotas are unlikely to ease pressures for agricultural intensification, at least in the short term. If possible, some farmers will switch to beef and sheep or arable cropping. Another consequence may be further efforts to 'improve' marginal grassland as specialist dairy farmers, with little or no opportunity to diversify, seek to reduce their reliance on expensive bought-in concentrates by maximising their grass yields. Moreover, if quotas do squeeze out many farmers, we can expect extensive rationalisation of holdings, including the removal of unproductive landscape features. This often occurs when farms change hands or are amalgamated.

The final means being considered to reform agricultural support is that of *direct income transfers* to smaller and poorer farmers. At first sight this may seem a long way removed from the problems of surpluses and of rural conservation. In fact it may have considerable relevance to the social and environmental well-being of particular rural regions, as well as being the key to the wider reform of the CAP. Within the European Community there are certainly pressures to reorient the CAP towards income supplements. The proposal arises from the significance attached to the maintenance of small farmers' incomes in fixing price levels. The majority of European farmers could survive on lower commodity prices but prices are kept unnecessarily high ostensibly to safeguard the livelihoods of small farmers.

One respected commentator on agricultural policy, J.S. Marsh, has concluded that 'some form of direct income payment must be included if there is to be any satisfactory CAP reform'. The idea, however, is not without its problems. Farming interests would resist such.a development if it were seen as a means to lower commodity prices. The farming lobby in Britain, dominated by large producers, would be particularly resistant to a support system which strongly discriminated in favour of small producers, although the NFU has accepted in principle the need for direct payments to smaller farmers. However, though income subsidies should safeguard the lot of this group, they might have a detrimental impact on the other deprived group within agriculture, the farm workers, especially if there was a sharp decline in the profitability of the larger farms where agricultural employment is concentrated. Indeed, in the British farming context it would be more sensible and equitable to work for income *and* employment subsidies. Even organisations representing smaller farmers, such as the Farmers' Union of Wales and the Smallfarmers' Association, might be wary of measures which singled this group out for special treatment as a 'problem', rather than encouraging them to play an integral and productive part in British agriculture.

Additional problems relate to defining eligibility qualifications for income support to ensure that government aid reflected need. A maximum level of production (or farm income) would have to be specified to prevent big farmers from abusing the scheme; and a minimum level too, to restrict it to *bona fide* farmers. A minimum financial dependence on farming would also have to be specified to take account of the fact that many small farmers in marginal areas are of necessity part-time farmers, but also to exclude wealthy hobby farmers. Considerable potential would still remain for gross anomalies in the eyes of rural workers (all too often on low wages) and those dependent on social security benefits (for which farmers are also eligible).

Some of those who have advocated special treatment for small farmers have suggested that it be done through European social or regional funds, leaving agricultural funds for their traditional purpose of stimulating farm production and ensuring satisfactory incomes for the average or viable farmer. However, this would sharpen any sense of injustice felt by the non-farming community. Moreover, there is an argument, of great interest for conservationists, that the problem is an agricultural one and should be addressed through the agricultural budget. After all, the difficulties of small and marginal farmers are an outcome of the competitive pressures and rising thresholds of viability fostered over the years by agricultural policy, and one of the prime justifications for subsidising agriculture to the extent that it is, is to maintain the livelihoods of agrarian populations.

Many of the problems with the idea of direct income support could be best alleviated by placing the measure in the context of a reformed *agricultural* policy that gave due — perhaps even primary — regard to the environmental and social problems created in the wake of the 'second agricultural revolution'. Conservation of the countryside could provide the necessary justification for a switch from production to income and employment support which would avoid the charge of 'farmers getting something for nothing'.

This shift would help farmers and farmworkers off the treadmill, whereby at present the only way they have to maintain their income is by producing more and more unwanted foodstuffs. It would also recognise that, though intensive farming systems may be inimical to wildlife, recreational access and landscape beauty, the continuance of farming of a certain traditional type is absolutely essential to maintain these qualities. Moreover, many conservation practices, such as woodland management and the maintenance of hedgerows and drystone-walls, are skilled and labour-intensive. As conservation and amenity are (like foodstuffs) socially desirable products of the country-side, those who farm or work in such a way as to produce them should be adequately remunerated.

CONSERVATION INCENTIVES

Management agreements under the Wildlife and Country-side Act do embody the principle that forms of agricultural production that conserve the environment should be subsidised. Though many conservationists accept this principle, they reject the way it is applied in the Act. The main objections are as follows.

First, the Act's mandatory provisions apply only to SSSIs and national parks, implying a retreat from the notion of caring for the environment as a whole, to the discredited notion that the conservation of wildlife and landscapes can and should be confined to specifically designated areas.

Second, the requirement that a farmer who is refused grant aid from MAFF on conservation grounds must be compensated with a management agreement seems to embody the notion that farmers have an absolute right to agricultural grants. This is patently absurd and of dubious propriety. In the past, agricultural grants have been refused on a variety of grounds including lack of technical or economic viability. Moreover it is implicit in the Act itself that where there are strong conservation objections the payment of an agricultural grant would be contrary to the public interest. In such circumstances, there should be no entitlement for grant and therefore no entitlement for compensation.

Third, the basis for compensation is the maximum possible production lost by the denial of grant aid and subsequent agricultural investment. This begs the question of whether a landowner would have actually achieved the postulated productivity levels. Indeed, these may not even be ecologically sustainable: yet conservation money is made available on the outrageous assumption that they are, and that they would always be achieved.

Fourth, the current system perverts the management agreement concept; for management agreements work best where both parties share conservation aims. They are not an appropriate means of resolving basic conflicts of interest. However, if management payments were calculated on the assumption that no grant would have been paid, this would weaken even further the bargaining power of conservation authorities in objecting to damaging schemes. The corollary, therefore, especially as capital grants are cut or withdrawn, must be to give powers to the authorities to prevent or to amend such schemes (see Chapter 14).

Fifth, compensation has to be paid from the limited budgets of the conservation agencies, rather than by MAFF, whose relentless promotion of agricultural output and new farming methods is creating the problem. Not only is this requirement unfair and impractical but it is also an irrational allocation of resources. If agricultural policy is creating external costs, then the socially most efficient response would be to get the agricultural budget or the farming industry to pick up the bill. This is the 'polluter pays' principle. It is particularly apt in the present case because MAFF actually *saves* money when a conservation objection is sustained; and because the agricultural support system greatly inflates the cost of conservation, compensation being calculated to include all public subsidies.

To take account of these objections would involve a major reform of MAFF. Its remit would have to be expanded to include rural conservation as a primary objective, to be reflected in the grants and advice it gave to farmers (see Chapter 14). Section 29 of the Agriculture Act 1970, which restricts capital grants exclusively to the purpose of an agricultural business, would have to be amended.

A practical scheme for new types of subsidies to encourage conservation-oriented husbandry has been put forward by Clive Potter in *Investing in Rural Harmony*, published by the World Wildlife Fund. Central to his proposals is an alternative package of agricultural subsidies and incentives (APAs). This is envisaged as a modified and more rigorously scrutinised form of the existing agricultural and horticultural development scheme, which promotes a planned farm development over a period of years, in contrast to the one-off capital grants for specific projects. Potter suggests that the latter, which are now awarded retrospectively, should be subject to prior approval by MAFF, who would have the power to refuse a grant on amenity grounds, to impose stringent environmental conditions, and to award supplementary grants for conservation purposes. As far as possible, though, farmers would be encouraged to adopt an APAs grant, whereby money would be paid for conservation management and investment according to a detailed and comprehensive farm plan, which combined environmental and food production objectives. There would also be specific payments and incentives for small farmers in joining the scheme.

In areas such as the Somerset Levels and the Halvergate Marshes with a high agricultural potential, but 'where it is considered desirable in the interests of conserving certain nationally important natural characteristics, that traditional farming practices be continued', Potter proposes that grants should not be available for purely agricultural investments. Instead, farmers would be eligible for 'special area grants' (under an existing LFA directive which has been largely ignored by the British government), which would protect income through supporting a farm plan 'aimed at balancing any burdens of managing a certain proportion of the land for conservation, with a careful development of the rest of the farm business'. The drawback is that under the existing Directive, they could only apply to 2½ per cent of the land of the UK, and to 4 per cent if revised EEC proposals are accepted.

Potter's approach of seeking progressive modifications within the existing statutory framework contrasts with the more radical stance of Bowers and Cheshire. However, there is more to this disagreement than a difference in tactics. Potter emphasises the importance for conservation of active management and is aware that vitally needed conservation investment will not occur unless the necessary advice and financial assistance are made available. He is also more realistic regarding the political possibilities within the CAP as there is much greater scope for national action and discretion over direct aids to farmers than over price-support. Bowers and Cheshire do not overlook agricultural grants. On the contrary, they point out that grants provide a significant incentive for bringing into production ecologically-important marginal land, such as wetlands, heathland and permanent pasture, and so should be abolished. This is in keeping with their thoroughgoing economism, of taking pressure off the rural environment by depressing the agricultural economy. But for Potter, to abolish grants would be to throw the baby out with the bath-water, because grants are a potentially powerful and selective instrument for translating national production and environmental policies into farm-level management and development decisions.

Bowers and Cheshire, however, argue that agricultural grants, in general, play a much less important role in determining the pressures of production than price-support. This is certainly the case currently in the lowlands, but not so in the uplands. And it is likely to become less so generally as prices are squeezed and quotas and levies imposed. Agricultural grants, reformed along APAs lines, could thus become an increasingly significant factor in farmers' decision-making, encouraging them to integrate conservation objectives into farming practice. We would agree with Bowers and Cheshire that grants should not be available for purposes inimical to conservation, such as clearing ancient woodlands. However, we also recognise the potential of a reformed system of production and conservation grants and income and employment subsidies to achieve a desirable integration of agriculture and conservation at farm level. Indeed, we go further than Potter and argue that *all* grants, whether for farming or forestry, should be made conditional on the preparation and implementation of a comprehensive farm management plan.

This would be a radical departure from the present

situation. Farmers who currently receive grants at the highest rates under the agricultural and horticultural development scheme do have to prepare a development plan; but this is concerned solely with the improvement of the farm as a food-production enterprise and not with its management for a range of purposes. A comprehensive farm management plan would look at the farm as a whole, and take into account both the income and the costs associated with every aspect of its management. The aim would be to incorporate conservation into agricultural and forestry practice, to promote environmentally-sound husbandry and to encourage the creation, where suitable, of new habitats and landscapes. The costs (direct and indirect) of specific conservation measures would enter the grant calculation in much the same way as the cost of a new building or machine. Aid would be allocated in a much more highly packaged form than at present, investing in the farm as a whole rather than in specific capital projects or management agreements, and in relation to the overall balance of costs and income. The labour-intensive requirements of various aspects of land care would be recognised — for example, the repair and maintenance of vernacular buildings and walls, and the management of hedges and woodlands. In areas where the pressures of agricultural change threaten to sweep away valued landscapes and habitats, aid would be directed towards supporting and enhancing the infrastructure of traditional husbandry. With experience, such a farm management plan would offer a clear indication of the real need of the efficient but conservation-minded farmer for support from public funds.

The preparation of such a plan would involve, *inter alia*, a survey of the farm's habitats and landscape features; the formulation of proposals for their management; identification of areas in need of rehabilitation or replanting; and guidance on the phasing of activities, sources of grant aid, and labour requirements. These plans would be prepared by the farmer or landowner, advised by local agriculture and conservation committees (see Chapter 14) and, where necessary, by accredited consultants, with access to expertise in ecology, soil science, landscape architecture and farm management. Already some FWAGs offer a consultancy service on similar lines. The farm plan would be the basis for any management payments, but also for other incentives. For example, it is now possible for land in SSSIs and national parks to be exempted from capital transfer tax. This exemption could be extended to other land of conservation merit being managed under an agreed farm plan. In addition, conservation expenditure under a farm plan could be made deductible against income tax.

The precise package of payments would need to vary according to circumstances. Chapter 13 describes the elements which could comprise a reformed system of support specifically for upland farmers; whilst realising the measures outlined above would require changes in the objectives, organisation and practices of MAFF and ADAS and these are discussed in Chapter 14. But first we must turn to forestry.

FORESTRY REFORM

The time has come to effect a radical reform of the state policies that are as much responsible for forestry as they are for agriculture in contemporary Britain. One element in any reform package should be the extension of planning controls to afforestation and woodland clearance. Exceptions given automatic consent would have to be small, perhaps no more than $\frac{1}{2}$ ha., and certainly nothing remotely like the 50 ha. exemption suggested by the Countryside Commission. Planning control would give some protection to open land in the uplands, where the pressure for afforestation is greatest, and to existing forests and woodlands in both uplands and lowlands. It would have to be applied very strictly, and with no exceptions, in the case of ancient and semi-natural woodlands.

Planning control is no more than an essential negative power, a device for stopping objectionable proposals. It cannot, by itself, begin to protect the existing broadleaved woodlands or ensure sound, continuing management and afforestation programmes and could, if rigidly or weakly operated, have some harmful consequences. We have to look elsewhere for the positive policies and programmes that are needed. In devising such policies we should not be over-influenced by the argument that for balance of payments and other reasons Britain should massively expand the production of softwood timber, if only because even the most expansive programme would still leave Britain dependent on imports for at least three-quarters of its softwood needs. We accept the case for extending the forested area, but the emphasis should shift from the uplands to the lowlands; from blanket afforestation to the integration of farming, forestry and conservation; and from softwoods to the more valuable hardwoods, of which Britain could in time produce half its requirements or more.

Afforestation programmes in both the public and private sectors continue to be based on the assumption that growing trees is a second-best use of land, and so should be concentrated in the infertile uplands where food cropping is difficult or impossible so as to give food production an absolute priority on the better lowlands. This approach makes little economic sense when the EEC is producing large food surpluses, nor does it make much sense silviculturally, for trees (and broadleaves in particular) like any other crop, will grow best on good soils and in mild climates. There is evidence that much recent afforestation has taken place on land that is too marginal for commercial forestry. Much of it is threatened with premature destruction by windblow. The foresters' response, to eliminate thinning, deprives the forest-owner of the income from thinnings and the local community of continuous employment. There is an overwhelming case for shifting the emphasis of grants, tax relief and research away from coniferous planting in the uplands towards the lowlands where there is great potential for growing broadleaved woodlands, including high-yielding, fast-growing species.

In May 1984 the Forestry Commission published a consultative paper, *Broadleaves in Britain*, which marked a significant shift towards broadleaved woodlands, and recognition of the ecological value of unproductive ancient woodlands. But the paper was, as the Council for National Parks observed, 'astonishingly complacent' about the continuing loss of broadleaved woodlands. Its target was to maintain the present extent of broadleaved woodland not to extend it, and to accept further losses provided they were compensated for by new plantations. There should, instead, be a firm commitment both to stopping the loss of existing woodland and to an extension of the broadleaved area. The paper's advocacy of a register of ancient and semi-natural woodlands, management to perpetuate their unique features, and the publication of management guidelines is very useful. But the Commission wishes to confine conservation management to 'the most valuable conservation sites' — a half-hearted policy that could actively encourage the destruction of those deemed less valuable. The biggest omissions from the paper are any references to the need for a broadleaved grant and a tax-incentive system that would encourage management, or to the need for grants, research and advice on integrating woodland management with farming.

The Forestry Commission's complacency is at odds with the Countryside Commission's 'second look' at the farming landscapes it first studied in 1974 in *New Agricultural Landscapes*. For the Commission found that, although there had been quite a lot of tree-planting in the intervening ten years, this had been confined to a few farms and showed little imagination, because 'many farmers have surprisingly little knowledge of how to plant and take care of trees'. The Commission's report concluded that in none of the seven survey areas could the countryside be said to be safe from the threat of sudden and devastating change. One reason for this continuing threat is the Forestry Commission's extraordinary requirement that replanting grants are conditional on felling the existing woodland, even in circumstances where the appropriate course would be rehabilitation rather than replacement.

Reform should start with an amendment to the Forestry Acts to place on the Forestry Commission a firm duty to further conservation, and to promote timber production only to the degree that this is compatible with the agreed conservation policies for specific areas. Timber production would then cease to be the Commission's overriding purpose, although it would clearly remain a very important one. It would then be much easier to reform the grants and tax incentives to ensure that grant-aided or tax-relieved forestry schemes contained a significant conservation, amenity and recreation element. Criteria for both tax incentives and grants need to be amended to encourage broadleaved planting and subsequent management, and to discourage any plantations that are incompatible with the conservation policies for the areas in question. There should be a new grant for managing existing woodlands, which need not be conditional on the production of usable timber. And there should be a specific scheme, with appropriate grants and technical advice, to encourage the much closer integration of forestry and farming within the land management strategy of individual farms. The time should soon come when no financial support from agricultural or forestry funds is provided to farmers unless they have prepared, and are implementing, a comprehensive farm management plan that fully integrates farming with woodland management and the conservation of nature and landscape.

Nothing less than a programme of reforms on these lines can halt the continuing loss and deterioration of British woodlands, or ensure that flourishing woodlands make an ever bigger contribution to the beauty and productive wealth of the British countryside.

13. A New Deal for the Uplands

It was not until the mid-1970s, when the Countryside Commission initiated a major study of agriculture's impact on the upland landscapes of England and Wales, that 'the uplands' were recognised as constituting a specific environmental problem. But the term 'uplands' has never been officially defined. It is not in common use in Scotland, where the greater part of the British 'uplands' are to be found, and none of the statutory or non-statutory designations of land or landscape refers to the uplands. The nearest the government has come to recognising their existence as a special category for policy purposes is in the definition of the land above what used to be called the 'hill line', and is now called the agriculturally Less Favoured Areas, within which farmers get special assistance (often equivalent to a farm's profit) to compensate them for the permanent natural handicaps they experience in hill and mountain areas.

To add to the confusion, agricultural terminology distinguishes between 'hill farming', where extensive use is made of rough grazings on the moor and fells, and 'upland farming', where the farm consists almost entirely of enclosed fields. The Countryside Commission uses the term 'uplands' to embrace all the agriculturally Less Favoured Areas of England and Wales, whether on hill or upland farms, together with the valley lands that are integral to hill or upland farming. We would also include those 'marginal' areas that suffer from similar, although usually less severe, handicaps in soil, climate or remoteness, over 1 million ha. of which were added in 1984 to the existing LFAs by the EEC following representations by the British government.

The term 'the uplands' robs the mountains and the hills, the lakes and the valleys, the rocks and the cwms, the walks and the climbs, the bogs and the woods, the stone walls and the field barns of the magic that gives such areas as the Lake District, Snowdonia, Exmoor or the Yorkshire Dales a unique place in the affections — and the leisure-time — of the British people. The uniform label obscures the immense diversity that is perhaps the greatest single characteristic of the uplands. And yet, although rash generalisations are to be avoided, and although the uplands share many of the trends and problems that are common to most rural areas, their problems are different in many ways from those of the lowlands, or they are experienced in different ways or to a higher degree.

AGRICULTURE AND UPLAND COMMUNITIES

Whatever measures are needed to bring farming and forestry into harmony with the needs of landscape, wild-life and recreation, there should be, as the Countryside Commission recommends, a package of reforms specifically designed to deal with upland conditions. But conservation-oriented policies are unlikely to be successful in conserving a man-managed, productive landscape, unless reasonably vigorous, self-renewing upland communities can sustain, and be sustained by, a reasonably prosperous economy. If people are to work on the land — and even more if the land-based workforce is to be increased — people need houses to live in, schools, shops, alternative employment, transport and the health and other services that are often taken for granted in less remote areas. Any 'new deal' for the uplands must have wide social and economic ramifications.

The most important influence in the uplands, if seen from an agricultural or a conservation point of view, are the sheep. The land within the 'hill line' is, by official definition, suitable for livestock-rearing but not to any material extent for dairying, stock-fattening or cash-cropping. Low-input/low-output systems of livestock rearing are most suited to the poor soils, harsh climate and short growing season. While it is essential to maintain a balance between sheep and beef cattle to sustain the forage value of the rough grazings, sheep are the dominant influence, particularly at the higher altitudes to which the hardy breeds of sheep are well adapted. Well-shepherded and in the right numbers, sheep maintain the traditional swards; badly shepherded, or in excessive numbers, they impoverish the flora and fauna, erode the soil, encourage the spread of bracken (which cattle keep down) and prevent the regeneration of trees. John Muir, the Scottish 'sheep herder' who founded the conservation movement in America, called sheep 'four-footed locusts'. However, understocking also upsets the traditional balance, allowing the vegetation to revert in time nearer to its natural climax.

It was assumed in the 1940s, when the post-war agricultural and conservation legislation was passed, that a reinvigorated traditional agriculture would of itself sustain the rural population and conserve the landscape. Hill farming in particular was seen in the Dower and Hobhouse Reports to be the natural way to conserve the hill and mountain landscapes. Even when it had become obvious in the lowlands that modern agriculture had become the main agent in changing the landscape and reducing the rural workforce, it was thought that the permanent physical handicaps would prevent the same pattern asserting itself in the uplands. Machinery, after all, cannot take over lambing or gather sheep on the fells; the scope for applying chemical fertilisers and pesticides was very limited and the farmer could not diversify or specialise in crops for the market.

Today, although the uplands are still livestock-rearing country, it is no longer true to say that land within the LFA boundary is unsuitable for raising fat stock in any numbers. On the contrary, advances in animal husbandry, grass management, land improvement and buildings, combined with high guaranteed prices for fat lambs under the EEC sheepmeat regime since 1980, have encouraged 'upland' farmers to fatten lambs in very substantial numbers. The Ministry of Agriculture's experimental farms at Liscombe in Exmoor and Pwllpeiran in Wales (both of which are technically 'hill' not 'upland' farms) both now sell the majority of their lambs fat. In this way the more favourably-located farmers in the LFA can pick up both the sheepmeat premia for fat lambs and the headage payments that were intended to compensate them for the 'permanent natural handicaps' that prevent them (in theory) from producing fat lambs in any quantity.

The dominant influence of the sheep in the landscape and in the farming economy of the uplands should not be allowed to obscure the fact that farming, although using most of the land in upland areas, has ceased to be the majority employer. In the Lake District, for example, farming only provides one job in six, and it is far outweighed in economic importance by the tourist and other service industries. Forestry is of less economic significance than farming, even if its influence on the landscape is often greater, and it too is on a capital-intensive treadmill, achieving higher productivity by displacing labour. One cannot approach the uplands from the standpoint of either farming or conservation in isolation, and expect that by so doing one can achieve either a balanced or an acceptable solution to the problems.

Although the Countryside Commission attempted to extend the discussion of upland problems that it launched in 1983 into the social, economic and nature conservation fields, its initial discussion paper *What Future for the Uplands?* reflected the Commission's statutory preoccupation with landscape beauty and its enjoyment by visitors. The Commission identified three main trends in the uplands: the scenery was becoming less attractive; the reduction of jobs in farming and the ageing population were threatening the maintenance of the landscape and the provision of services for visitors; and lack of coordination at national level was limiting the ability of the authorities to tackle these problems. This can be contrasted with a study of integrated development in Exmoor, Dartmoor and Bodmin Moor, commissioned by the EEC from the Dartington Institute. Its primary concern was to establish the needs and aspirations of the inhabitants as a whole which, to nobody's surprise, turned out to be neither scenic beauty nor keeping the visitors happy, but jobs, homes and services.

Although the Commission's discussion and the Institute's study approached the issues from differing standpoints, there was a large measure of agreement between them. Both directed attention to the lack of any coherent government policy for the uplands apart from agriculture, and to the lack of any mechanism for integrating or coordinating policies that were in conflict with each other. The Institute recognised the need for economic development to respect ecological constraints; and the Commission the need for viable upland communities if the landscape is to be conserved.

It can fairly be concluded from these assessments of the complex of upland problems that one of the keys to any 'new deal' is to integrate conservation with development. No approach that tries to conserve natural resources by denying a decent livelihood to the people can succeed; but neither can an unsustainable policy of exploiting living or finite resources that diminishes the scenic beauty and environmental quality which, all studies show, is a major economic asset. The way to success lies through the concepts embodied in the World Conservation Strategy which makes conservation an integral part of development, and rules out unsustainable development that destroys irreplaceable resources.

We have neither the expert knowledge nor the resources to develop a complete package of social, economic and environmental policies for the uplands. But it cannot be emphasised too strongly that the reform programme we are putting forward to reconcile farming and forestry with conservation and recreation should be seen as one element — albeit an important one — in a larger package that embraces job-creation, housing, education, training and a wide range of services.

The Countryside Commission's research, published early in 1983 in the *Upland Landscapes Study (ULS)* and in a popular version *The Changing Uplands*, has now proved that, so long as present policies and trends continue, neither agriculture nor forestry is capable of sustaining the population of the uplands or of conserving their rich heritage of landscape, wildlife and human artefacts. The main conclusion to be drawn from the *ULS* analysis of 337 farms in 12 representative but widely different upland areas is that the agricultural support system, ostensibly designed to conserve both rural society and the environment, has become the major factor promoting depopulation and landscape deterioration.

From a narrowly agricultural standpoint, that measures success solely by productivity per person employed or productivity per acre, the trends revealed by the *ULS* can be seen as a success story. Between 1955 and 1976 the stock density in the study areas increased by almost 80 per cent, and the bigger farmers had plans for further expansion. Labour productivity, measured by the number of livestock units tended per worker, rose more than $2\frac{1}{2}$ times, and if measured by the number of workers per acre it increased by 30 per cent. Between 1967 and 1978 the rate at which farmers were converting moor or heath to enclosed pasture increased 11-fold compared with the rate over the previous 95 years. The rate at which farms were being amalgamated into larger units, employing relatively less labour, more than doubled during the 1960s compared with the previous decade, and continued to increase in the 1970s. Hill farmers were responding positively to the incentives offered to them — so much so that, in the view of Geoffrey Sinclair (the principal consultant in the *ULS*), in the 1960s the hill farming industry had been lifted out of its pre-war depression and was achieving the increases in production that seemed to be necessary after the war.

Since the *ULS* data were compiled, the introduction of the EEC sheepmeat regime has given an enormous additional incentive to the production of lamb, by adding a variable premium which for much of the year has nearly doubled — and at times more than doubled — the price received by the farmer. In July 1983, for example, when the market price was £1.06 per kilo the farmer received in addition a premium of £1.20 per kilo, equivalent to £24 for a fat lamb. This can be contrasted with the headage payment for the lamb's mother which since 1981 has stayed at £4.25 for lowland ewes and £6.25 for hill ewes on the ground that overall the farmers in the LFAs are doing well. The sheepmeat regime has given an immense incentive to lowland farmers and to farmers on the better, lower 'upland' farms to increase sheep production. The price of store (i.e. unfattened) lambs has also tended to rise. But the 'hill' farmers in the high country, unable to raise fat lambs 'to any material extent', and therefore to take advantage of the premia, have seen the real value of their headage payments shrink. The sheepmeat regime has undermined the long-standing arrangements for the support of the disadvantaged farmer in the 'hard' uplands, and seems likely to provoke a new round of intensified exploitation of the landscape in the 'soft' uplands, even if (as the EEC proposed towards the end of 1983) some limit is imposed on the upper level of the variable premia paid on fat lambs. The EEC's decision to extend the LFA in the UK by more than 1 million ha. threatens to undermine still further the position of the farmers on the poorer land to whom the headage payments are a lifeline. For if the LFA funds are to be spread over a much larger area, those who now depend on them are almost bound to lose.

UPLAND DECLINE

Seen from a wider social or environmental standpoint the story takes on a different colour. In the *ULS* areas the number of farms fell by 40 per cent between 1950 and 1976, and their average size increased by 56 per cent in those areas where no significant amount of land was lost to afforestation. The number of farm workers was reduced almost to vanishing-point in some areas: in Snowdonia 79 per cent of full-time and 70 per cent of part-time workers' jobs disappeared in the eight years, 1965/73; two-thirds of the full-time jobs in Exmoor and Dartmoor disappeared between 1952 and 1972. Although, as the 1981 census has confirmed, the total population of the uplands is stabilising, the trend is towards an ageing population and a shrinking land-based workforce, with continued loss of population from the smaller and more isolated settlements.

The younger farmers tend to work the larger, more viable, expanding farms: almost two-thirds of the farms over 200 ha. are worked by farmers under 50, but 80 per cent of the farms of 10 ha. or less are farmed by people over 50. The likelihood that their children (or anybody else) will carry on as these older farmers die is small. The *ULS* found almost exactly half the farms in the study areas to be economically unviable. More than three-quarters of these, however, are run on a full-time basis and provide the family's only source of income, although many of them are categorised as 'part-time' by MAFF. And of these full-time farms more than half (30 per cent of the total number of farms) are classified by the *ULS* as 'vulnerable', either because the farmers have no supplementary income or run marginal dairy farms. It can be assumed that this broadly represents the situation in the uplands of England and Wales as a whole.

There is no mystery about the reason for these trends. Hill farming depends on government support to survive. The majority of those consulted by the *ULS* said that support was 'vital', and their opinion is borne out by the fact that farms in the study area received no less than 40 per cent of their gross farm income from LFA grants and subsidies (this totalled £118 million for England and Wales in 1983). But if, as the Ministry of Agriculture never ceases to proclaim, farmers are businessmen whose business is to make money by producing food, we should not be surprised that the farmers respond to financial incentives designed almost exclusively to help them to produce more food with less labour and at lower cost. Farmers tend to neglect those resources that do not contribute to livestock production, that do not attract grant, or whose management cannot be justified by the cash return.

The environmental consequences of these trends have been amply documented already, as capital grants encourage 'active change', such as land drainage, felling woodland and reclaiming moorland. Headage payments, in the words of a Peak Park study, encourage farmers to push sheep numbers as high as they think they can risk — in one recorded case ten times the number consistent with a flourishing heather moor. Shortage of labour, the drive for profit and the lack of spare resources encourage 'passive change' — the neglect or non-management of landscape features, buildings, field boundaries and woodlands. The *ULS* pinpointed in great detail some of these changes in the uplands, such as the spread of bracken, the loss of deciduous woodland (a decrease in area of 22 per cent between 1967 and 1978), the poor condition of hedges (only 20 per cent well-maintained or in fair condition), and the neglect of common land (where less than half the graziers use their rights fully). The uplands present the paradox of degeneration and decline proceeding in parallel with agricultural intensification.

If, as the Ministry of Agriculture claims, hill farming supports are intended not only to promote livestock production but also to make an essential contribution to the social and economic well-being of the uplands and to further conservation, its support system stands condemned as a model of both injustice and ineptitude. With no upper limits on eligibility, support goes disproportionately to the larger farms on the better land. Sinclair has calculated from *ULS* data that the help given to farmers in the LFAs is in inverse ratio to the degree of physical handicap, with those on the best land receiving four times as much per hectare as those on the worst. Of the 20,500 farms in the LFA in 1981/82, the 11,000 smallest, with less than 50 livestock units* averaged £590 each in grants and subsidies in 1981/82, whereas the 750 largest with more than 300 livestock units averaged £13,200. In a nutshell, 30 per cent of the money goes to 6 per cent of the farmers. There is a similar bias in the provision of capital grants. This regressive distribution enables the large farmers to maximise their receipts from grants and subsidies. They find it much easier to raise capital to pay their share of development schemes, whose purpose is to increase stocking levels, and so to attract more headage payments. But the *ULS* found that the smaller farms either could not raise the capital or could not risk servicing it, or were ineligible for grants because their businesses did not meet the target income from farming sources.

It is not always the 'inefficient' or 'non-viable' farms (to use MAFF language) that are most at risk when farmers

---

* 1 livestock unit = 1 cow or 0.15 sheep.

are caught, as increasingly they seem likely to be, in the cost-price squeeze with agricultural supports being held down and costs continuing to rise. The most vulnerable are often those who have been enticed into farm development schemes designed to raise their level of 'efficiency' but find themselves trapped by their indebtedness when profit levels fall or (as in the case of milk) production is cut back by a quota and a levy imposed on production in excess of the quota. It is significant, that despite MAFF's claims that its supports serve social ends, Sir Michael Franklin, the Permanent Secretary, reaffirmed in November 1983 that it is not the function of the CAP or of MAFF to give social support to marginal farmers whose survival is threatened by the cost-price squeeze (*Farmers' Weekly*, 18 November 1983).

The British government is alone in Europe in its interpretation of the Less Favoured Areas Directive, and it offers no supports comparable to those available in France or Germany to small or young farmers outside the EEC framework. Both these countries impose a strict ceiling on the number of livestock that can qualify for headage payments, and only offer the highest rates of payment to farmers in the most handicapped Alpine zones. A study by the Arkleton Trust has shown that although British hill farmers include the richest and largest in Europe, they get the lion's share (about 39 per cent in 1981) of the EEC's funds for Less Favoured Areas. The average subsidy to a hill farmer in the UK (an average which, as we have seen, conceals gross disparities) is 3 times that in Greece or France, $5\frac{1}{2}$ times that in Germany and 7 times that in Ireland. A German study, published in 1981, of the social consequences of LFA supports throughout the Common Market found that they are only of marginal importance in stopping depopulation (the principal aim of the Directive), and fail to facilitate the conservation of the landscape (its secondary purpose). They found, as Sinclair did, that the largest payments went to a small number of large farms, particularly in Britain, and they recommended that the entire concept should be reconsidered, so that the aid could be directed on a farm-by-farm basis to those farms with the greatest physical and social needs.

Not all hill farmers by any means take the Ministry of

Agriculture's view that they are businessmen first and foremost, whose decisions must be justified by the criteria of profitability. More than half the farmers interviewed in the *ULS* said that they would be prepared to modify their farming to conserve the landscape, although a few would do so only if compensated. Where incentives are offered for conservation farmers take them up, as they have done since MAFF made the laying of hedges eligible for capital grants. There is potentially a large body of support for conservation among upland farmers.

But the *ULS* interviews also enabled the study to construct a picture of the kind of 'businessman' farmer who is 'least sympathetic to conservation and who is least likely to make concessions to it, especially if it reduces profits. Predictably this farmer is young, depends wholly on farming, and has a large farm, and has increased the size of his farm taking over land from other holdings'. And the study found that it is precisely farmers of this kind who are 'being encouraged by government policy to run their hill and upland farms as efficiently as possible'. The Dartington Institute study, while confirming local findings that on Dartmoor, Exmoor and Bodmin Moor it is the larger farmers who benefit most from the present system, also noted that these larger farmers 'feel no particular sympathy' for the plight of the small farms that are under pressure. Correspondingly, it found that those 'at the bottom end' feel frustrated, and want the system to be geared to their needs. There are solid grounds, therefore, for believing that a package of reforms that helps the smaller and disadvantaged farmers and promotes countryside conservation will, if fairly presented, prove acceptable to many farmers.

Unfortunately, despite having stimulated a wide-ranging debate, the Countryside Commission came up with proposals for *A Better Future for the Uplands*, in March 1984, that fell far short of what was needed. In particular, the Commission ignored the overwhelming evidence of the maldistribution of farming support funds and its consequences — above all the growth of the large farmer and the squeezing-out of the small farmer. It retreated from its preliminary conclusion that lack of labour was causing landscape deterioration. It had clearly given in to the farming unions which, it says, were 'particularly forth-right' in arguing that government should not provide more assistance to smaller and marginal enterprises at the expense of the larger businesses. The Commission's decision not to seek the redistribution of the existing farm supports obliged it to look for new money to support conservation and the smaller or more handicapped farmers; but it was equally concerned not to ask for much from the government. In the event, it asked for more money for management agreements in national parks and SSSIs, and for £5 million to extend farm capital grants to cover the cost of expensive building materials and of protecting landscape features. It offered the smaller and more handicapped farmers little, apart from sympathy and a lower threshold of eligibility (150 instead of 250 standard man-days) for farm capital grants — a change that only a minority with access to capital could benefit from. The Commission made no proposals for higher grants or headage payments for the smaller or more handicapped farmers. It did not even discuss the sheepmeat premium, which is now the major support and one that greatly favours the bigger farmers on the better land.

This is not to say that the Commission's proposed package contained nothing of value. It urged on government the desirability of integrating conflicting policies, and of pressing for the EEC LFA Directive to be given wider objectives. Its boldest recommendations were that planning permission be required for farm roads and buildings; that all land improvement and drainage grants be withdrawn within those areas of moor and heath designated for conservation by national park authorities under Section 43 of the Wildlife and Countryside Act; that large-scale afforestation of bare land should be brought under planning control; and that farm capital grants should be given social and environmental objectives. But these recommendations are seriously weakened by the qualifications attached to them. Section 43 moorlands are but one part of the vulnerable areas that need to be protected from grant-aided 'improvements'. Moreover, each of the national park authorities has adopted different criteria when designating the Section 43 moorlands it believes 'particularly important to conserve', so that Snowdonia at

one extreme has excluded all aesthetic criteria while
Exmoor has adopted them exclusively. By proposing that
plantations up to 50 ha. be given 'deemed planning consent' the Commission is inviting landowners to disregard
existing voluntary arrangements to limit afforestation, and
to desecrate the moorlands with what are, in visual and
nature conservation terms, very large developments. And
the wider scope given to capital grants does not meet the
farmer's need for income to pay for unprofitable conservation management, although the Commission concedes
that income — not capital — help is what farmers need
most.

The Commission's timidity was exposed in an embarrassing fashion in December 1984 when, for reasons of
economy, the government withdrew all grants for land
reclamation, while retaining grants for the improvement
of existing grassland and introducing grants for the
management of moorland by burning and cutting. In
withdrawing land reclamation grants the government has
created problems for those farmers whose economic viability depends on the ability to improve small areas which
may have little conservation value, and it has failed to
relate the new grant structure to conservation. Neither
the Commission's timidity nor the government's crude
approach to grant-cutting means that the need for a more
realistic and radical approach to upland problems has disappeared. On the contrary, unless decisive action is taken,
the adverse trends that the Commission has identified will
continue.

The government's response to the report on the uplands
took the form of a letter sent on 31 January 1985 to Sir
Derek Barber, Chairman of the Countryside Commission.
Though strong on worthy sentiments concerning the need
to sustain vigorous upland communities and protect and
enhance their wildlife, landscape and historic heritage, it
proved disappointingly silent on specific proposals. It
described the report as 'a milestone, but a milestone on a
road which stretches far ahead' and drew attention to the
'interim flavour' of its response. Decisive action, it seems,
is on the agenda but as yet has only minimal content and
no timetable. Although conspicuously lacking in initiatives, the only significant, albeit modest, response to the

Commission's suggestions was the announcement of the government's intention to issue a consultation paper proposing that a new Landscape Area Development Order should be made covering the design and siting of all farm building and farm and forest roads in all national parks.

AN ALTERNATIVE APPROACH

The key to the prosperity of the uplands and to the conservation or enhancement of its magnificent heritage lies in a total approach to the land management. At government level this entails an understanding of the need for specific upland policies (within a framework of rural policies) and a commitment to conservation that should run like a thread through every aspect of policy and imbue the thinking of every department and agency. It implies some mechanism at every level to coordinate what would otherwise be discordant policies, although the machinery may often be of less importance than the attitudes of the people concerned. The approach here described is essentially an adaptation, to the specific conditions of the uplands, of the alternative package of agricultural subsidies outlined in Chapter 12.

On the land itself, it means that the farm ceases to be regarded either as a mere food-production factory or a business enterprise whose decisions are all made according to the criteria of profit or loss. Of course, every farm or estate is and must be a business; it cannot survive unless it yields a reasonable income to those who work it, or if it is wasteful of money or other resources. But it should be more than a business. Management decisions should also be justified by a range of criteria which include the need to sustain a sufficient land-based workforce and to conserve natural and other resources.

Appropriate use should be made of all a farm's agricultural, woodland, recreational, tourist, industrial or other potential. Income can be derived from farm and non-farm sources. Support should be available from public sources not merely to compensate hill farmers for genuinely permanent natural handicaps or to promote timber production, but also to encourage such financially unrewarding work as the management of ancient woodlands and other wild-life habitats, and the satisfaction of recreational needs.

Once it is recognised that a farm is more than a business, it becomes possible for official policy to recognise the positive role of small and part-time farmers, and to remove the disabilities imposed by the present support system on farms which are officially classified as 'non-viable' or 'part-time', or whose incomes are too low to enable farmers to benefit from the tax concessions available to large farms or forestry enterprises. A reformed policy should put more money into the management of the land for conservation, amenities, recreation and tourism, and into the promotion of craft and processing enterprises which add value locally to farm and woodland products. The incentives on offer should encourage the balanced development and management of the total resources of a farm.

The first step in this process must be to publicise the detailed maps of the Less Favoured Areas for public scrutiny. MAFF should revise its present narrow interpretation of the Less Favoured Area Directive, and the British government must press within the EEC for the reform of the Directive itself. It suffers from the fatal contradiction that although it is intended to achieve social and environmental objectives, the only incentives it provides (apart from small grants for farm tourism that the UK has not taken up) are calculated to stimulate livestock production. This remains the basic flaw in the proposals published by the EEC in November 1983 for changes in the CAP Directives; they even make things worse by extending the LFA Directive to forestry with the usual emphasis on production rather than woodland management.

A package of reformed supports designed to achieve wider objectives for hill farming would include comprehensive, multipurpose farm management plans (as outlined in Chapter 12), reforms in headage payments and capital grants, an upland management grant, a comprehensive advisory service and controls over certain agricultural and forestry operations (see Chapter 14). The reformed headage payment system would relate the level of payments on a sliding-scale to the degree of permanent physical handicap, measured by a farm-by-farm assessment which would classify land in the LFA in a number of handicap classes. It would also adjust the headage payments according to the number of livestock units on the farm, again on a sliding-scale, with the largest payments per animal going to the smallest farms, and a cut-off point beyond which no additional animals would qualify for subsidy. Farmers would be involved in the assessment of handicap, and in monitoring the scheme to avoid abuse. A payments ceiling would be fixed (probably so many £s per 'adjusted forage hectare' in technical terms) to ensure that the number of livestock does not exceed the ecological carrying capacity of the land, and farmers who exceed the limit would be penalised. The result would be to give the maximum support to the smallest farms on the poorest land, and the least support (or no support at all) to the largest farms on the best land. Although the system would be more complicated than the present one (whose 'delightful simplicity' MAFF officials constantly praise) it would be fair, practical and flexible. It would redistribute the payments in socially and environmentally beneficial ways, and should produce some savings, which could be used to provide incentives for resource management.

There is a strong case for eliminating altogether the flat-rate percentage capital grant system, as the grants are invariably taken up only by those farmers who can raise the balance of the capital to be invested from their own resources. If grant systems are to benefit the smaller farmers they should be progressive, with a higher rate for small projects on small farms, and they should be supplemented by other incentives such as loans at low rates of interest. All grants should be related to a comprehensive farm management plan and no capital grants should be offered for operations that are contrary to conservation policies for the area.

The withdrawal of grants for land reclamation in December 1984 — though it will take some time to have its full effect since it only applies to commitments entered into after 11 December — represents a significant retreat by MAFF in the face of sustained pressure from the conservation lobby. Grants for re-seeding and regenerating grassland, the laying-down of permanent pasture, and bracken control are now only available for work on already existing laid-down grass. The new schedule thus removes the major incentive to upland farmers to embark on environmentally damaging capital projects (though 30 per cent grants are still available for land drainage in the uplands), and severely curtails the potential for inventing spurious 'improvement' projects whose real purpose is to attract compensation in the form of risk-free and work-free indexed annuities. There would be no need to pay compensation, because the grant would not have been offered in the first place. If management agreements cease to be seen as a device for resolving conflicts (for which they are wholly inappropriate) they could be restored to their proper role of formalising understandings between farmers or landowners and conservation authorities. Their scope could be enlarged. Existing management agreements in Exmoor, for example, are usually confined to the management of a small part of the farm, typically a few tens of acres of moorland and to the compensation payable for loss of profit from that area. But, like the farm management plan, these agreements should envisage the appropriate management of the total resource — moorland, woodland, wetland, streams, the inbye land itself, and the potential for non-farm income from tourism or other activities. Neither comprehensive plans nor agreements would rule out the more productive use of farmland where this can be done on a sustainable basis and without serious loss of wildlife interest. The Lake District Special Planning Board argued in its contribution to the uplands discussion that there is considerable scope for increasing production and farm incomes by better management of the inbye land, and by reversing the continual spread of bracken over the hillsides.

The comprehensive farm plan and management agreement has to be matched by a new, comprehensive grant — an upland management grant. This would not be limited to a specific operation such as tree-planting, nor to the initial cost alone. Nor would it necessarily be a fixed percentage of the initial cost. It should provide support for any unprofitable but necessary action on the farm for conservation or recreation, provided it formed part of a comprehensive farm management plan or a management agreement. It would be particularly useful in encouraging

the integration of farming with the management of existing woodlands and hedges, and the planting of deciduous
trees. It would not only support the initial operations —
draining, fencing, planting, and so on — but also the
continuous but unprofitable management required more
or less in perpetuity for ancient woodlands and for some
years in productive woodlands. The amount of the grant
would be individually negotiated but as it will take time
for farmers to be drawn into such an arrangement, existing capital grant schemes for tree-planting would be continued, and even extended.

In this way the true integration of farming with forestry,
which has never been attempted on 99 per cent of the
farms in the uplands of England and Wales, could become
a reality. But, as a Countryside Commission study of small
woodlands has shown, only 1 per cent of farmers understand woodland management. It would be one of the
major tasks of a reformed advisory service to equip
farmers with the knowledge and the skills, and to offer the
financial incentives.

Jobs would be created in several ways: individual farms
that would otherwise go under could be kept going; other
farms could take on more labour (full- or part-time, or
through contractors). Farmers who are also contractors
would diversify into woodland management, tree-planting
and other conservation or recreation work. The national
park authorities in particular could greatly expand their
upland management services (which are largely concerned with the maintenance and reorganisation of foot-
paths and bridleways), and could increase both their
permanent staff and the number of jobs they could offer
to farmers and contractors. If the tourist boards would
interest themselves in small-scale farm tourism by offering
grants and cheap loans to small farmers, additional income might flow into many farms. The French regional
nature parks have demonstrated that there is considerable
scope for promoting small local industries to manufacture
wood, meat, cheese and wool products, thereby retaining
in the area much of the value added to them.

The answer to the question 'Where will the money come
from to finance conservation or recreation works, and to
assure the smaller hill farmers of an income comparable to

that of industrial workers?' is that it can all be found by savings in the existing agricultural support programmes. What we are seeking is, essentially, a transfer of resources: first, from the bigger, richer farmers on the better land, both to the smaller, poorer farmers on the poorer land and to farmers on farms of any size or quality who are undertaking serious conservation and recreation work; and second, from the agricultural support budget to the conservation and recreation budget. The Ministry of Agriculture spends 11 times as much on subsidies and grants to farmers in the Peak District as the Peak Park Joint Planning Board (perhaps the most progressive national park authority) can afford to spend on conservation. Clive Potter has estimated that nearly £50 million (in 1980/81 terms) could be saved in agricultural grants, subsidies and compensation annually and spent on conservation (particularly in designated areas) or additional help to the smaller more handicapped farmers, particularly in the uplands.

There is some evidence to suggest that hill and upland farmers will accept the kind of package we are suggesting. Ken Parker, leader of an EEC-sponsored research project into integrated rural development in the Peak National Park found, as others have done, that if they are given a real say in the decisions most farmers are happy to accept, and work to, a combined food production and conservation management package of policies and incentives. There is, therefore, nothing impractical in the package of reforms we suggest. No doubt it could be improved upon after debate and trial-and-error. We do not claim that it represents, in every detail, the only possible solution. But we have no doubt that its basic principles are sound, and will have to be adopted if the future of the uplands, their landscape and wildlife are to be assured.

14. Sticks and Carrots

Chapters 12 and 13 examined the possibilities for reform of the agricultural and forestry support system. We concluded that, whereas a reduction in support might well create a much more favourable economic climate for rural conservation, it would not ensure that particular features or areas of conservation interest would either not be destroyed or be actively cared for and managed. This final chapter therefore concentrates on the need for conservation safeguards and for changes in the administration of the countryside.

CONSERVATION SAFEGUARDS: CONTROLS AND ORDERS

The most contentious aspect of conservation reform relates to the regulation of farming and forestry developments, with positions polarised between the advocates of *laissez-faire* and the advocates of control. The Conservative Party, backed by farming interests and supported by the NCC and the Countryside Commission, argues for a minimum of compulsion and stresses the need to build upon the voluntary cooperation of farmers and landowners in conserving the countryside. On the other side, groups including Friends of the Earth, the CPRE, the Socialist

Countryside Group and the Labour Party stress the need to bring agricultural and forestry operations under statutory planning controls as the only way to prevent damage to the rural environment.

Presented as the opposition between voluntarism and controls, the debate has been falsely polarised, because these are not mutually exclusive or incompatible alternatives. Any system of regulation, whatever legal or administrative procedures or safeguards it incorporates, depends for its effectiveness on the ready compliance of the regulated — or at least the vast majority of them. It is quite spurious to maintain that controls and an ethos of stewardship are necessarily inimical. On the contrary, nothing has been more corrosive of the stewardship ideal than the historically recent notion that a farmer has an absolute and unfettered right to do what he pleases with his land. The critical question, therefore, is whether or not regulation is needed; and, if so, what degree and form of regulation would be appropriate.

The argument that no controls are needed simply ignores the experience of the last 30 years during which farmers and landowners, left to their own devices, have steadily impoverished the rural environment. But would controls be needed if we could radically alter the economic pressures on farmers in the ways discussed in Chapter 12? Bowers and Cheshire, in their book *Agriculture, Land Use and the Countryside*, seem to think not: 'Economic incentives, if properly designed, are to a greater or lesser degree self-policing and ... are in general superior to physical controls in influencing human behaviour' (p.143). There are two reactions to this argument.

First, no system of incentives, however well designed, is going to be able to tackle all the many and complex causes of agricultural development or to take adequately into account the full variety of personal, financial and physical circumstances facing every farmer. Therefore individual farming responses will vary considerably. Moreover, there will always be mavericks, and those who simply do not know or care about the incentives on offer. Second, no system of general incentives is going to encompass the full range of social, economic and conservation values attached to each particular area and feature of the countryside. The statutory planning system, in contrast, incorporates democratically accountable and responsive procedures for regulating the development of any and every piece of land.

Controls, if introduced, must operate effectively. They must be able to cope with the technicalities of modern agriculture without becoming an intolerable burden on the farming industry, but at the same time they must have a positive impact on farm development decisions, by discouraging, modifying or blocking developments which clash with the public interest.

The main fears of the farming community, apart from the loss of freedom, are that planners would not be able to understand the finer points of agricultural practice and that farmers would be subjected to bureaucracy and delays. Delays could be particularly serious in view of the seasonality of farming. Any new powers, therefore, would require the commitment of sufficient skilled staff to operate them efficiently.

The experience of the national park authorities in vetting notifications for farm capital grants is instructive. They were given this new responsibility in 1980 at just a few weeks' notice. On average each now handles over 500 notifications a year; and the average time taken to deal with a notification is 15 days. There has been general praise for the administrative efficiency of the authorities (though note the reservations we express in Chapter 7) which, like other planning authorities, had never previously had any formal role in farm management decisions. The park authorities have allocated on average the equivalent of one full-time member of staff to the task.

The notification system does not cover all farm developments, only those that are grant-aided. Nevertheless, this gives us some indication of the order of magnitude of the staffing implications of extending controls to agriculture. Contrary to some assertions, therefore, the *direct* costs should not be great. The *indirect* costs are more difficult to assess but are likely to entail a *net public gain* given that most farm developments involve considerable direct and indirect public subsidies both to the capital employed and to subsequent increases in output, all of which would be saved if a proposed development were not granted permission.

More formidable difficulties than the staffing and resource implications relate to the definition of development and its extension to incorporate significant farming changes, without creating too many legal loopholes or a system of controls which could not be enforced. Agriculture is subject to inherently unpredictable environmental conditions and deals with living systems, one of whose properties is inexorable change. The real scale of change and intensive overlapping of different interests on the same parcel of land bring a unique complexity to rural land-use issues. Any regulatory system would have to accommodate all these distinctive characteristics. In many cases the negative controls available to local planners would be insufficiently sensitive to deal with the dynamics of organic change. Such change is usually gradual, creating perhaps insuperable difficulties in defining or detecting a specific departure, and therefore in isolating the causes of change and allocating responsibility. Many of these impracticalities are overlooked by Marion Shoard in her forceful advocacy of planning controls over farming in *The Theft of the Countryside*.

Living systems also need to be managed. Yet, in themselves, controls can only prevent the construction, removal or material change of features; they cannot ensure that what is thereby not obliterated is managed in a sympathetic manner. It would be both impossible and inequitable to achieve desired management practices by the imposition of planning controls. They are too blunt and insensitive to deal with such activities as ploughing, fertiliser application, pesticide spraying, adjustment of stocking densities, coppicing, woodland and hedgerow management and the clearance of water courses, even though some of these activities may be inimical, and others essential, to the maintenance of valued habitats and landscapes. Where the intention is to oblige a farmer to follow a certain management strategy, this must be achieved by a farm management plan or by a management agreement.

None of these caveats concerning the difficulties of regulating organic change through planning controls applies to those agricultural operations which already fall within the definition of 'development', *viz*. the construction of farm buildings, roads and yards, and drainage works. Given the industrial character of most modern farm buildings, and the fact that many are badly designed and sited from any but an agricultural point of view, it is an indefensible anomaly that these and other construction and engineering operations on farms are exempt from development control. They should pose no technical difficulty for the planning system and could readily be brought within its ambit simply by amending the general development order.

To apply development control procedures to other farming activities would be to use a quite inappropriate and insensitive sledgehammer, since what is generally sought is the preservation and management of some traditional features. It would be quite inequitable to use the development control system to this end, since it is largely regulatory in nature. The presumption is that planning permission will be granted unless there are good grounds for refusal. If the goal is to preserve particular landscape features and characteristics either indefinitely or until a lasting management solution can be devised, then the ethos of the preservation order is more pertinent. The precedents include tree preservation orders, limestone pavement orders and landscape areas special development orders. To complement or supersede these specific powers a generalised notification and order power is needed which could be applied to any vulnerable features or areas.

Farmers would be required to give notice to the relevant authority if they intended to remove or alter a specified landscape feature or to carry out a notifiable operation which might damage the conservation interest of a site. The authority would then have time to assess the importance of the feature or site and, if appropriate, seek to make a financial agreement for its conservation. In these respects, procedures would follow and extend those already established under the Wildlife and Countryside Act for the notification of potentially damaging operations in SSSIs. However, in cases where an agreement was sought and the farmer refused, powers to impose a preservation order would be available *as a last resort* and subject to a right of appeal. The CPRE proposed such a scheme in 1975, and Lord Porchester, following his investigation of moorland conversion on Exmoor, advocated similar procedures to prevent the loss of scenically important moorland in the national park.

The advantages of a general order-making power compared with development control are that the period of notification and the area(s), the features and the activities subject to notification could all be adjusted in line with political and administrative feasibility and perceived need. Regulation could therefore be introduced on a piecemeal and responsive basis and amended in the light of experience and circumstance. The procedures could be made more or less specific in relation to the complexity and significance of local land-use conflicts. Selectivity and local sensitivity would be primary features in contrast to the blanket standardisation and bureaucracy that a uniform system of development control might foster. Management activities, including positive requirements, could also be included in an order without creating too many legal loopholes and problems of enforcement; in which case the term 'conservation management order' might be appropriate. In addition, the 'burden of bureaucracy' would be borne more by the authorities than by the farmers, in contrast to the situation under development control: for example, any delay on the part of the authority would work to its disadvantage, not the farmer's, who would be free to proceed if no response was forthcoming from the authority within a specified period. (The standard period of notification would probably be three months.) A further advantage is that a refused planning application might only lead to a succession of revised applications whereas an order is a clear statement of intent or policy, and as vulnerable areas were gradually covered by orders the administrative workload would diminish.

The final advantage of the order-making system relates to compensation. The introduction of the planning system in 1947 was accompanied by a scheme for a once-and-for-all compensation for the nationalisation of development rights. Though the scheme was only partly implemented it could legitimately be argued that the extension of development control to agriculture should follow this precedent. Order-making powers, though, set a different precedent.

Under a tree preservation order, for example, compensation is payable on refusal of consent, or the granting of conditional consent, in respect of resulting damage or expenditure. There is no compensation for effects on the value of land. There seems no reason why other features covered by a preservation order should not be treated similarly, with restitution limited to actual (not hypothetical) loss or damage. The right to compensation, introduced by Section 30 of the Wildlife and Countryside Act, for depreciation in land value due to the imposition of a nature conservation order is quite anomalous and should be repealed.

NEW STRUCTURES AND A NEW ETHIC

New procedures and policies require parallel changes in structures and personnel. So far as possible, these changes should seek to achieve two objectives: the delivery of aid and advice to farmers in an integrated manner to support the comprehensive farm management plan; and the bringing together of positive and negative powers within the same agency to ensure that safeguards and incentives are mutually reinforcing. The greatest obstacle to the integration of rural policies is the monolithic structure of MAFF. Since the second world war and with single-minded purpose, the ministry has pursued the objective of expanding food production, overlooking the social and environmental consequences of its policies. Now that the era of agricultural expansion is over, the structure and purposes of MAFF must be overhauled.

The coordination of policies always has a political as well as an administrative dimension. Administrative coordination without wider changes in structures and policies will tend to perpetuate and reinforce the *status quo*. This was the experience of the Countryside Review Committee which, between 1974 and 1980, brought together senior officials from the DoE, MAFF, the Welsh Office, the NCC, the Countryside Commission, the Forestry Commission, the Sports Council and the Development Commission to examine the range of policies affecting the countryside. The failure of this committee to tackle fundamental problems and conflicts fuelled support for reorganisation of central government responsibilities, to create a new Ministry of Rural Affairs. As proposed by the CLA and others, the core of such a ministry would be MAFF, to which would be transferred the DoE's responsibilities for rural planning and development, and oversight of the NCC, the Countryside Commission and the Development Commission.

Despite its attractions, this proposal as it stands has major drawbacks. For a start, it fails to bring together the positive and negative powers over rural land-use at the local level since the only controls that exist are with local planning authorities. Moreover, in overcoming some divisions at the national level, it would create others. Responsibility for food policy would sit incongruously with the social and environmental responsibilities of the new ministry. In addition, rural planning and nature conservation would be artificially removed from responsibility for urban and regional planning, environmental protection and local government.

Problems of internal coordination would supersede those of external coordination, though with the crucial difference that internal dissent is more easily suppressed than external dissent. In political terms, the transformation of MAFF into a Ministry of Rural Affairs would probably entail the subordination of social and environmental interests to agricultural interests. Conflicts currently aired on an interdepartmental basis would be internalised within the one department and stifled by the dominant interest and the cloak of official secrecy. If one of the major obstacles to constructive reform is the monolithic structure and power of MAFF, it would be a grave error to strengthen it further. As presently constituted it is neither able nor well equipped to assist in the diversification of rural economies and the conservation of the countryside. A Ministry of Rural Affairs, if it ever comes into being, should be very different from the old MAFF in new clothes that the CLA seems to have in mind.

Administrative integration could alternatively be pursued at a local, rather than the national, level. County councils have the general responsibility for planning and promoting the social, economic and environmental well-being of their areas. To these functions could be added specific responsibility for promotion of agriculture, rural employment and rural conservation. Each county council would have to establish an 'agriculture and conservation committee' to formulate relevant policies and exercise its new powers. The staff and functions of ADAS would be devolved to the counties, thus reverting to the situation which pertained before the second world war. MAFF would retain its overall policy-making role but would lose most of its responsibilities for implementing agricultural policy. In this way it would be possible to move away from MAFF's dogged insistence on the uniform application of national policies that has done so much to eradicate the diversity and distinctiveness of the British countryside. This would also help to redress the imbalance of power between MAFF and the other countryside agencies, although more would need to be done to strengthen the conservation agencies (see below).

The county agriculture and conservation committees would be responsible for determining local policy and for integrating advice and central funds not only from MAFF but also from the NCC, the Countryside Commission, the Forestry Commission, the Development Commission, the tourist boards and the Soil Survey. The committees would dispense grants to farmers and would also be equipped with the order-making powers described above.

However, this proposal too has its shortcomings. The county committees would be dispensing 100 per cent of national funds but without being subject to any specific control or accountability by central government. This is unlikely to be politically or administratively acceptable unless the county councils were themselves to provide a substantial proportion of the funds which might only be possible through the re-rating of agricultural land. Farmers, though typically well-represented on county councils, would probably resist any move to make them the agencies for administering agricultural policy. Conservationists might also be wary. Such decentralised decision-making, in which the national conservation agencies would have little leverage, could hamper the drive for more positive conservation programmes. The initiative would very much lie with the county committees, yet many councillors and local authorities are not especially suited to take the lead in these matters. Finally, the relationship between the county committees and MAFF would be most uncertain and potentially very fraught. It is difficult to see how MAFF could be the ministry for farming but have no responsibility at national level for initiating the necessary research, transmitting the results, issuing essential guidance, framing grant schemes and supervising them, and generally trying to ensure that policy is implemented.

A middle way between devolution to county councils and consolidation in a Ministry of Rural Affairs would be to seek effective coordination at both local and national levels. This would necessitate close liaison between MAFF and the DoE and its various agencies. Appropriate inter-departmental mechanisms would have to be established to make cooperation a reality. MAFF would remain as an agriculture department but statutorily committed to the conservation of soil, wildlife and landscape as an integral part of *farming* policy. It would be expected to promote in every possible way new conservation-oriented farming techniques and technologies.

Arrangements would have to be made to ensure that ADAS, while ultimately responsible to MAFF, was also responsive to environmental and socio-economic concerns. This could be done through the DoE providing a proportion (perhaps 25 per cent) of the finances for ADAS and for the comprehensive farm management plans, and by giving the DoE's countryside agencies a statutory right of representation on national and local boards established to oversee the policy and work of ADAS. These boards would be charged with responsibility for the integrated promotion of agriculture, rural employment and rural conservation.

ADAS would have to be recast to cope with the local realities of integrating conservation and agriculture, and would need additional sources of expertise in conservation management and land-use planning, to be able to offer comprehensive land management advice. It would also be equipped with the order-making powers described above. The national board for ADAS would be consulted on priorities for agricultural research, the issuing of

guidance, the devising of grant schemes and general
guidelines for the work of ADAS. The local boards, which
would probably be county-based, would have three functions: the interpretation of national policies, taking into
account local needs and resources and any relevant
countryside designations; the coordination of advice
and information from MAFF and the other countryside
agencies; and the vetting of grants and orders.

The major drawback of this model of administrative
reform, compared with the other two, is that the lines of
political accountability are indirect and weaker. The more
latitude that was given to the local boards the more potentially serious would be the difficulty. It could be alleviated
by reserving a proportion of the seats on each for the
nominees of the relevant county council, to facilitate local
accountability and coordination with county planning
policies. In addition, the new arrangements could be subjected to regular review by a joint subcommittee of the
House of Commons select committees on agriculture and
the environment.

Of the three models, however, this is probably the most
feasible. Indeed, it might even be thought of as a necessary intermediate stage, if one of the others were preferred
as the ultimate goal. Whichever model were chosen,
adjustments would have to be made to accommodate
existing arrangements for integrating agriculture and conservation that had proved their worth. In national parks,
for example, it would be appropriate for grant-vetting and
order-making powers to be exercised by the national park
authorities.

Just as important as new structures are new attitudes.
The stewardship ethic has been largely squeezed out of
modern farming and forestry by an attitude that is narrowly utilitarian, exploitative and profit-oriented. The
Wildlife and Countryside Act took this process to its logical
conclusion by introducing the principle of full compensation for farmers for foregoing the profit they could have
made by destroying valued landscapes or habitats. Conserving farmers or landowners, whether private or the
National Trust, are excluded from the financial benefits
which go only to those who make damaging proposals.
The Act, in other words, rewards the would-be despoilers,

discriminates against environmentally responsible behaviour, and places a high price on so-called 'good-will'.

Specific steps will have to be taken to build a new
conservation ethic, which will give a renewed sense of
purpose to farmers and foresters. As Mabey puts it: 'far
from being an abandonment of good husbandry, nature
conservation also requires a great understanding of the
land, and that combining it with the production of food or
other material crops is the greatest challenge to all a
farmer's skills'. The various policy reforms we have proposed should help to develop a consciousness of conservation in the farming and landowning community, but
a new ethic is needed in part to ensure a basic continuity
whatever the political machinations over the details of
grant, price, taxation and planning reforms.

A new ethic is not something that can be wished into
existence, nor will it appear simply through constant
exhortation or cajoling. It must be firmly rooted in the
pattern of land-holding and the motivations of those who
have interests in land. Of course, the county FWAGs have
an important role to play in giving advice to farmers, and
it is imperative that the agricultural colleges broaden their
curricula to ensure a more responsible outlook amongst
the next generation. Crucially, though, a new ethic is
dependent on certain arrangements for the administration
of agriculture and conservation. To revive a sense of
corporate responsibility within the farming community,
we need mechanisms by which more farmers can be
brought into the conservation arena and can participate
in local decision-making for the benefit of farming, the
environment and the local community.

An appropriate means might be through district agriculture and conservation committees comprising members
nominated by local farming and conservation organisations. These committees would work closely with the
restructured advisory service, helping to put local farmers
in touch with it as well as giving advice on their own
behalf. They would also make recommendations on the
award of grants and on tax-exempt status. The main function of the district committees would be to help local
farmers to draw up their comprehensive farm management plans and to monitor the implementation of the

plans. Such a task would require a deal of tact and local knowledge for which the district committees should be well suited. This would provide an opportunity for a degree of self-management within the agricultural community which could be of considerable political importance in mobilising farmers for changes in agricultural practice.

With the right structures, policies and motivation we could expect not only a conservation ethic to permeate agriculture but interesting initiatives arising from the farming and landowning community. Farmers might be encouraged to look to ways to 'market' conservation. A wealth of public interest already exists, some of which could so easily be transformed into economic demand for 'farm and wildlife holidays', nature trails, the sale of wildflower seeds, and so on. More conservative farming methods initially seen as a brake on agricultural expansion could provide vital inducements for more 'organic' forms of farming. Only a decade ago such farming was caricatured as 'muck and mystery' and dismissed as being incapable of meeting any of the food requirements of modern Britain. Now, slowly, more research is being directed towards it and societies made up of leading members of the agricultural community, such as RURAL, are turning their attention to the claims and possibilities of organic farming. Some of the findings are so commonsensical — for example, the importance of clovers in pasture to reduce the use of nitrogenous fertilisers — that it seems amazing that the agricultural establishment should have ignored them for so long.

UNITING THE AGENCIES: A NEW CONSERVATION COMMISSION

MAFF is not the only central agency in need of reorganisation. The present parlous state of rural conservation is, in part, due to the weakness, indecision and rivalry of the national conservation agencies. It is necessary, therefore, that their powers, constitution and objectives should be revised. The first important step would be to merge the NCC and the Countryside Commission (and the

Countryside Commission for Scotland) in order to overcome the artificial and enervating divide between nature
and landscape. Britain seems to be almost the only country
in the world to have separate agencies for these objectives.
The consequence is to perpetuate an effete and denatured
notion of landscape and a remote and élitist notion of
nature. In reality beauty is not skin deep; landscape conservation is not just a matter of keeping up appearances;
and nature conservation is not the preserve of scientists
working in nature reserves. Not only is landscape inseparable from nature, but both are inseparable from man's use
and management of land.

A field of rye grass may look as green as an old hay
meadow, and an aesthetically-sited clump of trees may
bear a superficial resemblance to an ancient woodland.
But they are not the same thing at all. 'Landscape', like the
German word *Landschaft*, has ecological as well as scenic
connotations. We prefer to use the word 'scenery' to
describe the visual appearance of the countryside, and
'landscape' to mean what the Lakeland poet, Norman
Nicholson, calls 'the living landscape behind the view'.
Scenery and nature are interdependent, and there is a
wide overlap between areas of great scenic beauty and
areas of great wildlife value.

However, there is a good deal of linguistic sleight-of-
hand in the countryside business. The Countryside Commission and the national park authorities have the job of
promoting countryside recreation and of conserving and
enhancing the 'natural beauty' of the countryside. But the
1949 and 1968 Acts interpret natural beauty as including
'flora, fauna and geological and physiographical features'.
In theory at least, the Commission's job is to conserve
both nature and beauty, although in practice it tends to
lose interest in nature unless it believes it to be beautiful.
What then is the job of the Nature Conservancy? It is to
conserve nature, but not its beauty! Nobody is coordinating the two.

The conservation agencies, in fact, encompass a spectrum of interests. There are sectional interests at either
end — such as the Conservancy's interest in species conservation or the Commission's research on leisure — with
an increasing overlap in between. The extension of the

common ground between the two agencies lays the basis for common action, directed at two objectives. The first must be to secure fundamental changes in government policy, so that the conservation of natural resources and natural beauty is built into the entire apparatus of subsidies, grants, tax incentives, farm development plans and dedication agreements for agriculture and forestry. The second must be to enable the agencies and the voluntary bodies to unify their forces, and to concentrate their influence and their support where it will do most good — above all, perhaps, in helping, persuading, informing and in some cases thwarting, the owners and users of land — both public and private. But as things are the split is the source of needless confusion and antagonism.

Its most serious consequence is that the nation has two weak conservation agencies that can be played off against each other, instead of one strong one. As shown during the passage of the Wildlife and Countryside Act (see Chapter 6) and in the controversies over Exmoor, the Berwyns and Halvergate (Chapters 8, 9 and 11), the NCC and the Countryside Commission all too often work at cross-purposes or in isolation. They seem to hold each other at arm's length, communicating largely by correspondence, if at all. Each likes to go its own way and pursue its own priorities, even if this means duplicating designations (for example, in seeking to make the Berwyn Mountains an AONB as well as an SSSI) or dispensing grant aid in an inconsistent and sometimes wasteful manner (for example, for the management of broadleaved woodland or amenity grassland).

We are not suggesting a shotgun marriage between the agencies, of the kind that might raise a cheer when the minister announced that he had got rid of a Quango and a couple of dozen jobs. We need more jobs in this field, not less. The Commission and the Conservancy possess complementary skills and strengths: the former with its planning expertise, its excellent links with local authorities, and its experimental and promotional approach to countryside management; and the latter with its scientific expertise and research capability, and its long, direct experience in practical conservation, both in managing its own reserves and giving advice to farmers and public and private landowners. A unified agency, carefully designed to achieve far more than its component parts can now do, might well be necessary to press for and oversee the wide-ranging reforms that we present in this book.

We propose that a Conservation Commission be established by amalgamating the NCC, the Countryside Commission and the Countryside Commission for Scotland. It would be largely independent of government, and responsible to a variety of ministers. The parallel that springs to mind is the Health and Safety Commission, which is accountable to the Secretary of State for Employment, but which reports to and advises a number of ministers and departments. Although the Conservation Commission would have its headquarters in London, it should also have national offices for Wales, Scotland and Northern Ireland with sufficient delegated power to exercise considerable national autonomy, and strong regional offices in England. This should minimise the danger of over-centralisation and top-heavy bureaucracy, yet ensure a coherent UK perspective and a strong input into government policy-making.

REFORMING COUNTRYSIDE DESIGNATIONS

Preparatory to the establishment of a Conservation Commission it is imperative that the conservation agencies begin to work more closely together, to harmonise their objectives and procedures. One very important topic which will demand their sustained attention is the reform of the hotch-potch of designations that cover the British countryside. The bewildering list includes national parks, AONBs, areas of great landscape beauty, national scenic areas, Section 43 moor- and heathland, green-belts, heritage coasts, country parks, regional parks, SSSIs, potential SSSIs, nature conservation review sites, national nature reserves, local nature reserves and forest nature reserves. Some of these are statutory, some are linked to planning powers, and some are merely advisory. They have grown up over the years in response to specific pressures and variations in political mood. Many are no longer relevant and the whole pattern is inconsistent and ambiguous. Whereas some choice spots suffer from an accretion of designations, such as an SSSI in a heritage coast in an AONB, half the countryside enjoys no designation status whatsoever. Only England and Wales have the same arrangements: Scotland has no national parks but national scenic areas, which at best guide planning decisions. Northern Ireland does not even have SSSIs, only areas of scientific interest with none of the protection available under the Wildlife and Countryside Act.

Not only are these designations confusing but they no longer reflect the contemporary purposes and future requirements of countryside management. For example SSSIs have grown up with the Nature Conservancy Council but only within the past six years has it produced a unified (though still not consistent) rationale for SSSI selection and designation. One benefit of the much maligned Wildlife and Countryside Act is that it has forced the NCC to be even more conscientious in justifying the scientific importance of each site and the national conservation value of the whole mosaic. Similarly, national parks were conceived and designated at a time when countryside recreation and the demand for open-air exercise were very different from what they are today. Consequently, the parks have to meet requirements for which they were not designed.

The crucial question is whether to reform the system of designations or sweep it away altogether and rely instead on strengthened national policies for conservation and the redirection of agriculture and forestry. The pitfall which is certainly evinced by existing designations is of creating a polarised countryside with certain areas seen as precious and the rest left free for single-minded agricultural exploitation. It is a division that rankles with farmers in the designated areas and arguably releases farmers elsewhere from having a true regard for conservation. Many environmentalists also dislike the 'carve-up' that is involved and the lower conservation priority given to areas that are not at the top of the designation hierarchy.

The argument for retaining some system of designation is that rural areas have quite diverse social and ecological characteristics and constraints which fit them for different purposes, and that national policies should be suitably tailored at the local level to respect these differences. Moreover, after 50 years of agricultural intensification some areas are inevitably less environmentally interesting than others, and the appropriate balance between conservation and production will vary across the country. The lesson to be learnt from the existing muddle of designations is that any new system should cover the whole countryside and not divide it up into areas for special treatment and areas for neglect.

An additional consideration is a pragmatic one. A few of the existing designations, including national parks, national nature reserves and green-belts, have proved their worth and, despite certain shortcomings, are well established both as administrative realities and in popular consciousness. It would be counterproductive to sweep these away, though there is considerable scope for improving their effectiveness. What we advocate therefore is selective surgery to create a more coherent administration plus a comprehensive overhaul of the policy context and powers in which countryside designations operate. As we have seen (Chapters 7, 9 and 10), the NCC has recently met strong resistance to the designation of new SSSIs, and the Countryside Commission has found it even harder to obtain political support for new national parks and AONBs even when its case is sound on landscape and recreational grounds. The reforms we propose below should help to make their task easier.

We suggest the reclassification of the British countryside into a new unified system of designation and administration, with clear management priorities and powers, and consisting of three categories, namely 'heritage sites', 'conservation zones' and 'agricultural and forestry landscapes'. The size of any particular designation will obviously vary but we would suggest that the target total contribution of heritage sites and conservation zones should be between a quarter and a third of the countryside.

Heritage sites would be areas with special and irreplaceable nature conservation qualities (of wild or semi-natural vegetation) and/or highly prized landscape beauty. They should be granted the strongest possible safeguards against undesirable alteration and should be managed so as to conserve their geological, biological, scenic and historic qualities. Heritage sites would include all renotified SSSIs and areas of scientific interest, the national parks, natural scenic areas, all heritage coasts, and parts of certain AONBs. The Conservation Commission would be responsible for their designation subject to the approval of the relevant environment minister. There must be a national purpose to the designation of heritage sites for these will be the jewels in the nation's countryside crown. The mosaic must also fit a nationally accepted policy of strategic site protection so that ministerial approval can generate maximum public support. As a rule, heritage sites will be designated and managed primarily for their existing conservation and amenity values: the concept would not apply to new or created habitats and landscapes.

It follows that many heritage sites could still be used for agriculture and certain kinds of forestry. The conservation interest would however, be paramount: any other land-use would have to be subservient to that management objective. Normal farming and forestry grants would not be available: instead, payments would be made to support traditional husbandry and woodland management. Procedures not unlike those already in operation for SSSIs would apply to proposed changes in the use or management of land; namely compulsory prior notification of any potentially damaging operation (as specified) and the use of management grants to assist conservation measures. In addition, as outlined above, preservation or conservation orders would be available for use as a last resort to prevent damaging change or to impose a particular management regime. Sympathetic forms of recreation, such as nature study and rambling would be encouraged in heritage sites.

Conservation zones provide a designation to protect and manage both existing and new habitats and amenity landscapes. Conservation zones would be designed to meet a variety of management objectives, for example ecological reservoirs for nearby heritage sites, 'green lanes' to connect heritage sites, the creation of exciting new landscapes and habitats *de novo*. They would include cherished pastoral and cultural landscapes and areas for accommodating a diversity of recreational pursuits. These zones, which would also be designated by the Conservation

Commission, would generally be larger than heritage sites and would include peripheral areas adjoining national parks, most AONBs, green-belts, country parks and regional parks. The sticks and carrots which apply to heritage sites would also apply to conservation zones, but there would be a more liberal interpretation of management objectives and hence what proposals would be acceptable and what would not.

Agricultural and forestry landscapes would cover most of the rest of the countryside. Here food and timber-production would be pursued according to the criterion of sustained utilisation outlined in Chapter 12. The retention or creation of wildlife habitat and landscape features at the farm level would be secured through the comprehensive farm management plans. In addition, to safeguard the small-scale features that constitute the parochial 'common ground' and which mean so much to local people, local authorities should be given a statutory duty to designate areas or sites of local conservation interest (SLCI) within structure and local plans. This designation could apply to particular features (e.g. ponds, historic hedgerows) or to landscape areas of special local value. The SLCIs would be equivalent at the local level to heritage sites and with similar powers. The main distinction would lie in the locus of action, with the local authorities responsible for identifying SCLIs and providing 25 per cent of the cost of conservation grants (the remaining 75 per cent coming from the Exchequer via the Conservation Commission).

THE PURCHASE OF SITES AND DEVELOPMENT RIGHTS

By far the best way to safeguard a site is to buy it. This was recognised by the founders of the National Trust 90 years ago. Voluntary conservation organisations now own and manage about 278,000 ha. — nearly 1.5 per cent of the total land area of the UK. The RSPB and county trusts are continuing to invest considerable sums in site purchase though they are often confounded and annoyed by the inflated prices demanded by landowners. This makes them very cautious about site selection, and particularly anxious to ensure that activities on neighbouring property are properly controlled. Similarly, both the national park authorities and a number of local authorities are willing to take the opportunity of purchasing choice land when it comes on the market. By the end of 1982 Exmoor National Park Authority, for example, owned around 2600 ha. of moorland and pasture.

Comprehensive site purchase should be seriously considered as a medium-term conservation tactic, while the wider reforms we have advocated are being discussed and implemented. The aggregate capital costs look formidable but should be compared with other national investments and with the possibility of open-ended management agreements which are costly, time-consuming to set up, administer and enforce, and give no lasting security. The NCC has estimated that the cost of buying the most threatened SSSIs would be about £20 million at 1981 prices, but they are only a fraction of all the potentially *developable* SSSIs. The likely costs of safeguarding these and other heritage sites through permanent management agreements, discounted at appropriate rates, should be calculated and compared with the total discounted costs of site purchase. One problem is that, in advance of the wider reforms, land values will remain inflated both by excessive agricultural subsidies and the extravagant compensatory payments available under the Wildlife and Countryside Act. Even so, as the NCC pointed out to the Commons select committee investigating the effectiveness of the Act: 'Outright purchase is at present the cheapest conservation option.' Moreover, it obviates the long-term, open-ended financial commitments of compensatory management agreements which threaten to encumber the conservation agencies for a generation.

Substantial additional funds would have to be provided by the Treasury to finance an accelerated programme of site acquisitions by statutory and voluntary conservation organisations. We support the recommendation of the consultants reviewing the economic efficiency of national parks that there should be a central fund, financed by the Exchequer, to assist the park authorities to purchase land as it comes onto the market or to stimulate the sale of strategically valuable property.

Encouraging the sale of land for conservation purposes requires greater flexibility in the tax laws. At present the Inland Revenue are prepared to offer a measure of tax relief on capital transfer and capital gains tax to owners who propose to donate or to sell land to a recognised official conservation agency. In the opinion of the Treasury this land must be of outstanding scenic or historic or scientific interest, and the vendor must agree to maintain the essential character of the property and permit access to the public. We believe that these important tax concessions should be considerably extended and made more readily available to landowners, by increasing the 'sweetener' (percentage tax relief) to the vendor from the current 10 per cent to at least 25 per cent, and by allowing sales to *bona fide* non-government bodies, such as the RSPB and the Woodland Trust, as well as to the official agencies.

An additional and largely untapped source of funds for land purchase could be through donations from companies and foundations. For example, in 1981 Rank Xerox provided for a 999-year lease at a peppercorn rent on 117 ha. of Holton Heath and adjacent foreshore near Poole Harbour in Dorset. Similarly, Streetly Construction Materials Ltd and the Sand and Gravel Association bought the 50 ha. Brandon Marsh SSSI in Warwickshire and leased it to Warwickshire Nature Conservation Trust to manage as a nature reserve. Such donations could be further encouraged if land purchase designed to protect important habitat were to be treated as a charitable activity and be subject to tax relief.

Another possibility would be for landowners to be encouraged to sell or donate their development rights to the nation. This could be done by sale of land to a conservation body who would then sell it back at a reduced price under a permanent restrictive covenant with tight legal conditions governing future use and management. To provide an incentive, the gains to be made through selling development rights could be exempted from capital gains tax. Sales should be conducted on a voluntary basis, but if part of a heritage site, conservation zone or SLCI were threatened, there should be reserve powers for compulsory acquisition.

Long-term management of land under permanent restrictive covenants may prove difficult to guarantee.
Probably the most desirable solution is for sites whose
development rights have been acquired to be managed by
voluntary conservation bodies on long-term leases paying
nominal rents. Some of the leased sites may produce sufficient revenue to offset the costs of management; in other
cases funds would have to come from charitable donations
or long-term government assistance.

A PACKAGE OF REFORMS

Some of the individual reforms we have considered have
their own standard-bearers who proclaim the exclusive
advantage of their particular prescription — whether it be
restructuring agricultural support, or conservation incentives, or planning controls. What we want to stress is that
these approaches are not incompatible. Indeed, the single-
minded pursuit of one or other of them would not yield a
satisfactory solution. A workable package of reform must
contain elements of each.

The limitation of the current approach which relies on
conservation advice and incentives is that, without reform
of the agricultural support system, there are much more
powerful and ubiquitous incentives pulling farmers in the
opposite direction towards intensification. Not only do
they weaken the appeal of conservation incentives but
they also make conservation *seem* expensive because compensatory payments are calculated net of all public subsidies. Thus, the full potential of conservation incentives
could only be realised in the context of a reformed system
of agricultural support which fully acknowledged conservation as a legitimate and integral objective of state
assistance to the farming sector.

If the economic pressures on farmers were so radically
altered, this would not invalidate the case for controls over
agriculture. Ideally, incentives and controls should be
complementary and mutually reinforcing — the one maintaining a favourable climate; the other policing and
mitigating farming changes, and providing an accountable
safety net for valued sites and features.

Controls and management agreements should also be complementary — the one ensuring that sites and features survive; the other that they are cared for. It is clear from experience of the Wildlife and Countryside Act that a notification system for farm developments is crucial to provide an opportunity, where necessary, for modifications to be sought or a management agreement to be negotiated. It is also clear that without an ultimate sanction, as would be provided by a preservation order, conservation authorities are in an impossibly weak bargaining position. Equally, the administrative changes we have proposed — the creation of county boards or committees for agriculture and conservation, the reorganisation of ADAS as a 'front-line' land management advisory service, the amalgamation of the national conservation agencies, and the establishment of a comprehensive system of countryside designations — are all intended to ensure that the necessary policy and procedural reforms are carried through in an integrated and coordinated, rather than in a piecemeal and dislocated, manner.

There will be an inevitable cry: 'who is going to pay for all this?' Nobody wants to see public expenditure unnecessarily increased. So it is essential to reallocate existing flows of cash. Part can be paid for from savings through not investing in grant aid and price-support for surplus products: CAP support prices fell by an average of 10 per cent in 1984; and in 1985/86 the money available for agricultural grants in the UK is being cut by £40 million. Part can be paid for by redirecting tax relief for landowners and occupiers. Part too must be paid for by those landowners and farmers who have long enjoyed too comfortable an income cushion. This could come from such sources as rating agricultural land (a long overdue measure and a vital source of revenue for the Shire counties), from charging the bigger farmers for agricultural advice, and by imposing higher taxes on energy, chemicals and machinery. The revenue from this last source could finance environmental restoration (e.g. taking nitrite out of water supplies) while the additional charges would act as a disincentive for excessive use of capital inputs. We are confident that, when full account is made of all the costs and savings of locking conservation into agriculture, it will show that the wider public interest would be served with no fear of food shortages, at lower overall cost.

Though we present our reforms as an integrated package, they need not be swallowed whole. There are various steps that can and must be taken in the short term while the ground is being prepared for the more comprehensive reforms to follow. These include revision of the Wildlife and Countryside Act and its financial guidelines, the establishment of working links between the national conservation agencies, an accelerated programme of acquiring conservation sites and the extension of the farm grant notification system to the whole country.

The agricultural industry has acquired so much momentum that effecting a radical change in direction is bound to take time, so firmly established are many habits of thought and practice. Just as a super-tanker cannot suddenly be stopped or made to change course through 90 degrees, so a lot of effort and imagination will be needed to redirect the work of Britain's farmers, foresters, agricultural workers, researchers, advisers and administrators. The signs are that the agricultural intensification pursued relentlessly for the past 40 years has run its course. There is now a unique opportunity to direct the skills and dedication of everyone concerned into more constructive channels, and into an entirely new partnership with those who, until recently, were their main critics. With farming under severe pressure, all farmers should appreciate what a few have realised for some time — that if they become full partners in the work of conserving landscape and nature they will forge new friendships, new alliances, and new purposes in justifying their role in a harsh economic and political climate.

FURTHER READING TO CHAPTERS 12–14

Over the past five years a number of books and reports have been published each with different proposals for the future of the British countryside. A distinction can be made between those advocating more controls and those advocating a change in prices. In the former category is Marion Shoard *The Theft of the Countryside* (Maurice

Temple Smith, 1980); in the latter are Richard Body's books *Agriculture: the Triumph and the Shame* (Maurice Temple Smith, 1982) and *Farming in the Clouds* (Maurice Temple Smith, 1984); and John Bowers and Paul Cheshire *Agriculture, the Countryside and Land Use: an Economic Critique* (Methuen, 1983). Three reports have assumed the middle ground, advocating a reassembly of grants and other incentives plus greater controls over notification and protection. These are Timothy O'Riordan, 'Putting Trust in the Countryside', in *The Conservation and Development Programme for the UK* (Kogan Page, 1983); Clive Potter, *Investing in Rural Harmony* (World Wildlife Fund, 1983); and Malcolm MacEwen and Geoffrey Sinclair, *New Life for the Hills* (Council for National Parks, 1983).

A stimulating vision of a reformed agriculture taking into account animal welfare and food quality as well as conservation is presented in *Working the Land: A New Plan for a Healthy Agriculture* (Maurice Temple Smith, 1984).

Provocative analyses of forestry policy are included in Richard Grove, *The Future for Forestry* (British Association of Nature Conservationists, 1983); and Philip Stewart (ed.), *The Wood from the Trees: The Developing Debate about British Forestry* (Packard Publishing, 1985).

Index

ADAS *see* Agricultural Development and
  Advisory Service
Agricultural Advisory Council
  Agriculture and the Countryside 239
  Modern Farming and the Soil 238–9
Agricultural and Food Research
  Council 77, 305
agricultural and forestry landscapes
  362, 364
agricultural and horticultural
  development scheme 318, 320
agricultural buildings 349
  restrictions on 26
  see also Farm Building Award Scheme
Agricultural Development and
  Advisory Service 51, 124, 193, 276
  cooperation with other agencies 260,
  281, 299
  Lofthouse Report 211, 212, 215, 218
  see also Berwyn Mountains
  national parks 167, 169
  proposed changes to role of 136, 184, 321,
  353, 354–5, 368
agricultural 'efficiency' 31, 38–9, 43, 334
Agricultural Marketing Acts 1931 &
  1933 40
agricultural policy, post-war 39–45
Agriculture Act 1920 40
Agriculture Act 1947 18, 21, 39, 43, 87,
  94
Agriculture Act 1957 43
Agriculture Act 1970 317
Agriculture and the Countryside see under
  Agricultural Advisory Council
Agriculture, the Countryside and Land Use see
  Bowers, J K and Paul Cheshire
Agriculture: The Triumph and the Shame
  see Body, Richard
Anglian Water Authority 269, 272
Annual Review and Determination of
  Guarantees see under National
  Farmers' Union
AONB *see* areas of outstanding natural
  beauty
APAs *see* Potter, Clive
areas of outstanding natural beauty 18, 97,
  150, 209, 227–8, 359, 360–1, 362, 363,
  364
Arkleton Trust 334
Association of County Councils 200
  see also Wildlife and Countryside Act
AWA *see* Anglian Water Authority

Berwyn Mountains 189, 209–29
  Berwyn Society 222–7
  comparison with other areas 248,
  262, 359
  compensation for designation 203
  designation of sites of special
  scientific interest 159, 165
  future prospects 227–9
  Llanbrynmair Moors 216–22
  Lofthouse Report 211–6
  map 210
  'Berwyn Mountains Feasibility Study –
  Assessment of Biological Interest' 212
  see also Nature Conservancy Council;
  Royal Society for the Protection of
  Birds
Better Future for the Uplands, A see under
  Countryside Commission
Body, Richard *Agriculture: The Triumph
  and the Shame* 51, 174, 175, 309
Bowers, J K 121

and Paul Cheshire *Agriculture, the Countryside and Land Use* 175, 310–1, 318–9, 346
British Association of Nature Conservationists 115, 161–2
British Ecological Society 19
    see also nature reserves
British Trust for Conservation Volunteers 115
British Trust for Ornithology 244
Broads Authority 269, 271
    compensation payments 203, 273, 285–6, 293–4
    control over developments 276, 278–9
    relations with the drainage camp 280–97
    see also Countryside Commission; Halvergate Marshes; Lower Bure, Acle Marshes and Halvergate Fleet Internal Drainage Board; Ministry of Agriculture, Fisheries and Food; Nature Conservancy Council
Broads Grazing Marsh Conservation Scheme 299–300
    see also Countryside Commission; Ministry of Agriculture, Fisheries and Food
Broads Society 271
    see also Halvergate Marshes
Buxton, Lord 285, 286
    see also Halvergate Marshes; Internal Drainage Boards; Ministry of Agriculture, Fisheries and Food; Melchett, Lord; Onslow, Lord

Cambridge University, Department of Land Economy *see* Land Economy
CAP *see* Common Agricultural Policy
Caring for the Countryside see under Country Landowners' Association; National Farmers' Union
Census of Trees see under Forestry Commission
Centre for Agricultural Strategy, Reading University 89–90
    Strategy for the UK Forestry Industry 47
chalk grassland 68
CLA *see* Country Landowners' Association
Clark, David *see* Wildlife and Countryside Act, Private Members' Bills
CoEnCo *see* Council for Environmental Conservation
Committee on Land Utilisation in Rural Areas *see* Scott Report
Common Agricultural Policy 1
    curbs on expenditure 109, 173
    Halvergate Marshes 277–8
    see also Ministry of Agriculture, Fisheries and Food

reform of 45, 186, 308–16, 319, 339, 368
surpluses 45, 89
workings of 44–5, 94, 276, 334
    see also Ministry of Agriculture, Fisheries and Food; National Farmers' Union
Community Council for Somerset 244
compulsory purchase orders 195
Conservation Commission 360, 363
conservation groups *see* local amenity and conservation groups
conservation incentives 316–21
Conservation Society 117
conservation zones 362, 363–4, 366
Conservative government 51, 199, 201–2
    voluntary approach 206
Conservative Party 4–5, 93
    Conservation and the Conservatives 177
    Conserving the Countryside: A Tory View 177
    voluntary approach 345
COPA 94–5
COSIRA *see* Council for Small Industries in Rural Areas
Council for Environmental Conservation 116
Council for National Parks 116, 180, 322
    Wildlife and Countryside Act 146–8, 152, 158, 170, 183
    see also Council for the Protection of Rural England; Ministry of Agriculture, Fisheries and Food; Sandford amendment
Council for Nature 126
Council for Small Industries in Rural Areas 107
Council for the Protection of Rural England 114–5
    attitudes towards agriculture 121, 129, 345, 349
    'Campaign for the Countryside' 177–8
    formation of 12
    see also rural preservation movement
    Halvergate Marshes 271, 285, 296
    urban encroachment 62
    Wildlife and Countryside Act 152, 158, 170, 176, 180–3
    see also Conservative Party
    Wildlife and Countryside Bill 135, 137, 139, 146, 147–8
    see also Sandford amendment
CPRE *see* Council for the Protection of Rural England.
Country Landowners' Association 1, 85, 90, 352
    attitudes towards conservation 2, 90, 98–109, 182
    Berwyn Mountains 220, 222

Exmoor 191, 194, 195, 202
Game Fair 106
organisation and workings of 92–4
    see also National Farmers' Union
publications
    Caring for the Countryside 104
        see also National Farmers' Union
    'Human Impacts on the Countryside'
    100
        see also Council for Nature;
        Royal Society of Arts
    'Landowners and the Future' 100,
    101
    Management Agreements in the
    Countryside 99
relations with Ministry of Agriculture,
    Fisheries and Food and other bodies
    88–90, 105, 182
relations with timber-growing lobby 96
straw burning 79
West Sedgemoor 244–6, 249–50,
    252–4, 256, 260, 262
    see also Mellanby Report
Wildlife and Countryside Act 149–52,
    154, 158, 172, 183
Countryside Act 1968 102, 127, 130, 194–5,
    201, 219, 240, 358
Countryside Bill 1978 see Labour
    government
Countryside Commission 2, 123–4,
    127–8, 130, 345
    Berwyn Mountains 227–8
    compensation payments 158, 160, 163,
    167, 203, 205
    Exmoor 197, 199, 201, 203, 205, 208
    Halvergate Marshes 269–70, 281, 283,
    286, 288–90, 292, 294, 297, 299
    proposed changes to role of 351–3,
    357–60, 362
    publications
        A Better Future for the Uplands (1984)
        125, 201, 208, 335
        The Changing Uplands (1983) 329
        New Agricultural Landscapes (1974) 28,
        104, 123, 178–9
        A Second Look (1984) 123, 323
        Upland Landscapes Study (1983) 329–30,
        331–3, 335
        What Future for the Uplands? (1983) 328
    relations with other groups 107, 116, 122,
    125, 154
    straw burning 79
    uplands 325–6, 328–30, 335–7
    Wildlife and Countryside Bill 133, 137–9,
    141, 154, 158
    woodlands 71, 341
'Countryside in 1970' conferences see
    Nature Conservancy; Royal Society of
    Arts
Countryside Link 116
'Countryside – Problems and Policies, The'
    see under Countryside Review

Committee
Countryside Review Committee 34, 51,
    101–2, 104, 351
    Conservation and the Countryside
    Heritage (1979) 104
    'The Countryside – Problems and
    Policies' 101, 109
    Food Production in the Countryside
    (1978) 104
county trusts for nature conservation 24,
    115
CPO see Compulsory Purchase Orders

Dartington Institute study 328–9, 335
    see also Dartmoor; Exmoor
Dartmoor 191, 208, 328, 331, 335
Dartmoor Preservation Association 168
Dedication Scheme see under Forestry
    Commission
deficiency payments 42–44
DoE see Department of the
    Environment
Department of Land Economy, Cambridge
    University see Land Economy
Department of the Environment 110, 176,
    180–1, 297, 309, 351
    Exmoor 138, 206
    funding for management agreements
    159, 203, 206
        see also Countryside Commission;
        Nature Conservancy Council; Walland
        Marsh
    Halvergate Marshes 269, 283–4, 286, 290,
    292–3, 296
    proposed changes to 352, 354
    relations with conservation groups 121–2,
    134, 269
    relations with Country Landowners'
    Association & National Farmers' Union
    122, 137, 256, 260
    West Sedgemoor 247, 256, 260
    Wildlife and Countryside Act 130, 171
    Wildlife and Countryside Bill 133, 134,
    145
        see also Countryside Commission; Nature
        Conservancy Council
Development Commission 351, 352, 353
Dower Report 18, 20, 327
    see also Hobhouse Report; Scott Report
Draining of the Somerset Levels, The see
    Williams, Michael

Economic Forestry Group 96, 212, 215, 217
    see also timber-growing lobby
Egg Marketing Board 42
Environment Coordination Unit see under
    Ministry of Agriculture, Fisheries
    and Food
European Wetlands Campaign 242
Exmoor 27, 130, 146, 189–90, 191–208, 328,
    331, 335, 337, 359, 365
    management agreements 138–9, 202–6,

207, 283, 292, 340
map 192
Porchester Inquiry 196–202, 350
voluntary approach 138–9, 195, 206, 223,
    235
see also moorland; national parks;
    Uplands
Exmoor national park committee 195,
    197–200, 202, 204–6, 208
see also Countryside Commission;
    Porchester Inquiry/Report
Exmoor Society 194, 244
    Can Exmoor Survive? 194
see also Sinclair, Geoffrey

Farm Buildings Award Scheme 107
Farmers' Union of Wales 90, 219, 222,
    224, 313, 314
Farming and the Nation see under White
    Papers
Farming and Wildlife Advisory Group
    103, 152, 320, 356
Farming and Wildlife Trust 152
see also Farming and Wildlife
    Advisory Group
'Farming – The Backbone of Britain' see
    under National Farmers' Union
Fauna and Flora Preservation Society 115
Field Studies Council 115
Fisons Limited 245
FoE see Friends of the Earth
Food from Our Own Resources see under
    White Papers
Forestry Act 1981 48, 97, 323
Forestry Commission 46–50, 71, 77, 95–7,
    124, 184
    Berwyn Mountains 211–5, 217–8, 227
    see also Lofthouse Report
    Dedication Scheme 49
    Forestry Grant Scheme 49
    Home-Grown Timber Advisory
        Committee 96
    proposed changes to policies of 72, 323–4,
        351–3
    publications
        Broadleaves in Britain (1984) 322–3
        Census of Trees (1983) 97
        The Wood Production Outlook in Britain
            (1977) 47
    relations with conservation groups 69
    relations with timber-growing lobby 47,
        95–6
Forestry Grant Scheme see under Forestry
    Commission
forestry policy 46–50, 321–4
    subsidies and tax concessions 49–50,
        96–7, 174
    see also Forestry Commission
forestry policy review (1972) 47–8
    see also Forestry Commission
Fountain Forestry 174, 183
    see also Nature Conservancy Council; sites

of special scientific interest
Fream's Elements of Agriculture (1949) 32
Friends of the Earth 115–7, 126, 254, 345
    damage to sites of special scientific
        interest 159, 171, 295–7
    links with Liberal and Labour Parties 153
    Proposals for a Natural Heritage Bill (1983)
        177
    Wildlife and Countryside Act 141, 152,
        183
    FWAG see Farming and Wildlife Advisory
        Group

Game Conservancy 105
    see also Country Landowners'
        Association; Nature Conservancy
        Council; pesticides
Game Fair see under Country Landowners'
    Association
Glenthorne Estate 196–7, 199
    see also Exmoor
Great Yarmouth Port and Haven
    Commissioners 269
    see also Broads Authority; Halvergate
        Marshes
Greenpeace 126
    see also Friends of the Earth

habitat and wildlife losses 27, 55–8, 60,
    63–72
Halvergate Marshes 161, 189–90, 265–300,
    359
    conservation and drainage camps 269–74
    controls over 'improvements' 171, 183,
        296–7, 318
    costs of management agreements 203,
        293–5, 299
    see also wetlands
Hardy, Peter see Wildlife and Countryside
    Act, Private Members' Bills
heathland 68, 319
hedgerows 27, 65, 333, 335
    see also habitat and wildlife losses;
        woodlands
heritage sites 362–3, 366
Hill Farming Act 1946 42
Hobhouse Report 18, 209, 327
    see also Dower Report; Scott Report
Home-Grown Timber Advisory Committee
    see under Forestry Commission
House of Lords Select Committee on
    Science and Technology 76–77, 181, 305
House of Lords reports 179–81, 297
housing problems 22–3
    see also rural depopulation and pressure
        areas
'Human Impacts on the Countryside' see
    under Country Landowners'
    Association

IDBs see Internal Drainage Boards
Internal Drainage Boards 271–3, 275, 284,

285, 286, 290
West Sedgemoor 234–5, 236, 238, 239, 246
see also Halvergate Marshes; Land
    Drainage Acts; Lower Bure, Acle
    Marshes and Halvergate Fleet Internal
    Drainage Board; Ministry of
    Agriculture, Fisheries and Food;
    Nature Conservancy Council; Royal
    Society for the Protection of Birds;
    Somerset Drainage Act; Wessex Water
    Authority
Investing in Rural Harmony see Potter,
    Clive

Kennet, Lord 194

Labour government 18, 40–1
    Countryside Bill 1978 131, 137, 146, 152
Labour Party 4, 153, 346
    see also Socialist Countryside Group
Lake District Special Planning Board 341
    see also Uplands
Land Drainage Act 1861 234
Land Drainage Act 1976 239, 272, 273, 281
Land Economy, Department of, Cambridge
    University 285, 287
    see also Broads Authority; Halvergate
    Marshes
'Landowners and the Future' *see under*
    Country Landowners' Association
LBIDB *see* Lower Bure, Acle Marshes and
    Halvergate Fleet Internal Drainage
    Board
Less Favoured Areas 5, 110, 229, 293–4, 297,
    318
    Uplands 325–6, 327–8, 331, 332, 333, 334,
    336, 339
LFA *see* Less Favoured Areas
Liberal/Social Democratic Alliance 4, 153
limestone pavements 70, 144, 349
Livestock Rearing Act 1951 42
local amenity and conservation groups
    associations with class 24–5
Lofthouse Report 211–6, 217, 218, 220
low input systems 64, 73, 74, 236, 268, 312,
    327
    see also Society for the Responsible Use of
    Resources in Agriculture and on the
    Land
Lower Bure, Acle Marshes and Halvergate
    Fleet Internal Drainage Board 271
    stance taken by 273, 276, 279–85, 287, 291
    see also Countryside Commission;
    Nature Conservancy Council; Ministry
    of Agriculture, Fisheries and Food
    workings of 272, 278
    see also Internal Drainage Boards
    see also Halvergate Marshes

MAFF *see* Ministry of Agriculture, Fisheries
    and Food
Management Agreements in the Countryside see

under Country Landowners'
    Association; National Farmers' Union;
    Royal Institute of Chartered Surveyors
Melchett, Lord 135, 136, 142, 153, 285
    see also Sandford amendment; Wildlife
    Link Committee
Mellanby Report 252–3, 254, 255
    see also Country Landowners'
    Association; West Sedgemoor
migration, rural *see* rural depopulation and
    pressure areas
Milk Marketing Board 40, 42, 312–3
milk quotas 1, 2, 45, 52, 94, 109, 173, 277,
    293, 309, 312–3
Ministry of Agriculture, Fisheries and Food
    39, 124, 305
    attitudes and policies towards
    conservation 103, 109–10, 138, 142,
    145–7, 168, 180–1, 184–5, 245
    drainage 67, 234, 237, 245, 261, 275–6
    see also Halvergate Marshes; West
    Sedgemoor
    Environment Coordination Unit 93, 176
    Exmoor 193–5, 197–8, 201, 204–5, 228
    see also Porchester Inquiry/Report;
    Sinclair, Geoffrey
    Halvergate Marshes 269, 271–3, 275–7,
    279–86, 290, 293–9
    low input systems 74
    see also Society for the Responsible Use
    of Resources in Agriculture and on the
    Land
    policies of 3, 50–1, 76, 108, 177, 312–3
    proposed reform of 316–8, 321, 351–2,
    354, 357
    relations with Country Landowners'
    Association and National Farmers'
    Union 79, 87–90
    see also straw and stubble burning
    Uplands 328, 332–5, 339–42
    West Sedgemoor 234, 237, 239–40, 242,
    244–7, 253, 256, 260–1
    Wildlife and Countryside Act 130, 145,
    171
    see also Agricultural Development and
    Advisory Service
Ministry of Rural Affairs 352, 354
Modern Farming and the Soil see under
    Agricultural Advisory Council
MORI public opinion survey on
    conservation 118–9
moorland 69–70, 135, 146, 157, 193, 336–7
    see also Berwyn Mountains; Exmoor

National Agricultural Advisory Service 37
National Farmers' Union 1, 85, 90–2, 94,
    154, 314
    *Annual Review and Determination of
    Guarantees* 41
    attitudes towards agricultural change
    50–1, 182
    attitudes towards conservation 2, 52,

102–5
Berwyn Mountains 220, 222
Exmoor 191, 193–5, 198–9, 201–2, 208
farming 'efficiency' 39, 86
publications
    Access, Recreation and the Farmer (1971)
        102
    Caring for the Countryside (1977) 104
        see also Country Landowners'
        Association, publications
    'Farming – The Backbone of Britain'
        (1982) 86, 90, 151
    Looking at the Landscape (1971) 102
    *Management Agreements in the
        Countryside* (1984) 99
    The Reclamation of Exmoor (1966) 194
        see also Country Landowners'
        Association, Exmoor
    *The Way Forward: New Directions for
        Agricultural Policy* (1984) 3, 182
    Wildlife Conservation and the Farmer
        (1971) 102, 103
relations with Ministry of Agriculture,
    Fisheries and Food 87–8
relations with other bodies 88–90, 92–3,
    122, 178
straw burning 78–9
voluntary approach 129–31, 138–9, 145,
    150, 195, 201
West Sedgemoor 245–6, 250–60
Wildlife and Countryside Act 149–52,
    158, 160, 172–3
Wildlife and Countryside Bill 133, 137–40,
    142–3, 145–7
National Heritage Memorial Fund 161
    see also Wildlife and Countryside Act
national park authorities 123–4, 130, 154,
    276, 342, 347, 358
proposed changes to controls over
    national parks 130, 136, 184, 336, 355,
    365
Wildlife and Countryside Act 154, 157,
    160, 162–3, 167–70
    see also Exmoor; Peak Park Joint Planning
    Board
National Park Management Plans 128
national parks 16, 18–9, 276, 321
funds for compensation payments 203,
    336
Halvergate Marshes 269, 292
pressure to 'improve' land in 69, 97
proposed changes in control over 355
Wildlife and Countryside Act 135, 147–8,
    150, 167, 174, 202, 316
    see also Council for National Parks;
    Exmoor; national park authorities
National Parks and Access to the
    Countryside Act 1949 18, 21, 59, 214
    see also areas of outstanding natural
    beauty; national parks; sites of special
    scientific interest
National Parks Commission 18, 59, 127

    see also areas of outstanding natural
    beauty; Countryside Commission;
    national parks
National Parks in England and Wales (1945) see
    Dower Report
National Trust 114, 115, 117, 355, 364
Nature Conservancy 19–20, 59
    'Countryside in 1970' conferences 100,
    126–7
        see also Country Landowners'
        Association; Royal Society of Arts
    see also under later name Nature
    Conservancy Council
Nature Conservancy Council
    Berwyn Mountains 209, 212–5, 217–28
    Exmoor 193, 200–1
    Halvergate Marshes 269–70, 279, 286,
        287, 289, 300
    proposed changes to role of 351–3, 357,
        359–62
    publications
        Nature Conservation and Agriculture
            (1977) 28, 50
        Nature Conservation in Great Britain
            (1984) 105, 110, 122–3, 179
        Nature Conservation Review (1977) 243
    purchase of sites of special scientific
        interest 365
    relations with conservation groups 122,
        180
    survey of damage to SSSIs 143
    West Sedgemoor 241–3, 246–63
        see also Somerset Wetlands Project
        Group
    Wildlife and Countryside Act 150, 154,
        158–67, 169–72, 174, 183
    Wildlife and Countryside Bill 133–7, 141,
        143–9
    see also under former name Nature
    Conservancy; sites of special scientific
    interest
*Nature Conservation and Agriculture see
    under* Nature Conservancy Council
*Nature Conservation in Great Britain see
    under* Nature Conservancy Council
Nature Conservation Review see under Nature
    Conservancy Council
nature reserves 16, 19, 20, 297, 366
    see also national parks; sites of special
    scientific interest; Society for the
    Promotion of Nature Reserves
NCC see Nature Conservancy Council
New Agricultural Landscapes see under
    Countryside Commission
NFU see National Farmers' Union
Norfolk Naturalists' Trust 271
    see also Broads Society; Council for the
    Protection of Rural England;
    Halvergate Marshes; Suffolk Trust for
    Nature Conservation
North York Moors 169, 170, 203
    see also Exmoor; moorland; national parks

nitrates in water 5, 76
see also pollution

Observer, The 178, 295
see also Council for the Protection of Rural
England; Halvergate Marshes; Wildlife
and Countryside Act
Onslow, Lord 285
see also Buxton, Lord; Halvergate
Marshes; Internal Drainage Boards;
Melchett, Lord; Ministry of
Agriculture, Fisheries and Food
organic farming 73, 357

Peak National Park 343
see also national parks
Peak Park Joint Planning Board 342
see also national park authorities
pesticides 27, 73, 75, 77, 306
Phillips Report 196
see also Exmoor national park committee
planning system, post-war 17–21
pollution 5, 63, 70, 75–6, 298
Porchester Inquiry/Report 130, 138, 195,
196–202, 203, 204, 208, 350
post-war agricultural policy *see* agricultural
policy, post-war
post-war planning system *see* planning
system, post-war
Potter, Clive *Investing in Rural Harmony*
318–9, 342
pressure areas *see* rural depopulation and
pressure areas

Ramblers' Association 13–4, 114, 115, 116,
135, 137, 148, 152, 153, 183
see also Labour Party; Liberal/Social
Democratic Alliance; Wildlife and
Countryside Act
Ratcliffe, Derek 55–6, 209
see also under Nature Conservancy
Council, publications
Rayner Review 136, 165
see also under Nature Conservancy
Council, publications
Royal Commission on Environmental
Pollution 63, 75–6, 79, 176
see also pesticides; pollution; straw and
stubble burning
Royal Institute of Chartered Surveyors
Management Agreements in the Countryside
99
Royal Society for Nature Conservation 114,
148, 183
see also under former title Society for the
Promotion of Nature Reserves
Royal Society for the Protection of Birds 14,
114–5, 117, 121, 161, 364, 366
Berwyn Mountains 211, 216–8, 222, 225,
262
Halvergate Marshes 299
loss of habitats 67, 69, 159

relations with other bodies 134, 180
West Sedgemoor 231, 235, 240–3, 245,
251, 253, 255, 257–8, 262
Wildlife and Countryside Act 134, 139,
148, 153, 159, 161, 180, 183
Royal Society of Arts 85
'Countryside in 1970' conferences 126–7
see also Nature Conservancy
RSPB *see* Royal Society for the Protection of
Birds
RURAL *see* Society for the Responsible Use
of Resources in Agriculture and on the
Land
rural depopulation and pressure areas 21–3,
47, 330, 331, 334
rural preservation movement 12–17

Sandford amendment 142, 146–9
see also Council for National Parks;
Council for the Protection of Rural
England; Melchett, Lord; Ministry of
Agriculture, Fisheries and Food;
Wildlife and Countryside Act
Scott Report 15–18
see also Dower Report; Hobhouse Report
Scottish Highlands and Islands 154
see also Melchett, Lord; Nature
Conservancy Council; West
Sedgemoor; Wildlife and Countryside
Act
SDP *see* Liberal/Social Democratic Alliance
second agricultural revolution 32–4, 108,
315
Sedgemoor *see* West Sedgemoor
Sedgemoor District Council 244
Selborne Committee 40, 41
Shoard, Marion *The Theft of the Countryside*
25, 141
Sinclair, Geoffrey 194, 197, 330, 333, 334
see also Countryside Commission; Exmoor
Society
sites of local conservation interest 364, 366
sites of special scientific interest 18, 67, 276,
321, 336, 365
Berwyn Mountains 209, 213–5, 218–25,
228, 262
damage to 68, 122, 130, 167, 171, 177, 311
duplication of designations 359–61
Halvergate Marshes 270, 279, 286, 300
proposed changes to 362–3
West Sedgemoor 231, 238, 246–51, 255,
257–8, 260–2
Wildlife and Countryside Act 135–7,
142–7, 149–51, 157–9, 161–7, 171–2, 174,
177, 183, 202, 316
SLCI *see* sites of local conservation interest
Smallfarmers' Association 314
Small Farmers Scheme 43
Social Democratic Party *see* Liberal/Social
Democratic Alliance
Socialist Countryside Group 153, 345
see also Labour Party

Society for the Promotion of Nature
Reserves 15, 19, 130
see also under later title Royal Society for
Nature Conservation
Society for the Responsible Use of
Resources in Agriculture and on the
Land (RURAL) 74, 89, 357
see also low input systems
Soil Survey of England and Wales 73, 74
Somerset Drainage Act 1877 234
Somerset Levels *see* West Sedgemoor
Somerset Levels and Moors Plan 259–60
Somerset Levels and Moors Study 247
Somerset Moors Panel 238
see also Ministry of Agriculture, Fisheries
and Food
Somerset Trust for Nature Conservation
242, 243, 245
Somerset Wetlands Project Group 242–9
SSSIs *see* sites of special scientific interest
STNC *see* Somerset Trust for Nature
Conservation
Stowey Allotment 196–7
see also Countryside Commission; Exmoor
Strategy for the UK Forestry Industry see
Centre for Agricultural Strategy
straw and stubble burning 78–80
Suffolk County Council 292
Suffolk Trust for Nature Conservation 271
see also Halvergate Marshes

Theft of the Countryside, The see Shoard,
Marion
Timber Growers UK 49, 95, 96, 107, 109,
213, 220
see also Country Landowners'
Association; Forestry Commission;
timber-growing lobby
timber-growing lobby 47, 95–8
see also Economic Forestry Group;
Forestry Commission
tourism in the Uplands 328, 339, 342
Town and Country Planning Act 1947 17, 21
Tree Council 116

Uplands 325–43
decline of 331–7
alternative approach 337–43
urban and industrial encroachment 13, 61–3

Walland Marsh 159
see also Department of the Environment;
Nature Conservancy Council; sites of
special scientific interest
War Agricultural Executive Committees 40
Way Report 253, 254
see also Mellanby Report; Ministry of
Agriculture, Fisheries and Food; West
Sedgemoor

Welsh Office Agriculture Department 169,
211–5, 217, 218, 227
see also Berwyn Mountains; national park
authority
Wessex Water Authority 234, 238, 239–40,
242, 245
1979 Land Drainage Survey Report
239–40
see also Ministry of Agriculture, Fisheries
and Food; West Sedgemoor
West Sedgemoor 189, 214, 225, 231–63
cost of management agreements 161, 259,
261
map 232
SSSI designation 157, 159, 165, 248,
249–55, 260–2
Somerset Wetlands Project Group 242–8
Wildlife and Countryside Act 154, 224,
262
West Sedgemoor Board 234
wetlands 66–8, 311, 319
see also Ministry of Agriculture, Fisheries
and Food; Royal Society for the
Protection of Birds; sites of special
scientific interest
White Papers
Farming and the Nation (1979) 51
Food from Our Own Resources (1975) 51
see also Conservative government; Labour
government
Wildlife and Countryside Act 2, 70, 125,
130–1, 133–55, 157–85, 189, 219, 308,
316–7, 336
Berwyn Mountains 212, 214, 219, 223
Country Landowners' Association and
the 93, 98, 130
Exmoor 189–90, 201–3, 205
Halvergate Marshes 274, 284–94, 298–300
Private Members' Bills 171–2, 183–5
proposed changes involving the 351,
355–6, 361, 365, 368–9
Wildlife Link Committee 116, 135, 136, 170
see also Melchett, Lord; Nature
Conservancy Council; Wildlife and
Countryside Act
Williams, Michael *The Draining of the
Somerset Levels* 237
WOAD *see* Welsh Office Agriculture
Department
*Wood Production Outlook in Britain, The see
under* Forestry Commission,
publications
Woodlands 95–8
World Wildlife Fund 115, 162, 318
see also Potter, Clive; Wildlife and
Countryside Act
WWA *see* Wessex Water Authority

Youth Hostels Association 14